To Hugh,

With very best

Happy Birth d

from Robert & Sonia

July '93

CW00555453

AEGEAN ADVENTURES
1940-43
and the end of Churchill's dream

AEGEAN ADVENTURES 1940-43
and the end of Churchill's dream

Michael Woodbine Parish

The Book Guild Ltd.
Sussex, England

*To my wife and family
and the many Cretan and
Greek heroes.*

The Book Guild Ltd.
25 High Street,
Lewes, Sussex

First published 1993
Reprinted 1993
© Michael Woodbine Parish 1993
Set in Baskerville
Typesetting by Southern Reproductions (Sussex)
East Grinstead, Sussex
Printed in Great Britain by
Antony Rowe Ltd.
Chippenham, Wiltshire.

A catalogue record for this book is
available from the British Library

ISBN 0 86332 788 5

CONTENTS

LIST OF ILLUSTRATIONS

Spartamint wins first prize at Show for Mare and Foal, 1938
Michael Woodbine Parish, 2nd Lieut. in the Notts (SRY) Yeomanry, 1938
Michael Woodbine Parish with C4 Troop SRY, Palestine, 1940
The author with Colonel Donny Player, Palestine, 1940
Charles and Godfrey Woodbine Parish before the marriage of Godfrey and Lord Blackford's daughter, Ann Mason
Flight-Lieut. Charles Woodbine Parish with his Lancaster bomber
Charles with his Pathfinder plane and crew
Clement's beehives at Batemans, 1940
Batesmans at Burwash, Sussex
Royal Scots Greys Trooper in full marching gear

Second Photograph Section (between pages 190 and 191)

The original photo of our escape to Turkey from Crete, September 1941
Michael Woodbine Parish and Vernicos in Alexandria
The Italians and their new-found allies
The author's MI9 caiques at Khiosti, Egrilar, Turkey
Agia Irene and Ali Bey in Kushadasi
Colonel Simonds and the author in Istanbul, 1942
Ninette, 1942
Antiparos, where Commander Vernicos was captured
Michael Woodbine Parish and Milton on the *Sentosa,* 1942
Capt. Miltiades Houmas with Michael Woodbine Parish and Kostas Demetrakis from Mytilene, 1942
Capt. Dino Koumoundouros with Captain Miltiades Houmas and Christophoros Confer, 1942
Michael Woodbine Parish and Ninette at their wedding in Istanbul, 1943
Ninette
The *Lillias,* my home for the first months of marriage to Ninette
Michael Woodbine Parish and Ninette, 1943
British officers take over Samos and Leros, 12 September 1943
Syros houses on the waterfront
Colonel Harold Lehrs Gibson in Istanbul, 1942
Outside the death cell, Calithea prison

Cmdr Vernicos after release from Italian prison, 1946
At the wedding of Ninette to the author in Istanbul, 1943
Mary Churchill, 1944
Michael Woodbine Parish sailing with Cmdr Vernicos, 1946
The plane believed to be the Corsair flown by Lt. Cmdr G.W.
Parish in 1945
Michael Woodbine Parish and Billa in Grindlewald
Billa in Grindlewald

Third Photograph Section (between pages 338 and 339)

Michael Woodbine Parish and Billa at their wedding, 1947
Lt. Cmdr Godfrey Woodbine Parish and Roly Ruck Keene at
their wedding, 1946
Spartamint with my Jaguar in the background, 1947
Billa with Suzanne and Rev. Buswell at the christening in Jersey,
1948
Michael Woodbine Parish with Billa and Air Vice Marshal and
Mrs Somerled Macdonald, 1960
Michael Woodbine Parish with Elefteris Rosmaris in Crete,
1960
Lambris, the author, Suzanne, Lambris's daughter Lakkos, in
Crete, 1966
George and grandson Constantinos Zegos at the wedding of
Emma Parish to Charles Houston, 1987
Michaelis and Elefteris Rosmaris, 1988
Costa Rosmaris, 1991
Kandamos, Crete – notice in Greek and German – with Cmdr
Vernicos's comments
New Zealand guard of honour at Galatos, 1991
Mr and Mrs Albert Stokes of the Sherwood Rangers
Yeomanry
The memorial case of the *Evangelistria* and Capt. Miltiades
Houmas in the Hellenic Maritime Museum, Piraeus, Greece,
1990
The Greek Distinguished Service Medal awarded to Michael
Woodbine Parish
The *Evangelistria* made in bronze by the Hellenic Maritime
Museum
Charles and Emma Houston depart from their wedding
reception on a hump

9

Florence Houston, the author's granddaughter, aged two
  years
Glenborrodale Castle where Billa and the author met in
  1946
Manly sports at Glenborrodale Castle
Billa and the author at Glenborrodale Castle in 1990

LIST OF MAPS

ACKNOWLEDGEMENTS

In acknowledgements, I must begin by thanking my wife who, three years ago, began to write the story in longhand; my daughter, Emma for all her hard work co-ordinating and putting it onto the word processor; my secretary Mrs Smith for all the extra work I caused her; my son-in-law Charles Houston for drawing all the maps and cartoons; George Zegos for driving me all over Crete during the 50th Anniversary of the Battle of Crete, and Junior Kumaramangalam for all his research; my son Robin for suggesting the title; Judith Parish for translating 'The Trial of The Italian Admirals'; my old friend, Myles Hildyard, for allowing me the full use of his diaries; Christopher Hohler (a brilliant Greek scholar) for the immense amount of work he put in, and John Louis Marc for his many translations. Yanni and Christo Houmas for their unsparing efforts in providing the mass of material on their gallant father and many others who gave me help including Colum Scott, and the excellent staff of the Book Guild. Lastly, and perhaps most importantly, my brilliant editor, Dr Audrey C. Davies.

COPYRIGHT ACKNOWLEDGEMENTS

Mail newspaper.

'Hitler's War 1942-1945' by David Irving, by permission of Hodder and Stoughton Publishers, London.

'The Aegean Mission' by Jeffrey Holland, by permission of the Greenwood Press, Westport, USA.

'Triumph in the West 1943-1946' by Arthur Bryant, by permission of Harper Collins Publishers Limited, London.

'The Caged Lion: Winston Spencer Churchill 1932-1940' by William Manchester, by permission of Michael Joseph Ltd, London; first published in 1988.

'The Age of Revolution', Volume III of *The Second World War*; 'Closing the Ring', Volume V of *The Second World War*; 'Triumph and Tragedy', Volume VI of *The Second World War*. All by Winston S. Churchill, by permission of Cassell plc, London.

'English History 1914-1945' by A.J.P. Taylor, by permission of The Oxford University Press, published in 1965.

'Shame' from *The Sunday Express,* 30 July 1978.

Banker's Magazine, 1911, 'The Late Mr Whitburn'.

The author is also grateful for permission to use the following photographs:

Mary Churchill, by permission of The Hulton Picture Company, London.

A very young house-party at Raynham Hall, Norfolk, by permission of *The Illustrated London News* Picture Library.

Rear Admiral Maschera with Italian and British officers at Leros, September 1943, by permission of the Imperial War Museum.

INTRODUCTION

People write books for many reasons, such as to make money, gain prestige and so forth. Although I had on occasions been told I should write my memoirs, I had never intended to. Flying back from our annual visit to Greece in September 1988, my wife handed me Lady Henderson's book *Xenia*. She thought it would be of considerable interest to me as my period in Greece coincided almost exactly with that portrayed in *Xenia*. After skipping through it on the flight I saw immediately that Lady Henderson and I had several things in common.

Firstly, she was Greek and married two Englishmen. I am English and married, firstly, a Greek, and then an English girl. Secondly, she came from Cephalonia, and some of my most poignant experiences were connected with Cephalonia. Thirdly, she was working throughout the war and after with the Greek guerillas and their British Liaison Officers, and, fourthly, she had the interesting experience of being held by the Gestapo.

I had all four similar experiences; I knew two of the three British soldiers wearing battle-dress in the frontispiece photograph of her book with Archbishop Damaskinos and was serving in the Aegean at the same time as they were, namely George Jellicoe and Frank Macaskie, both of whom were very brave men. I note also that she has the original in her house in Fairholt Street, which is about twenty yards from where I am sitting now.

The only reason I am writing this book is because of what I read once I had got deeper into *Xenia* – to the period describing the attempted capture, or takeover, of Rhodes, followed by George Jellicoe's subsequent capture of Leros and Samos. At this point I said to my wife, 'That has done it' –

and promptly decided to reply to Lady Henderson's book in the form of another book. Like her, I begin at the beginning; nearly seventy-seven years ago.

Jellicoe did not capture Leros and Samos, but he deviated to those islands, going away from the vital island of Rhodes. This, together with General Wilson's failure, and President Roosevelt and Generals Eisenhower and Marshall's determination not to co-operate with Churchill ended with catastrophic results for Britain, Churchill and the world.

The historical facts surrounding one of the most important events in the Second World War – which could have brought victory to Britain by the end of 1943 or early 1944, maintained Britain as the World Leader, obviated the human and material devastation occasioned by the Second Front and greatly diminished the German Jewish holocaust had – for the second time – been completely distorted; just as it had been in the previous excellent book I had read called *War in the Aegean* by Peter C. Smith and Edwin Walker.

In neither case was the author at fault, as until now the exact historical facts have never been disclosed. In my opinion, after almost fifty years of study and re-study of the run up to that date and the subsequent events, I have absolutely no doubt that Britain and Churchill lost their war on that day; the immense tragedy of which I will describe without fear of a convincing contradiction.

I am not saying that the Allies did not win the war; they obviously did, but with the Russians taking the jackpot in the form of immense territorial gains, both in terms of land and human beings.

On September 3rd 1939 our huge Empire, upon which 'The sun never set', went to war. We had the greatest Navy in the world and were the richest Empire on earth, with the lion's share of all the oil in the Middle East and Persian Gulf.

We declared war with the express purpose of saving and liberating Poland from the Germans.

If you go to war to honour a pledge and you fail to do so, you have not won that war.

Today, fifty years later, Poland has gone through every conceivable form of suffering at the hands of its communist masters, who were for many post war years praised and lauded by the world Socialist Left.

14

Exactly the same goes for all the people of Hungary, Romania, Czechoslovakia, Estonia, Latvia, Lithuania, Bulgaria and Albania. Only through their own courageous and painful efforts – and with absolutely no help from Britain, the US or the West are they now, after nearly half a century, reaching a certain degree of liberalisation, but that can never expunge two tortured generations.

Neither can it expunge one of the greatest war crimes of this century, namely the murder of 15,000 Polish officers and elite in the woods of Katyn in 1941. For forty years the Foreign Office has kept hidden the truth and enormity of this crime for fear of annoying the perpetrators: Communist Russia.

Equally well hidden are the prepetrators (in whatever exalted position they may have been) of Britain's most appalling act: shipping 70,000 Yugoslavs and Russian Cossacks to death or slow torture in the Gulag Archipelago, in order to please Stalin and Tito.

Furthermore, we started off as one of the richest and greatest industrial countries in the world, and we ended one of the poorest; vastly overtaken by Germany and Japan, whom we spent six years defeating. We subsequently lost virtually our entire Empire other than the Falkland Islands (the one possession we could possibly have given up in an honourable settlement of a 150 year dispute), resulting in a vast and continuing toll of human loss, tragedies, terrorism and economic bankruptcies scattered over Africa and Asia and Europe.

Some time ago I was sitting next to Montague Browne at dinner; he was Winston Churchill's Private Secretary for the last twelve years of his life, 1955-67 and I happened to ask him if Churchill had died a happy man. He replied, 'Quite obviously not; he went to war to keep Britain great, and he ended up seeing the skeleton of what Britain became.'

This reminded me of what Churchill had said to Robin Maugham and myself in his hour of defeat at 10 Downing Street on 25th July 1945, referring to the Socialists: 'Hardly had I put down the reins of office, when the horse was taken from me, only to be ridden into the quarry.'

Saddam Hussein's blatant and unprovoked attack on Iran in 1980 continued for eight years, resulting in over a million Iranian casualties (plus his own Kurdish villagers of Halabja),

15

many of them suffering a terrible death from poison gas and other chemical horrors. During these eight years the United Nations did nothing. Britain continued trading with Iraq whilst France and others provided them with billions of dollars worth of military equipment with which to continue their slaughter. 'Let them kill each other and not disturb our interests', was the accepted view. Many of the poison gas victims were brought to London hospitals for verification, which was confirmed and seen by all – only to have us looking the other way, and passing on the other side of the street. Now that the boot is on the other foot, with American and Western interests at stake, it is a different story.

In 1982, during the Falklands War, I wrote the following: 'I think for all our interests, and those of our Nation and children's sake, it is most important to get the whole strategy and possible enemy threat into proportion. I believe history will prove that the fall of Khorramshahr was of far greater significance to us and the West than the Falkland Islands is ever likely to become.'

Recently I was staying with the Marquis de Riencourt (author of *The American Empire, The Soul of China, The Soul of India* et al) at his lovely chateau Bellevue, near Geneva. I said to him, 'Amaury, when we first met fifty years ago Britain was one of the two richest and most powerful nations in the world. Where would you place us today, July 30th 1990, amongst the world's industrialised nations?'

'At the bottom of the barrel,' he replied.

He was perhaps too tactful to add that we are in this unenviable position in spite of the generosity of the Almighty in giving us, in North Sea oil, a largesse of $20,000,000,000 each year – or $400 for every person in the UK – which is not enjoyed by any other Common Market country. This is the reason why the people of this country are enjoying a standard of living far beyond what they earn, and even then we are running a balance of trade deficit of £5,000,000,000 a year.

As this book is also for my shareholders, it may interest industrialists and City people to read about the growth of the Exploration Company plc and the El Oro Mining & Exploration Company plc. Their last fifty years are covered in the book, showing how £267,000 has been turned into £75,380,158 – virtually without raising any new money.

Although not in the league of Patrick Leigh Fermor's books, this volume may be of some interest as a travel book. Paddy was walking to Constantinoupoli at the same time as I was going round the world, in 1935, and was also in the Battle of Crete, as I was.

Lastly, I come to the end of the USSR and to the mad and tragic Gulf War, the results of which I cover in full and the seeds of which were sown in September 1943.

1

The Beginning

Life for me began on July 6th 1916, the fourth day of the Battle of the Somme. I was born at Scotsgrove Manor, Oxfordshire, the house my parents were sharing with Hester and Maitland Wilson (later to become Field Marshal Lord Wilson); their son Patrick had preceded me by about eighteen months. They were sharing Scotsgrove because both my father and Maitland Wilson were serving in France.

My father, Clement Woodbine Parish, and my mother, Elsie Mary Bonham-Christie, were married in 1914. When asking his prospective father-in-law, Major Robert Box Bonham-Christie, for his daughter's hand in marriage, my father was asked to produce a list of his investments – to which he had to reply that unfortunately he had no such thing; nevertheless he was allowed to marry her. My brother Charles was born the following year.

After my father had come down from Oxford with a legal degree he was fortunate enough to be accepted by F.E. Smith (later the first Lord Birkenhead), and worked in his chambers in Lincoln's Inn from 1911 until the outbreak of war. Some months before they were married my father was appointed Liberal candidate for Hereford by Lord Chesterfield. This was just before Lord Grey's prophetic remark 'The lights are going out all over Europe.'

With the outbreak of war father joined the Army and, being a qualified barrister, was soon moved into the Provost-Marshal's corps where he remained, becoming an assistant Provost-Marshal by the time he was demobilised in 1918. I still have the diary he wrote during the final stages of the Great War. It describes the liberation of Belgium after four years of

German occupation, and as such is of great historical, as well as personal interest.

Later we moved to 35 Eaton Square, where my brothers and I spent our first few years. One of my earliest memories is of me, aged about four, getting into the family car – a Berliot – which was parked outside on a slight slope. I immediately took off the handbrake, whereupon we whizzed down the slope until we were brought to an abrupt halt by the iron railings surrounding the gardens. This brought a retribution in the form of a red slipper, which my mother rather frequently used.

After the war father left the Bar and joined Reeves Whitburn, which my mother's grandfather, C.J. Sofer-Whitburn, had built up into the largest private discount house in the city of London – big enough to have helped out in the great Baring crises. After C.J.'s death in 1911* my mother's uncle, Joe Sofer-Whitburn, had become Chairman and proprietor.

Father had a few very happy and successful years until Uncle Joe, who was very good at the discount and bill broking market, became terribly speculative. He was a pillar of White's club, had a string of race horses (his wife Tiddles won the 1000 Guineas with one of her horses, trained by Harry Cottrell) and had a magnificent estate near West Malling in Kent, Addington Park. He also had 38 Grosvenor Place, a villa in the south of France, a very fine sporting estate in Scotland, and finally, a hunting box, Warwick Lodge, near Melton Mowbray, where he kept about twenty first class hunters. It was well known at White's – which he had helped out financially when it was in trouble in the '20s – that anyone in financial difficulties could 'touch' Joe Whitburn for a thousand pounds.

However, his high living and enormous speculations in companies such as de Beers soon began to outrun his considerable fortune, and he began to borrow against my mother's and her brother's Trust money, which had been formed by his father for his grandchildren. This became a

---

* In the Appendix is the obituary notice by *Bankers Magazine*. It shows that it was people like C.J. Whitburn who made the City of London pre-eminent in the world.

matter of great embarrassment to father and Uncle Bob, both of whom were working in Reeves Whitburn, and there was ultimately nothing to be done other than to resign from their happy and successful lives in the City. They had to bring a major court action against Uncle Joe to reinstate the Trust money; this created an irrevocable breach in family relations, and we were not to see either Uncle Joe or Tiddles again for some fifteen years; in fact Uncle Joe never again.

All this obviously changed the life of my parents and us children as father was now out of a job, and bringing up a young family was very expensive.

I was about five years old and already boarding at a pre-prep school, Sandgate School in Surrey, which was run by the very able and likeable Miss Honeybun. I clearly remember when, having apparently done something wrong, although I do not think it was anything too serious, I was called out by Miss Honeybun at tea-time. She told me she was afraid that she would have to thrash me in front of the whole school in the morning. This, I remember, was not conducive to a good night's sleep, and next morning the sentence was duly carried out. In spite of this I was happy at Sandgate and always liked Miss Honeybun.

After about a year father got a job in a shipping company in Paris, and Eaton Square was let, first to Lord Suffield and then, partly, to Harold Macmillan, whom father had met when they were fellow guests on Lord Brassey's famous yacht, the *Sunbeam*.

We, meanwhile, emigrated to Paris, where we moved into a nice house at 15 Avenue Malakof. My brothers and I attended a local school just off the Bois de Boulogne. Apparently we became completely bilingual, later disproving the theory that if you learn a foreign language young enough you remember it for the rest of your life. My knowledge of French today is abysmal.

One spring my parents, who were both very keen on hunting, took Charles, Godfrey and myself for the season's stag hunting on Exmoor. We stayed at a Mr Pugsley's farmhouse on Exmoor, taking our ponies with us. The holiday started well, with many exciting hunts across the moors. One day we were all in the farmhouse having lunch when we heard the huntman's horn and the hounds giving tongue. Suddenly they all swept through the Pugsley's farmyard in full cry, whereupon I dashed out, closely followed by Godfrey, threw the saddle and bridle on to my pony and spent the rest of the afternoon well up with the field. Unfortunately Godfrey, who was aged about six, had a nasty fall and broke his arm badly, and had to be taken off and operated on by Sir Arbuthnott Lane, so there was no more hunting for Godfrey that season.

Mr Pugsley had a very tough and aggressive son, who was about two years older than Charles. One day he had the most almighty battle with Charles – a sort of bare-fisted boxing match, until he had virtually knocked poor Charles out. My parents took an exceedingly poor view of this performance and took us away forthwith.

Towards the end of our sojourn in Paris my sister Elizabeth was born, and to include the French connection was christened Elizabeth Yvonne. After two or three years father's shipping work came to an end, and off we all went again, back to England. My parents thought that, having four young children, it would be beneficial to move into the country, and so they bought a small Queen Anne manor house, Little Danby, near Northallerton in Yorkshire. We settled in here very happily, with ponies, dogs, hunting with the Hurworth and Bedale, duck-flighting on the Whisk, which ran through the meadows below the house, summer tennis parties all over the county . . . in other words a childhood paradise.

Father took a partnership with a small brewery, Metcalfe's, at Thornton-le-Moor, and I often remember seeing him start off on an enormous Raleigh bicycle, doing 15-20 miles a day visiting the country pubs in an endeavour to increase the outlets for Metcalfe's – a big contrast to arriving by car at Cornhill, EC1.

Nanny Goodwin, who had been with us since my birth, married Brian Metcalfe, the son of the brewery owner, but nevertheless stayed on with us, bringing Brian too. She remained with us intermittently for the rest of her life, helping also to bring up my own children some thirty to forty years later.

We led a very free, and sometimes wild, life at Little Danby, with frequent shooting expeditions over our land – and also over that belonging to our neighbouring farmer, George Atkinson. One day Charles and I wandered over one of his fields and were just about to shoot some rabbits at the edge of a wood. Suddenly Atkinson sprung up out of the thicket shouting, 'So yore poaching are yore, well I'll have to have you in the lock-oop.' That brought us temporarily to heel somewhat, as in those days (the 1930s) the Constabulary laws were very much stricter than nowadays, and we were pretty certain he meant what he said.

Over the years my parents, with their great friend the architect Philip Tilden, transformed the house into an architectural gem; we all fell in and did our share of work too. I remember having to pick up stones from the front drive when it was turned into a lawn, as the main entrance was being changed to the back of the house.

During the summer holidays one of the many activities was to take father's beehives up to the Cleveland hills near Helmsley, a distance of some twenty miles. The beehives, along with one or two of us, were put in father's trailer, which was then hitched up to the family saloon car – and off to the beautiful heather-clad North Yorkshire moors we would go. There the bees would stay until summer's end, producing enough delicious heather honey for father to sell, at 2s.6d. a comb, to Fortnum & Mason in Piccadilly, which went some way to paying the school fees.

We used to be loaned ponies for the hunting season by our cousins Marcus Kendall and Willie Pickard. Mine was a cream-coloured pony called Henry. I became very fond of Henry, and he would go at any jump one put him at – although I was not nearly as courageous as Van Burden, the Master's son from Constable Burton. Van was the same age as me but absolutely fearless, as was proved fifteen years later when he was an officer in the 11th Hussars fighting Rommel on the Western Desert.

However, thanks to Henry we were never far behind and when the school holidays came to an end I had to ride him to the railway siding at Northallerton, from where he was to return to his home at Ness Hall, Nunnington, Yorkshire. When it came to saying goodbye to him in his railway carriage I unashamedly burst into tears, but fortunately I was alone.

On one occasion I remember going with Nanny and Brian

to Northallerton railway siding; this time to collect two young horses that my mother had bought. We had to lead them back the three miles to Little Danby, and by the time we reached the bridge over the railway line near Yafforth it was almost dark. On reaching the summit of the bridge a fast train came through below us, belching a stream of sparks and flame from its funnel. To me, aged about nine or ten, trying to hold on to a terrified young horse was something I did not forget, although I somehow managed to hang on enough to get him safely home.

One summer holiday our parents took us all to Majorca, where they rented a small house near the sea in Puerta da Polienza. Puerta in 1928 was much the same as it had been in 1028; a small Spanish fishing village, except for one fairly large hotel, the Formentor.

Each day Charles, Godfrey and I would go fishing in our little boat, following the fishermen quite a long way out into the Formentor Bay. One afternoon we were fooling about, rocking the boat, until we eventually succeeded in filling it with water – whereupon it capsized, leaving us nearly a mile out to sea clinging to its keel. Some fishermen had seen our performance from the shore, and rushed to tell my mother about the shipwreck, suggesting they should send out a rescue party. My mother, true to form, replied, 'Of course not; if they have been stupid enough to get themselves into this mess they must get themselves out of it.' With that she thanked them for coming and returned to her sewing.

After about half-an-hour of clinging to the upturned boat we saw a returning fishing boat, which, as my mother had correctly foreseen, took us aboard and towed our waterlogged boat back to harbour.

Once I went to stay on my own for a week or so with my father's cousins Constance and Greville Irby (later Lord Boston). Although I was extremely fond of them I evidently did not show it in a way which they could understand, as one night I found a pair of nail scissors – with which I proceeded to snip holes throughout my fine linen sheets. If, sixty-five years later, one of my young relations behaved in a similar way I have little doubt that I would have got into a towering rage and would have shipped them back to their parents. Not so Greville and Constance, who took it all in their stride, merely

Lady Boston mending her linen sheets after my effort.

asking me not to do it again. They remained amongst my favourite relations all their lives.

For another holiday we went camping on the banks of the river Lune; this, in pouring rain, was not so enjoyable. After a few soaking wet days we made a retreat to Great-Aunt Winnie North's house, Lilymere. My mother and father and Elizabeth stayed in the main house, with our cousin Dorothy. Charles, Godfrey and I, however, were relegated to the boat-house on the edge of the mere. I remember clearly one extremely long and very uncomfortable night spent in one of the boats, feeling very cold and hungry and longing to return home to Little Danby. This expedition put me off camping for life.

On the way home we spent the day with our cousins the Kay-Shuttleworth's, at Barbon Manor. During tea my Great-Uncle Ughtred presided at the end of the table in the long gallery, while we all tucked into a rather good tea of hot scones and honey, followed by a variety of cakes. Not so his Lordship, who consumed only champagne. I was greatly impressed when told that because of his great age (he was born on 18th December 1844) his doctors had ordered him to drink a bottle of champagne every day. (Later in life when staying with John

25

Tennant at Edenglassie in the Scottish highlands, I found that his mother, May Tennant, followed the same routine.)

From Little Danby we went to our prep school, Ludgrove, near New Barnet in Hertfordshire. This was a long journey from Little Danby and we usually went by train, but during the General Strike this was not possible and father had to motor us the 200 miles in his Berliot. I remember hoping against hope that we would break down and not have to go back to school, which, alas, did not happen.

My mother always fitted us out in rather loud tweeds, which caused derision amongst the other boys, but we managed to weather the storm – unlike some other poor boys, including Lloyd Kenyon, who was mercilessly bullied – I can not remember why. He stoically survived, to become Lord Kenyon, a director of Lloyds Bank amongst other distinguished directorships.

After Ludgrove we went to Eton where I was in the same house as Patrick Wilson. This was firstly the kind Mr Leonard Todd's house, but after a year he retired.

The next three years were spent with the inimitable and wonderful Aubrey Claud Beasley-Robinson, who used to coach us in rowing whilst riding his stallion along the towpath. In later years he divested himself of all his worldly wealth, which was fairly considerable, and became a Cowley Father in Oxford. During his very short periods of leave he came to stay with us at Friars Wells, Wartnaby, near Melton Mowbray, and came out hunting with us. Off we would go, with the Belvoir and Quorn, with him wearing his full Cowley Father's robes!

However, soon after beginning at Eton tragedy struck; Mr Aubrey Claud Beasley-Robinson came into my room to tell me the perfectly shattering news that my mother had suddenly died. She was only forty-one years old, and there had been no warning whatsoever that she was ill.

This was to bring the curtain down on our happy and rugged life in Yorkshire, and my heartbroken father was landed with the job of bringing up four wild and unruly children all alone.

He decided to take us all back to London, where he owned a most attractive block of service flats, Park Lodge, which was next to the Hyde Park hotel and overlooked the Serpentine.

Little Danby and the small farm were sold in the worst of the 1931 slump for £7,500, which was considered a very good price.

Father got a job as the West End representative of the General Accident Insurance Company, and was shortly elected to their City Board. He also made his first venture into mining, by buying and restarting the Porkellis tin mine at Wendron in Cornwall. He was joined, as shareholders, by W.L. Stephenson, Chairman of Woolworths, and Lord Astor.

Park Lodge became our home from 1931 until 1936 and, although we were now based in London, father did a wonderful job for us children by enabling us to spend the school holidays in the country.

The summer holidays, for instance, were spent at splendid Scottish sporting estates. For the first three summers he took Glenmorvern, overlooking the Sound of Mull, which had a goodish grouse moor and a twenty-stag deer forest behind it. These Scottish holidays were always immense fun, with the lodges full of masses of friends. There would be boating trips, picnics, grouse shooting most days, stalking, and fishing trips on the Sound of Mull and Loch Etive after dinner – it was light until nearly midnight – all amidst the most beautiful Scottish highland scenery.

Glenmorvern was my favourite place; in fact, looking back over the past sixty years it was the most enormous fun, perhaps unique. Amongst the many friends who came to stay there were Jim and Peter Ramsbotham and their sister Joan.

Jim was a little older than me, a contemporary of Charles's, and was always top of everything at Eton both in games and work. Years later, after the war, he became a Buddhist monk and went to live in a cave in India. One day I was surprised to see a photograph of him peering out of his cave on the front page of the *Sunday Express.* The reporter had gone to tell him that he had just inherited his father's title, thus becoming Lord Soulbury. Jim's reply was. 'What possible interest could that be?' and withdrew into his cave.

Peter became the British Ambassador to the USA, where he did brilliantly until Mr Callaghan replaced him in favour of his son-in-law, Peter Jay.

Glenmorvern was a most happy and sympathique house, made of wood and painted white and standing right above the Sound of Mull, where we swam every morning. Every evening we would go fishing, either for mackerel, or, following the local custom, splashing for salmon and sea trout. This would be done into a very wide semi-circular net – about 100 yards wide. We also had quite a fast motor boat, which would take us in turns behind it on a surf-board; no-one ever seemed to worry about it being cold.

Other friends who used to come to stay on these holidays included Christopher and Tom Hohler, Edward Oliver, Rex Janson and Rivers Bosanquet. They all enjoyed the grouse shooting, which took an hour's walk straight uphill before reaching the moor. However, having spent the day on the hill we were always well rewarded with an excellent dinner, invariably organised by Joan Hulkes and Doris Oliver (Edward's mother). This would be roast grouse, accompanied by vegetables and followed by fruit from Archie MacDonald's excellent and prolific garden.

Charles used to roar us all round the Morvern peninsula in his two-seater, with a dickey in the back. This enabled him, with a bit of a squeeze, to get six on board.

Stalking was another great excitement, usually with only one rifle on the beat at a time. I loved my days with Macleod the stalker; he would take me out in the morning and we would walk for miles, right over the hills towards the descent to Lock Tiarchus, on the other side of the peninsula. It was here that the real stalking began in earnest. Macleod would see through his telescope a number of stags on the broken hillside or corrie, whereupon we would start to crawl – often for an hour – until a suitable shot presented itself. It was here that I got my first stag and with Macleod proceeded to gralloch it. Next he sent up a thin plume of smoke from a small heather fire to alert the pony ghillie as to where to come to collect the stag, which was carried down to the venison shed at Glenmorvern.

At the age of fourteen to spend twelve hours on the hill with my hero Macleod, and to come back exhausted but in triumph was one of my great boyhood memories. Sixty years later I have gone full circle, thinking the stags are far nicer than the people who shoot them – for which pleasure some of them pay up to £1,000 per head; I am afraid I find it rather repulsive.

One day my father suggested that Charles and I and himself should try to swim across the Sound, which is about one mile wide. We therefore covered ourselves in vaseline and, with the stalker Macleod accompanying us in the fishing boat, attempted this feat which apparently had not been done since the 1745 rebellion. Father almost made it and Charles and I, with youth on our side, achieved it.

After three seasons at Glenmorvern father took Ardchattan Priory on Loch Etive, from the Campbell Prestons. It was here that Macmillan happened to be staying many years later when the Profumo crisis broke out with the telephone lines to the highlands suddenly becoming red hot with reports on the attractions of Christine Keeler. However, in my days there in 1933 it was all much the same as at Glenmorvern, except that I was by now seventeen and much enamoured of Jeanne Barry. Jeanne was Colonel Barry's seventeen-year-old daughter and was an attractive and delightful girl. We spent much time together – including climbing to the top of Ben Nevis on a day's expedition from Ardchattan, which was some twenty miles away, and boating along Loch Etive in the midnight sun.

The last place father rented was Flowerdale, on Gairloch, although this one I missed as I was away on my world tour.

Clement must have had many worries bringing up three independent and often unruly boys, not least for the safety of our sister Elizabeth, who was frequently hung upside down by her ankles out of upstairs windows.

Sometimes we all went to stay with our grandparents Beatrice and Arthur Woodbine Parish, at their fine Georgian house Sellarsbrook, near Monmouth. My grandfather's father was Sir Woodbine Parish KCH (1796-1882), the first British Envoy to what was to become the Argentine. My grandmother was the eldest child of Clement Cottrell-Dormer of Rousham in Oxfordshire, famed for its William Kent furniture, ceilings and unique landscaped gardens. The Cottrell-Dormers had the honour of being Master of Ceremonies for the Royal Court through five reigns, beginning in 1660. Whilst in this hereditary office a medal was worn by the Cottrells that had

THE

DIPLOMATIC HISTORY

OF THE

MONARCHY OF GREECE,

FROM THE YEAR 1830,

SHOWING THE TRANSFER-TO-RUSSIA OF THE MORTGAGE HELD BY
BRITISH CAPITALISTS OVER ITS PROPERTY AND REVENUES.

BY

HENRY HEADLEY PARISH, ESQ.,

LATE SECRETARY OF LEGATION TO GREECE.

" Contempts against the Prerogative may also be, by preferring the interests of a Foreign Potentate to those of our own, or doing or receiving any thing that may create an undue influence, in favour of such extrinsic power."— *Blackstone*, Book iv. Chap. 9.

LONDON :

J. HATCHARD AND SON, 187, PICCADILLY.

1838.

The title page of the book written by the author's Great Uncle and published by Hatchard who are still at the same address.

My descent from Sir Thomas More, Lord Chancellor of England.

Born 1478. beheaded 1535. canonized at Rome 1935.

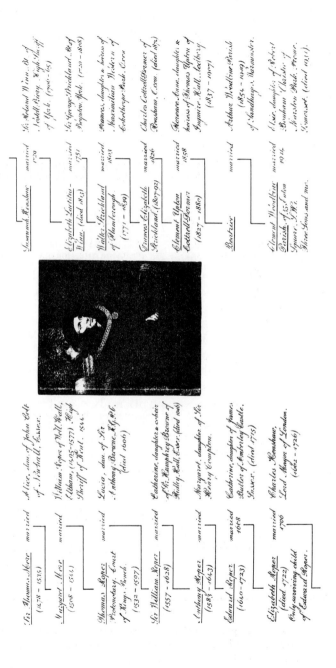

Sir Thomas More (1478–1535) — married 1505 — Alice, dau. of John Colt of Nethall, Essex.

Margaret More (1508–1544) — married — William Roper of Well Hall, Eltham (1495–1577) High Sheriff of Kent. 1544.

Thomas Roper, Prothonotary, Court of King's Bench. (1533–1597) — married — Lucia, dau. of Sir Anthony Browne, K.G.M.C. (died 1606)

Sir William Roper (1557–1628) — married — Catherine, daughter & coheir of Sir Humphrey Browne of Ridley Hall, Essex (died 1606)

Anthony Roper (1583–1643) — married — Margaret, daughter of Sir Henry Compton.

Edward Roper (1640–1723) — married 1668 — Catherine, daughter of James Butler of Amberley Castle, Sussex. (died 1715)

Elizabeth Roper (died 1722) Only surviving child of Edward Roper. — married 1706 — Charles Henshaw, Lord Mayor of London. (1662–1726)

Susannah Henshaw — married 1729 — Sir Roland Winn, Bt. of Nostell Priory, High Sheriff of York (1700–65)

Elizabeth Lætitia Winn (died 1813) — married 1751 — Sir George Strickland, Bart. Boynton, York. (1729–1808)

Walter Strickland of Flamborough (1771–1839) — married 1803 — Frances, daughter & heiress of Maximilian Western of Cokethorpe Park, Oxon.

Frances Elizabeth Strickland (1807–92) — married 1826 — Charles Cottrell Dormer of Rousham, Oxon. (died 1871)

Clement Upton Cottrell Dormer (1827–1880) — married 1858 — Florence Anne, daughter & heiress of Thomas Upton of Ingmire Hall, Sedbergh (1837–1907)

Beatrice — married — Arthur Woodburn Parish (1854–1919) of Sandheys, Warwickshire.

Clement Woodburn Parish, of 55 Eaton Square, S.W. Three sons and mar. — married 1914 — (our daughter of Robert Benham Cheshire, of Norton Hall, near Norton Priors, near Somerset. (died 1931).

31

been put round Sir Charles Cottrell's neck by Charles II at the Restoration. The King thanked Sir Charles for all he had done and for all he had suffered for the Royal Family.

This post was similar to what is currently Master of the Diplomatic Corps.

On one visit to our grandparents, during the very cold Christmas holidays, Godfrey decided he would like to be able to enjoy a warm bed. He therefore took the shade off his bedside lamp before pushing it down in between his sheets – thinking that when he came up from his supper he would have a nice warm bed. In this he was right, as by then the bed was almost on fire, with the sheets and blankets badly singed.

During the same visit my Uncle Henry arranged for us to be invited to a number of neighbouring shoots. At one of these, a fairly grand affair, the bag was laid out as usual at the end of the day and it amounted to about 200 pheasants. Considerable satisfaction was shown all round until Charles announced *en passant* that the tracer cartridges which he had been using had been of great help to him.

Unknown to Charles, but known to everyone else, tracer cartridges were poisonous to anything they hit. As it was impossible to tell which birds had been hit by Charles (who had only used about six) the entire bag, the efforts of eight guns and some twenty-five beaters and keepers, all had to be destroyed forthwith. Not surprisingly poor Uncle Henry was never again invited to that particular neighbour's shoot!

Long leaves were often spent with Christopher and Tom Hohler, and their mother and stepfather with whom we always shared our Scottish holidays. They lived at Long Crendon Manor, Thame (where the film of Henry VIII with Charles Laughton and Merle Oberon was filmed).

We shot partridge at Hampton Gay, their farm near Oxford, and hunted with the Bicester, and I still remember the wonderful breakfasts with that great character Snelgrove, the butler in charge.

During our Christmas holidays we often went to stay with the Townshends at Raynham; at the age of fifteen I had fallen in love for the first time with Elizabeth, George Townshend's sister. The drives down from London to Raynham, a distance of some 130 miles, usually turned into a kind of Le Mans race, and later we all tried to complete the journey in under two hours. I had just been given a Bugatti; a move up from the Lea Francis which I had had from the age of sixteen, and in which I used to motor up to Scotland for our holidays.

Our frequent visits to Raynham were always enormous fun, and there was always a large number of kindred spirits staying. George was a splendid host, as was his sister Elizabeth, although everything was organised and loosely arranged by their mother the Marchioness of Townshend; their father having died when they were very young. Raynham is a magnificent Georgian house surrounded by a very large agricultural estate which amounted to many thousands of acres and we went there most in the early thirties, which was the time of the great recession. During this time farm land in their area was almost unlettable and virtually unsaleable except at £5 or £10 an acre. In spite of this, and having huge mortgages on the estate, the Marchioness, and later George, did a wonderful job keeping the enormous house and estate going.

If we spent Christmas in London we always went swimming in the Serpentine on Christmas day. All five flats in Park Lodge were serviced by a most remarkable man called Martini. Martini seemd to think nothing of serving dinner to all five flats at the same time.

One summer my father took Charles and me to stay with his friends Lord and Lady Greenway; they lived in a lovely house called Stanbridge Earls, which had a famous beat on the Test. My father was very keen on swimming and we all used to plunge into the crystal clear waters of the Test before breakfast each day.

Lord Greenway was Chairman of British Petroleum and there was usually a number of other guests staying, as there were on this occasion. Lady Greenway's life revolved around her fox terrier, which, through excessive feeding, had become absolutely enormous, closely resembling an elongated balloon. Charles and I were so fascinated by its enormous size that one evening just before dinner, in front of the assembled guests, we proceeded to measure the unfortunate dog's girth with a tape measure. We were amazed to discover that it measured over forty-five inches, and reported this interesting observation to Lady Greenway.

Silence fell upon us all, until Lady Greenway drew herself

The butler consoling Lady Greenway's dog.

up and ordered the butler to put our suitcases into the car, as we would be leaving immediately. Poor Clement, always being let down by us, was asked to take us away.

In the autumn of 1934 my father rented a fine house and estate on the left hand side as you go up Kingston Hill, called Kenry House. Here we were able to have horses and could ride all over Wimbledon Common and Richmond Park, scarcely ever having to cross a road. We became very attached to Kenry House, in fact when writing to Clement from Jerusalem some months later I put at the top of the letter 'Get Kenry'. Unfortunately he did no such thing, and the following year it was let to the young King Farouk of Egypt, before he returned to Egypt to take over his Kingdom.

My brothers and I completed our education at Eton, although perhaps it would be more correct to say that Charles and Godfrey left with adequate marks in the School Certificate, but that was not actually the case with me. Although I had been accepted by Mr Bernard Manning for Jesus College Cambridge, and had passed the Jesus College entrance exam, I could not go there until I had passed what was then known as 'Little Go', the entrance to the university. This proved to be a major obstacle for me, and also for one of my contemporaries in my house.

This was Everard Bingham Hambro (known as Fatty Hambro), who, when confronted by 'Little Go' a few months after me, was approached by an Indian. The Indian suggested that for a certain modest fee he would sit in the hall and do all Fatty's exams for him. It would, however, be most important that Hambro did not appear at any time during the week's exam, or be seen by the invigilator, and that he, the Indian, would sign in each day under the name of E.B. Hambro.

As poor Fatty's chances of passing the exam were probably even worse than mine he promptly accepted the offer, and some months later it was announced with some pleasure –and not a little surprise – that Fatty Hambro had passed into Cambridge, where he subsequently spent two enjoyable years. However, having failed his first year's exams, and then his second year's, he was politely told not to darken the portals of Cambridge again.

Having received a rocket from his father, Brigadier-General Hambro, he then went into the city of London. In due course he became one of the head men in a leading merchant bank, I think Samuel Montague, but sadly he died very young – I always feared from a surfeit of city lunches.

As for me, the Beechers Brook of 'Little Go' probably changed the whole course of my life. Despite going to a crammer at Frant, in Kent, I was not as confident as Bernard Manning (with whom I got on very well), that I would pass the next time round. Also, I thought that I would have a much more interesting and practical time if I did the grand tour, spending the next eighteen months travelling around the world.

My father, after a certain amount of hesitation (and persuasion) agreed to my suggestion of going with a school friend, Toby Horsford, and we set off on January 1st 1935.

In the letters I wrote to my father every ten days or so, I can show the world as seen by an eighteen-year-old boy in the last great days before the twilight of the British Empire. These letters may be the subject of a separate book.

Whilst in China I had been fascinated by the Chinese

35

custom of fixing bamboo whistles to the legs of thousands of pigeons; when they swooped down it had the result of making them sound like thousands of dive-bombers. I bought a lot of these small whistles and on my return planned, with Charles, to fit them to some of the pigeons in Trafalgar Square. The idea was for them to dive bomb off Nelson's column, but sadly we never got round to bringing this scheme to fruition.

We arrived back on Cunard's SS *Georgic* on about April 15th 1936, having seen a large part of the world and many different people, races, industries and political philosophies. During my travels I had already formed a pretty shrewd idea of what I wanted to do for the rest of my life. This was to go into the mining world, as the whole of Africa, Australia, Canada, America and Mexico were awakening to the greatest mining boom of the century. This was almost certainly led by South Africa, with the opening up of the fabulous Witwatersrand goldfield centred on Johannesburg, known as the Rand – greatly enhanced by President Roosevelt's recent doubling of the gold price. There were also many satellite mineral fields such as the vast Merensky platinum belt, diamonds on and off-shore, also in South West Africa, and the vast copper deposits at Phalabora. These were all discovered by possibly the greatest of all geologists, Dr Hans Merensky. Fifty years later South Africa has produced thousands of tons of gold, hundreds of tons of diamonds, millions of tons of copper and millions of ounces of platinum, making a combined value of trillions of dollars.

My life's objective began in Rhodesia in 1935, whilst with A.A. Carnegie and Colonel, later Lord Robins, Chairman of the Chartered Company. Equally important was my insight into the great mining finance houses, many of whose leaders I had met whilst I was in Johannesburg. These included Sir Ernest Oppenheimer, founder of the Anglo-American, and his young son Harry, with whom we stayed at their Brenthurst home.

The older established mining houses included Sir Alfred Beit's and Werhner's Central Mining, and Sir Henry Strakosch's Union Corporation which, through judicious investments and outright loans and gifts saved Winston Churchill from bankruptcy just before the war, and Sir

Frederick Hamilton's (who was sentenced to death after the Jamieson raid) H.E. Propriety standing for Hamilton and Erlech, both of whom I met and did business with.

Barney Barnato's mining house, formed before the turn of the century, was Jo'burg Consolidated, otherwise known as 'Johnnies'. Other than by professional managers it was chaired by Jim Joel. (I was later to meet Jim Joel, with Alma Christopherson. He won the Derby with 'Royal Palace', and almost all the great flat classics. In 1987, aged ninety-six, he was flying to England from Cape Town when the captain announced over the radio that Mr Joel's horse 'Major Venture' had just won the Grand National, and promptly ordered champagne for all 450 passengers.)

An interesting sideline derived from Johnnies was the famous Bentley car. Barney Barnato's son, Woolf Barnato, was Bentley-crazy, and used to race them. He achieved a hat-trick by winning the Le Mans race three years running, in the early 1920s. By 1925 Bentley Motors were on the verge of bankruptcy and were successfully rescued by Woolf. In pre-war days his daughter Diana became a great friend of Charles and myself.

Another great mining house was that of Sir Abe Bailey. By 1938 he had virtually moved to England, where he lived in Bryanston Square. I remember going to a dance there for his two daughters, Ann and Noreen, where he was gallantly present in his wheelchair, having just had both his legs amputated. That, however, did not stop him watching his horse 'Lovely Rosa' win the Oaks the same year. His eldest son, John, who was maried to Diana, Churchill's daughter, did not want to carry on the business (which had the best part of the future Orange Free State goldfields) and thus it fell into the hands of Sir Ernest Oppenheimer's Anglo-American.

Amongst the newly formed mining houses was Anglo Vaal, formed by Basil Hersov and S.B. Meynell, always known as Slip Meynell. Whilst travelling out on the *Windsor Castle* with Charles in 1939 we saw quite a lot of our fellow passenger Basil Hersov, but sadly he died too young to see the full success achieved by Anglo Vaal.

An equally young and distinguished mining house was started by Punch Barlow whom I knew from polo playing at the Inanda Club in Johannesburg in 1935. He had come down from Cambridge with a rugger blue and in the 1930s started what is now known as Barlow Rand; it is now a huge 1000m rand operation.

Next comes Cecil Rhodes and C.D. Rudd's Consolidated Goldfields, which at that time was very much a waning star, but already on the springboard to take over the lead again. This was thanks to their brilliant move, originated by Carlton Jones and Dr Maclaren, of employing and backing a young German geophysicist, Dr Krahmann, straight from Charlottenburg University. He was the first person to have correlated the significance of the carbon leader which underlay so much of the West Rand. Furthermore Dr Krahmann, who had been introduced to Carlton Jones by Dr Merensky, was able to locate the carbon leader even at depths of 8,000 feet and more underground.

The great importance of being able to trace the carbon leader over hundreds of miles throughout the Far West Rand was that, wherever the carbon leader was, there was one of the richest gold-bearing veins with a remarkable consistency in values for mile upon mile.

Douglas Christopherson was the then manager of Consolidated Goldfields in South Africa (and the father of my friend Stanley Christopherson who was later to command my regiment the Sherwood Rangers with such distinction that he was described by F.M. Montgomery as one of the finest colonels in the war) and he gave Dr Krahmann a free hand over the next year or so to plot the carbon leader over the whole of the Far West Rand.

When he had completed this work the Goldfields management pegged, for their newly formed subsidiary West Witwatersrand Ltd, the entire area amounting to hundreds of square miles. This was to produce at least a dozen of the greatest gold mines the world has ever seen, or is likely to see, such as Venterspost, Libanom, Kloof, West and East Driefontein, Doornfontein, Blyvoorichtzig, Western Deep Levels and Western Ultra Deep Levels.

These mines, some of which will still be going in 2020, have already produced thousands of tons of gold, worth trillions of dollars – all stemming from Dr Krahmann's £50 per month salary.

2

Back Home After World Tour

As I leant over the *Georgic's* rails on arrival at Southampton the above scenario was very much in my mind, although I knew that I had been signed up and apprenticed to Sir Alfred Savill, of Savill's estate agents. I was happy at the prospect of working under General Cole, President of the Chartered Institute of Surveyors and the Chairman of father's recently formed company Porkellis Property and General Investment Trust, which was already making excellent progress in the property world.

Father had originally formed the company and allocated the first twenty-five shares to me who, he intended, was to become a fully qualified chartered surveyor before following in General Cole's footsteps. This was attractive and exciting, but my heart was already set on mining and finance, and the memories of the 'Little Go' exam – and thus the horrors that would have to be overcome to become an FRICS – gave me cold shudders.

However the homecoming, and the pleasure of being with father and my family again soon allayed these fears, albeit temporarily, and it was very exciting hearing how father's new ventures were progressing, such as the Porkellis tin mine.

My work with Savills commenced almost immediately, and I had to go round inspecting and checking up on damp and other such problems in people's houses.

It did not take me long to realise that this type of career would not thrill me for the rest of my life.

Father had a business friend, Herbert George Latilla, who was head of one of London's leading mining houses whose main companies were the Gold Coast Selection Trust,

Rhodesia Corporation and East Rand Consolidated, plus numerous lesser companies. I asked my father if there was any chance of getting me into the Latilla group, with a view to starting at the bottom of the organisation, which was housed in Finsbury Pavement House in Moorgate.

Thus one Sunday afternoon he took me down to Latilla's country house, Marlands, near Horsham in Sussex, where we arrived in time for tea. There was a large party of guests, including the portly Lord Portarlington and Dr Edward Papenfus, the eminent South African geologist who had been largely responsible for discovering the Orange Free State Goldfields.

I understandably kept a very low profile amongst all these important and opulent people, but was delighted when motoring back with Clement, to hear that HGL had agreed for me to start just as soon as I had extricated myself from Savills. This I managed to do without too many problems (I expect they were equally pleased with my departure), and I was able to report for duty at Finsbury Pavement House towards the end of 1936. Thus began my Mining House career, which has continued unbroken, with the exclusion of the six war years, until now.

Coinciding with my change in careers was also a major change in the Parish family life. My father, who had been a widower for six years, became engaged to Eva Lawson-Johnson, and they were married shortly afterwards with my brother Charles acting as best man for our father.

Eva was a very sweet, kind person, who had no fewer than twelve brothers and sisters. After their marriage we moved back into 35 Eaton Square as the last tenant had recently given up his lease.

Life became great fun, with much entertaining – at which my father was excellent – ably assisted by the superb cook, Mrs Hayes, Lawrence the parlour-maid and Ernest Bowles, the young chauffeur/valet.

In those pre-war days the London season was something never to be forgotten, with a large dance almost every night, given by the mother of a precious, and often beautiful, daughter. These were great occasions, often held in their large private houses, with every man in tails and everyone invited to lavish dinner parties before going on to the dance. We all had dance cards with pencils attached by white silk tassels, and of course there was always a scramble at the beginning of each party to book one's favourite girl for several of the dances.

There would always be an excellent band (often Harry Roy's), lashings of champagne, and delicious second dinners with all the delicacies, such as quails in aspic, that were freely available in pre-war years.

As I was now working fairly hard in the City I always tried to leave by midnight, but made many life-long friends from these three glittering pre-war seasons, 1937, 1938 and 1939 and immediately post-war.

At this stage Godfrey and Elizabeth were still at school, and Charles was working in Lloyds, in the City. He and I would leave home at about 9 o'clock in the morning and bicycle the four miles to the City, arriving by our clock-in time of 9.30 am. At the end of the day we would return by bicycle to the Bath Club in Dover Street, which in those days was almost an institution with a seven-year waiting list to join.

Every evening at about 6 o'clock we, together with many of our friends – of all ages and from all walks of life – would rendezvous for a swim in the exceptionally good bath. Because of the great height of the room there was never any condensation and there was a succession of rings suspended on ropes from the ceiling, on which we all swung, like Tarzans, from one end of the bath to the other.

Overlooking the pool was a balcony, going all around the room, and this was where many of the elderly, or less energetic members would congregate to enjoy a drink and a chat with their friends. Amongst these I would often see my future father-in-law, Jack Trent.

After swimming some of the members (not often myself) would go and do twenty minutes hard work in the gym, and amongst these I would often see Bernard Freyberg, who later commanded me in Crete. He had won a VC in the First World War for swimming across the Bosporus under gunfire at night, painted black, and was famous for many other exploits, during which he was riddled with bullet holes; this was most evident when he was wearing his gym shorts. He used to spar with an equally tough customer, Dr Hans Pirou, the South African Minister of Defence who was renowned for his pro-Nazi sympathies.

41

Sometimes at weekends we would go to the Ranelagh Club, which in those days was very much one up on Hurlingham. It no doubt would have remained so had it not been for one gentleman who had managed to buy up enough Founders' shares to gain control of the club. He sold its unique 200 acres of green belt for a housing project, which sadly put the shutters up on Ranelagh.

In July 1937 one of my dancing partners, Priscilla Bibesco, invited me to stay with her aunt and uncle, Prince George and Princess Marthe Bibesco, at their house near Posada in Romania. As it was 1,500 miles away I suggested that if I could bring a friend, Toby Horsford, we could come out on our recently acquired motorcycles, mine being a brand new 500cc Norton. This was agreed, and off we set, travelling through Holland, Belgium, France and Germany and doing the last leg by train.

As it was summertime the Bibescos were staying in their most wonderful summer house, on the hills above Bucharest. (Their winter residence was a huge palace of mellowed brick on the outskirts of Bucharest, remarkably similar to Hampton Court Palace, and of the same size and period.)

They had a huge house party of about twenty people staying, and these included Margot Oxford, Priscilla's aunt, and Violet Trefusis. Our hostess, Princess Marthe, was absolutely charming, and gave us all the most wonderful fortnight. Prince George showed us all over his estate and his fairly substantial industrial activities. I remember when he was taking us round his large brick works the manager, who was in attendance, had somehow annoyed him. The Prince caught him by the ear and twisted it round to such an extent that I thought it would come off – and at the same time continued explaining the various processes of the plant.

Being very interested in world affairs, politics and industry (probably stemming from my eighteen months travelling around the world), and having seen and felt the throbbing energy and re-birth of Germany, I appreciated that if war with Germany did come, Romania would be one of its most obvious targets – either as an ally or a captive. It had vast agricultural resources for Hitler to feed on and, above all, it had the Ploesti oil fields. These were not only very substantial but also the only natural oil fields in Europe, and would be vital in the event of war, for Hitler's war machine. These oil fields had a double interest for me, as my mining companies were amongst the original shareholders in Phoenix oil and transport, which owned the Ploesti oil fields (and whose shares, incidentally, we still have today). There was plenty for me to think about as well as enjoying the holiday.

One evening Violet Trefusis took Toby and me down to the casino at Posada, which was every bit as glamorous and sophisticated as Monte Carlo, and she entertained us to champagne on her winnings. I remember returning to the house, where everyone was still up, and feeling very much the worse for the champagne, having to sit down next to Margot Oxford and join in the general conversation.

On the return journey to England I wanted to see Rheims cathedral, and the Champagne area of France – which I duly did, but on my way to Paris I had an accident on my Norton and badly hurt my leg. I was about seventy miles from Paris, and rode to the Gare du Nord in a certain amount of pain – anyway, I somehow managed to get there and put the motorcycle on the morning boat train for London. I then spent the next few hours in one of the more fashionable Parisian nightclubs before catching the train myself, in the early morning. The journey home was exceedingly uncomfortable and painful, and I arrived to find all my family away in Scotland. My next stop was with the doctor, who X-rayed my leg, pronounced the fibula bone broken, and promptly put it in plaster.

Back in the City I seemed to swiftly get into the swim of things in the Mining House that I worked for; it was during the middle of the gold boom of 1936-7 and it was said that Herbert Latilla had been seen sticking pins into himself to see if he was really alive, and not in a dream. This was because he had made such a fabulous fortune in the gold boom he could not quite believe it was true. He was floating a number of sizeable mining companies in the Gold Coast, Nigeria, Rhodesia and South Africa, and I was a fly on the wall, watching and working and fascinated by the excitement of it all. I would decode cables sent by Latilla when he occasionally visited his new mining ventures on the East Rand in a company he had bought from Sir Abe Bailey, called East Rand Consolidated. He used to stay with Abe Bailey at his wonderful house Rust-en-Vrede, at St James's, in the Cape.

After about a year at Finsbury Pavement House I suggested to father that it was high time we started a mining house of our own. At some of my lunches at the Mining Club in Finsbury Circus I had come across two very distinguished and elderly mining engineers, Cordner and Trewarthur James, who, with a very fine Australian, A.H. Collyer, chaired, ran and managed a small quoted mining company called Star Explorations Ltd, in Finsbury House, Bloomfield Street. As they wished to retire they agreed to sell out and, for a modest amount of money they sold their administrative company and offices to a company which father and myself had formed called Danby Registrars. At the same time father was appointed to the board of Star Explorations, with the proviso that I too would be elected in due course, as I was soon to be twenty-one. I thus crossed my Rubicon, and we were away, albeit in a very small way.

At the beginning of 1938, on the friendliest possible terms, I left Herbert George Latilla and his dynamic organisation to go into my own small mining finance house. Before long I spotted other possible avenues of expansion, in the form of The Exploration Company. This belonged to the Rothschilds and was one of the first, and oldest, mining houses in the City, having been formed in 1886. In spite of this, and having a number of successes behind it – including building the Central London Underground line in 1890, and all the Paris Metro system – it had hit disaster in the Iron Cap gold mine in Rhodesia, and had lost the majority of its assets. This had so discredited the Board that when they were approached by Harley Drayton's Anglo Scottish Amalgamated Trust with the offer to buy from the shareholders all the shares in The Exploration Company, at a price of 3s.6d. – provided they obtained ninety per cent acceptances, the Board agreed.

From my new headquarters in Finsbury House I naturally watched this with the greatest interest, particularly when it was announced that Drayton had failed to get ninety per cent acceptances. I immediately asked father if he would go round post haste to see Lionel de Rothschild (whom he had known since his university days) at New Court to ask if we, Star Explorations, were to put in a bid for 2s.10d. a share, they

44

would accept it. Father agreed to do just that; he was still engaged in mining, with his now wholly owned Porkellis tin mine doing well, and he was also a Director of H.G. Latilla's National Mining Corporation. He also represented his brother-in-law Lord Luke for Ashanti Goldfields on the Board of London and African Investment Trust (which, incidentally, is still going strong today under the very able chairmanship of Michael Heller).

One weekend whilst staying with my great friend Marion Keilberg and her parents, Sir Michael and Lady Keilberg at their lovely house Stockgrove, near Leighton Buzzard, I was suddenly called to the telephone. It was my father, who gave me probably the most important business news of my life, namely that the Rothschilds had accepted our bid – on condition that we made it to all the other shareholders too.

This was quite stupendous news for me, and I instinctively knew that this was the beginning of my career.

On Monday morning we lost no time in getting our offer out to the 2,000 Exploration shareholders. The offer remained open for three weeks, and by the closing date we had received just under fifty per cent acceptances, which we accepted and the offer was then closed. We were delighted to have 1,000 shareholders who were happy to continue under us.

The Exploration assets were similar to those of Star Exploration, namely £125,000, so in one fell swoop my embryo group had combined assets of £¼m. However, we did not stop there as The Exploration Company in turn had a holding of 112,000 shares in its sister company, the El Oro Mining and Railway Company Ltd.

This company had been floated in 1890 to work and mine the famous El Oro mine in Mexico, and its eighty miles of railway network. For some twenty-five years they had been immensely successful, working one of the richest silver and gold mines in the world and paying substantial dividends. However, with the advent of the communist revolution in Mexico, the depletion of the ore reserves and the liability of running the railway, the future for El Oro was beginning to look rather sombre, although they still had net liquid assets of over £100,000.

I suggested to father that we should approach the Chairman, J.H.M. Shaw, to see if he would agree to retire and appoint father as Chairman and also for the company to join the Star Exploration/Exploration Group.

After two weeks of friendly negotiations this was all achieved, with the new Star Exploration group having combined assets of £350,000.

(That was in 1938, and now in 1990, the three companies are still together and under the same management. Having raised virtually no new money from the original 2,000 shareholders – a number of whom are still with us – the assets have grown – almost entirely self-generated – to over £50m, to be put against an issued capital of less than it was 100 years ago).

Having made this quantum leap we now had to reorganise and run these companies, largely beset as they were with problems.

For instance, the El Oro company was bound by statute and the new revolutionary government in Mexico to continue running their passenger trains from El Oro to the main junction, and the mine was under threat of nationalisation. We had an excellent general manager in Mexico, Mr Wasteneys, and we sent him a cable asking him to come to London. We wanted to draw up a plan which would enable a tourniquet to be applied as soon as possible, but which had to be done in conformity with the new laws of the Mexican Government. After a worrying six months Mr Wasteneys was able to report that in exchange for our Mexican assets he had been able to hand over the railways to the Government. The losses were quenched and the El Oro company was finally able to withdraw from Mexico with no further liabilities.

It was at this same time that other companies, such as The Mexican Eagle Oil Company, lost millions through nationalisation, to the great regret of the first Lord Cowdray, Wheatman Pearson, and Shell Oil.

In the case of The Exploration Company, their massive loss in their Rhodesian mine, the Iron Cap, needed urgent attention. I was shortly to fly out in a Sunderland flying boat via Crete, Khartoum and Lake Victoria to Rhodesia to see what could be done, and, if possible, to salvage something from the investment.

In the meantime life in London, and enjoyable weekend house parties, continued to be great fun, although the cloud, which had begun five years earlier no bigger than a man's hand, had grown considerably.

Hitler's shadow was casting a menacing threat over western Europe, when the house next door to us became the residence of the German Ambassador, Herr von Ribbentrop. He was known amongst my contemporaries as 'Herr von Drop-a-brick'. Often when returning home at midnight from a dance, I would see the Ambassador's car draw up outside number 36. As I went in to number 35 I would pause for a moment to watch 'Drop-a-brick' stand at attention, click his heels and salute his chauffeur with a 'Heil Hitler' – even though there was seldom anyone other than myself around at that time of night.

For the past few years I had been fascinated by world affairs, particularly foreign affairs and the relentless inexorable advance of Hitler's Nazi Germany. The only time I became seriously concerned that the odds against Britain and her Empire were showing signs of being overwhelming was when our neighbour pulled off the greatest diplomatic coup of the whole period, namely the Molotov-Ribbentrop Pact.

This, in a nutshell agreed that Hitler's Germany, allied to Stalin's USSR would contain the heartland of Europe, stretching for 5,000 miles – from Cologne on the Rhine to Vladivostock, including 300 million potentially very tough fighters. I knew that Stalin and his communist entourage loathed the capitalist Britain and her great Empire, and that he was hovering like a vulture over what he thought would be the corpse for him and his fellow dictator Adolf Hitler to dismember. Years later this terrible plan with Stalin's desires were exposed in their entirety by the opening up of archives in various chanceries.

It was in the light of all this that I considered the only possibility of arresting this coming avalanche. This was by going over to Germany in the guise of a pro-Nazi student and, at one of his mass meetings, shooting Hitler dead. I am convinced that if someone had had the courage to kill him at any time from 1936-1939, the greatest war in the history of mankind, and the loss of upwards of twenty million people, would never have taken place.

At this time Churchill, who was far from accepted as anything other than a war-monger – with the reputation of having created the disaster of the Dardanelles, was making speeches about the coming danger of Germany. My brother Charles had just joined the Auxiliary Air Force, and I, like many others of my age, decided to join the Territorial Army. I thought that if there was going to be a war (and I thought the chances were about even) I had much better be carried by a horse than march on my own two feet. One weekend I was staying at Brocklesby Park in Lincolnshire with Diana Pelham; her father the Earl of Yarborough was Colonel of the Nottinghamshire Sherwood Rangers Yeomanry, and he invited me to join them. As this did not entail any beastly exams, but gave me the entrée straight in as a second lieutenant, I promptly accepted.

I was never greatly enamoured with the thought of being a soldier, which I always imagined – and correctly so – would entail punctuality, being bossed about, and long periods of intense boredom. My only previous experience of soldiering was in the corps at school, and it had not taken me long to discover that the corps was a voluntary organisation – I horrified Beasley-Robinson, who had been through Woolwich, then a regular gunner and through the 1914-1918 war, when I told him that I had decided to resign; this set a precedent, as it had not been done before.

However, with Hitler now in the political driving seat I saw the necessity of pulling myself together, and proceeded to spend a number of weekends at my regimental headquarters in Newark.

I used to motor up in my almost new V12 cylinder Lincoln Zephyr which was just about the best car I have ever had, and was capable of doing 120mph.

Apart from the intermittent weekend training we had two weeks of summer camp, which was held at Welbeck, the Duke of Portland's seat. He had been the Colonel of our regiment before Lord Yarborough, and his brother Morven, who became a close friend, was also in the regiment. Regimental cavalry exercises at the gallop in Welbeck Park were quite an exhilarating experience, but I was not greatly amused by the horse-play in the Mess after dinner each night. My only other part-time military duty was a two-week course with the Blues at Combermere Barracks, Windsor.

When I was a child we often used to go to stay with our distant cousins, Geraldine and Marcus Kendal, who had a lovely farm at Ness Hall, Nunnington, Yorkshire. Charles, Godfrey, Elizabeth and I had many happy summer holidays hunting with the York and Ainsty while staying with them. We also used to chase rabbits as the binder cut the corn, converging in ever-smaller circles, until, in the last circle, about the size of a tennis court, there would be a mad rush of rabbits out into the open, with us helter-skelter after them.

Marcus Kendal, who had built up a wonderful breed of hunters which he called the Mint breed, was invited every year to judge the young horse class at Dublin Horse Show. He also supplied a large number of Yorkshire-bred horses to my father's brother-in-law, Colonel Sir Percival Lawrie who had built up, and was commandant of, the Mounted Police. These were based in Imber Court, and were one of the many prides of London.

Shortly after I had joined the Cavalry Yeomanry Regiment Marcus (who knew I was very keen on hunting) told me that he had just bred the finest colt he had ever produced, and that if there was going to be a war, which looked fairly certain, he would keep him for me until the war was over. I could then come back and have him broken by Willy Pickard, his neighbour, who was renowned as a horse-breaker. I was delighted, and paid Marcus £400 for the young foal Spartamint, and told him I would be back at the end of the war to take delivery.

In 1938 I went out to Rhodesia to see if anything could be salvaged from the Iron Cap mine. It had been fairly extensively developed, mostly by adits into the hillside, and it had a large mill and treatment plant, all complete and capable of treating 500 tons a day. The problem was that the ore reserves were reputed to run at between three and five pennyweights per ton, but in practice the first 10,000 tons had yielded less than two pennyweights of gold. I had to evaluate – with my old friend the mining engineer A.A. Carnegie – whether we could get the cost down enough to make a large scale 1½dwt mine profitable. On balance we decided it was worth a try, and we took on a manager, Mr McIntyre, and some staff and put it back into operation.

Having set this in motion, I then returned to England and worked very hard on the companies. Father was in the chair and the directors included Major W.M. Henderson-Scott. I became very attached to Max Henderson-Scott, who was a distinguished mining engineer, and also to his family.

I concentrated on the tactical and strategic planning side of the business, with growth and expansion foremost in mind, while the others handled the administrative operations of the companies. On the expansion front we had extended our little empire by purchasing control of a rubber plantation in Sumatra, called Pereulla Sumatra Rubber Co. Ltd, which was a quoted London Stock Exchange company. Their assets consisted of a valuable estate in Sumatra with a thousand acres of recently planted rubber trees, which would be in profitable production in some three years' time.

Likewise, with a view of entering British industry, we bought control from Berthold Woolfe of his publicly quoted textile Moratti Spinning Mills which had interests in the textile world, including a lingerie manufacturing company called Kempat. This had an extensive factory at Mitcham, employing a work-force of over 100, and was not only profitable – with a leading brand name in the trade – but had every latent possibility for industrial expansion.

On the mining front we purchased a major shareholding in a new, and what promised to be an outstanding gold mine called Nanwa, and I have the note that Herbert Latilla wrote when we increased our holding after the war, regarding our purchase, which was a binding contract – the way he always did business.

Nanwa, however, was to prove almost a disaster for us – in fact a millstone around our necks for the next ten years, which greatly impeded our group's growth. The main cause of the trouble was that Hitler and the approaching war prevented Nanwa being brought to production by 1940, and instead we had to keep the mine on care and maintenance for the whole six years of the war. Even worse – we had to build a treatment plant and power station and equip the whole property – costing over £1m – at least three times the pre-war cost. Then, to pile Pelion on Ossa, it was discovered that the gold grade of the mine was appreciably below that reported in 1939 by the

50

Australian mine manager.

However, at this stage, spring 1939, the Exploration Group had, in two-and-a-half years, become quite a factor in the mining house world – and very nearly a major factor. I had spotted a similarly sized mining company, Zambesia Exploration Co. Ltd, (the very distinguished Board of which combined three DSOs, two MCs and one VC) which controlled, through a large percentage shareholding, Tanganyika Concessions Ltd. Tanganyika in turn controlled Union Miniere de Haut Katanga, the company controlling virtually all the vast mineral resources and production of the Belgian Congo. The Belgian Congo was at that time by far the largest producer of lead, zinc, copper, radium and tin in the whole continent of Africa, and almost certainly comparable with any other mining province in the world. Within two years Union Miniere was vital to the war effort, with Flying Fortresses flying into the Congo to collect the vitally needed radium, for the first atomic bomb.

I saw in a flash that if we could buy control of Zambesia Exploration we would then, in one jump, be the most important base metal mining group in all Africa. I decided to make what was probably the first opposed take-over bid in England. We offered all the shareholders in Zambesia Exploration six shillings a share, as opposed to the current price of four shillings. The offer was reported in the *Financial Times* and the *Financial News*.

However, the offer went out during a period of growing uncertainty and depression in London and the world markets; Hitler was already on the move, Jews were being persecuted, the Saar had been reoccupied, the Anschluss had taken place and Austria had become part of Greater Germany. Dolfuss had been murdered and the house of Rothschild had had their great investments in the Skoda works in Czechoslovakia – and many other investments – confiscated. People were generally scared and apprehensive, and did not know which way to move, preferring to do nothing. So, while we got quite a response to our offer, we did not get nearly enough to gain control. We therefore reluctantly withdrew our offer.

Social life continued much as before, in spite of the now huge and menacing war clouds. A ray of hope briefly filtered through these clouds in the form of Neville Chamberlain,

51

who had just flown back from his famous meeting with Hitler at Berchtesgaden.

I remember with the utmost clarity hearing and seeing Chamberlain as he got off the aeroplane, waving a piece of paper and saying, 'It is peace in our time'; something which unfortunately proved not to be the case.

Business, however, had to be continued, in spite of the speculation as to whether or not war was coming. My father had just made a grand tour of the Gold Coast, and stayed at Ashanti Goldfields, of which his brother-in-law, Lord Luke, was one of the founder directors. He also visited most of the other mines and the Bremang dredging concern.

It was my duty and task to return to Rhodesia where the Iron Cap Mine was now back in production, and so I left, with my brother Charles, in the late summer of 1939. We went on the *Windsor Castle,* taking my fine V12 Lincoln Zephyr on the ship with us. Also on board with us was the Cambridge Boat, including Alan Burrough and Tom Langton; they were going out to row against the South Africans in the Transvaal.

We approached Cape Town and Table Mountain in the early morning; I had just had my twenty-third birthday and felt immensely proud to be British, and to be part of the great British Empire which contained some 300 million happy people made up of scores of different races, colours and creeds. We had the finest Navy in the world, the pound sterling was synonymous with quality, as was evident with five dollars and fifteen Swiss francs to the pound. Of equal importance Britain possessed over one fifth of the world's surface containing the world's greatest raw material resources – a glimpse of which through the cabin porthole reminded me that most of the 5,000 miles from Cape Town to Cairo was under the British Empire.

I probably knew the Empire as well as many of my contemporaries, having visited India, Australia, New Guinea, Hong Kong, Canada, Egypt, Kenya, Northern Rhodesia, Southern Rhodesia and South Africa, and I was confident that if war did come, however unpleasant and time-consuming it would be, Britain would win at the end of the day.

My faith remained unchanged – even after the terrible black days following the fall of Crete, by which time Hitler had victoriously conquered the whole continent of Europe and Britain stood alone against Germany, with the conspicuous absence of the USA (who twenty years previously, after enriching themselves at the expense of the European Allies, entered the Great War at the eleventh hour, after the Flower of France and England had been killed.) What I did not calculate was the total loss of the British Empire and the bulk of Britain's financial assets – a direct result not of Hitler, but of the United States of America, and in particular President Roosevelt, General Marshall and General Eisenhower, ably assisted after the war by various British politicians.

Having disembarked at Cape Town the Cambridge crew caught what was then the Blue Train for the thousand-mile journey to Johannesburg, via Kimberley. Meanwhile Charles and I, in our Lincoln Zephyr, proceeded to motor up on the dust road to Johannesburg. At each main town we passed the train containing the Cambridge crew, and, not without a little satisfaction, we arrived in Johannesburg several hours ahead of them. Three months after these happy times we were all, in one form or another, in the armed forces fighting Adolf.

Alan Burrough was to marry my future wife's first cousin, Rosemary Bruce, soon after the outbreak of war; she is wonderfully cheery and a great personality – in fact a most redoubtable person. Alan, within a year, had lost a leg fighting Rommel in the Western Desert, but this did not prevent him from managing the Cambridge Eight in Japan against the Japanese University after the war, nor did it prevent him building up his small distillery business, Burrough's Beefeater Gin, into a world-famous brand name.

Likewise Tom Langton, one of the personalities of the boat, was captured two years later after the fall of Tobruk. He made an amazing two-hundred-mile escape to freedom across the desert, which is vividly described in the excellent book *Special Boat Service in World War Two*, by G.T. Courtney.

Charles and I, after spending a few days in Johannesburg and seeing many of our friends, motored on to Rhodesia and the object of our visit – to see what progress had been made at the re-opened Iron Cap Gold Mine. We were due to stay at the mine for three weeks, to give ourselves time to decide whether the mine could continue in profitable production, which unfortunately still seemed somewhat doubtful – particularly with the news from Europe becoming more ominous with every new day.

On September 1st Charles and I had some business to do with The Exploration Company's accountant and holder of the power of attorney. We stayed at Meikles Hotel, Salisbury, for a few days, so as to be right on the spot.

WOODBINE PARISH

The author's Great Grandfather in the early days of his
diplomatic career was with Sir Thomas Maitland in the
Ionian Islands and stayed with Ali Pasha in his court at
Yanina. At the same time his younger brother Henry
Headley Parish was in the Embassy at Constantinople
under Lord Stratford of Redcliffe and subsequently
wrote his book which was published by Hatchards in
1838 and titled *The Diplomatic History of the Monarchy
of Greece from the year 1830.*

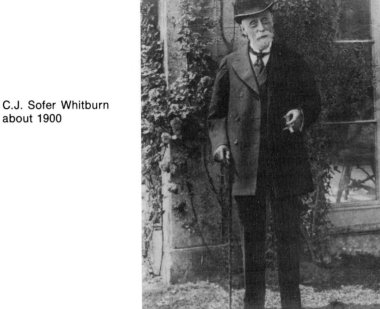

C.J. Sofer Whitburn
about 1900

Ali Pasha
of Yanina.

The author's Mother
and Father with
David Lloyd George,
1914.

Charles Woodbine
Parish and Michael
Woodbine Parish
aged 5 and 6 years.

A painting of Clement Woodbine Parish with Ypres
Cathedral in the background, 1917.

A car load of Boots. Jesse Boot driving his son John, later Lord Trent, the author's father-in-law; his wife Florence and daughters Margery and Dorothy in 1906. Having built up *Boots* into over 500 shops and defeated the establishment who opposed him. He would have been horrified to see the present board investing some £900m in a hotch potch of bicycles and car shops etc., just as the greatest recession since 1930 was commencing and the top part-time executive drawing over £500,000 in remuneration.

Lady Trent's house in the South of France, 1920-1960.

Raynham is the young Marquess of Townshend's family seat. He was born in 1916, and in this very young house-party, which was recently assembled, are included, left to right: Mr M. Parish, Miss Cherry Pinckard, the Marquess of Townshend, Lady Elizabeth Townshend, his sister, Mr P. Trevelyan Thomson and Mr G. Parish.

Michael Woodbine Parish in the Bugatti at Raynham, Norfolk, 1934.

Left to right: Sheila Graham – now Mrs David Bonsor, Tony de Cossan, Beryl Johnson – now Lady Hobson, the author, Doreen Johnson – now Mrs Edwin Yarborough.
The photograph was taken at Col. Johnson's home at Henshall Hall, Cheshire, 1938.

The author and Everard Bingham Hambro (*Fatty* Hambro), on right. They were staying at Ardchattan Priory just after leaving Eton in 1933.

Mrs Bonham-Christie, aged 96, the author's Grand-mother – the Queen of Brownsea. She could be described as the first 'green' or environmentalist in the UK. She owned the Island for some 30 years and turned it into a nature reserve.

The Queen of Brownsea's Isle.

Spartamint wins first prize at Show for Mare and Foal,
seen here with Marcus Kendall, 1938.

Michael Woodbine Parish, 2nd Lieut. in the Notts (SRY)
Yeomanry, 1938.

Michael Woodbine Parish with C4 Troop SRY, Palestine,
1940.

The author with Colonel Donny Player leading C
squadron SRY in Palestine, 1940.

Charles and Godfrey Woodbine Parish before the marriage of Godfrey and Lord Blackford's daughter Ann Mason at the Holy Trinity Church, Brompton, London 1942. Ann tragically died a year later from tuberculosis.

Flight-Lieut. Charles Woodbine Parish photographed in
front of the Lancaster bomber, of which he was the pilot.
He completed 54 raids before being killed.

Charles, on left, with his Pathfinder plane and crew
before the first raid over Berlin.

Clement's beehives at Batemans, 1940.

Batemans at Burwash, Sussex. Once the home of
Rudyard Kipling, where we lived for 20 years until
1965.

Royal Scots Greys Trooper in full marching gear, exactly
as the SRY was in the stampede in Palestine, 1940.

3

Charles and I were eating breakfast at Meikles Hotel when we read the banner headlines '*War declared against Germany*'.

From that moment on we had to make every endeavour to return to England as soon as possible – as a serving territorial officer in the Sherwood Rangers Yeomanry I knew that there would be a very poor view taken of my not already being with my regiment. Charles was in the same position; he had to go back to the Air Force in which he was an auxiliary reserve pilot.

Also from that moment I realised that my business life had come to an end, but my hope – providing the Almighty allowed me to survive – was that my father and Major Henderson-Scott would be willing and able to keep the companies on a care and maintenance basis for however many years the war was to last. As it happened they did just that; as did the Almighty – to my eternal gratitude.

We set off for the Cape in our Lincoln Zephyr, which was the very latest thing in cars – it had a 12-cylinder V engine which went extremely fast and was very comfortable. Unfortunately, the week before, whilst driving the manager of Iron Cap Gold Mine, we had had the misfortune to get off the 'strip road'. This consisted of two lines of tarmac going down the road, either side of which was the ordinary sandy soil. We suddenly hit some object and turned over twice, doing, I suppose, some ninety miles per hour. Consequently our Ford Lincoln Zephyr was not the car it was a few seconds before. Nevertheless it still moved, and we were able to drive the thousand miles down to the Cape, staying with Harry Openheimer in Johannesburg on the way.

We arrived in Cape Town in time to catch the *Windsor Castle,* which was sailing direct to the United Kingdom. This was an interesting voyage because many people were returning home to join up, including Bevil Rudd who had recently won a gold medal at the Antwerp Olympic Games.

Very soon we had to paint the ship battleship grey, because the menace of U-boats was already prevalent. Our first stop was Sierra Leone on the west coast of Africa, where there was a slight hazard as the captain ran into the boom which had been laid by the Navy to prevent submarines entering the harbour. This wasted some three days, but it enabled Charles and I and several of the others to have some very good surfing from the Bamboo Surfing Club.

After our enforced delay we arrived at Southampton without further incident, where we were met by Clement, our father, our brother Godfrey and our sister Elizabeth, and for the first two days of our reunion we all went to a hotel in the New Forest. This of course was overshadowed by the constant worry that time was very short until we had to rejoin our regiments, and as there was already a threat of petrol rationing, we spent much of our time getting all the petrol we could into jerry cans and hot water bottles.

After these two days we returned home to Eaton Square; I little knowing that it was the last time I was to see my brother Charles.

From there I went up to join my regiment, which was in Malton, in Yorkshire.

Suddenly, after a very free, enjoyable and interesting life in Africa, and in business in London, where I was already a director of several companies and inclined to get my own way, the situation at Malton was a rather hard landing.

Everybody was very worked up, trying to be frightfully efficient. We were a cavalry regiment, with all our horses – a thousand of them – and I was allocated to Number 4 Troop, C Squadron, with Donny Player as my squadron leader. Our Colonel was 'Sack' Yarborough, the Earl of Yarborough, of whom I was very fond, and the other squadron leaders were Flash Kellett, who was an immaculately dressed MP and had been in the Irish Guards and Tony Holden, who had been a regular. A number of other interesting characters included Dandy Wallace, of Wallace Brothers in the City of London and

Sidney Morse, from Suffolk.

I was stationed in Mr Elsie's house; he was a very pleasant person who had been one of the top trainers before the war – his gallops, with all his horses, surrounded the house.

My batman, Ernest Bowles, who had been our chauffeur/ valet in Eaton Square came up to join me. He was a most amusing and very independent person of Cockney upbring- ing. My father had sent him off to do an apprentice course at Rolls Royce, so he knew how to handle cars, and he did not think much of our being on horses, of which he knew neither the back from the front!

My old friend Second Lieutenant Stanley Christopherson was also there; we used to ride in Rotten Row together before going to the City. I think he was then working for the Consolidated Goldfields, of which his father, Douglas Christopherson, was one of the Managing Directors. (Five years later, when commanding the regiment, Montgomery described Christopherson as one of the finest colonels in the British army.)

Then there was Mickey Gold, who was to become, some eight years later, my brother-in-law, as he married Lord Trent's second daughter Mary (Meg), and I married her youngest sister, Elizabeth (Billa), within six months of each other.

There was also Jack Abdy, a First World War veteran; very amusing and young for his age, who told us a thing or two about the 1914-18 War. He need not have joined up, as he must have been approaching fifty. Then there was Stephen Mitchell, who was a Second Lieutenant like myself; he used to work for the Imperial Tobacco Company in Nottingham, and his father owned the pipe and tobacco firm of Mitchells, which presumably he had sold to Imperial. We knew him as Cheeny Mitchell. He was always very good company and went right on with the Regiment until the end of the war.

Another was Derek Warwick, who worked for his family's Nottinghamshire brewing firm, Warwicks. Derek was wounded at Alamein in 1942, and never returned to the regiment. His sister, who was a very pretty red-headed girl, married Jocelyn Abel Smith, who was also in the regiment and was later to be in Crete with Tony Holden and myself.

Yet two more were Lawrence Biddel and Dan Ranfurly, the

57

Earl of Ranfurly. I think the reasons why the Sherwood Rangers Yeomanry had so many non-local officers were the lack of locals and, more, the fact that it was still horsed.

After about a month at Malton we were all moved to be stationed at Brocklesby Park, the beautiful home of our Colonel, Lord Yarborough. We had a very happy two months there, because we were all able to hunt with the Brocklesby hounds, one of the oldest packs, if not the oldest, in the country. Lord Yarborough and his charming wife Nancy lived for hunting, and so we were able to have the best of both worlds.

Donny Player's 'C' Squadron was stationed in Brocklesby Hall and the officers of whom I was one, lived in the house. This was very agreeable for me as I had stayed there before the war and was slightly enamoured of Lady Diana Pelham, the eldest daughter, and was also very fond of her younger sister Wendy. We had all our meals in the main dining room, and they were cooked by Mrs Rugman – who was superb at crême brulée.

The daily routine consisted of manoeuvres on the horses and turning them out spotlessly groomed, with all the saddles and bridles and accoutrements looking spick and span. This happy period of eight weeks was brought to an abrupt close just after Christmas when the War Office notified the regiment that we were going to be moved to a secret destination. This was a major operation, and as the phoney war was still going on it was an exciting adventure for us.

We entrained a thousand horses at the Brocklesby railway siding and all moved down to Dover, from where we sailed to Calais, with the horses remaining in their trucks on the train.

Getting the horses into each truck was quite a job, but we eventually arrived at Marseilles, where we were stationed in Chateau Renard and its grounds. This was a huge old chateau and we happened to be there during the coldest winter for fifty years. It was so cold that all the water troughs were frozen; consequently watering the horses became a major problem. I remember going out there during the perishingly cold nights, and having to move the horses down to the local stream so that they could drink from there.

Apart from the cold the *esprit de corps* was good, and most of us were able to go out to the cafés and nightclubs in Marseilles in the evening.

One evening I remember dining with Patrick McCraith, Myles Hildyard, and one or two others at a rather amusing French restaurant where there were a lot of French sailors wearing their berets with *pom-pom de matelots* on top; a sort of red wool ball.

4

Pom-Pom de Matelots

It occurred to me that as we were sailing in forty-eight hours, and we had to load 1,000 horses onto the various ships that had been provided, it would be very difficult for me to recognise the thirty horses in my C4 Troop once they had been loaded. I therefore quickly did some negotiations with the French sailors, and was able to buy thirty *pom-pom de matelots!* I carefully took them all back to Chateau Renard after dinner, and went straight down to my horse lines, where I promptly fixed every head collar with a red pom-pom, between the ears.

When dawn broke and we were on duty with the horses, there was consternation when everybody saw my troop complete with their pom-poms, and there was all hell to pay when Colonel Lord Yarborough heard about it – he took an extraordinarily poor view of the whole affair. Nevertheless, I seem to have been allowed to keep the pom-poms on my horses; in fact, when we loaded them onto the ships that afternoon I think I am correct in saying that my horses were the only ones that anyone recognised, and I was able to get them all together in the same hold. There they remained all the way to Palestine, which was about a two-and-a-half week voyage.

On arrival in Haifa we were stationed with the Royal Scots Greys, and spent the next six months mounted and training in Palestine. I was in Major Player's 'C' Squadron, and had No. 4 Troop throughout. We managed to win Colonel Lord Yarborough's prize for the best turned-out troop in the regiment, and the best polished saddles and bridles.

We rode over practically the whole of the country, and it was really very enjoyable. We kept together as a regiment until we were doing a manoeuvre down from Latrun to Sarafand; the whole regiment had moved with all their equipment, every man with his rifle and bayonet and all the other accoutrements which are carried by a mounted trooper on the march.

We left early from Latrun and reached Sarafand at about midday. As you can imagine, with a thousand horses in line, we were spread over a considerable distance, perhaps half a mile. I was the rear-guard, the last troop, and we steadily made our way through the rocky countryside, interspersed with cactus bushes and other semi-desert plants. When we got the order to halt, we all dismounted and waited while the front troop watered their horses from some horse troughs on the outskirts of the village.

While I could not see from that distance, evidently a water pipe had burst in front of the leading troop which was being watered. This terrified the horses, and in a matter of seconds they had stampeded straight down the whole line, and were coming flat out towards me, collecting all the other horses in the regiment as they went by.

The entire regiment was completely demoralised; one thousand horses galloping flat out, terror in their eyes. Machine guns, Hodgekiss guns, and all the other things which were carried on the horses' backs were all flying and waving around as they stampeded downhill.

During the long march towards Sarafand from Latrun, I had done what was a very unwise and stupid thing to do; I had taken the revolver out of its holster, and put it in the saddlebag. When we dismounted I had unfortunately left it where it was pending putting it back in my holster. However, such was the speed of the stampede, that my beautiful horse Nanwa, together with all the others in my troop, were swept along by the rushing torrent of 1,000 horses, and I was not to see Nanwa again for quite some time. My revolver was lost for good, which could have meant a death sentence as the strictest orders were made to prevent the Jews getting arms.

At the very end of the column was our medical officer, Captain Geoffrey Brooks, and he was lying on top of a soldier who had just previously had a fall and broken his leg. Geoffrey had dressed and bandaged the leg, but seeing and hearing all these horses racing down towards him, he had lain on top of the soldier to prevent him being trampled to death, completely disregarding any personal safety. Fortunately the horses managed to jump clear of Geoffrey. They all went over him, and both men were unscathed.

It was a very brave act for which he was awarded the George Medal. At a later date, he brought my eldest daughter, Suzanne, into the world.

We managed to get most of our horses back within a day or two; some had gone up to forty miles – but we were re-established as a regiment (perhaps a little bedraggled), albeit not for long. After the stampede I think the penny had dropped in the War Office in London, or with the command in Palestine, that the sooner we had our horses taken away from us the better. In the Brigade we became known as the 'Stampede Rangers!' I imagine the Sherwood Rangers rather lost their name as a cavalry unit, and it was not very long after the stampede that we heard the news that we were going to be dismounted and turned into coastal defence gunners, which was always considered the lowest form of humanity.

Before that took place we had many happy times on the coast at Jaffa and Tel Aviv, with wonderful surfing and swimming, and weekend leaves up in Beirut. This was everything that a young officer could possibly desire, with a very fine hotel, I think called King George V, and a number of nightclubs with inadequately clad young ladies doing bicycle tricks on steel wires above the table, and all sorts of other excitements.

We were given a fortnight to learn how to shoot the big guns, and they were very big guns, six inches. We went on a course at Haifa and down to Port Tewfik at the southern end of the Suez Canal, where we spent two or three weeks learning gun drill.

But to return to the thousand horses which we had left behind in Palestine after we were dismounted.

I was extremely fond of my black charger who was about 15.2h, and I had named her 'Nanwa' after a West African gold mine that my father and I were interested in. I went all round the remount depots in Palestine searching for her; I spent hours doing that, perhaps days, but was never able to find her again. A little comfort was gained by the assurance that 1939-40 was not going to be a repeat of the 1918 effort when Field Marshall Lord Allenby's horses were all sold off to the Egyptians and subsequently appallingly treated. Thankfully, this time that did not happen.

After a comparatively short period when we were able to enjoy Cairo and Alexandria on leave, we were split up into four squadrons and sent to various destinations.

My particular squadron went to Cyprus. We arrived at the ancient and picturesque port of Famagusta, where we were stationed, and we were taught ordinary small arms fire, before getting our big six inch guns. We had a very enjoyable time in Cyprus for about a month; I had bought an AJS motorcycle for £5 and was able to go all over the island and up to Troödos, a ski resort in the mountains.

At that time the first batch of Polish refugee families had come out through Romania, Bulgaria and Turkey and then to Cyprus.

We had wonderful riding on small Arab horses when not on duty, and it was fun going up to Nicosia on the local train; about a fifty mile journey.

I remember Jocelyn Abel Smith, who was in my squadron, admired the Barclays Bank manager's daughter in Nicosia. She was called Ellwyn Jones and was a very pretty girl, who ultimately married Colonel Simmonds, my CO when I was later stationed in Turkey. But for now it was Joss's turn to court her. To make an impression he thought it would be a good idea if he rented the whole train from Famagusta up to Nicosia, where Ellwyn lived, and filled the panorama compartment at the front of the train with flowers. He thence arrived in state, with all the flowers, to take her out to dinner. I think the cost of hiring the complete train was £2.10s.

Shortly after that in Famagusta, which was a lovely old Venetian fortified town with everything extremely cheap and friendly, I experienced my first earthquake. At about four o'clock in the morning everything started to shake and for the first few seconds I could not think what was happening. Then everything started to crash down, so I got out of the building as quickly as possible. It was all over after a short time, but there was a lot of damage done.

The only other minor excitement was that the Italians, who had come into the war against us, were beginning to fly reconnaissance planes over Cyprus, and directly over us. We had strict orders not to shoot at them, so as not to draw attention to our defences, but Jocelyn managed to break that command and fired his Bren gun up at one of the Italian aeroplanes, which caused a severe reprimand.

Normal routine continued until we embarked on our next move, which was to Crete, another 250 miles due west along the Turkish coast.

We arrived in Crete in early February 1941, and docked at Souda Bay. It was rather wet at that time, and therefore a little depressing – the Greeks have a saying for that 'February should be cut out of the year.'

We disembarked, knowing nothing about the Cretans or their island. The two batteries which had been allocated to Crete were 'A' battery and 'Y' battery. Myles Hildyard, Michael Riviere with Sydney Morse commanding were in 'A' battery, and they were stationed at Kalives Fort at the entrance of the great Souda Bay naval base, which was on the south side of the bay and on the north side of Crete. I was in 'Y' battery, and we were based on St John's Hill, which is about one-and-a-half miles, on high ground, above the town of Hania, looking straight out to sea to the north, and to the west looking out along the coastal plain of Crete towards Maleme airstrip and then on to Kastelli.

My battery was commanded by Tony Holden and Jocelyn Abel Smith, who was senior to me in age and rank, and myself, and consisted of about 120 other ranks. We arrived there and found that the marines had just recently finished installing the guns, and had made underground accommodation with bunks etc, so that the entire battery could sleep and remain underground in extremely well prepared and fortified dugouts.

The guns were sited so that they could fire right out across the sea to the north, and they could, if need be, swing round to the west, to fire down the coastal plain.

5

Settling in to Crete

The first two months in Crete were very peaceful, with little interference from the enemy. We led a fairly routine life of doing gun drill, with little other excitement. I had one or two very enjoyable trips down the island; one with Myles Hildyard when we went right through to Heraklion on my motorcycle, to stay at the Villa Ariadne.

John Pendlebury was one of the leading figures there, and was already getting ready to work with the Greek resistance in the event of a German invasion, which was not considered, at that time, to be very likely. We had an amusing dinner with Pendlebury in Heraklion at a cafe Neon, and I noticed that he consumed a great deal of alcohol, seeming none the worse for it. He had a glass eye, which was always looking in a different direction to his good eye. Dilys Powell wrote an excellent book about Pendlebury, entitled *Villa Ariadne.*

Other trips took us up into the White Mountains, where we saw some of the Cretan villages, but during that period we did not really get to know the Cretans, other than on nodding terms, and it was not until several months later that we really got to know them.

As the days went on we heard of the collapse of the Greek and British armies under the onslaught of Hitler's troops, who had come to rescue their Italian allies. They had been completely defeated by the Greeks in the Albanian campaign, and there were quite a number of Italian prisoners who had been sent down from the northern front by the Greeks, to be put in prisoner of war camps in Crete.

Towards the beginning of May air activity increased considerably, principally from the Germans, but no doubt from the Italians as well. On about the 16th May we, in our gun positions on St John's Hill, overlooking Hania, became subject to very considerable and continuous bombing raids. These were largely by Stukas, which would dive from a height of about 1,000-2,000 feet with a tremendous whine and scream, and then let their bombs loose about 500 feet above us. That continued, with increasing intensity, until about May 19th.

We carried on using our Hodgkiss guns to try and shoot down some of the enemy planes. I remember well when the gun I was in charge of jammed, and I had to take the whole thing to pieces during an air raid, and reassemble it, so that I was able to fire many rounds at the oncoming Messerschmitts and Stukas.

Once, while I was all alone in the range finder control post on night duty I heard a considerable number of planes coming over. This, coupled with my first baptism of fire, was a rather eerie and frightening experience. Early the next morning – it was a very clear lovely day as usual – I looked out due west across the plain to Maleme, which was covered with olive trees and plantations, and suddenly saw a mass of JU52s, some pulling gliders.

The heavens seemed to open up and literally hundreds, possibly thousands, of gaily coloured parachutes were jettisoned from the aeroplanes, and I could see figures of the men hanging from the parachutes as they descended into the olive groves, amidst sounds of rifle and small arms fire at the parachutists, and also a certain amount of anti-aircraft fire at the planes as they dropped their passengers.

During the first day I think approximately 4,000 parachutists were dropped on the area stretching from St John's Hill to Maleme. They largely dropped onto the New Zealanders, and the other troops who were guarding the olive trees below us, and it appeared that the defenders would have a fairly straightforward task of defeating the parachutsists, unless some heavy guns and troop carriers were landed by the German transport planes.

They would not be able to do this until they had captured Maleme airport, so by the end of the first twenty-four hours it looked as if Crete would be the first British victory against the Germans (at this point neither the Americans nor the Russians were in the war) after a succession of disasters stretching right across Europe from Dunkirk to Athens. Providing General Bernard Freyberg had allocated enough troops to deny the Germans Maleme airstrip there was no way they could win.

The next day I was in the gun observation post, from where I could see everything perfectly through the Barr and Wallace rangefinder. I watched the JU52s endeavouring to land at Maleme airport – a large number of them turned turtle, and presumably the crew and contents were destroyed. It was not until the morning of the third day that it became evident that something had gone badly wrong with the defenders of Maleme, because these massive beetle-like aeroplanes were coming in at the rate of about one every two or three minutes, and appeared to be able to land, often with their gliders intact behind them.

We began to think that it was going to be a much stiffer battle than had previously been thought, and during all this the bombing of our gun emplacements on St John's Hill increased even more. They also began to bomb the town of Hania immediately below us, doing it in waves, and devastating whole blocks at a time.

As I have said, our guns were coast defence guns, and sited by the Marines to do just that. They were not designed or made for on-shore work, although they could be perfectly well utilised for that. The only target which would have been eminently suitable for this was Maleme airport, where we could have lobbed our six-inch shells straight onto the runway while the German planes were landing. Admiral Cunningham's cruisers and destroyers were patrolling off Maleme each night and the combination of these pounding Maleme from the sea – if only General Freyberg had asked them to – together with our guns could have devastated Maleme, making a German defeat certain.

For some unknown reason 'A' battery only had seven shells and were never allowed to fire them, whereas 'Y' battery had plenty of shells and fired plenty of them – but we were never allowed to fire them at the only place that mattered, Maleme.

We were probably the only people in the Battle of Crete who were in a fixed position throughout the whole period of the battle, spread over eleven days. Being on top of St John's Hill we could see everything that took place at Maleme apart from the ground fighting, hidden because of the olive trees. Our range was seventeen miles and the distance to the airport was about two miles beyond that. Nevertheless, we asked GHQ, which was situated just below us, if we could increase the amount of cordite in the loading of the guns, so that we would have the necessary range to hit Maleme. The answer came back that as our guns were coast defence guns, they did not want them used for land work. There was the possibility of them blowing up, which in any case we had to do a week later to prevent the Germans getting them.

This was a great disappointment, as if we had been able to fire 500-1,000 shells at Maleme airport whilst the Germans were bringing in their Mountain Alpine division with heavy guns, coupled with Cunningham's bombardment from the sea, it would have been impossible for them to have landed the Mountain Division and all their field artillery, and the loss of their planes would have been enormous. By that time the German High Command would have called off the whole operation, as General Student, the German C-in-C had already, after the first twenty-four hours, reluctantly decided he would have to go back and tell Hitler that his airborne division had been virtually wiped out and the whole operation was a failure.

At this moment he sent in one very intrepid German pilot called Hauptmann Kleyle with a light aeroplane to try a landing at Maleme; he found that the resistance from the New Zealanders at Maleme had been defeated, and no-one was shelling the airport, and he was able to land his plane, take off, and return to General Student in Athens. Once safely back he reported to Student that it was worth sending in the JU52s with all the heavy guns and equipment, as he thought it would be a success; unfortunately, it was.

Therefore, from complete disaster for the Germans after the first twenty-four hours, the battle had turned the moment the Alpine Division landed with their heavy guns. They were able to slowly advance through the olive groves, and by the ninth day the Germans were virtually the victors of the battle for Crete.

During these nine days the bombing went on continuously

on us at St John's Hill, and after the third day we did get instructions to swing the guns round and to fire at various points on shore, but never to the extent of being able to reach, or fire at, Maleme, which was the key to the whole operation – and, indeed, to the Battle of Crete. This was because we were not allowed to increase the cordite charges.

Apart from the continual menace of being heavily bombed day and night, it was very depressing watching the airport and seeing the JU52s coming in to land hour after hour. It could only mean that they were bringing in heavy equipment.

The whole Battle of Crete depended on holding Maleme, which was guarded by the valiant 22nd New Zealand battalion and their commander, Lt Colonel L.W. Andrew VC, from the strategically vital Hill 107 above Maleme. They, however, had not received any assistance or reinforcements from GHQ – even after forty-eight hours of intense and heroic fighting. There was ample time and troops available to mop up the rest of the scattered Germans and great success was being achieved in both Rethimnon and Heraklion. For now all that mattered was Maleme and Hill 107.

It was obvious that all this created the most serious problems for us of being able to withstand the Germans and hold the island. Once they had captured the airport they could bring in whatever they wished, whereas we would be unable to get many reinforcements or supplies from Alexandria because we did not have command of the air. Nor could the Navy bring in many because they were already fully stretched and were in the middle of a terrible battering from the Luftwaffe, and on top of this they could only operate during the limited hours of darkness.

Furthermore, we were not aware that the Cretans themselves had been deprived of their rifles (of which there were 2,000 stored in Hania) to defend their own country. Had the Cretans been fully equipped with arms, the paratroops, who had landed in widely spread areas, would have fallen straight into the arms of the Cretans themselves; the Cretans were brilliant fighters and it would have made a tremendous difference to the battle. However, once the heavy guns started arriving at Maleme it was a different kettle of fish, and they continued to do this, right under our eyes, until the end of the battle.

After eleven days the battle of Crete was lost, purely because Freyberg had lost Maleme airport – even though days before the battle Churchill had warned him, through Enigma Ultra, that the Germans were making it their main target – and he had failed to trust and arm the Cretans. This is excellently described in *'10 Days To Destiny: The Battle For Crete, 1941'*, by G.C. Kiriakopoulos.

Without this, Mr Churchill would have had his first major victory, instead of which he had to report another disaster to a rather antagonistic House of Commons.

It was a tantalising position for us to be in, on top of St John's Hill, unable to move or do anything to help other than occasional rounds from one of our big guns onto the olive plantations. We could see, and feel, the tide coming slowly in towards us from Maleme. This was about eighteen miles away, and after about the third day the Germans were beginning to advance towards us and towards Souda Bay and Hania.

On the eighth day, at about four o'clock in the morning, we had orders to abandon our positions, destroy our guns and to retreat to Sphakia, which was some sixty miles away over the mountains, for an evacuation of the island.

We hastily got together various pieces of clothing and equipment that we thought would be needed, and struck camp, after having taken the breech blocks out of the big guns and thrown them over the cliff into the sea. We then marched off, 120 of us, towards Souda to begin with, and then due south over the mountains towards the small south coast port of Sphakia. Directly it got light the Stukas were there again, machine gunning and bombing us incessantly on the withdrawal.

6

Withdrawal

It was a very shameful, demoralising and pitiful sight, seeing thousands of British troops in a bedraggled state, with morale at zero, heading south – later to be clearly portrayed by Evelyn Waugh in *Officers and Gentlemen*.

When I got to the village of Lefkos, about five miles from Souda Bay Fort station, where 'A' battery was, I ran into the General commanding the island, as Freyberg had already left and gone to Egypt by flying boat, and had handed over command to General Weston, a very fine Marine General. I asked him if I could be of any assistance, as he seemed to be very short of staff, and he said, 'If you can ride a motorcycle you would be invaluable to me as liaison officer on the withdrawal.'

Two years previously I had motored all the way from London to Bucharest on a 500cc Norton and there, lying on the roadside was a brand new 500cc Norton! I immediately jumped on it, and stayed with General Weston for the rest of the evacuation, whilst our troops staggered on (by night; by day they were hiding in the olive groves) down the road towards Sphakia. I well remember passing, on my Norton, my squadron leader Tony Holden – he was puce in the face with rage, and shouted after me that he would have me court-martialled for this. He was apparently unaware that I had been requisitioned by the island commander General Weston. I spent my time racing up and down the Souda-Sphakia road with messages to various commanders, such as General George Vasey, Brigadier Generals Puttick and Hargest of the New Zealanders and Major-General Sir Howard Karl Kippenberger, KBE, DSO & Bar.

Each time I had to deliver a message I reported back to General Weston, by which time he was ready to send me off on another mission. I well remember going down that road, and on some occasions, if I stopped for a few moments the bombs from the Stukas, which were bombing us the whole time, would come within three feet of me, but luckily the road was right on the edge of the cliff and the bombs carried on over the edge. I would see and hear them right next to me, and then the next minute there would be a terrific burst in the valley 1,000 feet below.

On one occasion, when I was alone with General Weston in a little sheep-shearing shed with bamboo rafters on top of it, there was suddenly a line of machine gun bullets which cut diagonally across the roof; somehow they hit neither the General nor myself. I noticed the General remained completely calm, and carried on writing his despatch while this was going on.

Through this operation I was able to see how the High Command worked, and I took a greater interest in the whole conduct of the war from that moment. After about the third day of the withdrawal, we were within five miles of Sphakia, and were up on the high ground before going down the rocky hillside where Sphakia lay. This was where the Naval ships were coming in during the night to take some 15,000 British troops off, and the General said to me, 'Our job is done, and I am going now to Egypt, by sea plane; you have my permission to go straight down and embark on the first convoy which is leaving tonight.'

I carried on, on my motorcycle until almost the end of the road, whereupon, with a most nostalgic feeling, I pointed it towards the cliff side, revved it up and jumped off. Over the cliff she went, lost to the oncoming Germans.

I then proceeded on foot towards what I presumed to be the embarkation point. It was now getting dark, and I went on down a very rocky sheep track, but it was very very difficult to find my bearings and be sure of where I was going. However, from my stalking days in Scotland, I had got a fairly good sense of smell, and I could smell the diesel fumes coming up from the ships three or four miles away. I therefore followed my nose, over very rocky country, and eventually approached the point of embarkation, where I ran into some of my regiment.

When we got right to the bottom a call went out for volunteers to carry rations up to the Maoris, who were about 500-1,000 feet up on the mountain doing a rearguard action to prevent the Germans capturing the troops before they got on the ships. The Maori rearguard was commanded by Major Dyer, with Captain Ranji Royal as his second in command, four subalterns and 144 other ranks. They had been told by Freyberg that they would be evacuated the following day.

Unattractive as it was, I thought it was my duty to volunteer for the job, and only about twenty others did the same (out of several thousand) including Sydney Morse, and we sweated back up until we reached the Maori rearguard, handed over the supplies of food and ammunition that we were carrying, and then returned. By this time we were greeted with the good or bad news, depending on which way you looked at it, that the last ships had sailed, and we were all told to surrender to the Germans. Our trip back up the hill had well and truly cooked our goose.

No-one else was to be taken off by the Navy except for the Maori rearguard regiment. General Freyberg, a New Zealander himself, had quite rightly made special arrangements with Admiral Cunningham for them to be evacuated at the eleventh hour, almost in sight, if it had not been dark, of the advancing Bavarian Alpine troops.

7

Surrender

It was dark; about one or two in the morning, when we were given this news, and there was nothing to do but wait for the dawn and see what took place. With the first light the aerial strafing continued, even though we were supposed to have been surrendered by then. Our much respected Sergeant Major Fountain was one of the many killed after the surrender, on the rocky shore leading down to Sphakia.

I joined up with Myles Hildyard, who had already found himself a nice Cretan house for the night, and had managed to capture a chicken which was running nearby. In a fairly short time he had turned the poor chicken into an excellent lunch. During that period one could see the German Alpine troops jumping from crag to crag, coming down to take us.

One predominate thought in my mind was the incredible bungle of the whole Cretan operation, and the far-reaching effect it would have on the wretched people at home in England, because we had now been swept right out of Europe. Crete was our last foothold in Europe, and now we were falling right back onto Cairo and North Africa, although we did not even have much of that as the Italians were right up to Benghazi and Tripoli. Of course it had occurred to me that the Germans might not be inclined to stop where they were in Crete and North Africa, and might press on to capture all of Egypt and the Suez canal, which would have made a very ugly situation. England was being heavily bombed, and the possibility of an attack on England herself was quite a probability. At that stage the Germans had not attacked Russia; in fact the Ribbentrop-Molotov pact, which had so depressed me, was still in operation, so we had the whole potential weight of the Third Reich ready to attack England and the Middle East.

It was really a very depressing picture for anyone who could understand the least bit about world strategy and the art of war, and with this in mind we started the long, hot and thirsty walk back over the rocky mountains from whence we had come.

However, the sun was shining, I was still feeling extremely fit, and on reflection I never had the least doubt that we would ultimately win the war. I therefore concentrated on the possibility of getting out of the mess into which we had all fallen.

Over and above all this, it was an entirely new adventure; we were on this fantastically beautiful island of Crete, and it appeared that there were quite a number of options to be taken, both on the way back to the prison of war camp and possibly afterwards.

The next four months I spent with Myles; he kept an excellent diary, written on any scraps of paper he could find, until he reached Cairo where he was able to write it out for his parents. The following pages come straight out of it.

A DIARY KEPT IN CRETE WHILE ESCAPING FROM THE GERMANS IN JUNE, JULY AND AUGUST, 1941.

Myles Hildyard

I had slept the night in Micky Riviere's house instead of in my tent, where from dawn onwards there had lately been a struggle between my love of bed and a certain restlessness as enemy planes started the day's work overhead. Micky and I took it in turns to sleep down by the guns. Sidney also slept in a village house but during the blitz he also slept in the BOP.

Now, calm and well dressed as usual, he came in and woke me up to say we were off in an hour. Crete was to be evacuated. He disappeared and I yelled for Yates to discuss the situation.

In my haversack, ready for all eventualities, were already some tins of sardines, my compass and so on. I added a few things and told Yates to destroy everything else. Down at the guns we destroyed everything we could with hammers and with bars, and threw the breech blocks into the sea.

During breakfast I went through my papers and gave Yates a mass of Intelligence stuff to burn in the oven in the garden. That attracted our friends who zoomed over the house machine-gunning. Meanwhile, the men had collected in the gateway of the prison. Some had had close shaves with the BOP and gun positions were machine-gunned after I left, though nothing like so severely as a day or two earlier when bullets went through the telephones, wireless and both officers' beds, and blast from rear bombs blew the whole of the front in. At the same time the Port War Signal Station got a direct hit and Commander Salisbury and his staff vanished completely.

I was told to lead the way out of the prison. We ran from house corner to house corner, and once out of the village from ditch to ditch and patch of corn or weeds to olive tree, while the enemy planes passed low overhead, machine-gunning when they saw anybody.

After a mile or two we reached the river and followed the tree-fringed bank. It was the fast flowing icy little river in which after a long hot solitary walk I used to love to bathe. We were hot now, but we hurried on. Sidney joined me. Michael brought up the rear, and very soon he was in difficulties. Men who in a period of tension we had not been able to take off the guns and exercise, some who long before Crete had never walked further than the messroom, now began to collapse. It

79

was with difficulty that at midday we reached a village, Neon Kerion, on the main road to Heraklion intact. Here our truck with food and ammunition was to meet us and Sidney went off to find it.

All the 15th Coast Regiment was there, and instead of letting us go on, the Adjutant said we were to stay till dark as no movement was allowed. Micky and I sat with the men under olive trees and were machine-gunned continuously. Then a message came from Sidney. We were to meet him and the Colonel two miles up the road. As the road was obviously suicide, we led the men up a dry river bed and so to a point we judged to be two miles above the village. We hid in a pine wood against the road and Micky and I looked and shouted for Sidney. No sign of anybody. So we led the men down again into the river bed and there we lay till dark, protected by a cliff behind us and hidden by leafy plane trees, while aeroplanes passed continuously just above our heads, spitting and crackling.

A little further up was a good spring. We refilled all our water bottles there just before dark and moved off in good order with strict instructions as to discipline on the march. The road was a streaming riot of flying troops, hurrying along in the dark. It was difficult to keep our column together and yet push our way through the stragglers past jammed lorries. We came to a village in flames some time before midnight, and at the rumour of water our men fell out in the darkness. We had to halt and try to collect them. The water was in fact an illusion. I jettisoned my heavy overcoat, and we went on. Soon after Matheson, Micky's servant, fainted – a tough man who had trained the battery's boxers.

Men began to drop out hopelessly, and Micky and I gave up all idea of keeping them together. We went on with a few of them, becoming very thirsty and weary ourselves as the road began to climb. In the ditches all the way along, men were resting or asleep. We pressed on, for our reading of the map had made us expect to reach a mountain plain, where we might get food, water and room to disperse off the road. But the road circled up and up in long sweeps and we felt thirstier and thirstier and were practically alone.

Just before dawn we came to a place where the road crossed a small open flat, and there was a well. We tied together all the water bottles we had and let them down and had just got water when General Freyberg, the C in C arrived with Force HQ in trucks (which they drove into the undergrowth and covered over) and he ordered me to disperse the men collecting round the well before planes began arriving. We took our men as far back from the road as we could get and settled down for the day. I slept on a ledge of rock, camouflaged with branches and tufts of grass.

In the afternoon I was sitting talking to Micky when a plane dropped bombs just below us. Buckingham, Sidney's servant got a piece of shrapnel in the arm. We put him on an ambulance with Force HQ. When it got dark we moved out again and when we reached the top of the mountain pass we began to look down and listen for the sea. In the mountain plain of Lasithi reached at last, crowds of soldiers were fighting round the wells.

We came about one o'clock to Imbros, a village on the road used as a collecting post, and there we found Sidney. The stony fields were crowded with sleeping men, but Sidney got us permission to move on and we marched out down the road, pretty well up to strength, for the stragglers who had not joined us during the day before had mostly walked on and joined Sidney.

We didn't get far before we were stopped and told we must take cover as there were already too many men on the road to the sea. So we went into a gorge off the road and slept very coldly on a rock till it was light and then told the men to hide where they could for the day. We officers found ledges on the cliff side, but it became too hot and Micky and I moved into a cave full of New Zealanders, charming people we thought. There we finished my sardines. We found we were eating very little. All day planes were over and we covered our faces in the mouth of the cave as they passed.

At dusk we collected the men and formed up ready to march down to the sea. This was now more or less organised – everybody had to be in a band of fifty under an officer, with a gap between each band. But we moved at about one mph, stopping every fifty yards, and when we reached a counting post we were chopped in half and I was given a band, half our men and half of the band next behind.

Next we stopped for a talk from an Australian officer, who

told us that the evacuation had gone well the night before, that if we made a sound or lit cigarettes we should be fired on by our posts on the mountains overlooking the road, that terrific air-raids by the RAF over Germany all week would keep the German Air Force off Crete for the next few days, and that we had had great success in Libya and reached Tripoli! *All* untrue.

We marched on, halting every instant because of the crowds ahead and to let rearguard parties go through. They were begging water as they passed, but we had failed to get any all day. Only some rum which a parson was doling out. The road began to swing down hill, and became much worse. Every moment in the darkness we expected to see the sea.

At one of our halts I was sitting on a stone wall by the side of the road when to my great surprise I got a bullet in the leg. Randall with me was hit in the hand. Two men had been shot and were lying also hit quite close, one very bad. But it is puzzling, and I accuse a Colonial, who is indignant! We put on first field dressings, and as at that moment some trucks came along with wounded on board, we got on them. They gave us to drink petrolly water and liver salts. I thought it was the best thing I ever tasted. We bumped and jolted downhill past bombed and burnt out trucks and ambulances.

At last we can get no further, the road is blocked by discarded trucks. I am on one of a lot of trucks with walking wounded. We get out. Nobody knows where we go next. We walk off down the road which twists down a steep hillside, embanked at the corners and finally just stops. All around a dark rocky hill, and far away a flatness which is probably the sea. But in what direction the evacuation is going on no one has any idea. Randall and I walk downhill, tripping over rocks and bushes, till he has a fall which all but knocks him out. We feel hopeless about it and decide to lie down and sleep where we are and wait for daylight.

Hearing a voice I shout out, and it is Bob Laycock, the commander of 'Lay force' our commandos. Another voice in the darkness ceaselessly calls for help. When it gets light we find we had stopped on the edge of a gorge, and climbing down into it we find that its cliffs are lined with caves, already full of soldiers. In the village on the further side of it we get water, and we go into a cave full of Australians. None of us have any food at all. There are caves all along the gorge side and in the bottom olive trees, and all chock full of troops, 'Bomb happy' troops at that, shouting if anyone moved out into the open, for fear of attracting enemy planes. We lie quiet all day feeling a bit weak from lack of food, and sleep well that night. We look at one another's photographs – Randall has hundreds (and four toothbrushes). Some of the Australians come from fine looking places; they are all mad about their own country, like the New Zealanders the day before.

In the morning there is a conference of officers in the village at the end of the gorge. There I find Tony Holden. They tell us at the conference that very few troops would be taken off that night. Tony tells me that Sidney and 'B' battery are right down on the beach, so I decide to go off and join them again, which meant leaving the Australians who wanted me as an officer to lead their party. However, first of all we managed to get a bit of food from the dumps on the beach – biscuits and marmalade – the best thing I ever tasted, which we drew for the whole party, and tinned stuff too, which I made them hoard. Then Randall and I went off to find Sidney. The gorge ran down to the sea, but one left it before the end and we walked about three miles across the open to the village of Sphakia. On the way we met Colonel Downes of the 15th Coast, who told us to find Sidney quickly as he should be getting off that night. We found Sidney in the village, very exhausted as they had had no sleep but spent the night taking up rations to the rearguard. They thought I had got off. We lay under a tree and there were planes over the village all the time.

Micky Riviere was there and Michael Parish, and they had a pot of golden syrup and some tea and biscuits. Sidney and the battery had gone on marching down after I left them and had come to the end of the road and actually found a guide to take them to the beach. But Sidney wanted to help some wounded men and the guide wouldn't wait and bounced off. So they got lost too that night.

Michael Parish had spent the last three days as Liaison Officer for General Weston, riding a motorbike between him and the other Generals, who had now all got themselves off. Michael, however, was sticking to 'B' rather than 'Y' battery, which wasn't together much as Tony and Joss were in a pretty good state. Most of the way down they got a lift from Sidney in our truck, but they were exhausted. Sidney was working all he was worth to arrange for us to get off, and he was given a position in the body for that night.

We formed up about 11 pm, and with some difficulty and jostling, got into our position. But unfortunately about then the rearguard began to arrive and pass through us. We moved slowly down towards the beach, down a steep and stony path, in bursts as a load was taken on board in front, and long halts. It was very slow and the fatal hour when all ships left for the night came closer and closer. We were getting quite near the water when there was a complete stoppage. At last officers were summoned to the front; we were told that the boats had gone and would not return, and that we would be surrendered in the morning.

We felt pretty tired when we heard that. We collected the men, told them, and said that from now it must be every man for himself. We officers went down to the sea in the dark. We could see a couple of half swamped rowing boats in the water. I threw in my revolvers and everything else heavy and unnecessary. Then we went back into the village for a bit of sleep. We slept in a house – deserted like all of them – high up on the outskirts of the village. It was quite empty. In the morning we went down and bathed – the best bathe I ever had. From the rocks on the shore the water fell clear and very blue and very deep below us. We felt a hundred per cent better. There was a young commando officer bathing too and we began to plan our escape.

While we were there we saw an army landing craft used for the evacuation put out to sea from a mile further along the shore. It moved out quite fast, picking up on the way the empty boats we had seen during the night, which had drifted far out. Left behind for lack of petrol a party of officers and men got this going. They were thought to have been attacked by enemy bombers in Crete. But I was told later that they got safely away. Halfway across, an Italian submarine stopped them and ordered the officers on board. All but one had crossed over to the submarine when an English plane came over and it crash dived. The remaining officer who had fallen crossing over to the submarine reached Egypt safely.

There were fairly large boats on the beach, but either rotten or machine-gunned. Our idea was to go to the next village along to the west and look for something there. As we walked up to our house again, German bombers came over and dropped bombs on us and on the village we had planned to go to. As we knew we had been surrendered we hadn't reckoned on this. We sat under a great ledge of rock till they had gone, and then we went up to the house.

Almost immediately we were being machine-gunned there by planes which patrolled the village backwards and forwards, firing all the time. It was impossible to leave the house. We had looked at the house next door in the darkness and turned it down in favour of ours which had a nice vine clad verandah to sleep on. But we regretted it now as the other house had vegetables and every kind of thing in it. It had since been occupied by Australians, and we were a bit frightened of them. However, when I saw a chicken walk into their front door I hurried in after it and said it was mine and cornered it. It was quite a young chicken and I found it quite difficult to pluck. Then I had to cut its head off with Micky's souvenir Cretan knife, and take its insides out, which I thought was the worst thing I'd seen in war yet. I filled an earthenware pot with olive oil from a great jar, put in the chicken and some potatoes and onions and made a fire under it. Meanwhile Sidney went out for a bathe and to look for some wine. We felt irresponsible and gay. After twenty minutes I took the pot off and it was done to a turn. We had just begun to attack it when Sidney walked in. 'Quick, give me some,' he said. 'I'm a prisoner and can only stay five minutes.' We looked out of the window and there was a German on the rooftop below, pointing a tommy gun at us. I shouted something to him and we settled down to the chicken, which was excellent, though we could have dealt with a couple each. Sidney rushed off and we followed. The Germans were a small party of Alpine troops in green uniforms. They searched everybody's haversacks and took weapons, binoculars, compasses etc. I talked to them in German, handed over my cigarettes and was not searched, thus saving two compasses as I had Michael's in my bag too.

They let us go and get some water at a well we had been to in the dark, and which we found now to be graced by the most revolting corpse I ever saw.

Really I was tickled to death at the idea of being a prisoner.

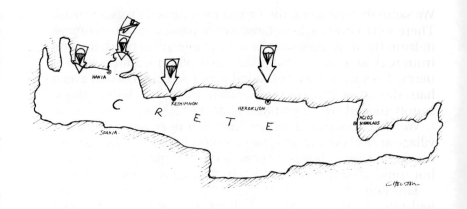

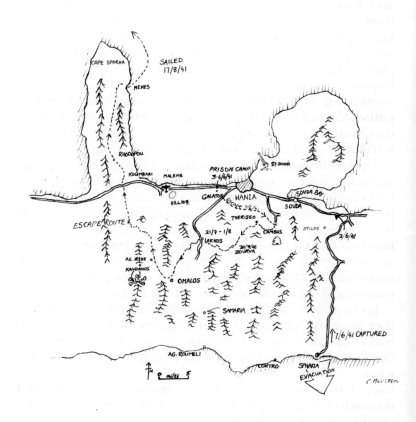

We sat in the sun while the Germans rounded everybody up. There were very few Germans; we watched one party coming in from the mountains to the west at a terrific speed, leaping from rock to rock as though they were at home in their native bergs. They were very neat, or seemed so beside us, in green hats, short coats and shorts, and all blond and well shaved and simply loaded with paraphernalia.

We were moved higher up into the upper part of Sphakia village and all the officers put together. I got permission from the German lieutenant in charge (a most unattractive looking but quite pleasant man) to go and look for our men.

Throughout the blitz neither Y battery nor ourselves had had a single casualty. We had been lucky in our one heavy raid and Y had survived several days of continuous bombing on their gun positions. (Y's six inch guns were used to fire landwards towards Maleme. They couldn't reach the aerodrome and permission wasn't granted to increase the charge. In fact the guns were only fired at all after strong opposition from (1) the General I/C area, who said they were *sea* guns. (2) His staff whose HQ was dangerously close if the guns became a target. And in fact they moved out as soon as they were fired. (3) Tony Holden OC Battery, who feared retribution.

They were at all times interesting guns, mounted far inland above the town, to fire over it out sea, or completely blinded by hills into Souda Bay, and out of range of Maleme. The battery personnel shortly before the blitz moved into dugouts built by the marines in a sandpit and never got hit once. At first I used to visit them when I drove into Hania for food etc. at night. It was quite an exciting drive, in pitch darkness with mysterious flares going off and patrols stopping us with rumours of parachute bands.

When I found our men it was to face disaster – deserted (as they obviously and openly felt) by us the night before – they had climbed back to the little valley at the entrance to the village where they had been encamped for several days. There when it got light they proceeded to cook the little food they had, and they were sitting around doing this, thinking themselves prisoners and perfectly safe, when the German planes came over and machine-gunned them. One of our men was killed outright. The wounded were in a little church, and among them was our Sergeant Major Fountain with twelve bullets in him. We heard later that he died. Three Germans who ran out shouting and waving to the planes to clear off were also killed.

In the heat of the afternoon we set off on the march back, a mile long column of men and planes overhead photographing us. We passed a few Germans going south, laying telephone lines etc. They mostly carried cameras. I talked to our guards and all came from around Berchtesgaden and Munich. They were the nice peasants of the Lederhosen and looked very much the same except they had no feather in their hats. Their doctor was bitter against us because his best friend was killed while tending a wounded man, knifed, but he thawed. And the rest were perfectly friendly and unconcerned. They told me of their walks into Poland and France and Greece, and how they'd like to be home. The only thing against them was the way they all had of shouting, in the most brutalized voices. Pappy (Graf Zu Pappenheim) always used to say that the Bavarian peasant really let loose was the most brutal fellow on earth.

We walked along parallel with the sea and into my valley of caves and from there back again north-west up the hill to the road where it ended meaninglessly, and up and up, taking every time the short cut where the road made a sweep.

Everywhere on the road Germans were getting our discarded trucks moving again. It was said that every parachutist had in his equipment the small part in the dynamo of our trucks which our men are taught to take out.

We became very tired. We came to a chapel and I lay down in it; it was cool, and was turned out by a German soldier. Micky Riviere was all in and dropped behind. 'A little further on,' the Germans kept saying, 'there's a rest camp and food.' We passed under some trees. Germans with commandeered horses (a thing we never thought of doing) and a few German graves on the road below Imbros along the gorge, and blown conduits and bombed trucks and hideous smells. The German graves with a cross and inscription and the dead man's helmet and cartridge belt on it.

We reached Imbros in the dark and there were big marquees, but not for us. We were tired and thirsty and the road seemed endless before we reached Lasithi plain. There in the first village crowds were fighting for water round the wells against the road. I threw one off it, and got water there with great difficulty, for the peasants saw themselves drink-waterless and the summer before them. And by still another well, undiscovered by most troops, I slept a bit. Then I walked on to the next village, for it was too cold to sleep, and there there was a staging camp, and officers all sleeping together in a field and Sidney and Michael there. But no food. I asked for a drink in a house and they had me in and gave me tea and a tiny bit of meat. They were refugees from the town and all sick from exposure.

We marched on in the morning. Our feet were becoming very sore and our shoes giving out. The bottom of my feet hung in places in shreds. We walked all morning; up the mountains and down again. And at midday we came to the village which was burning as we streamed south. And here at last we were given food, a tin of bully beef and some biscuits between four; and there was a shallow river in which we could bathe. A fair-haired boy, a soldier, gave a bit off a loaf – he had exchanged it for his gold watch.

Suddenly we found that the place was full of released Italian prisoners, taken in Albania and brought to Crete. They had refused to make use of the arms which the Germans dropped them by air, for which they were bombed. Now instead of standing and jeering at us they were all friendliness, and drowned us in red wine, which no doubt they were stealing in the village. We all had as much of it as we could drink and filled our water bottles with it, and when we moved again it was in high fettle.

But the long, hot road wore that off, and as it got dark we were almost past going on. In fact I tried to persuade the others to fall out, sleep by the river and get back to Kalives and our officers' mess, food and clothes. But we did not get to the next night's lodging place, by the village of Stilos. Here during the blitz one day when a great black cloud from the bombing of Souda was hanging over and darkening the whole countryside, I walked and watched Australians bathing naked in front of the village women, and admired the blue convolvulus and lilies on a roadside inn.

Now we were by the river bank, close by where it first

appears suddenly and almost full grown above ground. We were given m and v, and found a great barrel of black treacle, and slept. It was foully damp and bitterly cold though I shared the heavy fleabag Michael Parish had carried all through. He tried to escape from here and couldn't.

In the morning again we moved on. Michael and I dragged further and further behind until we seemed to lose sight at the tail with a few Germans. We passed through a grim little battlefield with bombed trucks and corpses under trees, sprawling about, and so to the road along Souda Bay. Souda was a complete ruin. The cruiser *York* and plenty of other ships still lay in the harbour; but all out of action. Between Souda and Hania the road was completely jammed. Off the road were thousands of Italians, apparently shut up by the Germans for looting.

Michael and I, very hungry again, stepped off the road and approached a party of these under an olive tree, and were received with open arms. They gave us as many fritters, freshly cooked, as we could eat, made lemonade for us out of citrons, and gestures of all possible friendliness. When we joined the column again we fell in with a most unpleasant German, who ordered us about in the nastiest way and annoyed us a lot. We felt quite sure he would shoot us if he got the chance.

Hania was an amazing sight. Every house apparently had some damage, a large proportion were completely destroyed. And this was not the old and crumbly part of the town. The streets were blocked with fallen stone. For two days Hania was bombed all day. It contained hardly anything military, but when after almost a week the blitz failed to make headway, the Germans revenged themselves on the towns, which they destroyed systematically, in waves, attacking one quarter at a time. Heraklion suffered the same.

We were marched on, on the road to Maleme, and at last we reached our prison camp. The Field Hospital which Michael and I had watched arise just round the corner from our bathing place, was bombed by the Germans who also set part of it alight, then parachutists captured it, destroyed the medical stores and made the walking wounded there work for them, and I believe walk in front of them as they attacked. It was recaptured later. Now the tents were full of men, and as the later arrivals came in they camped in the open ground.

90

The officers were more or less together. There was practically no organisation. We slept in the open that night, and it was cold and damp by the sea. Sharing Michael's fleabag was such a tight fit that any movement disturbed the other. We were right on the sea, and the first thing we did was to get into it. Throughout our long hot thirsty walk a bathe seemed the ultimate bliss, and yet when I got into the water I shivered with cold, swimming slowly with raw stinging feet, and hurried out again, disappointed. I was feeling too tired to be braced by it.

Next day we found a tent. Sidney and Michael P and me, Alexis Casdagli and D Gilbey and Venables the RC parson, and a few others. Venables, like many others, had never made the trip to Sphakia and he had a suitcase full of clothes, unheard of elegancies, which he gave and lent most generously. Derek had been next to me the last night at Sphakia, and when we were held up down by the shore he pressed forward crying, 'Embarkation Staff Officer' (which he was in Souda Bay). Alas! It didn't work, Tony and Joss were in another tent. Tony got a lift back in a truck all the way, but Joss had walked and survived. Considering that he was so rheumaticky that he would never walk fifty yards this was amazing. Micky Riviere had been brought in on a truck and was in another tent, not too well. Alexis Casdagli, a Major in the RAOC, is a brother of the Casdagli who married Pat Seymour.

We had one or two beds and mattresses in our tent, but I had only the sandy floor, and it was dirty to say the least. There was no water inside the camp, it had to be fetched from outside, and we were all in such a futile state that this seemed an unparalleled and impossible effort. Most of us possessed nothing – brushes, combs, plates and spoons were the most needed. I found a case of glasses which had been twisted but unbroken by the fire, and some hospital bowls, enamelled. We cut spoons out of wood and began cutting wooden sandals. I still had my knife, though they were supposed to be given up. The Adjutant of the camp, Milne, the Field Marshall's son commanding an AA battery on Akrotiri peninsula where he surrendered without trying to escape – gave me the bottoms of some hospital pyjamas. The CO of the camp was the Colonel of the Welch.

Apparently the Germans, finding we had people like Milne

who enjoyed organising things, simply left everything to them, which means to say that having chosen a site for the prison camp, on which a few tents already stood and buildings for themselves, they started to wire it in. They made no effort to provide further accommodation (nor did they during the two months the prisoners remained, although there must have been plenty of tents captured on the island, including my own). They provided no food or blankets or beds or latrines. Our guards were parachutists and resting from their labours. When they were dressed they wore our uniforms out of our stores and our topees. But most of the time they were lying browning on the beach.

Meanwhile Milne was organising the thousands of men into camps of about 500 each for feeding etc. Casdagli in a truck under guard was fetching ordnance stores which Teddy Parker and his REs were installing (they ran water later into the camp) so we got food and stoves to cook it. But it was very little. There was none for about a day and then we got some tea for one meal and some rice for another, and some stew for the big meal of the day. We were madly hungry. We would queue up and wait ages for our bit of porridge dumped in an enamel spittoon, and return and queue up hoping for a scraping more. And we would slip into the German cookhouse and see if there was anything to be pinched.

The Germans were eating enormously on the verandah, and their officers, on white tablecloths and all; while we looked like nothing on earth – half unshaven for lack of water and blades, unbrushed, dirty with sand and no change of clothes, ill with dysentery which began almost immediately.

Tony Holden got back to his old mess on a truck and found a sackful of books. Their store of bully beef had been systematically punctured by Michael P just before they left and was bad; their pig was blitzed and very dead. Still, that gave us some books.

Then Casdagli went to visit the village where he had had his ordnance HQ all winter. He had been generous to the villagers, and now when he returned as a prisoner, the whole place turned out for him. They made the guard so drunk he didn't know what was going on (but sat handing round pictures of Hitler which the villagers accepted gracefully and with the most dreadful imprecations). They feasted Casdagli till he could eat no more and they filled his truck with clothes and food. He brought it back to our tent, tins of butter and marmalade, fresh bread, chickens, tea, sugar, rice, potatoes, God knows what, but to us it was a miracle. And it made Michael P and myself think that the villagers were friendly and had food.

From the first Michael P had talked of escape. Nobody else did. Everyone was sick or exhausted, shoeless, fed up. Teddy Parker, a most brave and tireless man, who himself blew all the bridges as the Germans came to them on the road to Sphakia, and walked back barefoot, too proud to take a lift, a man moreover who knew all about sailing, said that it would be madness to try to sail away on our own. Crete seemed to most people as much of a prison as any prison camp. The Germans were presumably everywhere, their planes seemed to spot anyone who moved. It was difficult to realise that blitz conditions were already over. There was a feeling of resignation at best of putting off any effort till a better opportunity. When we mentioned the word escape to Derek Gilbey, he said 'Would that be quite playing the game, old man?'

Meanwhile, Milne put a stop to organised scavenging parties which had been getting out of camp searching nearby fields and villages. Anyone trying to escape, he announced, would be put under close arrest. He was obviously not the man to ask for help. We needed money, but rather than broadcast our intentions, merely got what we could from Sidney, about £10. The Germans announced that anyone trying to escape would be shot.

Among the prisoners was Tony McCraith, Pat's brother. He asked me to join him in escaping. His idea was to get out of the camp and go to Maleme aerodrome which was quite close. He had an RAF Sergeant Pilot, and they planned to watch their opportunity on the aerodrome, jump into a plane and make off. It was a tempting idea because if it came off you'd be in Egypt that same day.

But Michael and I decided to stick to our old idea, which was to walk to the eastern end of the island (the port of Sitia) where there had been no fighting, which we had not garrisoned and which most likely would be free of Germans and unblitzed, and there get a boat.

(Captured June 1st. Slept Lasithi.
June 2nd. Slept Stilos.
June 3rd-6th. Slept Galatas Camp.
June 7th. Escaped.)

Michael and I slept four nights in the camp. We had our own doctors and MI room in the camp and I had my leg and feet dressed, and my wrist which I had cut jumping away from a bomb on the way to Sphakia. Everyone was beginning to get what we thought was dysentery but really was a glorified diarrhoea. The sanitary conditions in the camp were awe inspiring. Sidney was down with it, unable really to appreciate Casdagli's treasure or think of escaping with us. Micky was too weak. We thought in any case that two was enough together, and we didn't even tell Joss and Tony (who would have been furious at the idea). Casdagli gave us tea and sugar. We hung on one day to fatten ourselves on his food. Michael pinched some tins from the German stores.

All this time we saw little of the men. One of us would go and lead them up to get their meals, otherwise there was nothing to be done for them. We were as badly off ourselves; we only wanted to lie quiet all day. The Australians and New Zealanders only stayed in the camp one night and then marched on to what had been the Italian P of W camp up in the hills. Which left three or four thousand in our camp – Marines, RAs, Commandos and oddments like ourselves. We learned that the officers were to be flown off almost immediately and that the Yeomanry would be in the first batch. So Michael and I had to get moving.

With practically no plans in our heads we set out after breakfast on June 7th. We both had bright blue hospital coats. I had also pale blue pyjama trousers. We jettisoned tunics, belts, fleabag etc. I carried my haversack containing compasses, tinned food, handkerchiefs, pullover, pair of shorts, extra shirt (from Venables), socks (from Casdagli), three books, cheque books, photographs, all inside a sack over my shoulder. I also carried a spade. Michael had a blue coat, shorts, his big infantry haversack, a spade and bucket, and on his head the leg of a bright blue pyjama. We climbed through the wire, wandered across a vineyard in the direction of a well where prisoners were washing and drawing water and

94

German guards sitting around talking. The atmosphere charged with unconcern and innocence we meandered on, looking under olive trees and crying, 'Is this the place – is this where we left it? It looked, I do believe, like that clearing over there.'

We crossed the main Maleme road. Among the olive trees were the trenches of the battle, and parachutes and ammunition cases. We cut bits of green grey silk off a parachute. After a bit we came to a village on a ridge. In the well below it children filled our water bottles for us. We walked up into the village and asked for food and rashly strolling into the main street we met two German soldiers.

'What are you doing here?' they said in German.

'Do have a grape,' we said in English, handing each a bunch of unripe grapes about the size of green peas and devouring them ourselves. 'How hungry we are. Notice our bucket, we fill it with these uneatable grapes. Notice our spades, we are a work party; our clothes too, so striking. And we are so pleased to see you, anyone can see that.'

'Where do you come from?' they said. 'Where are you going?' They point, we point, all in the same direction, back to the camp of course, where else? They walk on up the village, stop, look back at us. We sit, eating the uneatable grapes. They walk on and we leg it.

We get into olive groves again and look down on the valley through which runs the road to Meskla. Among the trees by the road we hear German voices, no doubt of soldiers collecting parachutes etc. We run across the road just in front of an empty German truck. Almost immediately we come to a river, with trees and rushes and high banks and we lie down in the shade. We found some little bakelite boxes there of stuff to put in contaminated water. Dropped by parachutists I suppose, who filled their water bottles there. It was difficult to read the labels but it seems to work in ten minutes while ours takes half an hour. I threw away here my razor as I had no more blades, and the spade and bucket. We went on towards the hills, with a gap in view, but lost it as we came to the foothills and began to climb. We passed German telephone wires laid among the vines but saw none.

We began to feel very tired, and Michael who had boasted of never having been in such good form as after the march, suddenly crumpled up with diarrhoea. In the groves of great old olives at the foot of the hills it was difficult to know which path to choose. Towards evening we hit on a lone farm hidden away among the trees – a most attractive place, built around a courtyard with a chapel in the middle. It all looked very old and peaceful. We walked in. There were people sitting in one corner. They gave us chairs. We asked for water; they gave it to us. 'You are Germans?' they asked politely. So we said, 'Of course not.' We shook our heads, pointed to our clothes, our bandages. They only half believed us and were none the more friendly for that. It was a big family, swollen by refugees, and there was a town bred granddaughter who spoke French. They thawed a little but told us the Germans often visited them. We asked for bread and they gave us some with miseethra – whipped cream cheese, which we still had to learn to like. We then took our leave for we were obviously unwelcome. It was the one and only occasion that we were not welcomed by the Cretans.

After that we climbed uphill, up and up, till we came to the top, and we were on a ridge looking across a valley at further ridges. In the valley was a river and a road. It was the valley of the gap we had been aiming for. There was nothing to do but climb down into it. As the sun set on the hillside opposite, ourselves already in the shade, we climbed diagonally down. It was covered in stiff undergrowth, over which we tripped and fell painfully and miserably. It took a long time to reach the valley bottom and it was already getting dark. We decided to sleep a bit. We lay down, but there was a cold wind, and by midnight it was altogether too cold. We got up and moved on. The path led us into a gorge which narrowed till it formed one of those 'natural phenomena' in which Crete is, I believe, rich – a narrow cleft between towering perpendicular cliffs, running for miles, sometimes in bright moonlight, sometimes in darkness. The path became a stone causeway built at some time at enormous trouble alongside a river bed, which from the size of its boulders must in spring be a rushing torrent.

We stumbled along till I could go no further, and despite Michael's determination to keep going, I lay down under a rock and slept an hour or two. It was protected from the wind there. Then as it began to get faintly light we went on again.

The gorge ended and a path went left and right. We took the right and it led west (the rising sun told us) we hadn't thought of using our compasses.

So we turned back and on the other path we came to signs of cultivation again, fields and olives, but no houses. We sat down in a grove and there came along the hillside a flock of goats and their shepherd. I rushed to him, while Michael sat, feeling very ill. He was a nice friendly man, filled a bowl for me and another for Michael. It took not quite three goats to fill our bowl, which was quite a good size. It tasted wonderful.

We lay for a bit and then, before the sun should get too hot, walked on. Neither of us felt too good. So following a rocky path we came to a village – Panagia, and we went up to the first house. They were the nicest people in the world. A boy from Hania spoke a little French, otherwise communication was difficult. They made beds for us and we lay down while they prepared a meal. The house was really all one room with a gallery for a bedroom and some store rooms under, but all open with the living room. It was nice and clean. The woman was charming, her husband back from Albania with frost-bitten feet, full of spirits. And the food! Fresh eggs! Chips! Hot marrow! Salad!

When it was all over the men took us down into the village to the café. It was Sunday and the café crowded, and the barber in one corner plying a great trade. People sent us drinks over. We got shaves and our hair cut. The barber spoke a little English, he had been in America. We pressed them to find us someone to mend our shoes, and he made quite a good job of them.

And then we returned for supper. People we had seen at the café drifted in and out. Conversation was a little difficult. They made us beds on broad couches built out from the walls, sheets and pillows, quite wonderful. And they mended our clothes, and gave us wine to take with us in the morning when we left, and were all the time so friendly and generous and helpful that they seemed the best people we had ever met. For we didn't know the Cretan people at all.

We left in the morning and took the valley east. But immediately villagers clutched us, crying 'Germania' and they led us up the hill side. There we met a man of the night before carrying a bucket to the well, and he dropped everything and said he would guide us. So we followed him through a nice pine wood with bracken underfoot, and up and down the steep ridges of the foothills, by paths which we should never have known to choose ourselves. But he was going homewards to where he was born, and he even lost his track, or perhaps there was none. We walked across country, through brush wood which tore chunks out of my bare legs. I was to curse that walk as long as I remained on Crete. The wine came unstoppered and leaked, and we by drinking rid ourselves of it.

We climbed down into a village where a white church stood by a dry stream full of oleanders in flower, and as we toiled up the farther side a Greek policeman passed us. We distrusted the police, but he took no action.

We followed a steep wooded valley running into the hills and at midday came to a village buried in olive trees. It was a small place and everyone turned out for us. A schoolmaster and his wife, refugees from Hania, gave us lunch, fried eggs and bread and wine, and after that we were taken to see an English refugee – Parry Shaw, a retired sailor with a Cretan wife, who was living next door, surrounded by his wife's relations. He had been working in the Cipher office. We talked to him about our chances of escaping. Everyone begged us to stay, and a man with two pretty daughters, refugees again, made us wait at least until he brought a chicken freshly cooked, and eggs and bread.

Then we moved on up under the trees, crossing and re-crossing the little dry stream bed, till we came to the village where our guide's wife and children were living. It was some time since he'd seen them, they were with a sister, and he led us to the house, promising us beds there. It was incredibly squalid. Everything looked filthy. It swarmed with children. Michael collapsed inside. I took a chair and sat in the yard. Lots of women walked in, none seemed very pleased to see us. Our guide seemed to lose interest in us altogether. There was one woman who obviously wasn't a village woman, wearing quite a nice dress. She asked us to her house. She was staying there with her husband in the house of her parents. We followed her gladly. She had some children too, and everybody lived and slept in one small room with two big beds in it. The husband looked like El Greco. They came from

Hania. We lay down on one of the beds. When it began to feel like mealtime we offered our chicken to swell the feast. It was accepted gratefully, but we were a little disappointed when for our supper we shared with the whole family our chicken and nothing else. Still, she was a very nice woman. The old people, her husband's parents, real old villagers, were put to sleep somewhere outside with the children (under a tree we discovered next morning) and we were given one bed, quite a big comfortable one, with sheets.

But hardly had we settled into it for the night, and the woman and her husband in theirs, when we began to scratch. It was alive with fleas. I stood it as long as I could, then I got out and lay on the floor. They were there too. I sat in a chair. There was no respite. I got back into bed and at dawn, when they tired, I slept. It was a dreadful night.

That evening among the olive trees I came on a man lying on a threshing floor, who jumped a mile when he saw me. He turned out to be a corporal in 151 AA Battery. He had a boy with him, who brought him food and news. And the boy had reported that we were Germans. In fact when we first arrived this boy had told me that he spoke German and so discovered that I spoke it (which he could not), but that convinced him. This soldier, an oldish and not very attractive man, was the first other free Englishman we had met. He was living up in the mountains with a shepherd, helping in the cheesemaking and receiving milk and cheese in return. The villagers brought him up food too, and he sometimes came down, as now. His story was that he was with his battery on Akrotiri peninsula and they had no news of the evacuation till Souda was in enemy hands and all chance of escape by land cut off. Major Milne, their OC (the Field Marshall's son) sent to the Germans to surrender. But this corporal walked out on them and went off to look for a boat in which to cross Souda Bay. He knew where there were some in the little bay, but when he came there it was noisy with German soldiers romping in the water. He hid, and found another, in which he crossed and made his way into the mountains. He had been on the island for some time, had made friends among the Greeks, and his idea seemed more to be to live peaceably with them till the end of the war, even to live with the shepherds as he was doing, than to try to escape. He wore civilian clothes and called himself

Johannis.

The next morning we walked out of the village, following the valley. We soon met up with two friends – a very good-looking boy and a young soldier just back from Albania, who guided us. We were both weak and found it hard climbing. A party of refugees we passed gave us handfuls of the almonds they were picking. We came to a village high up all in one straggling block, like a fortress, and at last, above it, to one lone house, the boy's uncle's. It was a really nice house, a little concrete chalet for the summer with proper rooms and windows, the owner having done well for himself in America. He was a nice man, but he only offered us water.

Here the boy left and the soldier took us on, down now into the next valley. He was obviously nervous, kept us up on the hills off the tracks, and after a bit he too pointed out our way and left us to it. Across the valley before us straggling up the further side of the hill we could see the roofs of another village. He told us to avoid that (for we were making for Stilos on the road to Heraklion). But Michael and I as we stumbled downhill, over vineyard retaining walls, and stopping and falling heavy from weakness on the rocks, we began to see the next village as something of a haven. Particularly me. We climbed down and up again to it and turned into the first house. They were a bit scared till they recognised we were English. It was nicely whitewashed; we sat down and asked for milk. There were lots of goats tied up outside, and they produced a bowl of it. So we showed them how to make hot bread and milk of it, and they gave us plenty of sugar, so it was grand. I ate enormously of it.

Then Michael lay on a couch and I on a blanket and sheet on the floor and the house was cleared for us. We felt better after that for continuing our day's walk, so we thanked them very much and went on through the village. It was less like a village than a number of scattered hamlets, all having one name, Cambus.

As we left one of these, we were surrounded by people who seized us by the arm, asked where we were going, assured us that we were walking straight into the Germans, begged us to stay. One extraordinary little fellow, with an apache cap over one eye, the most appalling squint I ever saw, a face all twisted to one side, and an excellent flow of French, assured us that if we cut open his veins, or the veins of this sister of his here (a fat old woman) or that sister there (a fat younger woman), or his brother-in-law here, we should find some English blood would flow out. Such was his and their love for the English, as anybody could tell us. He begged us to stay a week, a month a year, we should want for nothing. No, we said, we must press on.

An old Cretan like the Ancient Mariner, adopted us as his children. Michael began to weaken (I longed to sit down anywhere). So we said, right, if we might stay a day or two and rest we should be very grateful. For every day now we got weaker with a sort of dysentery. The little Frenchman led us off. He was a chauffeur from Hania, and with his two sisters and his brother-in-law, he was taking refuge with his aunt. 'Thea' was a fine old lady with a bad leg, widow of a captain of the hills in the eighties, who lived in the filthiest house I ever saw. It was a part of a conglomeration of hovels, all of whose occupants were cousins, and the ancient mariner was the 'papous' – the grandfather.

In one small room on the roof of Thea's house lived her nephew Georgio with his wife and four children. He was a handsome ruddy creature, young and jolly, with a stick of a wife like a ghost, who never uttered. There was a sweet little girl, Katina and three boys. We lay down on their one bed and at night they gave us blankets and sheets on the roof. One-eyed Kosta, our host, disappeared that night, so no one remained to whom we could talk. But Thalia, his fat unmarried sister, dealt most efficiency with my wrist, which was in a pretty good mess, having gone septic and spread.

They were all terrifically friendly and kind. People poured into the house to sit and stare at us and describe with much gesticulation the fate of their homes in the bombing of Hania, and what they would like us to do to the Germans. 'Germania' they shouted, with hideous grimaces, and drew their fingers across their throats. We nodded brightly back. There was one bearded giant of a man who like most of the men had fought the parachutists when first they landed. We were taken to dinner in the house he was living in, a very nice clean house and piles of food, and we said that if we could find a nice clean room like that we should like to stay a bit and help them in the fields for our keep. They wouldn't hear of that. So we slept very comfortably on the roof and next day rested mostly on Georgio's bed. Our insides became worse, and we felt pretty feeble. I decided to do Geoffrey Brook's cure and starve for two days.

Meanwhile, they took us down to Thea's well and vineyard, where the effort of collecting a few dry sticks for a fire almost killed me. There was some kind of a feud between Kosta's family and the papous. He had, like most of the old men, been in America and retained a few unintelligible words which he fired off at us, and at one moment we gathered he was trying to warn us against our hosts, but why we couldn't make out. Later, it really seemed that he longed to look after us himself. He was a strange, fierce, bone-headed old man. His main attraction was that he had *crassi* – red wine – and our hosts had none. He would disappear with a dirty old bucket and return with it full and pour it partly into a decanter and largely on to the floor, assuring us that it was his last.

The day after I began my starvation cure, Michael started on it too, and that morning, as we lay on our bed, in came papous and ordered us to come to his house and eat. We tried to explain that we weren't eating; he tried to drag us off. Finding us quite determined he retired, and reappeared with fried eggs and red wine. We were horrified and began all over again, begging him to take them back and eat them himself before they got cold. The fierce old man burst into tears. Horror-struck, we got out of bed and to appease him drank some wine, followed hurriedly by water to save the cure.

That same afternoon Thalia came back from visiting in a distant part of the village with the news that she had met some Australians there, and brought back one with her. He was a good-looking self confident fellow, and told us that with two friends he had escaped from the Australian prison camp. They walked across the mountains and they met a man who handed them a note. This note was addressed to any free English, and adjured them to keep their hearts up, for the writer was working to get them off. It was signed illegibly, Lieut. Commander RAR. They were expecting to meet him that same evening in Cambus.

This was wonderful news, and Michael threw up his cure and went off together with the Australian. I had our bed on the roof to myself that night and revelled in it, for we always quarrelled over our just shares in it. Michael was gone all next day. He met the naval officer that night and returned very early next morning to collect me and our things. The naval officer was a Greek, which explained the slightly odd tone of his note. As owner of a salvage boat he had been working in Souda Bay salvaging and in the Boorns. Because he had his wife and children on the island and they couldn't go too, he didn't leave with the fleet, but had taken to the hills. Now he was planning to get a boat to take them to Egypt, and with them a party of ten British soldiers if he should find any hiding in the mountains. He told Michael what he must do – move immediately right up into the mountains and stay there till they found a boat. Michael was impressed with his energy and confidence and we moved at once.

My cure had done me good and I made the climb quite easily. Georgio gave us one blanket and some food and helped us into Cambus with it where we met the three Australians and a guide with a donkey, who was already loaded with a great sack of potatoes and more blankets. Walking carrying nothing was a hundred times easier. We left the village, climbing gently up into the mountains. After the first hour it became really mountainous and steep, climbing up the side of a ravine.

After two hours we reached our new home – a cluster of amazing dome-shaped beehive dwellings built of rough stone. Here lived the shepherds from Cambus in the summer months. A little further on was a second cluster, of two beehives and a pen, and this was handed over to us. Michael and I took the smaller house. Inside half was built up a couple of feet above ground level to make a seat. There was just room on the ground for the two of us to lie, and it was already covered in fairly clean-looking branches. The rest of the house was filthy and had recently contained goats.

The Greek Officer, Emmanuele Vernicos, whom we never called or spoke of as anything but 'The Captain', had assured us we should do well on his potatoes and the milk and cheese we should get from the shepherds. Fortunately, however, we had brought up with us presents of eggs, bread, chicken, etc. We had a good deal of tinned stuff, but we wanted to keep this for our eventual voyage. We added considerably to our stock of this, as we were given some by various villagers.

103

In the first days of confusion after we withdrew from Hania the villagers went down and carried off all they could find in our NAAFI or anywhere else, and they all had British boots and oddments of equipment.

We made a fire in the open and settled in.

We were high up now in the mountains and at night it was cold. Michael and I had one blanket under us and one on top, and all our clothes on, and we were very cold. There was only the doorway to give light or air to our beehive; it had no door and opened straight on to our feet. The bigger beehive with the three Australians in it had such a small doorway you had almost to crawl in. We kept all the food in our house and issued it out. Our three Australians – two corporals and a private – were very nice fellows. The private – George – had won a £1,000 sweep and spent it all racing. He was attractive and probably rather useless and a great one for the girls. Of the other two, John was a most frightfully nice person, a hat manufacturer in civilian life and doing very well. The other, Rex, was almost equally nice, very quiet and capable.

They had all been through the great attack in Libya, followed immediately and without any leave by Greece. In Greece their Battalion, the 2nd/2nd, did the withdrawal on foot with terrific hardships, beside which our walk to Sphakia and back paled. They failed to get taken off, escaped from Greece in a caique which took them to Chios, got another sailing boat there and were brought to Crete. They were one of the completely disorganised units which came to Crete from Greece, but should never have been allowed to stop there.

The Australians came to Crete after having had a very stiff time (whether they acquitted themselves well in Greece or not). Many of them had been sick on the way and picked up with nothing but what they stood up in. Few had much more, for the landing craft which carried them from the shore out to the destroyers would not take arms or equipment (though it had been carried in many cases for days and without it the men were useless).

Arrived in Crete they camped in the valleys, by the sea or rivers, and lay all day in the sun. Very soon they began to live up to their reputation. Women were attacked not only in Hania, but in my own quiet little huddle of cottages at Kalame. Civilians were shot. The NAAFI was broken open and employees held up with a tommy-gun. All day shots went off in all directions for no apparent reason. Col. Donnes, maddened by the lack of respect with which they treated him, and they were the least smart soldiers imaginable – forbade any to enter the prison, no matter their rank. They hung round our café however, outside the walls, firing revolvers vaguely into the air till one shot his hand off.

I myself had not yet begun to hear that they were far from being the soldiers in the field they were puffed up to be, though I knew that they had not by any means won the Libyan campaign for us as our papers suggested. One felt they were uncivilized animals, but no doubt terrific fighters. Now, sitting alone on a rock with three of them, I discovered how very much easier to talk to they were than our own men. Completely democratic, without any class consciousness, they were perfectly reasonable companions, where an English soldier would probably have been either dumb or tiresome. In fact, like most people, the Australians seem full of contradictions.

While I was a prisoner, I talked quite a lot to the Germans. The Alpine troops were typical Bavarian peasants, pleasant, speaking their strange dialect, not very talkative, but willing to talk of home. The parachutists were a very different cup of tea, well educated, mostly from universities, not professional soldiers, delighted to discuss or argue anything, as nice a lot of young men apparently as one could meet anywhere, and it was they who were accusing us (or at least the Australians and New Zealanders) of atrocities! My friend Hans Wilde, the pilot officer, who was my prisoner at Kalame, was undoubtedly one of the nicest people I ever met. He thought I was crazy to believe the stories I reeled out about Poland and yet before I left Crete I knew quite definitely that the tales of Nazi brutality and cold bloodedness were absolutely true. (In the same way since then I have talked with Simonds, under whom Billy McLean and Frank Pilkington served in Abyssinia. He told me that stories of atrocities committed by the natives there are without any foundation and that on two occasions his native troops made representations to him on his treatment of Italian prisoners.

On the other hand he says that the Italian cruelty was appalling and he detested the Italians. Wherever I have come up against Italians, either the prisoners taken in Libya or those in Crete, before and after they were freed, I found them charming, if rather contemptible persons.)

The Cretans say they would like to do the most awful things to the Germans, and I believe that both in Albania and in Crete they mutilated their prisoners. I am not sure whether this is true, but I can believe it of them, as they are almost fearless. They say that several hundred Germans were evacuated to Chios minus hands and feet. The Cretans were besides attacked in their own homes, when I think there is more excuse than when carrying war abroad.

The shepherds whose guests we really were, but of whom we never saw a great deal, were a wild-looking lot. In the morning they drove in their herds to be milked. I watched a shaggy bearded fellow milking his goats. He came to one which had been naughty when he was driving it in. To my astonishment and horror he seized hold of it, bit it madly in the face, threw it down, stamped on it, twisted its head back as far as it would go and trod on it, picked it up again high in the air and threw it away. The goat trotted away, no doubt chastened.

With the real shepherds are some genuine bandits staying the weekend. They wear the Cretan dress with baggy trousers and top boots, and belt chock full of cartridges, into which is stuck their long ivory handled knives. The sheaths of these are really superb, heavily chased silver with ships and trees and animals, ending in a fish's head. Apparently these bandits are all escaped murderers, released by the Germans from prison. They carry at least two revolvers and a rifle wherever they go, though the chance of their needing them without very adequate warning is remote. They are simply friendly souls, and delight in showing off their not very dangerous wounds. Still, one says he killed twelve Germans beside a Greek policeman.

Life up in the mountains is extremely dull. My legs continue to fester and I feel very dull and feeble. Water has to be fetched from a spring about a mile further up the mountain, a very good walk on the bare rock. It's an attractive spring though, a trickle running out from the bare stone flank of a cliff into a deep hole, shaded by boulders. The valley where we are has a little scrub, but it is the last, and above us there is nothing but naked stone. It is awful ground for walking, all rough stone ledges. All the plant life seems tough and prickly and unfriendly to my bare and tender legs. All the same, some are making a belated attempt to flower, little yellow and purple flowers, quite pretty. There is a silvery thing like our 'lambs ears', which is good for bedding and various plants which make a kind of tea concoction if put in boiling water. It may be senna.

After we'd been up in the mountains for a bit, Michael and I went down to Cambus to forage for food and news. We went to the house of an English speaking girl named Phyllis. Not her house actually, as she was an evacuee from Hania, but her aunt's. Phyllis was nothing great to look at, but when I compared her in her autograph book to Nausicaa, it wasn't half what we felt as we sat down to fried eggs, fried bread and tea in a nice clean house – full of nice clean friendly people (and our fat Thalia). Thalia, alas, dragged us back to her filthy house, where we slept the night, but got in a lunch with Phyllis before returning to the mountains again.

At Phyllis's we met 'the Captain', which was the first I'd seen of him. He was a smallish perky little grey bearded fellow like a youngish Shylock, with a loud voice and an authoritative manner. He hadn't left yet for the south, which saddened us, as mountain life palled. Thalia washed our clothes by the well, and we returned to the mountains with a paralytic donkey loaded with potatoes, seven loaves of bread (baked by Thalia from flour given us by Phyllis's relations) eggs, rice, dried beans, another blanket and some wine.

Our forage for news was equally exciting, for the Germans had just attacked Russia, and no one could help speculating on 'the beginning of the end'! In any case we imagined it would mean the withdrawal of many troops from Crete. They told us also that all the prisoners had now been taken off the island. (This was not true.) We got hold of a German newspaper printed in Crete in German and Greek, with fantastic claims of success against Russia. We learnt from that for the first time definitely that we had never retaken Libya. The German soldiers told us of great British successes there, God knows why. They told us too, that General Freyberg had been killed, crash landing in Egypt (a universally popular piece of news) and that Mr Churchill had been succeeded by

Mr Attlee!

There is no doubt that the Germans are simply loathed by the Cretans, who tell one all the time of people being shot. We reckon it is always the same people. But though I continue to give the Germans the benefit of the doubt (particularly after their treatment of us prisoners, which was at very worst neglectful) they appear to be doing their best to put the population against them by shooting civilians – for firing on parachutists during the blitz – burning houses and robbing everything.

In the mountains it is getting quite hot during the day and warmer at nights. We bought a whole sheep for about a pound, and having eaten it began to cast eyes on a little black pig 'Mickro Mavro' – to distinguish it from a very large white one.

John Hills, our nicest Australian, stole an extra cup of milk to our daily supply and it was from the tub prepared for cheese making, and turned our whole lot sour. A major disaster.

All scratches still go septic and spread, and we have nothing to dress them with. I managed to set fire to my small supply of cotton wool when burning a needle, which was the end of that.

On July 5th, a fortnight after we went up into the mountains, Michael and I went down to Cambus again. We slept the first night at Phyllis's aunt's. Next day we visited the Captain's wife, blonde, beautiful and cold. I decided she came from a seaport cabaret – she is English – but actually she is from Newfoundland. She has charming children. She wasn't at all pleased to see us, as too many escaped prisoners visit 'the Englishman' on their way through Cambus, and she is terrified of being betrayed.

Next night we slept at Thalia's and the following day there was a scare. Just as we were starting out for a meal with Phyllis's cousins, one of them came running the whole way, almost two miles, to say Germans were entering that end of the village. So we spent all day in the rocks.

Michael at this time was suffering agonies from a festering foot and not at all amused by scares and scamperings.

We were made to spend the next day down by the well, where Thalia brought us some very mediocre food, but we sleep on the roof as usual. We decide to stay till the Captain returns and we know definitely how things are. In the mountains we feel so very out of touch. By the well, Michael holds court and a procession of passing escapees are led up to him and discuss identical rumours and projects and possibilities. It is most difficult for us to advise them what to do, as we are at a low ebb ourselves. The noise of tree locusts is everywhere terrific and nerve-wracking. We long to hear a radio as the most fantastically contradictory reports of the German-Russian campaign continue to come in.

The Cretans exaggerate everything past belief and will invent the most impressive tales without foundation. I ceased believing anything, but we heard that the Russians were in Romania, Poland and Bulgaria; that Berlin was in ruins, that the Germans were using gas, that they were tearing the gold out of the teeth of our prisoners. Such rumours were repeated and believed enthusiastically.

At moments I appreciated the simplicities of Cretan country life – Georgio with his half dozen goats and his cow, winnowing the chaff in a small rocky field, around him his wife and children and female cousins. One sits under a tree spinning wool on a distaff. There is not overmuch work to do and it is done leisurely. The sun makes everything pleasant, and in the mountains it is never over hot. But here in the winter with many feet of snow it must be appallingly squalid – the houses dark and dirty and uncomfortable to a quite unnecessary degree.

But oh, the tedium! Oh! The stifled irritation – and they are so incredibly kind. Unfortunately they go into fits if we take walks away from their sight.

After a week the Captain arrived back from the south coast, with the great news that he had got a boat. *But* he went west first and then south, and in the villages to the west of us south of Hania he found hundreds and hundreds of Australians and New Zealanders, which has altered all his ideas. Now his suggestion is that four Australian sergeants should go in the boat and we remain in charge of this new army. The sergeants would carry a note asking for an evacuation to be arranged. We decided in a week's time to walk over with him to the south and see the boat off.

We were asked to Sunday dinner by Elefteria and were as

pleased as schoolboys on a treat to go over there. But to our rage Thalia turned up with one-eyed Kosta (a very rare visitor), and a Cypriot sergeant from Hania.

We tried and failed to get the BBC on a hidden wireless, but next day we got it. It was very exciting. They said the German claims were very exaggerated and their losses very heavy, and then they began talking about Lord Byron. Next morning early I went off up into the mountains by myself and down again in the evening with the rest of the party and all our blankets and stuff. During the day there had been a Germania scare in the village. At midnight we were woken up and very unwillingly, we are hustled off to the mountains. I lead a party of nine. After a bit we sleep behind a ridge and go on at daybreak. On the way up a young Englishman who had appeared at Thalia's the night before with Greek pseudo-parents who had saved him from the Germans, packed in and turned back. We were pretty bored to see our mountain again and this time we had a record small amount of food. And the milk was going dry. During the morning there were sounds of machine-gunning in the far distance. All the week there had been explosions somewhere beyond the hills in the plain. From up the mountain I could see some going off in a village north east of Hania. We suppose they are blowing up our dumps of shells etc. But now a terrific explosion well our side of Hania made the whole mountain shake and clouds of smoke rose slowly from below the foothills far up into the sky (possibly the destruction of Kandanos).

The constant sound of aeroplanes of the last week has completely stopped. They were probably carrying away German troops. A convoy went out, said to be carrying English prisoners, most of whom we think have now left the island.

On July 17th Lambros came up with food for the Australians he was looking after and we all went down. He told us of great Russian advances. Three RE (42nd Field Coy.) NCOs have arrived in Cambus, having escaped from Galatas just before the prisoners were shipped off. They say that the Bavarian and Hitler Jugend troops who took over the prison guard from the parachutists maltreated the prisoners disgracefully. They shot indiscriminately, knocked out people with their rifle butts and beat them with iron rods.

On July 19th we were to dine with Elefteria but there was a scare and we were hustled off into a hole, where we slept. We left with the Captain next day, very full after lunch with Elefteria, with whom we left everything we didn't need to carry. With us we took one of the REs, Cpl Bert Murfet, in theory because he was dark and could spy out the land before us dressed as a Greek, but in fact as a pack horse.

We walked west across the mountain valleys. The Captain is a great walker in spurts – that is to say he dawdles and then runs. We sat for a long time on a charming loggia shaded by vines overlooking the olive clad valley of Thernia and then ran to Dracona. The country was the most beautiful I ever saw in Crete, with many pine trees, but the sweat blinded me. We picnicked by a well and a dry stream beneath a plane tree, and hung our shirts out to dry. Excellent cold veal and bread and cucumber and cold water and hot tea. Then on, and as it got dark we reached Therisso. On the way we picked almonds off the trees. Therisso was always a great stronghold, which the Turks never once reached. It has over fifty soldiers living somewhere outside and a few whom we met inside. All the women carry them food, and they do some work in return.

There was a big party for supper in the house of a friend of the Captain's who had been an officer in the Greek army, and afterwards we were given blankets and sheets on the roof.

We made an early start next morning and crossed some very steep hills to reach Zonnia for an early lunch or late breakfast. Our next halt was at a shepherd's hut, where I made myself perfectly sick on yoghurt, like French sour cream and a miseethra just like Devonshire cream and a great mug of milk, and climbing up and down over valleys and ridges (in one dry stream bed I found campanulas in flower growing on rock) very exhausted we reached Omalos – a perfectly flat plain high up in the mountains, entirely surrounded by mountains. Deep under snow in the winter it is excellent for vegetables. Most of it belongs to the village of Lakkos, whose inhabitants have summer residences up there. There we found the Captain's four Australian sergeants, living with a charming Americanised gentleman named Steve. One of the sergeants was in bed with jaundice, but they performed on him their famous and apparently invariably successful operation of cutting the thread under the upper lip, and in two days he was well enough to leave with the Captain for the south coast and the boat.

With them went Fred Embrey a captain in the 1st Bn. AIF whom the Captain had met on his first journey to the south (and suspected of being a German, exactly as the inhabitants of Lakh Omalos suspected the Captain himself of being a fifth columnist and very nearly shot him).

Michael and I remained in Omalos alone. Steve gave us the most excellent food and my first cigarettes for a month, smoked most economically through a cigarette holder cut from a grove of walnut trees just by his house. Under them I lay most of the day. It was hot there in the sun and chilly in the shade, and at night really cold. We slept on a threshing floor which made a fine bed, though we got up looking like lunatics with our hair full of chaff. Neither Michael nor I had shaved by this time for over six weeks, and I had a handsome chestnut beard and Michael a fair Renaissance affair which made him look like Christ.

Omalos was the most pastoral scene I ever saw. Shut away from the world into a little world of its own, there seemed an extraordinary patriarchal dignity in the great herds of sheep led by colossal billy goats, in the groups round the wells down the centre of the plain, in the yoked oxen moving round and round on the little threshing floors and the men throwing the chaff and grain into the air with wooden forks, most of all in Steve's nieces as they took the crackling chipped potatoes off the fire in the dark smokey room and beckoned us to sit down to them. Steve in the morning would sit on a wall quietly watching his chickens on the hillside behind his house, to see where their nests were hidden. Now we were to reap the benefit of his patience. We eat with alacrity.

A few days later the Captain returned with the whole party. The plan had failed. The Germans in the south, perturbed probably by the news of stray parties of English, had probably scared all the fishermen and put sentries on their boats. The Captain had made arrangements with a fisherman who had to report to the Germans twice a week, that he should take off our party immediately after reporting, when he would not be missed for several days. Now he was afraid for his family and would not play.

We had decided before that if this plan should fail, we should try the north, and if possible leave together with the Captain's wife and children. We left Omalos now for Lakkos to put this plan into action. It was a long rough downhill walk, and I rode the last part proudly on a sleek cream donkey on a red saddle and wondered why I'd ever used my feet. We entered the village in the dark and were led by Lefteris to the house of his father Nicolas, just a few yards below the main road to Hania which ends in front of the café. The road was used by German patrols but no one seemed to mind.

They had a very good house compared to what we were used to, two storeys and fairly large. There was a separate dining room for instance. Nicolas's mother was there, a refugee from Hania. Of great age, she had walked all the way after being imprisoned by the Germans along with Steve. She was a real old peasant to look at, but *une grande dame* among peasant grandmothers, large like Steve and full of character. The children seemed to take it in turns to go from Lakkos to Omalos.

The Captain is the first person I can ask about many things that have puzzled me or interested me there. He says that the Greeks fight for two things – their family and their religion. Their family life is very close, their religion very real. I guess Greece is very backward. No one seems to have any money. They get up early and work off and on all day to produce enough to live on, frugally. They could in fact easily produce more to make themselves comfortable, or if comfort is nothing, pleasant, more interesting. Just as they could wash more if they chose and rid their houses of fleas. But long years of brigand life have made and kept them rough. What of it? The cattle trample the grain – muzzled for all the law of Moses, the men cast it to the winds, the women sift it in sieves, everything is serene, slow and laborious. They go to bed tired, not needing Miss Dell or gramophones or cinemas. They sleep in their clothes.

Their food is very poor, though they can and do manage a fine meal for strangers. But mulberries, almonds, pears, apricots and plums, drop almost unpicked from the trees. They make no jam or preserves, no cakes or pastry or biscuits.

113

In Crete the women do practically all the work. They wait on the men and eat after them. They give up their chairs to them. (Michael and I made a point of rising for a woman, to their consternation.) All this is a remnant of the days when the men were all fighters and the women did the work in the villages. The Captain says that in Greece they have good women and bad men, and in England it is the other way round.

We love Lakkos. The side of the valley is covered in the most magnificent olive trees with fantastic dulac boles and of a great height, quite hiding the houses. There are mulberries too and walnuts and plane trees and the houses are scattered among them. German patrols visit the village along the motor road, but we have never been so free.

We can sit and play backgammon in the café on the square, and eat grapes and drink coffee and cognac. The square with its three cafés is the centre of village life. Here we meet all our friends. The barber works ceaselessly in one, our good friend Paul the Mayor plays backgammon and there is a continual cocktail party atmosphere.

Both my legs have been improving miraculously. But with the great heat I got a shocking cold and felt wretched.

Lakkos has many quite important inhabitants, who only confirm one's impression of the democratic character of the country. For indeed here all are really peasants, and there is nothing to choose between the general's family and the shepherd's.

Because they treat all men as equals they can afford to be really courteous. Continually they are on the lookout to do someone a service; to such an extent that one has to preserve a numb passivity, for one's least move is interpreted as an unspoken cry.

Lakkos has produced five living Generals. We lunched with one, a most distinguished old man called Lureidis, who had been Governor General of Crete. I think our lunch there was the best we ever had. We sat out of doors under a vine. With difficulty we forced Spiros, our host, to sit with us. None of the women or girls (of whom there was a crowd) sat down. We had:

Rice
Fried Eggs
Chicken
Mutton
Chipped Potatoes
Tomato & Cucumber Salad
A National dish covered in
Yorkshire Pudding
Water Melon
Honey

Red Wine   Grapes   Cognac

I have had my beard removed. I regret not being able to photograph it first. It came away without any trouble, with the clippers. It was two months only, and really impressive, curly and chestnut in the very best late Georgian tradition.

The village has a water supply over which they have taken quite a lot of trouble. It has a tank and taps in a little concrete house and a filter. It is a quarter of a mile from this house and the women have to go there fifteen or twenty times a day and carry back the really extremely heavy earthenware water pot.

Although the house is only just below the road we sit peaceably outside at all times, and in the cool of the evening walk along the road with the villagers, as if there were no Germans on the island. We sit on a built up corner a couple of miles down the road and look down on Meskla very far below in the valley.

Yesterday after lunch a German truck did drive into the village, apparently on a reconnaissance. We went down among the olive trees, our host Nicolas saying, 'Don't hurry'. Shades of Cambus! We hear thirteen New Zealanders have been caught working in a cigarette factory in Hania.

We had a proper bath in a shallow pool the other day. We had to walk miles with the General's grandson to find anything suitable. There is no privacy in village life and absolutely no arrangements for taking a bath all over.

We lunched with Theodore Tzotzolakis, whose son was a Greek liaison officer, and afterwards he brought me a pair of breeches to try on as he had noticed how bad my shorts

115

were.

They regard such generosity as a duty. It is most shaming to us. When one thinks of all they do for us (and how little we deserve it) one cannot but wonder whether strangers would fare as well in our homeland. Would our mothers give them the bread for lack of which their little children will starve this winter?

On July 31st I dined with the village priest, a handsome young man with a beard, who only spoke Greek. We had a most lovely conversation notwithstanding. There was also there his small sister and a hobbly sweet old nun, and a younger one, who all ate with us. We had rice, eggs, roast pork, mutton and lashings of very good old wine. August 1st begins a fifteen-day fast (for the purification of the Virgin Mary, I think). The cigars were produced and I was pressed to stay the night and slept outside in a beautiful white painted iron bedstead with springs. I was still in bed on August 1st when I am told that there are Germans in the village. So I get up and dress and drink a glass of milk and retire into the trees, regretting my breakfast. I had been two hours in a ditch when Athene rescued me, and took me to a house where I got some milk and on to another house, Carolambris's. Then men begin coming in obviously excited, and tell stories to the accompaniment of female groans. They all come in armed. Carolambris, who is a fine oldish man, wounded in the blitz attacking parachutists, has loads of arms. Apparently the Germans are up to something bad.

We return to Nicolas's house and I find the others all set to move off and I am worried about how many of my things are going to be left behind. I did in fact, never again see my nice ivory pocket knife. We set out with Lefteris and several of his friends and a long string of villagers making for Omalos.

Apparently at four o'clock that morning the Germans surrounded the neighbouring villages of Fournes, Skenes, Alikarnus and Prasses, pulled the men out of bed and after making them dig their own graves, lined them up and shot them. Those who ran away they machine-gunned. The village of Skenes where the Germans met resistance was burnt to the ground. Some English, dressed as Greeks, shared the fate of their hosts. We saw wounded men from the machine-gunning flying also to Omalos. In one place they held a sort of trial and let out three who were not from that village. They have somehow obtained lists of names. What the trial was about the three had no idea, but everyone had to sign something, presumably an admission that they attacked parachutists. One hundred and twenty men were shot in Fournes alone, including the Mayor and the priest. There seems no reason for this sudden outburst. But when a deputation visited the German commander not long after the blitz and asked him when the persecution of civilians was going to end, he replied that there were still very many parachutists unaccounted for and that everyone would be revenged. The Germans at the start demanded eleven Cretans' lives for every dead German, and at another time they threatened to kill twenty per cent of the male population.

We don't go very far on the road to Omalos. We rest in shady places, while Lefteris goes back to Lakkos for news. In the evening we all climb the nearest hill, high above Lakkos, where there is some water. There were a lot of people up there. We have blankets (and a donkey) and bed down in a small sheep pen. Paul, the Mayor, is up there – a man like G.K. Chesterton.

Suddenly we are woken by the most terrific explosion imaginable. We leap up and through a gap in the hills we can see the sea and Maleme aerodrome, on which there is a red glow. More explosions follow and we can see distinctly the tracer bullets of our aeroplanes firing on the aerodrome. The explosions were so heavy, although fully ten miles away, that the Cretans all threw themselves on the ground. We were thrilled.

Next day we move on to a place on the road to Omalos where there are several wells and corn under trees. There are a few shepherds' houses.

The news from Lakkos is that the Germans have come into the village and are apparently settling down there. They pretend to be friendly and ask where all the men are. They are told that they are out with the sheep. All the men have left the village and are now high up in the mountains above us. They are all armed. Their women bring them food at night. There is much talk of starting a revolution.

In the evening the Captain arrived to join us. He had left us in Lakkos and gone over to Cambus with Bert to collect his wife and children. He had a mass of clothes, food etc, in Cambus, papers as well, and with his wife pregnant, they had a pretty tiring journey. Just short of Lakkos they stopped the night there and there they heard that Lakkos was full of Germans and we'd all left.

August 2nd. The Captain called an officers' conference and suggested we start a revolution without waiting for the Greeks to make up their own minds. Michael and Fred had been discussing revolution all morning, down to medical supplies. They are full of it. Very largely, in desperation I say that in my opinion we should still try to get off, and we decide to carry on with our present plans for leaving the island unless the Greeks rise in the meantime. The position seems to be that the local Greeks will rise if the Germans attempt to advance further into the mountains. As they point out, they would rather die fighting than be shot in their beds. Personally, I don't think the Greeks would make a good job of a rising. They might carry on guerilla warfare in the hills. But their villages would be burnt, and where would their food come from? I believe that under the Turks, when the Cretans contemplated revolution, they sent their womenfolk to the mainland, and the Germans are as unscrupulous and far more efficient than the Turks. The Cretans have arms, but very little ammunition indeed. Practically no one has a decent pair of boots, the leather is unprocurable – and without boots, how can you carry on guerilla warfare? The same with our men if we joined in with them. As we are now, without any connection or hope of aid from Egypt, we should in no time be out of food, ammunition and boots. We should be exhausted by the rough country. Admittedly we could cause damage to the Germans. But it would be a suicide squad. I thought it would be much better to combine a rising with a proper British landing, or at least time it to coincide with British advance in Greece.

The conference decided to carry on with our plans to get off. But we did plan now to ask in Egypt either for an evacuation or for aid for a revolt. Of course all the Cretans are certain that we will send troops to retake the island. At present that would not be very difficult if our information of the German troops is correct. But it's a most expensive island to hold.

It now appears that the Germans killed five hundred in this

district yesterday. Nicolas's wife walked up in the dark from Lakkos (which it is a death's sentence for women to leave) carrying on her back our heavy radio and news that the Germans have given the men five days to return or they will burn the village. Any women leaving with food will be shot.

The Captain brought some books over from the house in Cambus, so we can lie about and read again. There is plenty of shade under the pine trees. In the night I was stung, just as I was at Kalame, and wonder if it could be no animal but some kind of poisonous prickle. A New Zealander told us that when they first arrived here they were given lectures on Maltese fever, which they were told was rife here. As we have drunk huge quantities of unboiled goat's milk this rather horrified us.

On August 3rd, the Captain and some men went off to Therisso to collect some things he had left there on his way back from Cambus. He got back at dawn next day. The Cretans on the hill above us were a bit jumpy and pointed out how easily we could be surrounded where we were. Therefore that morning we officers kept a lookout from 3.30 onwards.

We pressed the Captain to get a move on and so it was arranged that we officers should set off before him, making for the peninsula beyond Maleme. We were to take the boy Lefteris with us; but at the last moment he wouldn't go (we were to take him right through to Egypt). We started at dusk and our guide went off to leave his rifle in his house. Nicolas led us the first bit till we should meet up with him. Nicolas didn't know the way, there was no sign of the guide. It was quite dark. Within one mile of the HQ we lay down on a cold windy ridge to sleep. What it was all about we couldn't understand but we were very cross.

In the morning (the 6th) we sat and watched planes taking off from Maleme. We were carrying an overwhelming amount of tinned food and cached half of it among the rocks to collect on our way back if this expedition should fail. It now appears that our last night's guide was deterred from going with us by his women folk. The Captain arranges for another but he has to go off and get his shoes mended first.

☆　☆　☆

End of the first part of Myles Hildyard's Diary.

THE SECOND HALF OF A DIARY KEPT IN CRETE WHILE ESCAPING FROM THE GERMANS.

Myles Hildyard

August 6th, 1941

I may say that we actually bought shoes for yesterday's guide, who failed us.

It is my opinion that a revolution wouldn't come to much if

(1) People make promises they are afraid at the last minute to carry out. Considering that most of the men in Lakkos are wanted, to be shot, it is odd they should be so scared of guiding us in the opposite direction. We ourselves think it monstrous and absurd we should have to kill ourselves moving by night instead of by day.

(2) Nobody has shoes, as I've said before.

(3) They don't know the country at all well, e.g. we have difficulty in finding anyone at all to guide us now, and Nicolas got lost at once.

Michael, certain as usual that he would do something splendid, cooked flour in water and produced a glutinous dough. We had some rice, cheese and a little yoghurt, and continued to feel cross.

Yesterday Michael and I each gave the Captain a cheque for £50 and a letter for Cairo (mine to Longmore, Michael's to Wilson) in case we got separated. We are keeping all the time in separate parties.

About tea time, just as we were about to cook a leg of goat the Captain sent up, Steve arrived looking almost warlike, and after eating a little miseethra of his we followed him up to Omalos. We are amazed that we should take this route to reach the north coast. The Captain joined us in Omalos with our two guides, one of whom is Carolambris and the other the famous 'fire dog'. We had a good dinner of rissoles and chips and heard news of a Russian advance. We slept up the hill, which all the people there are doing for fear of the Germans.

At dawn, a very cold misty morning, we set off across the plain, leaving it by the pass at its western end where there is a little lone white church, and so downhill mostly on a paved road to Agia Irene which lies in a wide valley. It is the highest village in Crete, very rich and quite delightful. Houses scattered along the village, a stream fast running between flowering oleanders and large trees, walnuts and chestnuts and sycamores and mulberries, loaded with the biggest and juiciest mulberries I ever hope to see. Lady Macbeth's hands were nothing to mine, and little fields of marrows, potatoes, maize, all watered by little runnels and channels. Actually it is not very far from the south coast, and we are making a big detour to avoid the plains and valleys behind Maleme. At the house we went to there was a nice Colonel's daughter who spoke French and gave me a French book and a letter to her father in Egypt. We had a big meal (though we had to wait a long time for it) and immediately after had to climb a mountain feeling horribly full. It was very hot.

For a long way after that we followed the crests of hills with little gullies and springs of icy water. We stopped in one at a shepherd's hut and were bitterly disappointed not to be offered milk. The Captain continues to keep his party separate from ours, but we catch up and pass him at intervals. At the shepherd's hut his dog, an alsatian, which from the start was a summons and six months from the RSPCA, but which had now been banting continuously for a week and looked like something stuffed in alongside his royal master in an Egyptian tomb, chased and caught a lamb. He didn't eat it, but neither did he improve it. Towards evening we looked down on Rumata and rested, eating cold goat's meat produced by Carolambris. The Captain went on ahead again. We officers followed with Carolambris down into the valley. Arrived at a stream in the bottom Carolambris made 'what do we do next' gestures at us, which infuriated us, and we made 'you're the guide blast you' gestures back. There were three Australians by the water and they said the Captain hadn't passed that way, and Lambris apparently had no idea where to meet him. Immediately after villagers appeared and told us there were Germans in Rumata which we could see a little further down the valley. In fact all the male villagers were sitting under the trees, toying with rifles. The Germans had only come in that day, and were apparently settling down there. We thought we would find the Captain somewhere in Rumata; now we didn't know what to do. We discovered a Greek who spoke English and was wanted by the Germans, he was very discouraging about our chances of getting a boat. Just as it was getting dark a little boy came from the Captain and we climbed the mountain again, simply furious with the Captain for keeping his plans to himself and let us get into such a jam. It was apparently impossible to go through Rumata, and we had to climb right up to the top of the mountain in the dark, looking for some other village. It was a murderous climb, very steep, rocky, prickly and abominable. Arrived at the top we followed the crest along till we found ourselves at the end, looking into space. All the way our two guides quarrelled. The famous 'fire dog' sat down like Satan on the Mount of Temptation, and we left him there. Down we climbed again. The Captain and Lambris rushed ahead and soon all sign or sight of them was lost. It was very dark and very steep indeed and the undergrowth had been burnt. As a result it was all black stumps about knee high, completely invisible but agonising and irritating beyond words. Arrived at a more level bit we sent Fred to shout for the Captain, Germans or no Germans, and he was found and led us into a small village. On the way we passed a deserted shepherd's hut, with the day's milk hanging up in a great cauldron and a poor little puppy tied up. What was really in that cauldron I don't know. It was half way to being something else, but we attacked it with spoons. In the village we went to the house of a poor woman whose husband had fled to the hills. She was going to have a baby and had several already. We found a basket of figs and they were gone before you could look round, and we devoured some wheaten cake and felt very gay and light-headed. From there we went to another cluster of houses, one of which we woke up and it contained among others a crazy woman who kept beating her breast and tearing her hair. I think her husband had been shot. From there a woman led us down into the valley, though she was also going to have a baby, and sick and risking her life. We crossed the valley and climbed up the further side. Half way up this new mountain there ran a main road. The Captain was certain it would be heavily posted with German machine-guns and as it ended, as Cretan roads do, just nowhere on the mountain, when we reached it he wanted to find the end of it and creep round it. However a road was good enough for us, and we got on to it and walked along it, finding imaginary machine-guns in the shadows to please the Captain. It was a well built road, quite overgrown with weeds. We left it after a bit and climbed up again to the very top of the ridge and begging I was to know when this marathon was going to end. I didn't think I should ever make that one. Just over the top there was the main road to Kastelli, which we hit and crossed in a desolate burnt out village where no doubt the Germans had met resistance on their way to the south.

As it began to get light we made down into another valley, and to a village and knocked up a big house. I longed to lie down, we had been walking twenty-five hours. They led us down to a secret place, where we slept a little. We were in a river bed, opposite us high perpendicular cliffs with oaks leaning out and over us from the cliff's edge and the stream forming a pool beneath our feet. A bit higher up the pool was dammed to make a long shallow pond, where I bathed with a boy from the village. We were very tired and stiff. It was shady all day in our little gorge and wonderfully pretty. The villagers brought us a marvellous lunch – chicken soup and potatoes, chicken, pears and grapes and water melon and most excellent wine. And bread and boiled eggs and a chicken for us to take with us and they sent to warn the villages ahead that we were coming. There was one English soldier in the village, with the priest, who was a grand man with the head of a world-loving Mazarin and helped us enormously. (We discovered later he was Kytherakis Elefteris's father-in-law Kolimbari.)

We left at six in the evening and walked to a village almost on the sea, through vineyards, stuffing grapes as we went. We were taken to a very nice house and had hot milk and decided to send on to find out how things were on the peninsula and sleep the night where we were ourselves, just outside the village. We slept in a vineyard, so that in the morning we could breakfast without stirring. But the rising sun soon gets one up. So we lay under a tree with vineyards all round us, but not very good grapes. Aeroplanes kept flying low right over us. I tried to boil tea and after half an hour without a sign of boiling, upset it all. Our breakfast of boiled eggs, bread and cheese, pears, grapes, cognac and tea and our lunch of two chickens, sugar melon and the best cream rice I ever swallowed were nothing to grumble at. I was lying reading a sexy American novel all about country clubs; it was a nice picnicky sort of day. In the evening our spy returned. We went first to the house in the village, where our clothes were ready washed for us and they gave me a new khaki shirt, mine being in rags. It had

126

detachable cuffs. The house was a police officer's and new and very nice, with a ceiling of matting and a separate kitchen and bedroom – amazing modernities. The village hadn't a window pane in it after being bombed for holding up the Germans. It was only just off the main coast road. Our spy's news was that, as we feared, the near port was patrolled by the Germans, but that the further one was quite hopeful – the far point of the peninsula. We started off about eight o'clock in the evening and crossed the main road. Just across it they showed me where the Germans had taken the village priest and some men and released them and made them run and shot them, so that they could say they were trying to escape. Though why they bothered I don't know. We climbed in the dark down into a rocky valley and crossed a stream. Our guides were going all out and we were strung out and falling over rocks and cursing and sweating. The hill above the stream was much worse, all shrubs and prickles clutching at my bare legs. I sat down and nearly cried with vexation. But at the top we all sat and ate a boiled egg and a little further on we came to a shepherd's hut where we were made very welcome. We sat in a row and they passed along sliced cucumbers and wine, buckets of it. The moon had risen as we rose to go and I went rolling. Some of the shepherds came with us, and helped carry our things. We passed through the only two villages on the peninsula. In the bright moonlight the first was charming, sloping away from us to the sea out of sight, across shadowy fields and orchards. Just beyond it we met our next guide and with him the lawyer cousin I met at Carolambris! I was amazed to see him and still more so to be told quite calmly that he was coming with us. He was nicely turned out in a grey suit, panama hat, overcoat over one arm and a suitcase. He had no food. It had all been arranged by Lambris and sprung on us without a word. The Captain was livid. In the next village, the only other one on the peninsula, big and straggling, our new adjunct sent a message back to his family. This enraged us as our movements were supposed at least to be secret. In point of fact Lambris talked in every village like a burst gas main, and while we were only passing through, we said, because it was such nice weather for a walk, we could hear Lambris explaining to any one who would listen that he was going to Alexandria to see General Skulies.

After this village we got on to a broad paved track. Midnight was just striking in the village. They said this was the old Minoan road leading to the Minoan port at the end of the peninsula. It is in a remarkable state of repair if that is so. At least twelve feet broad, paved with large stones, but foul to walk on as the stones now lay at all angles; with our practically soleless shoes it was most trying. We had the most amazing guide, Stratis. He insisted on carrying practically everything we had. He told us quite accurately how long the walk would take. Not that we believed anything so hair-raising as that we still had four Cretan walking hours before us. For definitely on the map the peninsula was a snub little affair about five miles long. It was mountainous but a series of level plains lay down the centre, which we thought could have been put to better use than sheep grazing. In fact it occurred to us to move all the escaped prisoners there and raise vegetables. We stumbled along, with the Captain ahead giving Lambris hell, over his cousin. The unfortunate Nicolas was very soon completely out and I'm certain as sorry as a live man could be about it all.

Passing over a ridge and entering a small plain we saw a body of men ahead of us. We approached them carefully. On the moonlit path we eyed one another with hostility. They were Cretans from Greece, landed that very evening.

Such concrete evidence that we were not on a fool's errand was wonderfully heartening and sent us hurrying on. But their news was not altogether good. They had been without food for a week in Greece before sailing, though they had plenty of cigarettes and pressed whole boxes on us. When they landed they were attacked by a German patrol boat. They ran off, but they believed their boat was captured. They were full of stories of Germans on the end of the peninsula. We hurried on.

The next people we met were a band of Cretan Muleteers with loads of olive oil, returning disconsolately from the sea after failing to get their olive oil on board because of the Germans. We longed to hear that we were nearing the point, they said it was still two hours. Our fantastic guide told us that we must keep going, because having brought us to the point he was going to hurry back and intercept the Muleteers before they could reach their village and spread the news of our movements. I kept on kicking one ankle with my other foot, till I had it so raw that the least touch was an agony and sent me swerving across the path. I stuffed my sock with handkerchiefs. My shoes were in tatters, the Captain's had no soles at all. Only Frederick had good soles, given him by Theodore in Lakkos. Michael had a good pair of army boots, but one was at the shoemakers when we fled from Lakkos and now he wore one black boot and one of his practically useless buckskin tennis shoes. They were already held together by string when we lived in the white mountains. It was really typical of British officers that for our evacuation walk Michael chose ten-year-old buckskin tennis shoes dyed brown and I a pair of Fortnum country shoes to which I was devoted but which had long reached the annuity and a cottage stage. I gave a pair of new boots to an Australian scrounger, the only Australian I ever knew salute. The Captain was more exhausted than I ever knew him before. It began to get light, and there was no point in going much further. Our guide went off and found two cousins, Elefteris and Michaelis Rosmaris, who lived alone with their goats at the end of the peninsula, and leaving us to them, he hurried back. We were in an open valley and the shepherds led us down into a little gorge in it to hide. They were afraid of a villager who had not yet returned from the beach with his olive oil. His small son was going to a German hospital and they got a lot of information out of him there. Twenty thousand men are said to have passed along that Minoan road in the last two months. Cretans returning to Crete and Greeks to Greece. All I suppose like us hurrying and struggling along in the dark, doubtful of the future, wanting only to get home. There is something weird about these walks by night, the whispering, the hidden cigarettes, like a band of smugglers.

All night the moon had been cloudy. It was an unattractive little gorge – all rocks and prickles and not a level yard. We had hardly found a place to lie down when there was a downpour of rain. I had crept under an overhanging rock with about eighteen inches headroom and only I kept dry. We slept, not for long, for the sun rose and there was no shade, so we sat up and ate our chickens, and slept again. Lambris said his shoes were too bad for him to go back to the last village for more food.

Just before dark we moved down towards the sea, turning

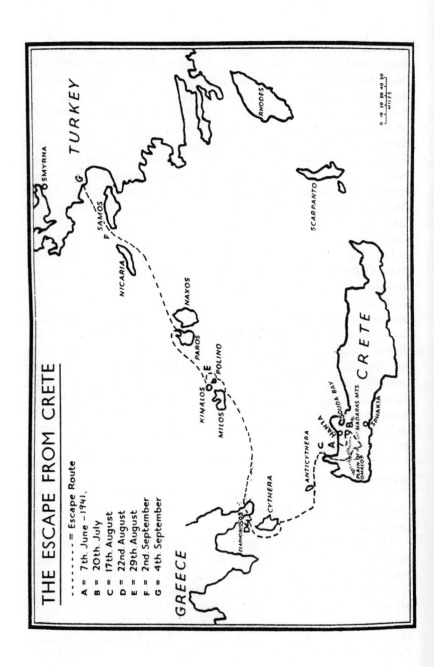

THE ESCAPE FROM CRETE

------ = Escape Route

A = 7th. June –1941.
B = 20th. July
C = 17th. August
D = 22nd. August
E = 29th. August
F = 2nd. September
G = 4th. September

east. We were furious with the Captain for waiting till it was dark, so that we should lacerate ourselves with the going so bad and our shoes terrible. But he had been right the way down once already to reconnoitre. We slept under a lotus tree not far from the sea, while the Captain and Lambris watched by the shore. We aren't allowed down on the beach because there are a lot of Greeks there waiting to get off and the Captain is terrified of our being betrayed. No Greek trusts every Greek. About midnight we could plainly hear a boat's engine, but no message came. It was a German patrol boat; they said in the morning that two had been around. However, later we discovered that one was a caique which saw the Germans and landed round the point instead.

It is August 11th. Our lotus tree is infested with flies which makes life almost unbearable. Due east of us about a mile is a little hole in the rock cliff, where caiques also sometimes put in. In the afternoon we went down there and bathed, one of us keeping a look out for German patrols. It was a difficult climb down to the water and must be desperate at night. On the way down to the sea there is a German glider. Two landed here in the blitz. It has very clear thick celluloid windows, the men sat one behind the other down the centre. It is pretty big, and very lightly, but well built. Near it is an unexploded shell, probably fired by a 25-pounder from Maleme. We tore off bits of canvas to tie round our feet and cotton binding which was proper ersatz and useless.

I keep on wounding my head on the lotus tree and that goes septic too.

That night there was no German patrol and no caique. To our fury we hear that one came in somewhere else on the point.

The next morning, August 13th, the Captain came back with the news that a caique had come in at 4 am and that it was waiting for him till nightfall. It has a German permit and is flying the swastika. At breakfast the shepherds came shouting and the Captain and Lambris ran off after them down to the bay. A caique with an engine had come in and they were just in time to prevent it taking Greek soldiers on board and making off again. Instead it moved round to the end of the point to await us by night. We sit and pray for no German patrols.

We hear now that the Germans have taken 800 women and children from the villages they shot up on August 1st to Hania, presumably as hostages against a revolt, though possibly to bring the men down from the mountains. Near Lakkos apparently the Germans met some armed Greeks. There was no fighting, the Germans merely told them to return to their villages, which naturally they have not done.

We had a fright during the day when we saw a boat in the bay of Hania, but it turned out to be going away. Lambris and Michael went off to locate our caique and came back to say they couldn't find it. At 6 pm the Captain went down to Menes bay and soon after we saw the sails of a boat being rowed slowly northwards below the cliffs past us. At dark we all packed up and followed down to Menes.

There was no boat.

There had been a muddle.

The sailing boat understood we had sailed on the motor caique and so had taken on thirty-three Greeks and it was her we had seen passing. The motor caique never appeared either for us or for the 500 okes of oil waiting on the shore. We realised that this was the boat we saw out in Hania bay, it had evidently taken fright. A friend of the Captain's, the master of the caique captured by the Germans, had been put on board the motor caique by the Captain to hold the fort for us, so we felt very betrayed. We climbed up again out of Menes valley and slept on the top of the cliff. During the night we heard a German patrol boat. In the early morning we returned to our lotus tree, discouraged.

Stratis had been told to find out about boats, and he brought news of one for sale for 30,000 drachmae. The Captain told him to go back and arrange for it to come to us. His other news was that the Germans had been into the peninsula villages and threatened with death any one feeding Greek soldiers, and it looked as if they meant to wire off the whole peninsula. He also told us that all the women and children of Lakkos had gone up into the mountains, which was good news for the Captain, who feared his wife might be among those carried off by the Germans.

That night, August 13th, two caiques came in on the other side of the peninsula and went straight out again.

The Captain went down to Menes for the night and learnt that quite unknown to us a caique had come in at 8.30 in the morning and taken off all the Greeks. The English were away getting water.

That night two more caiques came in on the other side and the Captain said they would always be coming in there now because of the German patrol our side. The Greeks all left Menes and we are in two minds. For there is a high wind and Menes is a much more likely place for boats to make for in rough weather. Also the sailing boat Stratis told us about has been bought and paid for and should have come here to Menes yesterday, loaded with provisions. All that has been arranged for us by a priest, we don't know what has gone wrong.

That evening we walked over to the western side of the point but no boats came in during the night.

We decided to stay, hoping the sea would go down, and we tried to arrange for the boat we have bought to come round here.

At midday we hear that a caique has come in to Menes. We hurry to a hillside where we look down into Menes cove and see a sailing boat on the beach and many Greeks. It is a great sight.

In no time the Captain is on board. Then there is an altercation between the Captain on the boat and the Greeks on the shore. We can see that there are too many of them for everybody to go. First we hear that the boat is only going to take the English. An olive oil seller turns nasty and the Captain goes mad. He draws his pistol, screams at us to leave as we aren't going in the boat and begins to get off himself. The Greeks round us tell us to stay where we are. The Captain climbs along the bowsprit, falls off still clutching it, drops his revolver in the sea, and gets ashore green with rage and still shouting. The quarrel dies down without our knowing what it was about. Half the English are to go. We had expected touble from the Australians who had to remain, but they took it very well. Lefteris is with us and we owe it to him that we are taken on the boat. He insists on Michael getting in first. Altogether six of us, the New Zealand officer and two men and thirty-four Greeks get on board. The boat is twenty foot long. At dusk we leave, the sail is hoisted, Lefteris kisses us all and fires off his

133

revolver. We sit round the edge of the boat with the Greeks huddled into the hold in the centre. The crew row the boat out of the cove. We eat some bread and cold pork, given us by Lefteris. It is all unbelievable.

We get out of the cove and there is a heavy ground swell as we move very slowly up the coast, one oar aft and one astern and no breeze at all on the great dhow-like sail. We pass over a sunken German plane which they say was pulling the glider we saw. It lies shivering pale green on the rocky bottom. The Greeks waste no time in being sick, and press forward to the side one after the other, shoving their heads between us. Apart from the hold, into whose bottom the Greeks begin to subside like corpses in a common grave, there are two tiny holds. We are all sick, me last of all, but I don't feel bad. Our bags are in the hold and buried under Greeks and I can't get at extra clothes for the night. We huddle together on the edge of the boat and doze.

August 18th. As it gets light we see a mountain rising out of the sea a mile or so behind us. We ask what that is. It is the end of the promontory, and all we have done during the night is tack across the bay to Hania and back again.

Just as we begin to think we are going to look extra-ordinarily stupid lying there by day, a breeze gets up and we run for the island of Anticythera. We tried before that to row the boat taking turns on the oars and feeling wretched. Opposite Anticythera the wind dies. It is a rocky and deserted island. Further on we can see a tiny island called Praesu and the Captain gets us to row towards that. The boat does not seem to move. The Greeks lie in a ghastly heap and won't help on the oars. The sun glares down on our bare heads. There is no shade. Practically no food, but we don't want that. It is terribly uncomfortable. It is all frightful. Apparently the boat doesn't move because her bottom is so weedy. It is definitely the worst thing I've ever been on.

During the night a breeze springs up and takes us past Praesu and half way to Cythera.

Next morning, August 19th, I am more or less in a stupor. We run in a high wind for Cythera, the sea very rough and splashing against the side all the time and soaking us. The boat's side where I sit is only two feet above the sea, but she rides very well and ships no water. It is a huge sea. Suddenly the sail boom gives a crack and looks like breaking any moment. We turn into the wind and lie rolling horribly. The Greeks stir and those that are conscious cross themselves desperately. The master of the ship remarks that he is a shoemaker, not a sailor. There is grave danger of the sail being carried away, and he can only think of turning and running before the wind. The little foresail does carry away. Our Captain takes command. We are almost out of water. If we turn and run before the wind we shall not hit Crete. If we hit anything at all it will be Bizarta. More likely we shall die of thirst somewhere in the Mediterranean. So the Captain turns the ship once more towards Cythera and battles on. The mast stands it, and suddenly to our salvation the wind veers round to the west and we run smoothly forward. It has been a near thing. The master of the boat swore he would never sail again. But in the crisis he had remained very cool. He climbed the mast and roped up the boom while we lay flapping and rolling. And they certainly were rollers. The Captain's plan was to try and get within distance of Cythera before the sail went. The wind changing saved our mast and sail, and when it died completely away we were not very far from the island. She might be a monster to row, but very few boats would have stood up for that sea. Now we had to row her.

During the evening we moved slowly up and along Cythera. We'd hoped to land there, but with a slight breeze the Captain decided to go straight on for Greece.

In the night a wind got up and for some never explained reason we used it to run into harbour in Cythera to get news of patrol boats apparently. We run in in the dark, like smugglers again. We had passed close to an Italian destroyer during the afternoon and now passing a hulking rock in the dark I could have sworn it was another. We crept in, past the dim shapes of boats, and the Captain whispered to us to be ready to swim for it if we ran into Italians. There was a light we aimed for, it seems to be on a jetty. In fact it came from a house of friendly Greeks, in a small fishing village. We anchored and the Captain went ashore and got fresh water. Michael managed to get into the boat with him but it was the wrong side for me and I sat longing to be on dry land, if only for five minutes; and when Michael got back he said there had been a peach waiting for me. But we crept out again, quietly still, for they said there were a great many Germans and Italians on the island and machine-guns on the cliffs. They said we must get round the north cape before dawn. The wind had dropped entirely and though we rowed till dawn, we had only just reached the cape and we had to turn east and coast along the north side of the island. And we never saw a man or gun. We went on rowing slowly along, in a broiling sun and the sight of vineyards on the islands made us sick. We decided to put into a bay for shade. Just as we'd dropped anchor among some rocks a breeze got up, so out we rowed again and the breeze sent us speeding towards Greece. We could see the mainland now, and it looked extremely like Crete, all bare mountains. But after a short crossing – when we saw some big caiques – we entered a beautiful sound, the water as clear as anything. We tacked up it and passed a fisher-boat from which the Captain bought some fish. After what seemed a desperately long time tacking about in the sound, the Captain found a spot to land the Greeks – and the other English (whose plan was to get across Greece by train and into Turkey). We sailed across to the island of Elaphonissos where a fishing village stood on a sandy beach. The Captain went ashore after battening us down in the hold, to which we objected, and it was unbearable.

Very soon after we landed there was some heavy firing the other side of the island. We heard later that a submarine had sunk a large caique full of currants. (For days afterwards the villagers were bringing in salt damp currants in boats from the wreck.) We went ashore in the dark and ate our fish in a house in the village, with lots of water melon. On dry land I felt quite dizzy and light in the head. We were given blankets and pillows and slept on the sand dunes by the sea.

The next day, August 21st, we stayed under some trees on the dunes and fed on water melons, very unripe sugar melons and grapes.

The Captain returned from a visit to the mainland. He had sat down in a café in Neapolis and some Italians came in after him and he had found some diesel oil for us if we can get a motor boat.

We ate in the dark under the trees, a whim of the Captain's. He is not well. He cut his leg to the bone during the storm on the way across, falling on the anchor, and now he is sick inside as well.

Next day the Captain announced that for 50,000 dr. he had bought the very pretty newly painted blue sailing boat which is tied up alongside our old horror on the beach. The wind has been favourable since we have been here and we are to leave in the evening. Lambris got a lot of figs and I started to wash my clothes at the well furthest out from the village but was stopped because a policeman had come over from the mainland. Actually he was harbour-master and came about the torpedoed caique. In true Greek fashion he had given the villagers time to pinch what they could. The captain of this boat was killed, because although the submarine gave the crew time to row off, the captain went back for his wallet.

During the day the Captain changed the boat he was buying and for an extra 10,000 dr. got a pink boat with brick coloured sails. We loaded her with two big baskets, one of grapes and one of vegetables and at dusk we rowed off southwards down the sound. We passed the village which stood out black against the sky and along the island for five miles. Then we waited a bit hearing the engine of a patrol boat and there being no wind. Then we rowed across from the island to the mainland with the sail up not helping much. Michael started off rowing in fine Eton style; it was very tiring after the first hour and we decided the others must learn to row. My oar was a brute of a thing, all warped. The sail was difficult to put up in the dark. The ends of the boat are covered in and two people can just crawl under each end. Michael reports ours full of bugs. They are probably also in the two blankets we bought off the last boat.

As there was no wind we fell asleep where we sat, but about 4 am the Captain heard another patrol boat and woke us up, and we rowed round the end of the cape and eastwards along, hearing patrol boats all the time. We came at last to a little cove and rowed quietly in just before dawn. There was a building on the cliff which the Captain thought might be an Italian post and boats in the cove he thought were patrol boats. So we made out again, but outside we ran into a fishing boat and they told us it was quite all right. We stayed there all day and it was lucky we stopped there for they told us that further along the Italians were stopping every boat passing by day, even fishing boats. Finding nets and a sail in a church, I slept there on them. We lunched off the most delicious small fish – two fisher-boats went out at dawn and fished with explosives. Last night we saw my first comet with a blaze behind it so bright I thought it must be a searchlight. Shooting stars are very common. My hands, which I scraped getting off the old boat in deep water have gone septic and are very stiff. I bathed in the cove in the afternoon, diving off a rock. The rock is all just like concrete, splitting in flat surfaces and made up of conglomerate.

We slept on the water's edge. The Captain decided we must cross the cape on foot while he brought the boat round by sea. We were also to try and get bread on the way, which he assured us would be easy. So, early next morning, August 24th, Michael, Fred and I left with two boys. We made first back NW to the village of Agios Nicholaos at the foot of the mountain range. There we had some milk with honey in it in one house, and bread and milk in another and in a third Michael was just settling down to a huge meal when our boy guide dragged us off. We climbed and crossed the mountains, which were greener and less rocky than those we were used to and reached a valley on the further side, where we sat down by a well in a vineyard. We were given the best grapes I ever ate, huge bunches of black ones and figs. In the village of Sklavouna we talked to the Mayor, who was long in South Africa and we thought probably a very rich man. But a tiresome one. They gave us some cognac, but no food, and seemed unnecessarily afraid of the Italians. He took us to two Englishmen who had just arrived – they were in fact two of the Australians we left behind in Menes. After we left the Germans machine-gunned Menes from the sea and practically everybody left. Then a motor caique came in which brought them across in ten hours.

A bit further on we came to Kastania. Nobody took much notice as we entered the village, so we sat down on the road in the shade of a house and started in on some cheese Michael had. A crowd soon began to collect and from one person and then another there appeared bread, then tomatoes, hot potatoes and marrow, cheese, finally scrambled eggs and superb grapes and figs and wine. We almost burst, watched all the time by a friendly crowd three deep. We were led from the roadside to a house, the crowd following, and there Fred and I had ourselves shaved and I had my first haircut for two-and-a-half months. Curiously enough it had hardly grown at all in the time, and Michael was the same. We were given beds in the house to rest and then went on down seawards, to the little village of Agios Phocas near Monemvassia where we were supposed to meet the boat. We thought we had seen it setting out from the mountain above Agios Nicholaos and again rounding Cape Malea, but when we arrived very exhausted at 6 pm, there was no boat there. We went to a house in the village and were given a very good meal and blankets, and slept down below the house in a field.

We breakfasted off figs then we were taken down to a small bay where there was shade all day and fresh water within a yard of the sea. The villagers are as usual afraid of the Italians, who declare they will kill any one helping the English. Michael and Fred were already discouraged and making plans for getting on without the Captain, possibly in a large lifeboat there, which brought eight English soldiers ashore. At the same time three bodies were washed up and the villagers have a strange assortment of eastern banknotes and cheques and photographs off them.

Quite early two boats were reported in the distance and about midday ours appeared. Although we had had plenty of wind crossing the mountains, they had met none at all and had to row most of the way. At midnight they had put in to shore to rest. There was an Italian post on Cape Malea, but it took no notice of them.

A fisherman had given us fish and now he gave the Captain more and we feasted on them in the village and had the rest cooked with a preservative sauce for the voyage.

Pressed by Michael the Captain left soon after lunch instead of waiting till midnight to see how the wind would be and mending the big sail as he had first intended. We ran fast out to sea and everything seemed splendid. But after an hour the wind veered to NE. Just the one we didn't want. It died down, and we rowed towards the bare rock which lay between us and the Aegean Islands.

At dawn it turned very rough with an easterly or NE wind and a big sea. It continued all day and the Captain feared we should have to turn back. He was afraid particularly of our southerly drift, which might make us miss the islands. Then if the mast carried away we should be lost. Like the Greek sailors of old he wasn't really happy out of sight of land.

At dusk the wind died down and we rowed for five-and-a-half hours and then a little wind got up and it was NNE. With our rowing this took us a bit north and saved us.

[The author here adds his own gloss to the Hildyard diary . . .

On the third day out in the fishing boat we were all rather exhausted. The Captain had fallen on an old tin and badly cut his leg, which was now going septic. Having steered the caique for three days through the Aegean, from the Peloponnessos towards the island of Milos, in fairly bad weather and with the melteme wind continuously coming from the north east blowing us back towards Crete, the Captain decided he could not go on steering the boat any longer.

I, Michael Parish, realised that I should have to take over, and it was vital that we should make, or at any rate be in sight of, the island of Milos by dawn the next day. This was because the wind was blowing so hard that we would almost certainly be blown back onto Crete, arriving somewhere in the vicinity of Heraklion. This would have put paid to all of us, because the Germans would have taken an exceptionally poor view of a motley crew of British and Greeks trying to evade them in a Greek caique. I was determined, therefore, to steer into the wind. I had Myles's oil compass, and with the help of this I understood that I had to steer about ten degrees to the east of the north star.

This I did all night, and by dawn we saw what to me was the most wonderful sight; the lovely island of Milos, beginning to show in the dawn. It was certainly a stupendous moment, as the alternative did not really bear thinking about i.e. being blown back to Crete, which was some fifty miles due south, and our four months of evading the Germans doubtless ending with a bullet from their firing squad.

When I was absolutely certain that we were within sight of our objective, I woke the Captain up and asked him to get one of the others to take over and get us safely to the island. As the wind had by now largely died down, they did just that, and had to row for the last one-and-a-half hours to get into the small cove, so ably described by Myles, on the south east coast of Milos.]

Myles Hildyard's journal resumes. . .

Next morning, August 27th, there was a very strong wind from the NE and the sea terrifically rough again. We were thankful to God just to make the south coast of Milos at midday. In weather like that we all have to lie in the hold to balance the boat and it is like an aquarium with the sea continuously pouring in. We none of us think much of sailing.

We sailed along the south coast of Milos and then the wind dropped and the Captain made us row for a cove at the SE cape. As we had had no food and no sleep I persuaded him to put in at a little creek and cook some food and rest. I heard cries from the Captain and thought he had bumped his leg as he was always doing. Instead Michael was lying at his feet, while he wrung his hands. Michael had climbed the cliff, which gave way just as he reached the top and he had fallen backwards on to the rocky beach, striking his forehead, which knocked him more or less unconscious. His wrist was obviously out of place. (He did in fact sustain a fractured skull which paralysed the nerve centres and prevented one eye and ear working, and a badly broken wrist). Bert was most efficient, and my curly-handled walking stick, which I had clung to as a souvenir, went for a splint, and his head was bandaged up. We moved him to a more comfortable place and covered him up with our coats and rugs. We fed off 'ladies fingers' a cross between leeks and cucumber which I think quite filthy. We slept the night there.

Next day at dawn we got Michael on board, walking on to a rock supported on each side. He had no idea when he was upright. There was no wind and we rowed for three hours till we reached the Captain's bay. I went ashore and showed myself and was given some fine grapes. The Captain was livid at my going ashore. There are about fifty Germans on Milos, on the aerodrome they have built there.

From there we sailed and saw Syphnos, the Captain's own island, and our objective, not so very far off in the distance.

We headed for Poliagos. But there was no wind and after rowing all afternoon with the sail up the drift had taken us far to the south. There was a current running against us and at the moment the Captain despaired of making the island and we thought of turning back to Milos again. However, we rowed on and just as the moon rose we entered a little cove. The beach of smooth white stones was merely the end of a dry watercourse. The island is not inhabited. But when we leapt ashore we met lying spread-eagled on the moonlit beach a month-old corpse,* clad in British shorts and shirt. I fled from his welcoming smile.

Next morning, the 29th, we woke to a stormy wind of which the Captain was afraid, but it died down somewhat and after burying the lonely corpse we rowed out and into the channel between the islands. We tacked slowly up it, with a high but unfavourable wind. It was too fresh to allow us to reach Syphnos, and so we made for harbour and food on Kimolos. There we could see quite a town on the hill and a little port. We put into a cove just beyond the port. There were no Germans or Italians on the island, nor food either – they had had no bread for three weeks. A doctor came and looked at Michael on the boat and he was got up into a cottage on the cliff and into bed. They all spoke well of the doctor, who seemed to know his business and put Michael's arm in plaster and dressed all our various wounds.

Lambris and Bert went up into the town and brought back fish, grapes, tomatoes and a little bread – one little loaf from the priest with a pattern stamped on top, used in church. So we had a marvellous lunch of fried fish cooked as they used to do in Kaleris – three together by their tails fried all floury and eaten whole like whitebait. We bathed with the boys of the place and sat in the shade of a boat by the sea.

The cottage Michael is in belongs to a sailor who was once in England with the Captain and served on one of his ships. It is one room only, spotlessly clean, whitewashed and neat. A chicken sits clucking under the settee, but that's nothing. The fireplace opening is halfway up one wall and hidden when not in use by gaily painted doors. Underneath the cottage, all the way round the cove, lockups for boats are cut out of the rock, and a landing stage and steps. Everywhere the houses with proper windows and doors look very different to the Cretan

---

* It was either Charles Mills Gaskell or probably Lady Caccia's brother from the British Embassy yacht *Calanthe* which was sunk here when Peter Fleming and eighty others were evacuating Greece.

hovels.

There is a radio set somewhere, so we heard some news again, and they say Laval has been shot, which is grand. One of the little boys brought me his kid to see, called Lefteria (freedom).

Fred and I went for a walk up the hill, avoiding the town and the first person we met sitting on a wall was the Greek Sergeant of Police. He looked rather like Count Ciano, but seemed friendly, so we invited him to walk with us and let him talk a lot. I reckoned he was saying that we put him in a very unenviable position and the Germans would shoot him if they found out and the town had two well-known spies and there was a telephone to Milos, and really we'd better not stop. So I patted him and said we wouldn't and we parted friends.

The Captain slept the night in the town. By some wizardry he got masses of food although the people were almost starving – seven loaves, cheese (a special local brand), thirty eggs, fish, beans, grapes, pears and tomatoes. He also arranged for the motor caique anchored below us to tow us as far as Paros, the furthest island. It was great news. No more rowing.

Kimolos is a very poor island. They produce very little but grapes and figs and of course they catch fish. On Syphnos apparently you get olives, tangerines, oranges and lemons. But I'm afraid we look like missing this idyll of an island, particularly as we hear now that there are Italians on it. The story is that an Italian troopship was sunk on its way to Rhodes and the men on it were first landed on Paros and then scattered throughout the islands. If we couldn't land openly on the island and go inland to the Captain's village and dance on his whitewashed streets and revel in his spring-mattressed beds, there wasn't really much point in going there.

We bathed again with the boys, and the Captain brought two quarters of a small calf and we ate some fried for lunch. Most of it was roasted for the voyage.

The wind has turned to south. On our return from a walk we had to hide because of a secret policeman who had come over from Milos. Our motor caique has gone over to Milos to get an official permit to leave harbour.

Next day, the 31st, the Captain decided not to wait for the motor caique, but to use the south wind, and the boat was loaded up. We only wait for the priest to come and bless it. We christened the boat by the holy name of *Agia Irene* but we put down our ill fortune on her to the fact that she has never been blessed.

Last night the BBC announced that in Crete British soldiers were fighting side by side with the Cretans. We rather doubt this.

The priest came, a big old man with a grey beard, in a long blue gown, followed by his little daughter carrying his grey umbrella. He climbed down over the rocks on to the boat and us after him. Standing in the hold, with in front of him on the water barrel, two candles and incense on charcoal, he read Mass and afterwards special prayers for the ship. When he took off his high black hat, a pig-tail fell to his waist. Round his neck he had a red and gold stole. At the end he blessed us all and the boat and scattered sacred water over everything, us, the boat, the pink sails, the great basket of blue, red and golden grapes and we kissed his cross. With many good wishes he departed, his little daughter behind him, leaving with us holy water and bread to take tomorrow.

Michael got down to the boat without too much difficulty, and at 1.30 we left, our host and his family in their boat circling round us and blowing a trumpet encouragingly as we dealt very inefficiently with the sail. The wind was high and soon we were away and past Syphnos going fine. The sea became so rough that it was difficult to keep the huge following rollers from splashing into the boat. It was fortunate we wanted to run before them, for we could have done nothing else. As it got dark the wind was reaching gale force. We averaged seven miles per hour for forty-five miles that afternoon. It got dark very early and we sailed along the island of Paros. There in the dark we made into a small bay for shelter. Taking the sail down it caught and tore and the Captain mended it by the light of holy candle ends and the clouded moon.

Next day, September 1st, the wind if anything increased. It is annoying not to be able to use a south wind now we have it. Paros is of course the home of Parian marble, and I wandered along the beach and a short distance inland and found some bits of white and pinkish and green marble and saw a hoopoe. We moved the boat into a good little cove, where we found a

144

trickle of fresh water right on the sea. I should like to see the famous church of St Mary of the hundred doors built by the Empress Theodora, but there are a lot of Italians on the island. Only ninety-nine doors are visible today and something dramatic is due to happen if anyone digs up the hundredth.

Next day, at midday, we set sail. We passed the famous Delos a very low uninhabited little island in front of Mykonos, and crossed over to Mykonos. In the evening the wind veered to north. We could see Chios in the distance and at nightfall we were opposite Samos. After a wretched night of veering and disappearing winds, ending up with our lowering the sail and merely drifting, we found ourselves fifteen miles further to the south off the coast of Nicaria. It was beastly cold at night. Michael had the blankets. We discovered a colony of young bed bugs on the woodwork of the hold.

Next day, September 3rd, there was a little wind in the morning. It rose in the afternoon and we had to go under hatches. They were most ineffectual and water poured in over us. We steered NW and by tacking got up near to the cape of Karlovasi opposite Chios. All day it was cloudy, like England almost, and at night it was very cold and damp and we were one and all miserable.

The Captain couldn't find a suitable landing place on the cape and so at dawn we steered south along the coast for Ephesos opposite Samos, which was marked on our map. (We had a map we found on the beach in Crete, a map of the islands we got in Kimolos, and our compasses.) We reckoned we were in Turkish territorial waters. A big convoy passed us steaming north, under a Turkish destroyer. It was a lovely day, smooth with a good breeze, and the boat swam along nicely. The town called Kushadasi on our map, Eresus by the Italians when they held this part of the coast after the last war, at last appeared before us. The plains and the mountains of Turkey were far greener than anything we had seen for many months. The little town climbed up a hill from the sea, white with red roofs, a little island before it with a Venetian fort, and a mosque and a minaret near the shore. We hid under hatches and anchored opposite the harbour-master's house. As the hatches covered two-thirds of the hold, we were prefectly visible to any one above us on the quay. The Captain went

145

ashore. We came ostensibly asking for provisions before carrying on to Cyprus, but he soon returned with the glorious news that all was well. Within an hour we were on land and free. It had just begun to get rough, and we had some difficulty getting the boat up to a jetty. Food on board which a few hours before had seemed priceless was discarded. We were led before the harbour authorities and spent hours with them and the police. Everything was formal and apparently efficient. In the ridiculous what-is-your-father's-christian-name-taken-down-phonetically-in-Turkish-manner. We were helped enormously by the Assistant British Vice-Consuls Gregorious and Demetri Marc, who had dealt with many hundreds of escaped Greeks. Free at last we made for the hotel, stopping to be photographed in the main street and myself darting into shops as I saw meringues and chocolates in the windows. The Turks seemed friendly but uninterested. We ate in a restaurant, pilaff; the hotel was quite clean, with bedrooms all round a central hall which was crowded with a party of Greeks also passing through. I managed to get a hot bath about two o'clock in the morning.

Next morning we breakfasted and got ourselves shaved and the naval defence officer arrived from Smyrna, a typical jolly old RNR Commander. We are in trouble over a steel box of papers which the Turks want to hold for examination and from which we refuse to be parted. The Turks have also seized Fred's diary and my family photographs for further examination. The tin box offered more possibilities. Its history was as follows. The staff of the British Embassy left Athens in the yacht *Calanthe*. It was thought unsafe to sail by day and arriving at Poliagos most of the party landed and spent the day ashore. At midday German aircraft came over and bombed the yacht. The crew were on board and a few others, including a friend of mine, Arthur Forbes (Wing Commander Viscount Forbes. His plane was held up waiting for a woman passenger and destroyed on the ground, so that he had to go on the yacht. When the ship was hit he was nearest the bomb and sent to the bottom of the ship. The boiler burst and shot him up to the surface again. Several of the crew were killed which explained our friend on the beach at Poliagos). Most of the secret cyphers on the ship were saved, but all the embassy plate and jewels to a great value were lost. The party were chased by Germans but had time to tell a fisherman on Kimolos (whence they left by caique) that there were important papers on the yacht. If they should be found they were to be handed over to the first trustworthy person to be carried personally to General Sir Maitland Wilson, our C-in-C in Greece. Hearing of the Captain's arrival on Kimolos the fisherman came by night bringing with him an iron box, full of papers. His story was that he had salvaged the box from the only partly submerged yacht. He reported his find to the Greek policeman on the island, who told him it was of no importance and advised him to throw it away. The Greek police did, however, report the matter to the Germans who in the meantime were using divers to try and collect papers from the yacht. The Germans therefore sent for the fisherman who told them that he had thrown the box into the sea, as he had been told to do. Now he brought it to us. When the Captain opened the box he found it contained the secret orders which passed between Sir John Dill, General Wilson and the King of Greece regarding the evacuation of Greece by their troops, and all the top secret meetings between Eden, Dill, Metaxas, Wilson and Wavell on the war.

The Turkish officials at Kushadasi refused to return us this box, and eventually we left for Smyrna with the box attached to a Turkish officer, whose turned up moustaches cut across his eyes in the most intriguing manner.

We travelled in two cars. As far as old Ephesos the road was Italian-built and quite good. Michael said the country was very like Rhodesia. The old villages lie deserted. Ephesos was of course a Greek town, Greek since the days of the Ionians. It was today clean, the people not at all eastern to look at.

Before entering Smyrna we got on a good road again, and stopped to look down on the lights of the town on both sides of a long bay. Very gay with the illuminations of the Smyrna Fair.

We drove to the police station and were kept there till midnight. The main trouble being the famous iron box. The wires to Ankara are humming.

There is a detachment of REs in Smyrna busy building aerodromes and they took charge of us. They wore civilian clothes of course and were charming but while we wanted to go to the most gaudy hotel they insisted it was full of Germans and we must keep hidden with them. At least till we had proper clothes. So they took us to their Colonel's house and a pension next door, where we ate and I shared an attic with Lambris.

Most of next morning we spent again with the police. We sent cables home and after lunch we were cross-examined by the RE Colonel (Hughes) and the Vice-Consul (Noel Rees). We made a short expedition to buy clothes and I got a white coat and a pair of grey trousers I can't get on. But everyone lent us things. We stayed in Smyrna a week, both on account of the iron box and because the train to Ankara only ran three times a week and it was difficult to get seats with the fair on. Since most of the city was burnt down in 1922 it is now quite modern to look at, and the largest town in Turkey after Istanbul. The shops were good, there were one or two reasonable restaurants, and the fair was gay if not exciting. The British, German and Italian flags flew side by side over the entrance and the same palais d'art housed the British and German pavilions. The British was, I should think, good commercial propaganda though rather like a hardware store to look at, and always full. The German was well laid out and uninteresting and empty. Both German and Italian had some very good china. The Turkish exhibits included some beautiful old carpets and some modern ceramics which I thought excellent and longed to buy. Very little else of interest. We had dinner in the open and lots of caviare, the Captain talked much too loud. Everything he said got round to Noel Rees next day.

Instead of resting, the pension not being wildly comfortable, we spent most of our time outside it and had a very gay time. Michael was much better. Fred, however, was feeling ill and suffering from a carbuncle. Bert found old RE friends and went off and lived with them.

We were extremely well entertained by the Levantine colony. Just as I had a completely false idea of Turkey before I saw it, so I had always supposed Levantines to be a race of swarthy swollen-nosed gentlemen; a low form of dago. Levantinos apparently are those resident in the Levant, with European passports. The leading European merchants in Smyrna had for a century been an English family named Whittall, who settled there in the 18th century. After the last

War their prosperity rather declined and the wealthiest family is now a French one, which started with a clerk in the Whittall office. The English, French, Italian and German families had all intermarried, but retained their nationalities and the Whittall children were every generation sent home to England to be educated. We visited several of the clan, who all lived in large houses in the village of Bornova some miles outside Smyrna. They all had attractive gardens surrounded by high white walls and arched gateways, and they all produced the best teas, cakes, scones, jams and buns I ever ate. Though they were liable to have a slight foreign accent, they were more English than the English, and talked about shooting and shooting dogs. They gave us nicely knitted socks and pullovers but war seemed far away.

Our best friends, however, were the Rees – Noel Rees, the Vice-Consul being of a very rich Alexandrian family, and his wife, previously a Mrs Ralli, was, I think, Greek. Noel, before the war, had a yacht and a fine villa on Rhodes, but the family had long had interests in Smyrna and possessed there a large house in the country. We spent the whole day there several times. It was a completely Edwardian Italianate house, occupied in 1921 by the Turkish GHQ, and Noel hadn't been there since he was a boy. There were deer, and vineyards and fig trees and a private way to the railway station. Their food was something quite excellent, and after lunch we would be given a room each to rest in till it got cool for a walk in the garden. I used to lie in the hall, with a heavily carved oak staircase ending in a statuette, a chandelier of antlers, a number of large heads and a stuffed deer in a glass case, and particularly a stuffed bear holding a card tray, all delighting my heart. For there were a very comfortable sofa, books, and acres of room. There was a fine ballroom behind it. One might easily have been at home.

The war seemed very far away. In 1922 the English residents fled to Malta, and now again they were a little afraid of disturbances. But it was said that if Turkey was not invaded within ten days, they were safe for the winter, for in wet weather the mud there is quite impassable. No one had much faith in the Turkish Army. The Levantines keep themselves very much to themselves, nor do the Turks make any attempt to interrupt their privacy. The Turks are extremely suspicious

149

of European penetration. They know that in the past the Levantines have made huge fortunes out of Turkey, and now in many cases they have taken over their businesses from them and attempt to run them nationally with very poor success. For instance they took all one man's chrome mines except two which were hardly worth working. Now this man gets more from the two left to him than the Turks from those they took. They will not allow western capital to be invested in the country, though it is hardly developed at all and enormously rich in possibilities. We were told how an American company offered to build roads all over Turkey if they were given a ten year monopoly of bus transport. At the end of ten years they would sell out to the government. Although Turkey had no roads the offer was turned down. It was the general opinion that the progress made under Ataturk was not being sustained.

A week in Smyrna and Crete seemed very far away. We were outraged when our pullman berths on the train to Ankara failed to materialise. The journey took rather more than a day. We crossed the rich coastal plain and climbed up on to a plateau land of bare plains and barren hills. Turkey on the map is broken and mountainous looking, but all we saw was merely steppe, and we reckoned Hitler wouldn't let that stop him. In any case a few parachutists at the nerve centres and Turkey's two million bayonets would look about as bright as the Yugoslavs! We never saw a soldier but he was making himself useful carrying a sack of flour or a sofa or something. Rifles – never. There was a soldier on the train, a jolly fellow who spoke English. Next morning he appeared dressed to the nines in civilian clothes. He explained that if you are conscripted in Turkey you join the ranks, as a private only has to wear uniform once a fortnight and the rest of the time he can attend to his business. Being an officer, however, is a full time job. In contrast to their men, Turkish officers are extremely smart.

Though Turkey is so progressive it isn't safe for nice girls to go out alone. Most girls we met had suffered some incident or other. One, for instance, had been walking on the beach when a most dashing Turkish officer galloped up, sprang from his horse, threw her to the ground and would have shared with her a fate worse than death if she hadn't hit him in the face and screamed the house down. Under Turkish law assault is nothing so long as no blood is shed, and it is far more serious to make a man's nose bleed than to leave him for dead with a blunt instrument. One day at Bornova we were taken to see Uncle Edmond's (Giraud's) 'Koolah' i.e. farm – in fact dude ranch or summer residence. Uncle Edmond, a Frenchman with £100,000 a year, leads an idyllic existence here with his native bailiff's wife and offspring. The villa stood on a rise, surrounded by terraces, and beyond are neat rows of pine trees, planted to form a forest beautifully spaced and pruned and whitewashed. There were endless kennels of strange dogs, cows, deer, ducks, horses etc. and the pride of the place was its squash court and swimming pool. Not very long before, an English Air Force officer had remarked that the place would present a fine target from the air. The villa was then all black outside and the terrace walls and steps white stone. Next day both wore khaki.

We never saw a sign of habitation after leaving the coastal plain till we began to approach Ankara, when there were a few farms and large stretches of stubble. Turkey's wheat crop for this year has been sold to Germany. There is quite a shortage of bread and also of coffee, without which Turks cannot exist but which they do not grow. It comes from Mecca.

Ankara stands in a desert plain, not unlike the old part of Cairo with an escarpment crowned by a fortress, nondescript buildings on its flanks and on the level ground below the modern buildings of the new capital. The station is extremely impressive. We were met by a military attaché, who took Michael and me to his flat, passing on the way the Ministries lining a fine avenue, all exactly alike. His flat was the most 'shee-shee' thing I ever saw, in a delicious chrome and marble villa.

The same night we caught the Taurus express. We were not at all surprised to hear that the Embassy had made every effort to obtain sleepers for us, but that somehow or other none on the train were reserved. We watched a German Embassy official escort his wife to theirs!

When the sun rose next morning we were passing through level hill-encircled plains, which seemed well supplied with water. When we entered the Taurus we saw for the first time what Turkey could produce in the way of mountains. Terrific

151

ravines and gorges, soaring bleak precipitous ranges dropping vertically to rocky torrents made a plaything of Lefka Ora. The railroad clung to the mountain sides and passed through and down to a plain running seawards. As evening fell we passed a crusader castle on a rock guarding the last entrance to the dwindling hills.

In the darkness we crossed the hills or mountains which lie along the Turkey-Syria border and round midnight we reached Aleppo. We were home.

Aleppo, my guide-book tells me, *qui a la prétension de devenir la plus grande, (ville de la Syrie) puisqu'elle est l'embranchement où les employés peuvent crier maintenant 'Les voyageurs pour Paris' et où ils crieront un jour 'Les voyageurs pour le Caire et le Cap ... Les voyageurs pour Calcutta et Pekin! En voiture! ...'.*

Our conquest of Syria was not long over. We were met and taken to the barracks of the DLI where in their officers' mess, lately the NCOs quarters of a French Colonial regiment, we were provided with a perfectly filthy meal and a palliasso with a couple of blankets. We removed ourselves early next morning to the Hotel Baron, lately German Staff HQ.

After the drab westernisation of Turkey it was delightful to see again the turban, the tarboosh and flowing Arab robes. *'Chaque nuit d'Orient est un poème'* says my guide-book. Michael and I stayed in bed all day recovering from the palliasses. So we missed the famous citadel on its precipitous rock, and reached Damascus. My only purchase was sufficient brocade for Toby to make a dressing-gown of gold, with dancing girls before a monarch on a throne, the only colour a green tree.

We saw some hideous intricately inlaid furniture which my companions greatly admired. We were told that for this work the Jews worked on the brass, the Christians on the mosaic of coloured woods, the Moslems inlay mother-of-pearl and carve the wood. The Armenians confine themselves to rugs.

We were shown the gateway in the town wall from whose ramparts St Paul was lowered in a basket. The wall still contains the city and outside one stream escapes from its bonds to water the gardens, 'the gardens of delight' of the Koran.

We were two nights in the town, for the Area Commandant

had thoughtfully ordered us to present ourselves too late for us to catch the train next day. I had time therefore to see the Great Mosque of the Ommayads – who followed immediately after Mahomed and reigned here as Califs, sending forth their armies as far as Spain. There is a long wide court, arcaded on three sides, with the mosque prayer hall on the fourth. In this is the tomb of John the Baptist, over which there was once a church. He is venerated by the Moslems as precursor of the Prophet. In the court is a heavenly fountain. Above the cloisters three huge minarets point to the sky – the brides' minaret square and solid, the minaret of Jesus, prodigiously pointed, the western minaret octagonal, a mosaic of coloured stone. By the main entrance still stand the remains of the monumental entrance to the 3rd century Temple of Jupiter which occupied the whole site. This in its turn replaced the pagan temple of Hadad, which flourished under the Aramites, the Assyrians and the Persians.

By far the most enchanting building in Damascus is the tomb of Saladin, a domed chapel sheltering under the massive wall of the mosque, in a green garden of orange trees and roses. Vines and convolvulus droop over a broad basin, and, as we entered, the guardian of the place rose from his couch by the chapel porch, white-robed in a golden turban.

Infidels are not allowed in Mosques at the times of prayer. Unlike the Mosque of Ibn Tulun in Cairo, whose plan it resembles, the floor of the prayer hall of the Great Mosque is covered in carpets. One old man knelt reading the Koran on a cross-legged stand, the long pillared aisles were avenues of serenity, in which we were strangers. Against one pillar stood a grandfather clock.

That is all I remember of Damascus.

We drove to Jerusalem by car, by way of Lake Tiberias, entering again the familiar stony hills of Palestine. We passed through Nazareth on its hill sides.

. . . And so after Turkey, Syria, the Lebanon and Palestine we finally arrived in Egypt, with its green unchanging delta water buffaloes and its egrets, Cairo and GHQ white sofas and tuber roses, the Mosque, the Gezira, clothes shops and cinemas, civilisation and war. Our party went its several ways. That journey was over. [That ends Myles's diary.]

8

Hospital in Jerusalem

I left the train in Palestine, and was sent straight to the British hospital in Jerusalem, where I was examined by the medical people, and I somehow managed to catch sand fly fever at the same time. There were a number of my friends at the same hospital, including my cousin Charles Chichester and

Michael Lycett, of the Royal Scots Greys, who were both recovering from various ailments. In Jerusalem Hermione Ranfurly then working for Sir Harold MacMichael came to see me.

I had several communications from General Maitland Wilson (C-in-C Middle East, based in Cairo – I had known him all my life) and I remember sending him a report pointing out how, on the evacuation from Crete, during the long arduous march from Hania to Sphakia the British troops of all ranks were quite unable to collect water in buckets from the wells on the roadside. This was because however hard they tried the bucket would always hit the side of the well, and then bump on the water, but would not sink, so you could not pull it up full of water. It was a knack, which the Greeks had learnt over the centuries, but we were unable to do it. The result was masses of very thirsty, bedraggled troops. That was a typical problem, and I'm afraid that it compared very unfavourably with what I saw of the Bavarian Alpine Division who had captured the island and us.

This was near the time that Singapore fell to the Japanese, and similar inexperience was apparently evident between the British in Singapore and the rugged, tough little Japanese.

However, once my sand fly fever had gone and I had been temporarily patched up, I was motored down to Cairo by Captain Henry Trotter, who was in my regiment. Once in Cairo I began to meet various people who were very interested to hear the views of somebody who had 'come from the other side', so to speak.

I knew Oliver Lyttelton slightly, who later became Lord Chandos; he was the Minister of State in Cairo, and took a great interest in everything I told him. He favourably received my suggestion that if I could take a few carefully picked personnel back by Greek caique all the way to the Aegean, we could probably bring out a number of other British escapees. At the same time we could lay the foundations for a network of sabotage and plan for a future re-entry into this important area. I said I would have to go back with Commander Emmanuele Vernicos, who had done such a brilliant job bringing us out and who had, by now, rejoined me.

Lyttelton arranged for us to see Henry Hopkinson, who was the first secretary at the Embassy and who later became Lord

Colyton. He signalled to the Foreign Office in London to get a report on Commander Vernicos before deciding what we should do. Next morning I got a message to see Henry Hopkinson at the Embassy, and he gave me the very disturbing news that the reply regarding Commander Vernicos stated that he was *persona non grata* with the British Government.

Apparently, before the war, he had made one or two sea voyages with his ship the *Irene Vernicos* taking Russian, and other, Jewish refugees from Greece to the newly formed Jewish community in Palestine. At the same time this was against all British Government orders, to the extent that the Navy was patrolling off the coast of Palestine to prevent such landings taking place. On one of his trips he was stopped by a British destroyer and all the Jews were arrested and sent back to where they had come from in Europe, presumably only to reappear in Hitler's gas chambers some four years later.

That put the kibosh on our return expedition to Crete for the time being. I was sent off to see Colonel Simonds, who had just been put in charge of forming the Cairo branch of the new MI9. After discussions with him and his superior officer Brigadier Dudley Clark, who was a splendid person at improvising and running clandestine operations, it was decided that my scheme would be adopted.

I was to be in charge of taking back the first expedition, in Greek caiques, right from Alexandria, or rather Cyprus, to the islands which I had come to know so well. This was a journey of some 500 miles, and it needed fully equipping with stores, arms, ammunition and supplies for a prolonged stay.

During this period my wounds had not by any means recovered from my accident on the island of Milos on August 27th. My right wrist was still in plaster, and although I was unaware of it at the time, the fall had cracked my skull. My right eye was still paralysed and closed up and my right ear was stone deaf due to the nerve having been killed.

I had to go to the 15th Scottish hospital in Cairo to have my wrist re-broken to try and improve the Collis fracture, as my hand was very nearly at right-angles from my arm. It had been put in a splint by Doctor Logothetes, on the island of Kimolos after my fall two months previously. This was all done under, if I remember rightly, quite a lot of pain. A number of people were kind enough to come and visit me in hospital, and amongst my visitors were Flash Kellett, my Colonel, who came with Mary Newall. Mary was known throughout Cairo as 'One Gun Mary'.

I also met up with one or two friends in the hospital; one of these was Alistair Timpson, Scots Guards, whom I had known at Eton, and he had joined me in mining in Rhodesia before the war. While he was at Cambridge he was wagered that he could not walk from Cambridge to London (St Paul's) and back in under twenty-four hours. He won his £100, doing it in twenty-three hours and twenty minutes. After serving with his regiment on the Western Desert he volunteered to join the Long Range Desert Group, where he was badly wounded, and so we met again in hospital. When talking to him in July 1990 he reminded me of the very attractive Sister Gill, whom I apparently chased down the corridor of the hospital – only to run into the matron, who said, 'Captain Parish, I do not think you understand hospital procedure!'

After about ten days in hospital I contacted Colonel Simonds of MI9, and began planning a return trip to the Aegean.

The next three or four weeks while we were getting everything ready, I was able to circulate a lot in Cairo, seeing all my old friends in the regiment and having many happy lunches and parties at Shepheards Hotel and the Gezira Sporting Club in between my hospital days and working at MI9.

Towards the middle of November it was decided that I must go over to Cyprus with Commander Vernicos (who, by now, I had got 'De-*persona non grata*-ed') and select two or three boats and crew for the trip. I was allocated three excellent Australians, Captain Greenway and Sergeants Brewer and Bezley, to take with me.

At this time I was still in hospital, and would no doubt have been there quite a lot longer had Colonel Simonds not heard about a certain Captain Atkinson.

Captain Atkinson had escaped from a prison of war camp in Athens and had then been able to collect some twenty-seven British and Australian escapees, assembling them on the island of Despotico. Despotico, which has an interesting history going back to 400 BC, was a very small island lying off

157

158

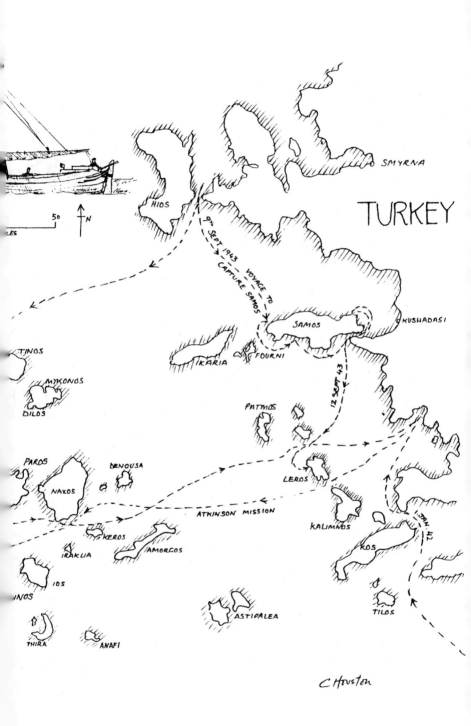

SMYRNA

TURKEY

HIOS

50

N

LES

9ᵗʰ SEPT 1943 VOYAGE TO CAPTURE SAMOS

KUSHADASI

SAMOS

IKARIA

FOURNI

12 SEPT 43

TINOS

MYKONOS

DILOS

PATMOS

PAROS

DENOUSA

NAXOS

LEROS

ATKINSON MISSION

KALIMNOS

KEROS

IRAKLIA

AMORGOS

KOS

13 JAN 42

IOS

INOS

ASTIPALEA

TILOS

THIRA

ANAFI

C Houston

159

Antiparos, which in turn is half a mile from Paros. It was hoped that my trip up to the Aegean could be synchronised with the meeting of Captain Atkinson and his party of escapees, and that I would bring them back.

A British submarine called the *Thrasher* had gone up there and had been in contact with them, but was shortly lost and sunk by enemy action; this meant there was no-one to rescue them other than ourselves.

I had hurriedly to say goodbye to the 15th Scottish hospital and left immediately for Cyprus, having got a new passport from the Embassy in a matter of hours, because it was evident we would be using the Turkish coast quite a lot.

Once in Cyprus we collected the two ships and the small boat we were towing. One was called the *Evangelistria,* and she was commanded by an absolutely splendid smuggler-fisherman called Captain Miltiades Houmas, who was from the island of Samos. Not only had Milton been the first Greek to escape to Cyprus with his caique to join the British war effort, then volunteering to return, but he was also the last to be demobilised five years later after innumerable epic expeditions. He was awarded the DSO and the OBE and invested by Admiral Talbot in Piraeus.* The other was a big caique of two hundred tons, the *Agios Demetrios* which had run out from Crete in the early days of the evacuation and was commanded by a very fine Cretan, Captain John Stambodakis.

I spent the next two or three weeks getting all the supplies necessary, from Cairo and Cyprus, and had to make several flights back to Cairo. These were to see my CO, Colonel Tony Simonds, and to collect equipment from the ordnance, including a large anti-tank gun, several Bren guns and several thousand rounds of ammunition, plus considerable quantities of food stores, including several 100-pound sacks of sugar.

It was all very different to one's regimental discipline; I was on my own, I was my own master, I could walk into the ordnance department or the Foreign Office and order more or less whatever I wanted, and it would come in double quick

---

* See the Citation in the Appendix.

time.

My organisational trips back to Cairo were great fun, and I saw many of my friends, including Eric Sanders and Robin Maugham, who came to see me at Shepheards Hotel. Robin was doing intelligence work with the Trans-Jordan frontier force at the time; he had immense charm and was great fun to be with. Sometime I went up to Gezira, where I saw, amongst others, Donny Player and Flash Kellet, both of whom were killed commanding my regiment, The Sherwood Rangers Yeomanry.

By the end of the year I was back in Cyprus and we were finally ready to go. The supplies were complete and all on board, thanks to the tremendous work done by Commander Vernicos. The small Greek crew were assembled; we had one or two Cypriots, one of whom was the engineer who let us down badly the following month in Turkey, as you will read.

We set sail on January 1st 1942, from the north-west fishing port of Paphos. I decided – foolishly – to leave in the morning, regardless of weather forecasts or Admiralty warnings, and off we went, heading straight up towards Fethye Bay on the Turkish coast, some 220 miles north-west.

We had not been going for more than four hours when a *megalo fortuna* blew up. It was beginning to get dark, and before we knew where we were we found ourselves in the middle of a force nine gale. This was a most terrifying experience, with the whole ship lurching and diving into the huge waves. The gale continued throughout the night and most of the next day, with Commander Vernicos doing a splendid job on the bridge, and myself with nothing to do other than fervently hope and pray that we would reach the Turkish coast rather than the bottom of the Mediterranean.

During this storm we lost the small boat that we were towing, which contained part of our arms and a large amount of ammunition. It had broken loose from the two very strong tow ropes and we never saw or heard of it again.

Eventually we reached Fethye Bay, a most impressive horseshoe-shaped bay, about two miles wide by two miles deep, and were able to pull in close to the shore for a little respite. This, however, was disturbed by the occasional rifle shot from the Turkish gendarmerie on the shore.

From there we proceeded along the Turkish coast, through the straits of Rhodes to Bodrum, where I was amazed to find Milton and the much smaller *Evangelistria,* which he had somehow managed to keep going. I soon learnt not to be amazed at what Milton managed to do; in six years he never once failed on any mission. We arrived in the dark, and by good fortune were able to get the two ships alongside each other. After a short stop we proceeded to Bucillius Bay, about fifty miles north of Bodrum, where we decided to tranship on to the *Evangelistria,* and to continue in this small caique of about three tons with her owner, Captain Miltiades Houmas, the indomitable Commander Emmanuele Vernicos and Sergeant Brewer.

We left the larger, 200 ton *Agios Demetrios* in Bucillius Bay with my second in command Captain Greenway, the Australian officer, Sergeant Bezley, her captain John Stambodakis and the two or three Greek crew. They were instructed to wait there for thirty days whilst we proceeded deep into the Aegean for our rendezvous with Captain Atkinson and his party of escapees, who we were planning to meet on January 27th 1942.

Having left Bucillius Bay and the safe three miles of Turkish territorial waters we sailed due west into the enemy-occupied Aegean. As it was January it was the coldest and certainly the roughest time of the year, and we were constantly on the look-out for German or Italian patrol boats and aircraft. There were twenty days to go before we were due to meet Captain Atkinson and his twenty-seven British troops. We planned to meet them either on Despotico or on Antiparos, where there was a massive labyrinth of caves near the summit of the highest hill, at about 1,000 feet. (This was described by the poet Achilaos as long ago as 700 BC.) They were full of stalactites and stalagmites, some of which had been destroyed by hand grenades, presumably during the capture of Captain Atkinson. The caves were 600 feet wide and up to 240 feet deep; quite large enough to hold a whole brigade of soldiers and an obvious place for Atkinson's party to hide, pending our arrival.

In the meantime I had a big programme of forming a supply dump on the barren islands of the Makares group, which lay about five miles east of Naxos. We reached these islands on January 9th, and left a small supply of tinned food and some 250,000 drachmae in sealed cocoa tins which we hid under the rocks near the summit of the largest island.

(Incidentally, some twenty-five years later my mother-in-law rented a magnificent old 300 ton steam yacht, the *Hiniesta,* for a three-week cruise in the Aegean. She took a party of six, including my wife and me, and I took the opportunity of suggesting we visited some of the islands I had known in the war. One of our fellow guests was Admiral Renouf, who had played a leading part in the capture of Castelorizo in 1941, and was later to suffer the loss of his ship in the Battle of Crete. Having told them the story of the hidden drachmae and sardines we decided to have a treasure hunt on the Makares islands. We all went ashore and had a very enjoyable two days searching – without success. Either my memory of the exact spot was at fault, or someone else had found the hidden goods. What had amounted to some £2,000 when I had hidden it would now, due to Greek inflation, be worth not much more than £2.)

This island had an ideal protected bay, from where we could observe all the enemy shipping moving from Piraeus to the Dodecanese and Samos and its surrounding islands.

It was here that I realised the value and importance of Denousa, which lay about ten miles north of the Makares islands, and upon which I was later to formulate my plan of seizing it. It would make an excellent observation post for all traffic, sea and air, from Athens to Rhodes, and could be used as a base from which to mount raids on to the islands and shipping. I later discovered that Denousa had been used by the German battleship *Emden* for similar purposes during the Great War in 1917.

This plan was subsequently approved by GHQ Cairo.

On the night of January 11th we set sail west again, passing Naxos, Paros, Antiparos and Despotico. We were heading for the island of Poliagos (Goat island), which was some forty miles west south west of Despotico, and to which I had been with Myles Hildyard after our escape from Crete. However, my previous visit was immediately after my disastrous fall on Milos, when I had a cracked skull and was almost blind, so I could not remember a great deal about the island. It was here that the British Embassy yacht *Calanthe* was sunk; so ably described in Peter Fleming's biography by D. Hart Davis.

We reached its eastern coast on the morning of January 12th, anchoring close in to the shore, from where Sergeant Brewer and I climbed up to a rugged stone building several hundred feet above sea level. The plan was for Brewer to do a 'recce' of the western bay of the island, where we planned to anchor the *Evangelistria* and create a large supply dump. To make certain that all was still clear of enemy troops I covered the eastern part of Poliagos, while Brewer had orders to check all was clear on the west and then to return to me as soon as possible.

I estimated his work would take him about two hours and myself likewise; the others, meanwhile, were waiting below in the ship. I duly returned to our meeting place after a couple of hours, but there was no sign of Sergeant Brewer. I then had an extremely worrying time, during which I imagined every possible horror that may have befallen him. Of course I could not leave our meeting point in case he did reappear, which, thankfully, he did, after five hours. We then went down the cliff to rejoin the others, who likewise were beginning to fear the worst and were greatly relieved to hear the good news that the island was still unoccupied; with that we proceeded to the western bay.

Here we unloaded all the supplies; several tons of them. Two of the valuable sacks of sugar unfortunately just touched the water, and as a result of capillary action were shortly to become like a deflated balloon, their contents gone. This was a great catastrophe, having carried them safely through 600 miles of enemy territory.

During the next few days we got ourselves well established and spent some time with old friends on Kimolos. This most lovely island was only three miles west of Poliagos, and we were able to spend a few days here, fishing and getting ready to sail back to Antiparos for the rendezvous and collection of Captain Atkinson and his party.

We left Poliagos in the afternoon, arriving at Antiparos in driving rain in the middle of a very black night. Having endeavoured, without success, to locate Atkinson, we decided to wait until daylight.

With the arrival of first light we were amazed to find ourselves anchored within 100 yards of four armed Italian ships; something similar to stepping right inside a major wasps' nest. Without further ado we weighed anchor and moved to a small hidden bay about two miles away on the south coast of Despotico, before our Italian neighbours were alerted to our presence. We were stuck in the middle of enemy territory, 500 miles from our base at Famagusta, with no possible chance of help.

The rest of this episode is told from notes in my diary, written in the extremely wet and uncomfortable hold of the *Evangelistria*.

'Italian Day. Believe it to be 23rd, Friday. Awake to find us alongside four Italian steamers and move down to a bay on Despotico. After breakfast Vernicos goes over to contact Atkinson by the small boat. Brewer and I leave by land to watch the progress through the Zeiss glasses; we arrive at our point of vantage slightly after V has landed, and are surprised to see three men hurrying towards the boat. Soon a shot is fired, and we see someone running up the hill flat out. Then we see V and his party joined by these three men in black and a few others. After some talk and another shot being fired they all embark into the sailing boat and I think all is well, but after 200 yards we can see that they are not coming triumphantly back to us, rather they are going to the main landing stage. Upon disembarking here we observe some fifteen dark-clothed men with rifles approaching the party in the boat, and we immediately realised that we had fallen into a trap good and proper, and that the key to our party was in the hands of the enemy.

We watched for another fifteen minutes and saw the miserable little procession proceed to a red house, which was presumably where the island commander HQ was. When they had all disappeared out of sight we spent another ten minutes looking at everything else and saw some fifteen soldiers in all, some leaning up against houses, some sitting down and some lounging about. Our reaction was pretty bloody but we decided to attack the island and release our friends, when one of the big patrol boats and a steam launch of some 300 tons steamed out towards our boat, presumably the others had been forced to speak.

I go back to warn the crew and get our rubber boat ashore and some supplies and then destroy my papers, while Brewer watches for any future operations on the part of the enemy. After an hour he comes racing down the hill to say that they were taking V off to Paros on his own boat, under armed guard of four. Immediately we decide to intercept the boat, save V and capture the enemy, so in great haste with all arms on deck we race out to intercept them and do so some fifty yards from Antiparos's south point, a perfect place. Upon closing in and making ready to board we see V in the bows waving us to go away, and thinking that this means we are going to be fired on we get down and go on. On coming up to them we see four smiling Ities and Vernicos comes aboard saying that we must go away as he has got everything fixed but Atkinson and thirty-two soldiers have been captured.

(Note: our main objective of finding Captain Atkinson and his party did not succeed because they were betrayed and captured by the Italians on Antiparos, just a few days before we were due to meet them. I heard subsequently that he had been appallingly treated by the Italians whilst in prison in Athens. This brave British Captain was one of the first officers to work for MI9 in the Grecian war zone.)

The senior Italian comes aboard and apparently thinks that we are Jerries and is very gushing. The others sit goggle-eyed, at any rate V is so determined for us to carry on with our plans that we let the Ities go back and V takes over the party who are going to Paros. I have misgivings, thinking that I should have captured them, and so go back to Vernicos who is again as insistent as ever that all is well and it is better to leave them as friends than enemies, so we continue on to Turkey and he agrees to meet us as prearranged.

But first I have to go back to the bay in Despotico to collect the rubber boat and stores that we had dumped ashore at the initial emergencies. By the time we had completed this the wind had changed and there was a huge sea running, which, although she was tied to the rocks on either side, almost crashed the *Evangelistria* on to the rocks. We were held in this small bay for the next forty-eight hours by the wind and sea, terrified that the Italians would have seen us and could attack us overland from the north of Despotico. However, this did not happen, and after a very worrying forty-eight hours the sea abated and we headed west for Bucillius Bay in Turkey.

Brewer showed the greatest foresight, and it was due

entirely to him that things turned out so well – I can not praise him and the crew highly enough.

Incidentally, while they were in the HQ house an MTB boat, possibly from Kos, came in at about thirty knots, and we presumed this was to take V back in, as a very wanted spy. There are quite a lot of sailing craft in these waters around Paros and Naxos; I can see them at the moment.

The southern point of Naxos seems to have no habitation and is very bare – there is a house but I can see no fortifications. We pass Mykonos, with Denousa visible to the north, in a freshening sea at 21.00.

Spend a terrifying sleepless night of hell at sea in a full-scale gale. Thanks to God and the magnificent courage of our captain of the *Evangelistria* (Miltiades Houmas), who stood alone for sixteen hours steering in a gale by night without using his compass, we were brought safely to the southern bay of Fourni by 12.00 hours. Again and again it is brought back to me that the fury of the sea in such a small craft is much worse than the malice of the enemy.

At 16.00 hours, while we were all asleep, a fishing vessel with sixteen Greeks and two armed Italians appeared. Two Greeks come aboard and, seeing our rifles, warn us to leave because a patrol boat will soon be coming. So, in raging gale we put to sea for Turkey but after two miles it becomes apparent that the ship will probably not stand the magnitude of the sea, so we shelter behind the tiny island of Arki without which I do not know what we would have done, and so hot tea and rum – biscuits and *glico,* then one hour's radio and so to bed.

It was as we sailed east, south of Mykonos, that we saw an eclipse of the moon; not an experience I am often accustomed to, particularly as we expected at any moment that the Italian and German MTBs would find us.

Early the next morning, as we approached the island of Fourni, we spotted what appeared to be an Italian schooner, heading in our direction at about twelve knots. I told Milton to pull in to the south coast, which was the lee side of the wind, where we could see a small bay. I reckoned that if it came to a fight we would be in a stronger position firing back from the shore, so we tied up to some rocks and got the anti-tank gun ashore, plus the two Bren guns. We lay there, hidden under the cover of the rocks, awaiting events as the schooner came directly towards us – it was now about three miles away, and steadily closing in. I ordered that there should be no movement in or around the *Evangelistria,* and that if they came in to inspect us we would hold our fire until they were virtually within 100 yards of us. The next half hour was one of considerable stress, as I was hoping that by keeping absolutely still the Italian captain would consider our caique to be a normal island boat, and would therefore turn away after bigger and better game. He came to within 500 yards of us when, to my immense relief, he veered round and pursued a south-easterly course. This was perhaps fortunate for him, as he would have been at the receiving end of our anti-tank gun and the small arms fire from the Bren guns. We waited for him to gradually disappear over the horizon before untying from the rocks, weighing anchor and proceeding in a north-easterly direction.

Next day: the gale has abated considerably and I suggest to Milton that we make a run for it, which we do. All goes well as far as G. Nix when a great *fortuna* gets up and it again appears to be about evens. I suggest sheltering at G, preferring the wrath of a handful of Italians every time to that of the sea. At any rate Milton sticks it out and after one hour's undiluted hell we reach the calm Turkish waters, and chug down to Bucillius where, to my great joy, we see the old *Demetrios* covered in smiling joyous faces. They were delighted to see us return as they only had a few more days to wait, because I had told them that if we were not back within one month they were to assume we were lost, and were to return to base. The rest of the day we spend telling of our experiences and planning those of the future.

Although in the comparatively well sheltered Bucillius Bay a *megalo fortuna* starts at about 12.00 hours and continues with ever-increasing anger. So formidable is it that the life of both ships depend on anchor and chain. We spend a depressing day below deck, for me relieved by a book on Leonardo da Vinci that I had brought with me.

27th. A day of no importance and dying wind. Decide to sail

for Kushadasi at 3.00 hours. The *Demetrios* to leave on 29th.

28th. Have an abortive start in sun and it starts to blow accompanied by hail, so I put off leaving and try again and set to the point, but meet a big sea and a maelstrom. Try and pull in to the first bay, but we are met by the crackle of rifle fire so go steady. Eventually after more firing we pull into a rotten anchorage and Milton and I proceed ashore in to the Turkish bayonets, ten of which await us. After talking pompously saying, 'My dear fellow you simply must grow up and not be such children,' the tension relaxed somewhat, but I was only just able to stop them firing at our ship when she endeavoured to get clear of some rocks. They gave me permission to go back on the boat and I spent a most depressing day in intense coldness; lunched in my cabin. Luckily at 16.00 hours an officer, charming as always, came aboard and gave us permission to join the other caique and apologised for shooting at an Englishman. Am so much gladdened by the sight of the others. And so to bed.

29th. Spent a pleasant morning walking ashore; two Turkish officers came aboard at 12.00 hours and we entertained them. At 15.00 hours I decided to sail for Kushadasi as the wind is SE and getting stronger. We sail in a terrible sea and have a very bad journey, arriving at 24.00 hours, but thanks to God the weather continued to come off shore.

30th. Awake in comfort at 8.00 hours and meet all my old Kushadasi friends, who give me the big hand. I go in to see Noel (Lt. Cmdr Noel Rees) and arrive at 16.00 hours and stay at his excellent house and discuss plans.

31st. Buca. Spend all day at Noel's house, awaking at 11.30 hours and spend afternoon writing reports; all exceptionally comfortable.

Feb 1st. Leave Noel's house at 9.10 to catch train at 9.35 in great haste. Noel sees me off and gives me a bottle of whisky. My police escort and Marc accompany me and I am met in state by the chief intelligence officer and arrive at Kushadasi at

169

14.30 hours. Much worried by having left Noel's charts in the train. From then on things go badly, very badly. I hear that the bloody engineer refuses to go aboard and has spent his time telling Italian agents about my plans, and then every Turk in the place asks to be given something. Eventually at 24.00 hours after failing to start the engine the consul Marc agrees to see Noel the next day to get an official order for the engineer to be forceably put aboard. And so to bed, after eggs and sausages, most depressed.

Feb 2nd. A wet dreary day but Marc wins the day and the engineer is put aboard by secret police after lunch. I have to go and see the Kaiberkum. Things seem better and everyone is friendlier later on and the outlook better. All night in rain they fight to start the engine and at 05.00 hours we leave, thanks to God.

Feb 3rd. A gentle smooth journey, the latter part in sun from Kushadasi to Khiosti (Friday) where we see two of N's ships and a Turkish MTB. It is a delightful bay, the countryside covered in fallen masonry which brings back to mind the 1922 Smyrna massacres. And so, in great peace and considerable happiness I enjoy the evening doing odd jobs in my cabin.

Feb 4th. Spend all day at Khiosti and await Noel, imprisoned by the rain and wind. Brewer next door, happy as ever, laughs and jokes with the Greeks, particularly the two boys on Noel's yacht, who sit around him admiringly as if he were some amusement at a fair. Marc comes for me at 20.00 hours and says Izmir but when I am about to get into the car he tells me *Avrio* (tomorrow), and I go back to the boat swearing.

Feb 5th. Enjoy a nice peaceful day but am anxious because the car from N has not turned up, but it does so at 19.00 hours and Demetri Marc and I travel in state to Noel through fallen houses with weeds growing out of their walls which foretells the 1922 massacres. Noel is charming as ever and has forgiven me for losing the charts, something I did not deserve. We talk until midnight, and so to bed.

Feb 7th. N is at office all day. I lounge about the house,

spending my time intermittently with Zoe, Alice, Miss Hakin etc. N comes back at 19.00 hours obviously worried. He has had a cable from the Ambassador; the gist of which is that I have behaved like a bull in a china shop and am on the point of causing an international incident. He explains that the others are forbidden to leave because one letter was missing, but that he would send for them on Sunday.

Feb 9th. Sunday. Go for a very long walk with Noel. Eat an enormous breakfast and lunch and the other two arrive in the evening, having fixed everything at Ayasmat (Secret Police HQ).'

9

Smyrna

The next week or so I spent with Noel Rees at his palatial house at Bouja, on the outskirts of Smyrna. Noel was the MI6 representative in Smyrna and occupied the first floor of the Consulate. He had done a brilliant job getting established there and in Alexandria, which his family had been associated with since Nelson fought there 150 years ago. (His family victualled Nelson's fleet at their own expense during the battle of the Nile.)

I began organising my plans for a major build up of MI9 operations based in Turkey. Colonel Simonds flew up to Istanbul to meet me to discuss the next few months overall plans and operations.

It was decided that I should work in liaison with Commander Wolfson, who was the DNI in Istanbul. I was to have my own office and personnel in the British Consulate in Smyrna, amd was to build up a fleet of Greek caiques and crews who would be able to enter the Greek mainland and the islands. This was for the purpose of intelligence; to be in a position to evacuate British and Royal Hellenic personnel and others and to assist in sabotage operations.

As a result of all this I spent several weeks in Cairo and Alexandria, mostly in the MI9 headquarters with Tony Simonds and his chief, Brigadier Dudley Clarke. The Brigadier was a most delightful and charming man with a splendid sense of humour and also quite unflappable. He had the entreé to all the senior people back in London.

The MI9 office had ben rapidly building up a number of schemes for assisting the operators in the field, one being in charge of the department for forged passports, ships' navigation papers etc. This was handled by Captain Maskelyne, the famous impressario and conjuror who, with his assistant, performed at many of the big parties in London before the war as Maskelyne & Devant.

Life in Cairo and Alexandria was very pleasant for those few weeks. One evening I dined at the American Embassy as the guest of Walter Kirk, the American Ambassador, and amongst the guests were David Smiley and Julian Amery; it was either just before or just after Julian's adventures in Albania with Billy Maclean (Colonel Neil Maclean DSO, late Royal Scots Greys). Billy, like me, was always popping in and out of Cairo between missions – I had little idea, and I did not like to ask, what his particular department was, but I assumed it was something to do with SOE.

One weekend I went to Luxor, as a guest of Mona Aboud. Mona was the daughter of Aboud Pasha, who had the most superb country estate on the Nile.

Aboud Pasha had massive sugar plantations, mills and refineries in the area, which we went over, but like so many others, he unfortunately lost everything in the Neguib/Nasser revolution some ten years later.

I saw quite a lot of my brother officers from my regiment who were still based in Palestine and Egypt, and I stayed for a few days with Eric Saunders; he had a very fine flat in Cairo as he had been seconded from the regiment to be GSOI Transport for Montgomery's 8th Army.

My visits to Alexandria, when not on duty, were equally pleasant, because I had made several friends including Lt. Commander Willis Rees; his wife, Nadia, was Russian, and was generally considered to be one of the most lovely women in the world. Willie had to spend most of his time holding off Aly Khan and others from his treasured beauty.

Alexandria was particularly gay because I stayed with Gabriella Barker and her husband Cyril and it was almost a home from home. Gabriella organised a troupe of the prettiest girls, mostly daughters of her friends, and they put on shows for the troops stationed in Egypt and the Western Desert. We had many wonderful parties in the evenings in her house.

On my return to Smyrna I took over from Captain Zangas RHN, and set up the organisation for MI9 to continue, and to greatly increase the evacuation of Allied Servicemen and many others. I stayed with Noel and Alice Rees for the first few weeks while I settled in, and soon got to know everyone in that happy community. It consisted of many French, Italian, Greek and other expatriates – some of whose families had been there for more than a hundred years.

The Girauds were one such family; Bill Giraud was the acting French vice-consul with a Legion d'Honneur and a fearfully attractive wife, Gwen, who remain to this day the closest of friends. Another such family was the Whittals – they were an old English family who had been inhabiting Asia Minor for the last fifty to one hundred years. Arthur Whittal worked in the Embassy in Istanbul – he was the passport control officer (which encompassed more than the name implied). One of my assistants in the office was Vem Whittal, who spoke perfect Turkish, as apart from his education in England he had spent most of his life in Turkey.

There was also the Louis Marc family – Gregorios, who looked like an Old Testament patriarch and was the British Consul in Samos, from where he was evacuated just before the Italians seized the island – and his brother Dimitri. Dimitri worked in the Consulate and helped with Noel Rees's very special work for MI6, and it was he who extricated us when we arrived at Kushadasi after our long escape from Crete. Their family had been the British Consuls in Samos for over a hundred years, and still are today. (After the war, in the Attlee era during the cut-back on Foreign Office expenditure it was decided that a number of the smaller consulates should be closed. I was very pleased to be able to help Gregory Marc by taking the matter up with Ernest Bevin, then Foreign Secretary, and he overruled the order. (The present Consul is Dimitri's daughter, Mrs Guiyot Garoufuli Marc, who recently appeared in the British newspapers after the tragic air crash off Samos on July 4th 1989.)

From Cairo I was sent two more assistants; they were Captain Jackie Vlasto and Alex Caridia, both of whom were from Anglo-Greek families. I also chose a brilliant young man aged about seventeen, who was studying at the English high school in Istanbul.

He was John Louis Marc, son of Dimitri Marc. I ran into considerable trouble from Sir Charles Morrison-Bell, an old school friend and colleague of mine, who was the MI5 representative in Smyrna, for employing John. They reported me to Colonel Thompson, who was the head man of MI5 in Istanbul, because they thought employing a young student could easily be a security risk. Luckily, after a rather rocky week I was able to convince them all that John Louis Marc was 100 per cent sound and in no way a security risk, and I am delighted to say that he continued to serve MI9 in the Smyrna office long after I was captured, and indeed right until VE Day, in June 1945.

I also had a young trooper who was in my regiment, the Sherwood Rangers, from the beginning of the war, called Louis Brown. He had been in the Cretan campaign and had been successfully evacuated from there, and I had met him again on one of my visits to Cairo when he applied to join me up in Smyrna.

For the next few months the build up of my fleet of caiques and personnel steadily increased, together with my knowledge of the Turks and also my friendship with the head of the Turkish Secret Police, Shefket Bey. Whenever he and his wife were invited to dinner he would always go through the regular routine of accepting for them both, but would then turn up alone, regretting that his wife was unwell. I got used to this, as it was standard practice with most of the Turkish officials that I met.

The build up of our operations was enormously assisted by Noel Rees. He got on extremely well with the Turkish officials and Government, and was wholly responsible for getting our secret fishing bay of Khiosti, near Chesme, and its surrounding area put into a militarised zone, where no-one was allowed to go except our various services operating from the Smyrna Consulate.

One of Noel's assistants was Christo Gonatas, who had been the British Consul in Mytilene (Lesbos). After Mytilene was taken over Christo came to Smyrna, where he did a fine job working about fourteen hours a day for the Allied cause. Christo became a very close friend and I saw him frequently in Athens after the war. He was a great friend of Mr Kanellos, a fellow Mytilenean and probably the most famous manager of the Grande Bretagne Hotel in Athens. Christo spoke perfect English and had been to the Wye Agricultural College in Kent, because his family had owned huge estates on the Asia Minor coast opposite Mytilene. Unfortunately they were deprived of them all when the Turks defeated the Greeks in 1922, thereby making the Greeks evacuate the entire Asia Minor coast and some of the best agricultural land in the eastern Mediterranean.

This was followed by the dreadful massacre of the retreating Greeks in Smyrna, when Prince Andrew, who was a Greek General and the Duke of Edinburgh's father, was condemned to death with five other generals by General Plasteras. The Prince, unlike the other four generals, was fortunate in having his sentence commuted.

In the Consulate there was also the official Foreign Office staff under the Consul-General Mr Hole, and his assistant Mr Edwards. Then there was Mr Melioressi, the Greek consul, who was always considered to have very left-wing views and to be pro-Russian.

We also had a very splendid ex-Regular Major from the First World War, who had served with Lawrence of Arabia and spoke Turkish fluently. He was CTC Taylor (known as Cape-to-Cairo Taylor), and he had emigrated to Rhodesia with two thousand other regular officers who had been retired in the great cut-back in the 1920s. They had been encouraged to go there, with grants of land, and he had built up a very successful tobacco plantation. However, with the outbreak of war he had very gallantly offered his services, with particular reference to his knowledge of the Turkish language and of Turkey. He abandoned his large tobacco estates, and his gallant American wife managed them single-handedly, with great success, until the end of the war.

On the SOE front, we had David Pawson, who was ably assisted by Pamela Lovibond; so much so that he later married her, and they became resident in Athens where he was in charge of all Lord Cowdray's immense industrial undertakings. These consisted of all the buses, electricity power stations and Hellenic electric railways.

David had a number of able assistants including Con Webb. She was a very attractive girl and had been married to Captain Webb, a Palestine policeman whom I later met in Oflag 7B in Germany. He also had a number of Greeks with him, including an outstanding wireless operator called Harry.

176

Harry was to prove invaluable to us later on.

I believe Harry, like many of the SOE people, was very left wing and pro the communists who were to cause so much trouble in the coming Greek Civil War, when more people were killed than in the whole of the Italian-German war. The beastliness of the Greek Civil War is vividly told in the book *Eleni* by Nicholas Gage, and also in Lady Henderson's book *Xenia*.

Amongst the others working from the Consulate were Brian de Jongh, who was always known as de B. He worked for Noel and was liked by everybody; a most sympathetic character. His mother had a lovely house outside Athens but since the German occupation had come to live in Bouja – we had many happy parties both then and after the war, when de B was working for the British Council in Athens. Two other ex-patriates working from the Consulate were Christophoros and Diamandaras, both of whom were indefatiguable workers from Chios, which was immediately opposite our base at Khiosti. They handled a great many of the incoming refugees, the intelligence work and the administration of the port of Khiosti – all extremely efficiently. Christophoros also did practically all the briefing with me of the sea captains before each mission. I show a photograph of them at Khiosti with Billy Maclean.

10

Istanbul

I had to go to Istanbul fairly frequently and I would go up by sea from Smyrna – there was a very good Turkish passenger boat which sailed, I think, every day. It took about twenty-four hours and went along the lovely Asia Minor coast, passing between the islands of Chios, Mytilene and the Turkish island of Imbros, up through the Dardanelles into the Bosporus and thence to the wonderful harbour of Istanbul. It was very romantic and beautiful scenery which was invariably accompanied by glorious sunshine.

My visits to the Embassy in Istanbul were very busy as there was always a great deal of work for me to do; I also had a number of friends there.

I came immediately under Commander Wolfson who worked from the Embassy; he was a likeable man who was brilliant at his job. (He had had a rather bizarre early life, a little of which I knew about then, and the missing links of which were filled for me later by R.A. Butler. They were as follows:– After the White Army in Russia was defeated by Lenin's communist Red Army the British Navy was sent to Odessa to evacuate British personnel and others who were helping the White Russians. The Captain of one British cruiser had taken on the full complement, and was about to raise the gang-plank when a young Jewish boy, about ten years old, came running up to it. The sailors ordered him off, but the Captain saw what was going on from the bridge and told them to let him come on board.

From that moment on the Captain took complete care of him, taking him back to England with him and educating him. This included university, where he was at Cambridge with

R.A. Butler. Wolfson subsequently joined the Shell Oil Company and progressed well with them, serving in Palestine and Egypt. With the outbreak of war he joined the RNVR and, with his knowledge of Russian and other languages, soon got promoted to the rank of DNI Istanbul. There he remained until the end of the war, when he joined BOAC. He soon became Chairman of their Cyprus company and as a result was due to take R.A. Butler, who was then Foreign Secretary, on the first Comet flight to South Africa. At the last minute Butler was prevented from flying with him due to international complications. This turned out to be a life saver for Butler as the Comet crashed a few miles off Elba, killing everyone on board. It had disintegrated due to the then unknown metal fatigue).

Also working from the Embassy was Nicholas Elliott who was in MI6. He became famous years later when he narrowly missed bringing Philby back from Beirut, from where he defected to Russia. Nicholas was great fun and amused everyone who came into contact with him, and was the son of Claud Aurelius Elliott, late headmaster of Eton. He has just published a book about his life and Philby.

The chief of MI6 was Colonel Harold Lehrs Gibson, always known as Gibby, who was generally considered to be the most intelligent man in the Middle East on matters to do with intelligence. He contributed as much as anyone to final victory and it was he who was responsible for *Enigma* and *Ultra*. I saw a lot of Gibby, and stayed with him in Istanbul. Gibby spoke perfect Russian, having spent his early life in Russia, and was very much in love with a Romanian girl who had been a ballet dancer in Bucharest, whom he married after the war.

Working with Gibby was a very amusing and brilliant, but rather lazy, Irishman called Bernard O'Leary. He had a very dry sense of humour and was extremely erudite. Some months later, after our capture of Samos and Leros, Wolfson decided he would like to capture a small Greek island but was forbidden to do so by Nicholas Elliott for security reasons. When telling O'Leary of his plans to capture the island of Ios, O'Leary retorted, 'All you want to capture is kudos!' – which was probably nearer the mark.

Back in Smyrna things were revving up; I now had ships

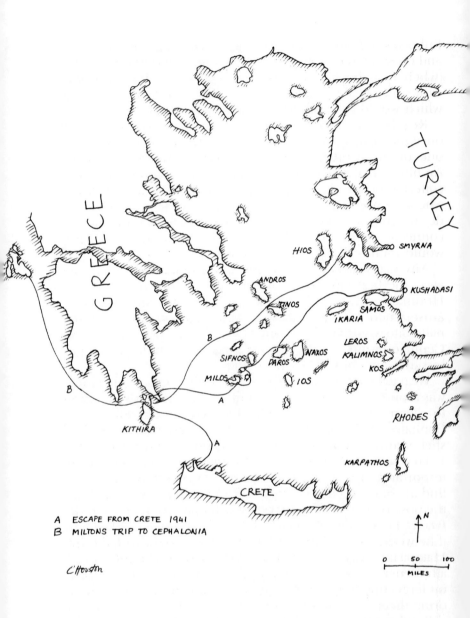

A   ESCAPE FROM CRETE 1941
B   MILTONS TRIP TO CEPHALONIA

C.Houston

going to the three main areas on the Greek mainland more or
less regularly once a week. These were the Peloponnesos,
Euboea and the Mount Athos peninsula. They all carried
forged German papers and they all had a rendezvous: the

180

Euboea ship at Kimi (this was the collecting point for Athens and central Greece), the Peloponnese one near Monemvassia (where I had been to on my escape from Crete) and the Mount Athos one at the southernmost monastery on the peninsula, which would cover all northern Greece and Salonika.

Regular arrivals amounted to several hundred a week, and once included the future Prime Minister Kanellopoulos and one of his cabinet ministers, Major Tselos and also the Archbishop of Athens. Numerous British personnel were also collected. They all landed at our little port of Khiosti, from where they were taken to the Consulate to be interviewed by de B who took down all the information they had in connection with enemy ships and troop movements etc. They would then be put on the train to Cairo.

Any really difficult missions I usually allocated to far and away the best of our Greek sea captains, Captain Miltiades Houmas, and his ship the *Evangelistria*. One such occasion arose when C-in-C Mediterranean Admiral Harwood signalled to us that they had lost the submarine *Perseus* off Cephalonia, and were most anxious to find out the cause of its loss and any information about it.

We had heard, through our network of informers, that there was reputed to be one able-bodied seaman who had managed to swim ashore when his submarine went down near Cephalonia. It was believed that the Greek islanders had sheltered him, and hidden him somewhere on the island.

That was all the information we had, but in view of the importance that Admiral Harwood attached to being able to find anyone who could give them information, coupled with the possibility that this rumoured seaman might be from the *Perseus*, I told the whole story to Captain Houmas. I asked him if he would be prepared to take his caique right round Cape Matapa and up to Cephalonia, a distance of some 400 miles – all in enemy waters – with a view to finding out through the underground population if this story was true, and if it was, to bring the seaman back to us.

Immediately he replied '*Malista! Oraia!* Of course I will!' – and proceeded to get his caique ready without further ado. We kitted him out with some false German papers in case he was stopped and inspected (which he was), and also gave him a cargo of potash, because potash was badly needed by the vineyards in Cephalonia and therefore seemed as good a cargo and excuse as anything else.

Off Milton went on the 20th May, thus beginning a most worrying and nerve-wracking time for us.

He sailed from Chiosti to Cape Malea and round Cape Matapa – heading for Argostoli, which was the main port of Cephalonia. When he was within about ten miles of his destination he saw a large convoy of Italian tankers and cargo ships sailing south towards him. Just as he was about to get near them he saw a squadron of British Beaufighters dive on them, bombing them with great effect, as a number of them were sunk. Milton was immediately requisitioned by one of the Italian Navy craft, and ordered to pick up as many survivors as he could, and to take them back to Argostoli, which he duly did.

Having deposited the Italian seamen he then had to go through the formality of having his papers stamped by the harbour-master, and after this he went ashore to enquire about the submariner.

After a day or two he had correctly located where he was being hidden, which was in a house a few miles from Argostoli. On reaching the house he was taken, in great secrecy, up a ladder stairway to the attic, whereupon he was introduced to Able-Seaman Capes by his host. Milton explained his reason for visiting him; namely to take him back to Turkey for the C-in-C Mediterranean, Alexandria, Admiral Harwood.

The immediate problem was that it was not safe to take him to where his caique was, to Argostoli, as that would immediately alert the Italians. The second problem was that, as Capes had been kept incommunicado in his attic bunk for sixteen months, hardly moving at all, he was unable to walk more than a very short distance. As Milton had planned to take him off from a small cove in the south east of the island, some twenty miles away (in order to solve problem number one) this in itself created a very great problem.

However, Milton, whose life consisted of solving problems, arranged for a donkey to be brought to the house at nightfall. Capes was then strapped to the donkey and taken to the cove, where he was greeted by Milton and the *Evangelistria*. Milton then proceeded to retrace the 400 miles back to Chiosti, where he arrived on the 8th June, mission completed, to a tumultuous congratulatory welcome, some three weeks after I had seen him off – and a congratulatory signal was sent to us all at MI9 Smyrna from the C-in-C, Admiral Harwood.

11

MI9 Smyrna

The Smyrna operations were the springboard of access to the islands and mainland of Greece, and were very important to the Greek Naval Intelligence side because it operated through our caiques. Captain (later Admiral) Alex Levides was in charge of this; he was one of the most unassuming, modest and yet heroic people that I met during the war. His department was on the same floor as mine, and I saw him daily for the next year; we often organised special missions together.

Working with me was Captain Dino Koumoundouros, a brilliant Greek barrister/lawyer. He was aged about thirty-five, and came from a famous Greek family – in fact, the small island lying just south of Athens is called Koumoundouros island. He had been on the Skopelos/Sciathos/Volos and Northern Sporades escape route to Smyrna, and brought out many people including a number of important government officials and politicians. He also brought out valuable information on enemy activities in Greece and the Balkans.

There was also Captain Cyril Cribb; he was in charge of a company of Royal Engineers, which included John Fermor Hesketh. They were frantically building up the Turkish aerodromes in the hope that the British and Turks would use them if, as Churchill had planned, Turkey came into the war on our side.

Cyril came under Major General Arnold, who was my ultimate superior officer in Turkey, and was the very likeable British Military Attaché in Turkey. He used to give wonderful parties on the *Marquop,* which was the Ambassador's yacht on the Bosporus, but sadly he had a tragic end and was found dead in his flat.

Occasionally the Ambassador, Sir Hughe Knatchbull-Hugessen, KCMG, of Cicero fame, came from Ankara, and I had the pleasure of meeting him at some of the parties that Cyril had organised on the *Marquop*.

In his earlier years as a diplomat Sir Hughe had been His Majesty's Minister in the Baltic States. After his only diplomatic secretary had been transferred to Moscow, and whilst reflecting on his hardship, he heard the *Quicunque Vult* in church, and wrote the following immediately afterwards. It was sent as a dispatch to the Foreign Office, and is said to have produced a secretary by the next boat.

QUINCUNQUE BALT (The Athanasian Creed)
Whosoever will be saved, before all things it is necessary that he hold the Baltic Post;

Which post except that a man keep for a few years, without doubt he shall go to Bogota or La Paz everlastingly.

For the Baltic Post is this, that we have one Minister in three capitals and three capitals in one Minister.

Everyone confounding his person and dividing his substance.

For there is one Minister for Lithuania, one Minister for Latvia and one Minister for Estonia;

But the Minister for Lithuania, for Latvia and for Estonia are all one; the uniform equally uncomfortable and the travelling almost eternal.

Such as Riga is, so is Tallinn and so is Kovno;

Riga remote, Tallinn remote, and Kovno remote;

But Kovno in particular is uncreate and incomprehensible.

As also Riga is a Legation, Tallinn is a Legation and Kovno is a Legation;

And yet they are not three Legations but one Legation.

So also Riga is expensive, Tallinn is expensive and Kovno is expensive;

And yet there are not three salaries but one salary.

For like as we are compelled by the Private Secretaries to say there is one Legation and one Minister; so we are forbidden by the Chief Clerk to say there are three salaries or three *frais de representation.*

So likewise there should be one Secretary for Riga, one Secretary for Tallinn and one Secretary for Kovno; and yet there are not three secretaries but no secretary.

No secretary, not by reduction of the Chancery work to nothing but by taking of the secretary away to Moscow.

Absolutely none, by confusion of the Private Secretaries and not by desire of the Minister.

The Minister is made and created but forgotten.

The Secretary is neither made nor created but proceeding to Moscow.

So there is one Minister, not three Ministers; one salary, not three salaries; no secretary, not even one secretary.

And in this Legation none is afore or after the other, although a good many people seem to be continually after the Minister.

The whole thing is most unequal and incomprehensible.

He therefore that would be saved might sometimes think of H.M. Minister in Riga.

Such is the Baltic Post, although any reasonable soul would find it hard to believe faithfully.

Colonel Simonds came up from Cairo to meet me in Istanbul and together we planned the major build up of the MI9 activities and the caique fleet.

It was decided that I should not command any more missions to the mainland and islands of Greece, for reasons of security in the event of capture, so for the next few months I gradually increased the number of missions to two or three a week. This went on successfully on a regular basis, and I had to make several trips down to Cairo, going by sea with Captain Milton in the *Sentosa,* a Norwegian pilot boat that I had taken over. These were fascinating trips, going right along the

Anatolian coast sometimes to Cyprus and sometimes right on to Beirut.

Sometimes I had to go to Alexandria, where I saw a lot of Colonel Humphrey Quill, CBE, DSO, MVO, Royal Marines, the exceptionally able DNI. Humphrey was ADC to the King and perhaps the greatest expert on clocks and chronometers. He wrote a classic book entitled 'John Harrison, The Man Who Discovered Longitude', and was a Fellow of the British Horological Institute. Humphrey said he was anxious to have photographs of all the bays suitable for anchoring and hiding craft on the Turkish coast between Cyprus and Bodrum. So, with my Zeiss-Ikon Mk111 camera, and Milton at the helm of the *Sentosa*, we set off, going down the whole length of the coast and taking some three hundred photographs.

It was a fascinating coastline with numerous bays, many of which had narrow entrances leading into deep indentations like the Norwegian fjords, with cliffs either side rising sheer up to 1,000 feet. Each one of these secluded bays was absolutely still and completely silent, with no sign of any human activity whatsoever.

As we proceeded past Rhodes, before heading north to Bodrum and Smyrna, I listened, fascinated, to my small portable radio. The account of Montgomery's great offensive at Alamein had just begun. As the crow flies this huge battle was taking place only two hundred miles south of us in the *Sentosa*. It gave me the greatest thrill, and I knew then that it would not be so very long before similar preparations would be made for the ultimate attack and capture of the vital island of Rhodes, only a mile or two from where I was.

When I returned to Smyrna I was told by General Arnold that I had been promoted to Major, and had been given an immediate award of the Military Cross. (Due to pressure of work I never went to Buckingham Palace to be presented with it by King George VI, nor, indeed, until I came to write this book forty-five years later, did I ever ask what the citation said.)*

Back in Smyrna I was, as usual, extremely fortunate with my numerous friends amongst the European community. When

---

* See Citation in the Appendix.

I needed something more permanent than impinging on the hospitality of Noel and Alice Rees I was lent the superb 'J' class yacht, the *Cambria* – renamed the *Lilias,* which had been built for Lord Camrose to race in the Americas' Cup. She came fully equipped with one of the best cooks in the Mediterranean, called Dhoxie, and a living-in sailor/steward. All this was generously lent to me by Bill Giraud and his father Harry Giraud, who owned the yacht.

From here we continued very active operations, increasing our caique fleet and making certain that all the single cylinder Bolinden and Skoda engines were in 100 per cent working order as so many lives, and so much, depended on their reliability.

It was about now that the Allied advance and initiative was becoming a factor on the Western Desert, and, later, in North Africa. GHQ Cairo had general plans to capture Rhodes, which would open up the sea route to Smyrna and Istanbul so that we could use the shortest route to supply Russia. At the moment there was the choice of either the immensely difficult supply route going right up through Persia, or the even more costly and hazardous sea route to Murmansk being convoyed, at great risk, by the Navy, in which my brother Godfrey was, with the Fleet Air Arm.

I formed a plan to seize the almost uninhabited island of Denousa, where the German battleship the *Emden* had hidden and operated from in the First World War, during the Dardanelles and Gallipoli campaign. I was therefore called down to Cairo to outline it, and it was accepted by the G.Ops' committee, under Admiral Maud, at a meeting where Brigadier Hackett (later General Sir John Hackett), Captain (later Full Admiral) Couchman RN and others were present.

The plan was that I should take a party of about thirty commando-type personnel on my own caiques and occupy Denousa unobserved. We were to have ample machine guns, anti-tank guns and enough supplies to last for several months. Our job was to be in a position to observe, and lie across, the main German air and sea supply routes from Athens and Piraeus to Crete and Rhodes etc.; to report by radio all movements by sea and air and to hold the island against any attack. This should have been possible because there were no beaches, only cliffs rising steeply from the sea, thus favouring the defenders of Denousa rather than the attackers.

I spent about three weeks in Cairo preparing for this; it was timed to take place well in advance of the projected attack and seizure of Rhodes by Force 100, which was rigorously training in Cyprus for this ambitious operation.

At this time, on the overall war front, the Germans were still massively successful. They had conquered the whole of Europe and were making enormous advances against the Russians. The occupation of Denousa would have been, although infinitesimal, the first recapture of any land in the whole continent of Europe. The timing for the capture of Rhodes was dependent on the speed of Montgomery's 8th Army advance along the coast of Cyrenaica and the Western Desert, and then linking up with the 1st Army, under General Anderson. The 1st Army was getting established in Algiers and was going to move east, join Montgomery and then jointly capture Tunis.

The Germans, however, put up tremendous resistance, and a very costly and bloody campaign ensued, postponing the attack on Rhodes. This was then put on the back-burner, and my Denousa plan likewise, so I resumed my Smyrna operations as before, continuing to live on the *Lilias* which was moored on the Smyrna waterfront.

On one of my many visits to Istanbul, I went out with Billy Maclean and several other young people on a boat trip from the Istanbul yacht club. It was a beautiful sunny day on the Bosporus and on the boat was the lovely Ninette Sgourdeos; until then I had been both heart-free and carefree, but from then on I was gone for a six.

I returned to Smyrna, having done my official duties with Commander Wolfson and others in Istanbul, to find my life completely altered. I could not get Ninette's image out of my mind even if I had wanted to, which I did not. In the next few days I sent Hassan, my excellent servant, by sea to deliver a huge bouquet of flowers to Ninette at her home in Istanbul. She lived with her mother in a small and quite charming house, rather like a Chelsea mews house. Her father had died about three years previously, and had been a much respected and famous surgeon. He was described to me by their great family friend John Mavrodi, *The Times* correspondent in

Istanbul, as the only complete man he had ever known. Ninette's mother's family were the Eliaskos, a very old Greek family who owned the prestigious Bank of Athens, of which her brother had been Chairman.

Ninette had two sisters and one brother. Her eldest sister Dora was married to the Swiss Ambassador to Cairo, Mr Brunner, and they kept a major establishment with a lot of entertaining. They had one son who is now in charge of the Swiss Foreign Office, Chef de Protocol and the Swiss Ambassador to the United States.

Her second sister, Vivi, had been married to a Swede but was now divorced and worked as a journalist for a Swiss newspaper. Because of her Swedish passport Vivi had the entrée to all the Germans, including Von Papen, the German Ambassador. As regards intelligence she was second to none. Vivi became a great ally of mine and it was she who told me that Ninette had fallen in love with me. Ninette's brother, Alexander, was rather shy but a very kind person who went on to be the Greek Ambassador in Moscow and the Consul General in London.

The good Hassan returned to Smyrna with a brief note of thanks from Ninette and the message that she would be happy to see me when I was next in Istanbul. I saw to it that that was fairly soon. I stayed at the Park Hotel and had several romantic days with her in that beautiful city overlooking the Bosporus.

Before returning to Smyrna I made arrangements for her to come down and stay with Noel and Alice Rees at Bouja. It must have been there that I proposed to her in the garden, and after some procrastination I was provisionally accepted. In due course I went to see her mother and uncle, who, happily for me, accepted me as a future son-in-law – quite an important hurdle to overcome in Greek families. A date was set for the wedding, which was to be first in the main Greek Orthodox Cathedral in Istanbul, and then followed, in early May, by a ceremony at the British Consulate in Smyrna.

I returned to Smyrna to find many activities hotting up and a coded signal from Colonel Simonds in Cairo. This said that Colonel Frank Macaskie, who had been working for MI9, had been captured with Captain Alexis Ladas by the Italians on a small Greek island. They had been taken to Samos and put in

This is the original photo of our escape to Turkey from Crete. *Left to right, back row:* Hildyard, Murcot, Lambris; *front row:* Emery, Vernicos, Parish. 9th September, 1941.

Michael Woodbine Parish and Vernicos in Alexandria,
Egypt, just before sailing for The Aegean.

The Italians and their new-found allies. *Left to right:* Rear Admiral Maschera, the Italian Governor; Brigadier Brittorous; Commander Borgh, the Italian Chief of Staff; Brigadier Turnbull; Lieutenant Colonel Li Volsi, the Commander of the Italian Infantry Units. *Back row, centre:* Major Jellicoe, SBS and Captain E.H.B. Baker RN, Senior Naval Officer. Admiral Maschera, who joined us with his Leros command at 0200 hrs on 12th September 1943 was executed by firing squad in May 1944 for his heroic action of joining Churchill and Britain.

The author's MI9 caiques at Khiosti, Egrilar, Turkey.

Agia Irene and Ali Bey in Kushadasi after we had given her to him, after our escape in 1941. The boat is still in service after 50 years, having had an engine installed. Ali Bey was the Kaiburkum of Kushadasi, Turkey.

Colonel Simonds and the author in Istanbul, 1942, for MI9 Planning.

Ninette, 1942.

Antiparos, the place where Commander Vernicos was captured – also the Atkinson Party. Despotico is on the left.

Michael Woodbine Parish and Milton on board the
Sentosa on an MI9 mission in 1942.

Capt. Miltiades Houmas with Michael Woodbine Parish
and Kostas Demetrakis from Mytilene with the
Evangelistria in the background, 1942.

Capt. Dino Koumoundouros with Capt. Miltiades Houmas and Christophoros Confer on plans for an expedition to Cephalonia on behalf of Admiral Harwood to collect Able Seaman Capes, 1942.

Major Michael Woodbine Parish and Ninette at their
wedding in Istanbul, May 1943.

Ninette.

The *Lillias*, my home for the first months of my marriage
to Ninette.

Michael Woodbine Parish and Ninette, 1943. Just weeks before I was captured and we were not to see each other again for nearly 50 years.

British officers take over Samos and Leros, 12 September 1943. *Left to right:* Capt. Levides, Col. Pawson, Major M W Parish with Greek Antarries Zaines, the first allied officers to capture these islands.

Cmdr Wolfson, Mrs Arnold, Zoë Rees, Arthur Whitall,
Mrs Giraud and Gen. Arnold at the wedding of Ninette to
the author in Istanbul, May 1943.

Staying with Colonel Harold Lehrs
Gibson in Istanbul on his birthday in
1942. Before the War he was the
MI6 Resident in Prague he obtained
Enigma and Ultra whose success
almost certainly enabled the allies
to win the War.

Colonel Frank Macaskie and Cmdr. Vernicos outside the death cell, Calithea prison. The door behind is for the cells of the dangerous. This photo was smuggled out of Calithea prison by Cmdr. Vernicos whilst he was there under sentence of death, and he wrote the above on the back of the photo.

Cmdr Vernicos after release from Italian prison. The inscription on the back of the photograph reads – To my only Pal. E Vernicos, just after Italy, 1946.

Syros houses on the waterfront. A German naval captain shot at an old lady looking out from a top verandah on the night that the author arrived there as a prisoner, 19 September 1943.

Mary Churchill, 1944

Michael Woodbine Parish sailing with Cmdr Vernicos, 1946.

This plane is believed to be the Corsair which Lt. Cmdr G W Parish flew from Puttnam in Ceylon to Yeovil, UK, over 5,000 miles. 1945. It is in the Fleet Air Arm Museum in Yeovil.

Michael Woodbine Parish and Billa in Grindlewald. They
intended to get married. 1947.

Billa in Grindlewald when she was unofficially engaged
to the author.

an extremely rugged concrete cell where he was frequently badly beaten up by his captors, pending being shipped to Calithea prison and condemned to death, to be shot as a spy.

The signal also said that a large Italian vessel was going to take Macaskie and others, plus the normal complement of soldiers going on leave etc. to Athens. Admiral Harwood had instructed a British submarine commander to be present outside the main Samos harbour of Vathy and to torpedo the vessel about half a mile outside the harbour, as it was heading west to Athens. My instructions were to take my best caique, the *Evangelistria,* and patrol up and down the Vathy strait so as to be able to rush to the stricken boat and rescue Frank Macaskie and his colleagues when they were in the water. This was all quite feasible and I was confident that it could be achieved successfully.

We patrolled in glorious weather and a moderate sea for the two days in which the attack was due to take place. We saw the ship pull out of Vathy harbour and gradually steam to the west heading for Piraeus, but unfortunately no attack took place, and so, deeply disappointed, we returned to our base at Khiosti. On returning to my office in the Consulate I was met by another signal from Colonel Simonds regretting that the Admiralty had, at the last minute, been forced to cancel the attack. This was because the submarine in question was needed in an offensive against a major convoy of ships carrying oil and supplies for Rommel to the Benghazi harbour for his Western Desert offensive.

The next I heard of poor Frank Macaskie was when my great friend and colleague, Commander Emmanuele Vernicos, smuggled out a photograph of himself and Frank with their Italian guards in the death cell block of Calithea prison.

I later heard that Emmanuele's father had organised a petition. This was signed by several thousand people and pleaded for the death sentence to be commuted to life imprisonment. Archbishop Damaskinos, who was magnificent throughout the occupation, sponsored this petition which fortunately was granted – neither Vernicos, Macaskie nor Ladas were shot, although probably a considerable amount of gold had to be provided as blood money to help bring this about.

191

Still very much in love, I saw a lot of Ninette in Smyrna and Istanbul, but some three weeks before the wedding I did not feel completely certain that this was the real thing, or that I was overwhelmingly in love with her. To my shame, I may have expressed some doubts to her, which caused her the greatest sadness, probably largely due to the loss of face as all the wedding invitations had been sent out. However, it was only a fleeting doubt, something which, I presume, happens to many people as the date of this all-important event approaches.

In my case I think this was particularly so, as since January 1st 1935 I had spent six out of those eight years abroad, away from my family, and the last four years had been totally absorbed by the winning of the war. No member of my family was within two thousand miles and I was enormously fond of and close to my father and his presence would have been very, very welcome.

As it was, I received a cable from my father just before the wedding, informing me that my brother Charles had been killed, on his fifty-fourth bombing mission. Shortly after this my father wrote a beautiful memorial to him, which in the Appendix I have used to give my own account of his death.

As our wedding day approached I completely overcame any doubts and was very much in love with Ninette, who, to me, seemed more beautiful as the days went by. We were married on April 29th 1943, followed by a reception at the Park Hotel. Afterwards we had a wonderful dinner at Uncle Nico's house at Heybeli Ada – a Wilton Crescent type house – where there were, apart from Ninette's family, Noel and Alice Rees and their daughter Zoe, who was our bridesmaid, Bill and Gwen Giraud, General and Mrs Arnold and Commander Wolfson.

We spent the first two nights in Ninette's mother's lovely house on the Prince's island in the Bosporus, at Halki, near Prinkipo – a more romantic and attractive place would be hard to find.

After two days at Halki we went to what was to me at that time the fantastic Chefket Palace Hotel at Brusa, overlooking the Bosporus. It was built on hot sulphur springs, and one could have either a hot sulphur bath or a fresh water bath in the bathroom whenever one wanted, as there was constant hot water at an ideal temperature. Having spent a week at Brusa, we then went down by sea to Smyrna and took up residence on the *Lilias*. This was absolutely ideal because she had one state cabin with bathroom attached, and two or three other beautifully fitted out cabins, so that we were able to have some of our friends to stay.

Ninette got settled in and I continued with my MI9 operations, which were becoming considerably more active as the war was hotting up in the Middle East theatre. I note that I recorded in my diary in early June 1943 that 'I expect the Germans to attack Turkey within the next few weeks.'

Life went on, and for me it was a period of great happiness. However, in retrospect I can see that, having spent all day and every day working in the Consulate, I may then have spent too much time taking Ninette out to parties in the evenings, and not spending enough time on our own. I am sure she would have preferred the latter, particularly as our time together, although we were then quite unaware of it, was rapidly running out.

12

Samos and Leros

In these months of July and August I was constantly aware of the vital necessity of capturing the string of islands beginning with the northern-most island of Samos, followed by Leros, Cos, and finally Rhodes.

In 1940, when General Sir James Marshall-Cornwall (who in later years became a great personal friend of mine) had been sent to Turkey by Mr Churchill to endeavour to get President Inonu to enter the war on our side he also asked him to grant us the use of Turkish airfields so that the Ploesti oil fields in Romania could be bombed to destruction. A large part of the German war machine and industry was wholly dependent on Romanian oil, particularly as Marshal of the Royal Air Force Sir Arthur Harris (Bomber Harris) was rapidly knocking out the huge synthetic plants at Geldsechurchen and other areas. These two operations could, on their own, gradually strangle the German war effort.

Inonu, apart from being a statesman/politician, had been a brilliant General with Kemal Ataturk, and he told Marshall-Cornwall that it would be useless for Turkey to come into the war until the sea route to Smyrna and Istanbul was assured, and this could not be done without the capture of Rhodes, Cos, Leros and Samos.

Not only would the capture of these strategetically vital islands bring the above immense advantages, they would hugely facilitate the supplying of Russia with raw materials, thus providing an easy, short and safe route to Odessa. Lastly, the possibility – in fact the probability – of winning the trump card of getting Turkey, with her forty-five mobilised divisions to join us in the war, would enable the Allies to mount their

Second Front. This was not the hugely expensive (in men and materials) one across the channel and into France but, as Churchill so rightly planned in his Dardanelles campaign in 1917, up along the Danube through Romania and the Balkans, via Vienna to Munich and the heart of Germany. The following letter from Churchill to Anthony Eden clearly shows this plan:

'Prime Minister to Mr Eden (Moscow)   20th Oct. 1943

Our present plans for 1944 seem open to very grave defects. We are to put fifteen American and twelve British divisions into France in May, and will have about six American and sixteen British or British-controlled divisions on the Italian front. Unless there is a German collapse, Hitler, lying in the centre of the best communications in the world, can concentrate at least forty to fifty divisions against either of these forces while holding the other. He could obtain all the necessary forces by cutting his losses in the Balkans and withdrawing to the Save and the Danube without necessarily weakening his Russian front. This is one of the most elmentary war propositions. The disposition of our forces between the Italian and the Channel theatre has not been settled by strategic needs, but by the march of events, by shipping possibilities, and by arbitrary compromises between the British and Americans. Neither the force built up in Italy nor that which will be ready in May to cross the Channel is adequate for what is required, and only transferences of the order of seven or eight divisions can physically be made between them. I am determined that this situation shall be reviewed.

2. If it lay with me to decide, I would not withdraw any troops from the Mediterranean and would not debouch from the narrow leg of Italy into the valley of the Po, and would engage the enemy strongly on the narrower front while at the same time fomenting Balkan and Southern France disturbances. In the absence of a German collapse, I do not think we

should cross the Channel with less than forty divisions available by the sixtieth day, and then only if the Italian front were in strong action with the enemy. I do not accept the American argument that our metropolitan Air Forces can flatten everything out in the battle zone or on its approaches. This has not been our present experience. All this is for your internal consumption, and not for deployment at this stage. It may show you, however, the dangers of our being committed to a lawyer's bargain for *Overlord* in May, for the sake of which we may have to ruin the Italian front and Balkan possibilities and yet have insufficient forces to maintain ourselves after the thirtieth or fortieth day.

3. You should try to find out what the Russians really feel about the Balkans. Would they be attracted by the idea of our acting through the Aegean, involving Turkey in the war, and opening the Dardanelles and Bosporus so that British naval forces and shipping could aid the Russian advance and so that we could ultimately give them our right hand along the Danube? How great an interest would they feel in our opening the Black Sea to Allied warships, supplies and Allied military forces, including Turkish? Have they any interest in this right-handed evolution, or are they still set only on our attacking France? – observing that of course in any circumstances the steady building up of forces in England will hold large German forces in the west. It may be that for political reasons the Russians would not want us to develop a large-scale Balkan strategy. On the other hand, their desire that Turkey should enter the war shows their interest in the south-eastern theatre.

4. I remain convinced of the great importance of our getting a foothold in the Aegean by taking Rhodes, re-taking Cos, and holding Leros, and building up an effective air and naval superiority in these waters. Do the Russians view with sympathy our effort to hold Leros and desire to take Rhodes? Do they understand the effect this has upon Turkey,

and how it opens the possibility of a naval advance into the Black Sea? Again, all the above is simply for your inner thoughts.' (Taken from Winston S. Churchill, *Closing the ring, Volume V, The Second World War.*)

This campaign would have had every military advantage on our side as, in the initial stages, Hitler, who was fighting a gigantic battle stretching from Stalingrad to Leningrad, using upwards of 180 divisions, was stretched to the very limit in his lines of communication. To have had to support another major front one thousand miles south east along primitive roads and railways would have been virtually impossible, as he would still have to keep fifty divisions manning his Atlantic wall to guard his western front from a seaborne invasion. (I knew this area well, as a result of my motorcycle trip from London to the Romanian Black Sea coast in 1937.)

In July 1943 the Allies had begun an attack on Sicily and were beginning one on the heel of Italy. If they were allowed to rest there – as Churchill wished – this, whilst continually keeping up the pressure, would yet again have stretched Hitler's resources, and was infinitely preferable to the terribly costly and strategically absurd long hard slog up the whole length of Italy, every inch of which was favourable to the German forces in its steady withdrawal action. Nor was it likely, as events have proved, to enable the Allies to break through the German final defensive line in the mountainous country south of the Austrian border, where they would have been confronted by Hannibal's Alps.

This Italian campaign, fighting the whole way up six hundred miles of difficult territory, with no carrot at the end of it, was one of the great strategic follies of the last war, and made no comparison with a potential thrust of ninety divisions through the flat country of Romania and Hungary, up the Danube right to the walls of Berlin, which was Churchill's earnest desire from 1917 to the time I am writing about, 1943.

On the advance north-west the additional bonus would be to capture the Ploesti oil fields, Hitler's only natural oil supplies, and deprive Hitler of Europe's bread basket which stretched for a thousand miles from the eastern Ukraine, through Romania and to the plains of Hungary.

The third supreme advantage was that we would have been able to reach Germany and Poland first – before the Russians.

We would thus have been able to fulfil our commitment of support and liberation for the Poles, for which reason we went to war.

I am not saying that we would have advanced on Germany quicker or better than the Russians to our north, but without the least doubt, when it became clear to the German High Command (The Wehrmacht) that their war could not possibly be won, the top Generals, to a man, would have decided to hold the Russians on their north-eastern front, as the last thing in the world they wanted was to be occupied by Stalin's Red Army. They would therefore have allowed, if not welcomed, an Allied army progressing up the Danube to enter and occupy Germany, whilst holding the Russians on their eastern front.

The key to all this was the planned capture of Samos, Leros, Cos and Rhodes.

Hitler could have won the war had he not wasted six vital weeks in attacking Crete in May 1941, thus delaying his gigantic attack, called Barbarossa, against the Russians. Although his troops did brilliantly, reaching the banks of the Volga and coming within three miles of Moscow, those missing six weeks brought the German armies to a standstill as the unexpectedly early and terrible Russian winter closed in on them. Also against them was the fact that they were without their only élite paratroop division and the 300 planes that Student lost in Crete.

Unprepared for such conditions, many of the soldiers, still in their Afrika Corps desert uniforms, suffered untold hardships. That was the moment when Hitler lost the war; six weeks earlier, before the winter had set in, would have enabled him to give the *coup de grace* to Stalin and his Red Army. This is abundantly clear from Stalin's letter of 4th September 1941, as follows:

'Premier Stalin to Prime Minister Churchill': A Personal Message from Stalin to Churchill dated 4th September 1941.

'I express thanks for promise to sell to Soviet Union a further 200 fighters in addition to the 200 previously promised. I do not doubt that the Soviet aviators will succeed in mastering them and putting them to use. I have however to say that these aeroplanes, which apparently cannot be put into use quickly and at once, but at different periods and in separate groups, will be incapable of effecting serious changes on the Eastern Front. They will be unable to effect serious changes not only because of the large scale on which the war is being waged, which necessitates the continuous supply of a large quantity of aeroplanes, but chiefly because the situation of the Soviet forces during the last three weeks has considerably deteriorated in such important areas as the Ukraine and Leningrad.

As a matter of fact, the relative stabilisation at the Front which we succeeded in achieving about three weeks ago has broken down during the last week, owing to transfer to Eastern Front of thirty to thirty-four fresh German infantry divisions and of an enormous quantity of tanks and aircraft, as well as a large increase in activities of the twenty Finnish and twenty-six Romanian divisions. Germans consider danger in the west a bluff, and are transferring all their forces to the east with impunity, being convinced that no Second Front exists in the west, and that none will exist. Germans consider it quite possible to smash their enemies singly: first Russia, then the English.

As a result we have lost more than one half of the Ukraine, and in addition the enemy is at the gates of Leningrad.

These circumstances have resulted in our losing Krivoirog iron ore basin and a number of metallurgical works in the Ukraine; we have evacuated one aluminium works on Dnieper River and a further aluminium works at Tikvan, one motor and two aircraft works in the Ukraine, two motor and two aircraft works at Leningrad; and these works cannot be put into operation in the new localities in less than seven to eight months. This has weakened our power of defence and faced the Soviet Union with a mortal menace. The question arises how to emerge from this more than unfavourable situation.

I think there is only one means of egress from this situation – to establish in the present year a Second Front somewhere in the Balkans or France, capable of drawing away from the Eastern Front thirty to forty divisions, and at the same time of ensuring to the Soviet Union 30,000 tons of aluminium by the beginning of October next and a monthly minimum of aid amounting to 400 aircraft and 500 tanks (of small or medium size). Without these two forms of help the Soviet Union will either suffer defeat or be weakened to such an extent that it will lose for a long period any capacity to render assistance to its Allies by its actual operations on the fronts of the struggle against Hitlerism.

I realise that this present message will cause dismay to your Excellency. But what is one to do? Experience has taught me to look facts in the face however unpleasant they are, and not to fear to express the truth however unwelcome it may be. The Persian affair has in fact turned out pretty well. The joint operations of the British and Soviet forces predetermined the issue. So it will be in the future as long as our forces act jointly. But Persia is but an episode; the issue of the war will not of course be decided in Persia.

The Soviet Union, like England, does not desire war with Japan, the Soviet Union does not consider it possible to violate agreements, including its treaty of neutrality with Japan. But if Japan violates the agreement and attacks the Soviet Union she will meet with a due rebuff on the part of the Soviet forces.

Finally, allow me to express thanks for the admiration you have expressed at the actions of the Soviet forces, which are waging a bloody war with the robber hordes of Hitlerite bandits for our

common cause of liberation'.
(Extract from *The Second World War* by Winston Churchill, p405 Vol III).

Other than Garrison troops he would have been free to move his two hundred divisions from the Russian front to wherever the Wehrmacht decided: very possibly through Turkey, where Von Papen was waiting to help him, down through Syria and Palestine to seize Egypt and the Suez Canal and thus seal off the whole of the Mediterranean and our route to India. From there on to Iraq and Persia and unlimited oil, where Rashid Ali was already waiting to welcome them. Persia would have fallen like a ripe peach into Hitler's lap.

Fortunately, thanks to General Student's attractive personality and persuasion, he allowed his better judgment to accept a quite unnecessary diversion. This was to attack Crete with his only airborne paratroop division, the absolute élite of the whole German armed forces which included Max Schmelling, the world heavyweight boxing champion. Within forty-eight hours the New Zealanders, British and Cretan farmers had wiped out half the entire ten thousand paratroops.

It was here that Captain Upham VC, holder of two VCs, was awarded his first, and were it not for the incredible bungle of the later stages of the Battle of Crete they would have captured the entire paratroop division, together with all the forces and equipment that General Student had committed to the island of Crete.

We had Hitler and Germany trapped in his fortress Europe with no escape. He was being subjected to appalling damage by Marshal of the Royal Air Force Sir Arthur Harris's Bomber Command. He could inflict harm on to Britain with his V1s and V2s, but he was trapped, and given a four month build up after the capture of Rhodes, Leros and Samos in September 1943 for our forces to sweep up from Turkey in Europe and north eastern Greece Macedonia he would have been trapped and strangled.

The Germans were at the very end of their lines of communication, desperately short of shipping and aircraft to take early reinforcements to Rhodes – they virtually did not exist, apart from Greek caiques and the like.

It was at this moment when the German High Command in Berlin told the Führer that they must abandon Crete and the other islands, thus saving their forces on these islands and on the mainland from being cut off and lost on a forthcoming withdrawal.

Hitler utterly forbade any such move, stating that it would have a catastrophic psychological effect on Germany's allies in south east Europe, and more particularly, the reaction on Turkey could prove one of the greatest danger. He therefore ordered General Helperman, his senior officer in Rhodes, to stand fast and hold the island. This was a virtually impossible task, as he was outnumbered by a ratio of six to one without counting any air or land forces likely to be sent by General Wilson.

Hitler had sent Helperman to Rhodes a few weeks previously in anticipation of an Italian collapse.

The only two people on either side to appreciate the vital importance of Rhodes were Hitler and Churchill.

At the same time that Hitler was ordering Helperman to hold Rhodes, Churchill was writing his brilliant far-seeing letter to General Ismay (whom he had ordered, on December 2nd 1940, to have models made of Leros and Rhodes, and on January 21st 1941 he had told the government to prepare to capture the eastern islands, particularly Rhodes) for COS Committee – which would have been in General Wilson's hands the same day – August 2nd 1943.

In the letter Churchill ordered Wilson to be ready to land on Rhodes immediately the Italian Armistice was signed, and, with the help of the Italians, seize control of Rhodes.

'Prime Minister to General Ismay, for COS Committee, 2 August 1943. Here is a business of great consequence, to be thrust forward by every means. Should the Italian troops in Crete and Rhodes resist the Germans and a deadlock ensue, we must help the Italians at the earliest moment, engaging thereby also the support of the populations. (And the Italian troops DID resist.)

2. The Middle East should be informed today that all supplies to Turkey may be stopped for the emergency, and that they should prepare

expeditionary forces, not necessarily in divisional formations, to profit by the chances that may offer.

3. This is no time for conventional establishments, but rather for using whatever fighting elements there are. Can anything be done to find at least a modicum of assault shipping without compromising the main operation against Italy? It does not follow that troops can only be landed from armoured landing craft. Provided they are to be helped by friends on shore, a different situation arises. Surely caiques and ships' boats can be used between ship and shore?

I hope the Staffs will be able to stimulate action, which may gain immense prizes at little cost, though not at little risk.'

Helperman did not fail Hitler, but Wilson was unfortunately to fail Churchill, thus creating for Churchill 'THE SHARPEST PANGS I SUFFERED IN THE WAR.'

13

BBC announces Capitulation

Returning to my own life and work, it was about now that Harry Giraud wanted the *Lilias* to be moved into dry dock for her annual overhaul, and I had to hastily find other accommodation in Smyrna. This was not easy, but I managed to find a rather squalid bed-sitting room that was within easy reach of my office in the Consulate. Ninette and I moved in, and spent the next few weeks in these very disagreeable quarters.

Ninette had virtually no family or friends of her own in Smyrna, as they were all either in Istanbul or with her sister in Cairo. The following month, with me being frantically busy, out all day and not paying enough attention nor giving enough love to my young bride must have been a sad period of unfulfilled expectations for her. A further disturbing factor for both of us was that there was a certain amount of hostility between the different departments in the Consulate. I was not party to either side – getting on extremely well with everyone in the Consulate and keeping my MI9 department entirely outside inter-party hostility, but it made social life much more difficult for Ninette.

This was the position when I was sitting in my office at about 8 o'clock in the evening of September 8th 1943, listening to the news from Britain. Suddenly, to my astonishment and thrill I heard the momentous news that, since Mussolini had been deposed, Marshal Badoglio had signed a Peace Treaty with the Allies.

Its immense significance for the Rhodes, Leros, Samos area hit me like a flash of lightning.

Having spent the last two years in this vital area I knew it like the back of my hand, and was fully aware of the great importance attached to the capture of Rhodes – a full scale invasion of which, I knew, had been planned and rehearsed for months by the assault force in Cyprus.

I had been with the G. Ops in Cairo and had had my Denousa plan, with Rhodes in mind, accepted. I knew our Royal Engineers (with John Hesketh and Cyril Cribb) in civilian clothes (mufti) were feverishly preparing the Turkish aerodromes in readiness for the RAF, and I knew several of their officers. I had not forgotten that President Inonu had told General Marshall-Cornwall that it would be useless for Turkey, with her forty-five fresh divisions, to come into the war until their sea route to Smyrna and Istanbul was assured – which could not be done without the capture of Rhodes, Cos, Leros and Samos. Therefore the capture of Rhodes alone would probably not be enough to push Turkey over the brink and into the war on our side.

What was needed was the grand slam – in other words, all four islands.

Even with the successful capture of Rhodes the Germans could, and would, with air cover from Athens, make the immensely fortified naval base of Leros virtually impregnable – even more so than, for instance, our Malta. I knew that HQ Cairo and London had no immediate plans to follow up the capture of Rhodes with storming Leros and Samos, although Rhodes itself would amount to a vitally important territorial gain and would also advance our striking power by 300 miles.

In a flash this incredible chance presented itself to me; not in a dream but as a million to one opportunity of changing the whole course of the war, and with it the certainty of bringing victory and all its consequences, the saving of millions of lives and untold trillions in devastation and destruction.

INSTANT ACTION

I did not waste a minute, knowing that the Germans, whose High Command was just across the water from where I was, would be thinking likewise, and unless we went immediately they would get there first, which they would very likely do in any case.

To my eternal discredit – without a word to Ninette – I raced round to my closest friend and colleague, Captain Alex Levides RHN, and said, 'We must go NOW and take over Samos and Leros before the Germans do.' Alex, as usual, was superb, and rose to the occasion saying, 'Yes, we must form a mission of three and get David Pawson to be the third member,' whereupon, at break-neck speed we dashed round to David who immediately agreed to join us in the mission to the Italian C-in-C Aegean based on Samos.

It was a journey of some sixty miles from Smyrna, and the only way we could do it was to go in my best caique and with my best captain, namely Captain Miltiades Houmas.

We decided then and there that we should immediately proceed, unauthorised, to Samos, to take over all the islands down to, but excluding, Rhodes – as I knew a major offensive was already being mounted to capture Rhodes.

My position was very different to that of the other two, firstly because I had my bride of four months with me (neither of the other two had their wives in Turkey); secondly because I was under orders (the same orders that the late Airey Neave operated under in London when he was my exact contemporary in MI9) not to do any operations in enemy territory in view of the security risk related to being captured and, thirdly, time being the essence of the operation it was impossible to get a clearance from Colonel Simonds at GHQ Cairo, or from General Arnold in Ankara. It was also highly unlikely that they would have agreed; therefore the only answer was 'the telescope to my blind right eye'.

I was certain that the ponderous General Wilson and GHQ Mid-East 600 miles away would do nothing in time to save the islands from the Germans even if they did move at all, which they did not, even though this was Churchill's wish.

Against this I knew that I was the only person who had a fleet of caiques with the ability to go and land anywhere in Greece or the islands, especially as I had the best captain of them all, Captain Milton, whose birthplace and home was in Samos.

For the next six hours I had my own personal terrible mental anguish which I shall never forget – in Biblical terms my Garden of Gethsemane. If the mission was a flop I had every reason to expect to be court martialled, in view of my standing order not to jeopardise my person in enemy territory. And was I, in the event of failure, to abandon and lose Ninette perhaps for ever?

My assistant, Vem Whittal, who was a source of great encouragement, begged to be allowed to go on the mission in my place, but, after six hours of hell, I refused.

From that moment on the die was cast, and I concentrated on rushing supplies, equipment and personnel, including David's wireless operator, Harry, down to Khiosti where Milton and the *Evangelistria,* with his deckhand, were lying. As usual, with a broad grin on his face, when I told him the plan he said, *'Horalo!* Off we go.'

Off we went the following morning, the 9th, and headed for the north-east coast of Samos where there was a suitable small bay for us to lie up and make preliminary soundings as to the Italians' position. This was about sixty miles south of Khiosti, but when we drew near to Samos there was a fairly major sea running, with a north-west wind, straight into this selected bay. This necessitated a reassessment and change of plans to a similar bay on the south-west coast, and the next morning Milton skilfully put in there.

It was not long before a group of *Andartes* (Samos guerillas) came to see what we were doing, and they reported that the Italians appeared to be in a state of pandemonium. We got Harry and his wireless, together with all our stores, ashore and radioed to Cairo for permission to go to the Italian C-in-C in his Vathy headquarters and take over command of the island. Their reply, which came at four o'clock the following afternoon, was in the affirmative. We then re-embarked and headed east for fifteen miles, in glorious sunshine, along the very beautiful southern coast of Samos.

At dusk we pulled in to the delightful little harbour of Tigani (where, two thousand years earlier Pythagoras had lived, and Tigani is now called Pythagorean) to an acclaim from the population the like of which would have had to be seen to be believed.

They had been oppressed and occupied since 1941, and they rushed onto the *Evangelistria* to such an extent that the poor boat nearly sank.

There was an Italian guard of company strength on the quay, and we ordered them to take us, in their vehicles, to their HQ at Vathy, leaving Milton to be cheered and admired by an ever-increasing number of his countrymen.

Before leaving Smyrna, to give our self-appointed small mission some semblance of authority, we had typed out a document purporting to have come from General Wilson, instructing the Italian High Command to hand over control to our mission. I said it would be more water-tight if we promoted David, who I am not certain had any military rank, but was ten years older than me, to the rank of Colonel –which he may actually have been, but he never used it in Smyrna.

This was the only document with which we were armed as we motored up north through the beautiful vineyards and olive groves either side of the mountainous road to the capital Vathy, leaving Pythagoras's historic birth-place on our right. It was growing dark as we drove up the General Solderelli's headquarters, in a state of very considerable uncertainty as to whether the Germans had already arrived and – even if they had not – would we be clapped straight into the dungeons that had been occupied, one month before, by Colonel Frank Macaskie and Captain Ladas – and by many other prisoners only yesterday?

Amazingly enough, our bluff worked perfectly, and we were taken stright in to see the General and his Chief of Staff and other officers including his ADC. As it happened, fortune was on our side, as Solderelli was not of the extreme Fascist-Black Shirt Military type, but rather a more conservative old-type regular army officer. He commanded the Cuneo Division and virtually all the islands in the Eastern Aegean down to, but not including, Rhodes. The very fact that he had accepted us and our orders was a supremely brave action on his part, and meant a certain hideously unpleasant death if he, or any of his officers, were captured in the event of a German counter-attack. The Germans were, of course, in force only one hundred miles away on the mainland, in Athens – and actually even nearer, on the island of Syros, where they had troops and ships. However, we had beaten them to it even though our nearest troops were in Cairo and Cyprus, some five hundred miles away.

Now, on this lovely warm September evening Solderelli invited the three of us to join his officers for dinner in the very large Officers' Mess. We all sat down to a very correct and formal late dinner, and a very good dinner it was too. Solderelli had the best of Italian chefs and toasts were drunk to the new spirit of co-operation; this was within twenty-eight hours of changing sides.

After dinner we had a conference with the General. We explained that we must immediately take over Leros, the key naval base, without which even after the capture of Rhodes the route to Istanbul would remain blocked. Solderelli agreed the importance of this move, but, whilst saying that Admiral Maschera, the Commander of Leros, came under his command, now that Admiral Camponi of Rhodes had possibly been captured he was uncertain in these very different circumstances which way he and his senior officers would jump.

The only thing to do was go straight away; it was now nearly 1 am and Solderelli said he would allocate to us his best and fastest MAAS (motor torpedo boat) which had recently arrived from Italy and was capable of doing some forty knots. We were to take the Deputy Chief of Staff, Brigadier T.C. Gaudioso, with us, and without a moment to be lost we went straight down to the harbour and boarded the MAAS.

Within minutes the engines were roaring like a jet fighter, and we found ourselves racing south through the clear moonlit Aegean. We rounded the eastern point of Samos and then went through the straits between Turkey, completing the sixty mile journey in under two hours.

We arrived at Porto Largo at 2.45 am on September 12th, and were met by the Italian guard at the harbour. Our Italian Brigadier, a splendid person throughout, explained the purpose of our mission and it soon became evident that this time our bluff was not going to work as swimmingly as it had seven hours earlier in Samos.

It appeared that the Germans, through their signals, were also putting immense pressure on Admiral Maschera to receive a mission from them and to hand over this vital fortress and naval base, and to remain with them for the rest of the war.

The Brigadier was then taken off to see Maschera and explain General Solderelli's commands and the purpose of our visit. We, meanwhile, were shown into a very cold, damp and dark underground ammunition bunker. We were left for

PARTENI BAY

AEGEAN
SEA

GURNA BAY

LEROS

Leros

Porto Lago

PANDELI BAY

PORTO LAGO BAY

S. Giorgio

0   1   2
MILES

X = Landing point of Col. Pawson, Capt. Levides and
MWP who took control of the island at 0200 on 12
September 1943 from Adml Maschera.

210

some two hours in tense anticipation, while Brigadier Gaudioso remained closeted with the Admiral and his senior officers. They had the awful and unenviable task of deciding which way to jump, as their lives depended on it. Any miscalculation would mean certain death.

(After Leros fell on 11th November Admiral Maschera was taken to Parma, Italy, tried and died a hero's death in front of a firing squad, on May 15th.)

To our immense relief we heard the massive steel doors of our underground tomb being opened, and in came our red-haired Brigadier accompanied by a number of senior officers. They announced their decision; it was to come over to us.

By now it was getting on for five o'clock in the morning, and already the first signs of dawn were appearing in the east over the Turkish mainland. We had a short discussion with the Leros command, and they told us that a British officer had just parachuted into Rhodes with a view of effecting, with the Rhodes Commander Admiral Camponi, what we had so successfully just achieved with General Solderelli and Admiral Maschera.

They were uncertain as to what decision the Italian command had taken, other than, possibly, procrastination. They did tell us, however, that the Italians were resisting and fighting the Germans in the south of the island. We knew that Rhodes was garrisoned by some forty thousand goodish Italian troops, as opposed to six thousand Germans, and we also knew of the long planned preparation for the assault on Rhodes.

The above factors, together with the spirit and co-operation of the Italian forces that we had seen, made it inconceivable, in our eyes, that General Wilson and whoever else went on the mission in Rhodes would not have the necessary impetus and guts to consolidate the capture of Rhodes, as all the advantages were on our side. It would be an easy run for the British fleet based in Alexandria and Cyprus, and also in ideal bombing range from both places.

We re-boarded the MAAS 522 in Porto Largo harbour, and, with the now familiar roar of the engines, raced off in the early morning due north to Samos.

Suddenly, when we were about halfway there, a German Stuka appeared above us. I have never felt so naked and exposed in all my life, and feared that our successful take-over of Leros had already got through to the German High Command in Athens, who had sent us their response. The aircraft shadowed us for about ten minutes, without attacking, and then, thanks to the Almighty, headed off in the direction of the Greek mainland.

On reaching Vathy we disembarked with a hasty wave and a *'Kalimeras!'* to Milton who was on the deck of the *Evangelistria,* and then let the Italian Deputy Chief of Staff report to General Solderelli that Leros, in my words, was 'In the bag'.

We were still virtually in complete control as it was a day or two before more senior officers of General rank were to reach us.

It is appropriate here, as our million to one gamble had completely succeeded beyond our wildest hopes, to relate our adventures with the teachings of Sun Tzu Wu. Of all the military experts going back two thousand years, opinions now accept that Sun Tzu Wu in his *The Art of War*, the oldest military treatise in the world, was superior to most – perhaps even to General Carl von Clausewitz in his *Principles of War.*

> In the passage dealing with attack by strategem, Sun Tzu Wu says 'In the practical art of war the best thing of all is to take the enemy's country whole and intact; to shatter and destroy it is not so profitable. So, too, it is better to capture an army entire than to destroy it, to capture a regiment, a detachment or a company entire than to annihilate it. Hence to fight and conquer in all your battles is not supreme excellence. Supreme excellence consists in breaking the enemy's resistance without fighting, and Rapidity is the essence of War.'

It was scarcely four days since the news of the Italian surrender on the 8th September. In those few days, without a single shot being fired and with no loss of life on either side, we had acquired – by bluff and speed – the islands of Samos and Leros together with numerous lesser islands; an area of some 5,000 square miles, plus twenty thousand troops and all their military equipment, stores, supplies and naval ships. The entire enemy force, together with their vital strategic islands, had been turned from enemy to ally.

Our most important achievement, however, was the absorption of the all but impregnable island of Leros only hours before Rhodes should have been taken – throwing open, in one fell swoop, the route to Istanbul and therefore the entry of Turkey into the war on our side.

Looking back through history I am unable to find another occasion when so much had been gained for so little, or when the course of world history could have been so strategically changed for the better.

The Leros commander had told us that the Italians were resisting the small German garrison on Rhodes, and that on September 10th Major Earl Jellicoe, SBS, had been parachuted into the island with orders from General Wilson to negotiate with Admiral Camponi and take over the island.

As we had had no sleep during this time we decided to requisition the finest house on the hillside above Vathy, which I think, had been occupied by the German Consul.

We repaired to our new headquarters and settled in with Harry and the wireless, unpacked what few things we had and tucked in to a good breakfast.

Hardly had we finished when a dispatch rider came rushing up on his motorcycle to our front door with a message from General Solderelli saying he wished to see us immediately as a matter of great importance had arisen. When we reached him he was obviously greatly shaken, as were the officers around him, and he hastily showed us the signal he had just received from the German HQ in Athens.

It demanded that they, the Italian command in Samos, should hand over the command of Samos and the islands forthwith, and that Solderelli was to reply within the hour.

We gave the reply immediately, using General Solderelli's wireless network to the effect that 'The islands have already been handed over to the British and any attack by the Germans would be fiercly resisted and repulsed.' This was of the utmost importance as it prevented the Germans from coming.

Considering the gravity of the situation Solderelli took it very well, and put all his troops on emergency alert while we returned to our new headquarters for a little much-needed rest.

Not much happened for the rest of that day, other than communicating with GHQ Cairo and with General Arnold, the Military Attaché in Ankara. He asked if it was safe for him to come over in the next few days with his Chief of Staff, Colonel Greer, lately assistant Military Attaché in Moscow. We gave him the All Clear and said we would send the MAAS to meet his vessel just outside Turkish territorial waters, as he was going to embark from Kushadasi. This was all put in train and arranged for the 15th. In the meantime I did a reconnaisance of a possible air strip on a flat hill about a mile south-east of Vathy, and found it could be made suitable for small planes to land. Then fairly exhausted, I returned to a makeshift meal and some sleep at last.

The next day saw us consolidating our position on Samos which, at that time of year with the grapes and figs fully ripe and the sheer beauty of the island, was Arcadia itself. During the morning the General's dispatch rider came roaring up to our building again, saying that we were wanted once again on a matter of great importance.

This time we were told that the Samosan/Greek *Andartes* were attacking his troops and their outlying garrisons in the more remote villages and towns on the island, and would we, as the mission, tour the whole island and speak to the guerilla leaders. We were to explain that we were now a united force, and that, whilst in the last two years the Italians had committed war crimes and atrocities, these would be properly investigated and punishment meted out where guilt was proved. This could not be done until the war against Germany had been won, and, for now, we asked every Greek to loyally co-operate and fight for final victory.

We went with the guerilla leaders Zaimis and Betsos, speaking in the towns and villages of Kerki, Kastania, Marathokambos, Karlovasi and Vathy. It was a most awe-inspiring and wonderful journey right through the length and breadth of this most beautiful island, both in the mountains and on the coast. We were overwhelmed by the spirit of the people and their leaders; it was a mystical feeling that I can still feel now –nearly fifty years later. They were not the sort of people to be on the wrong side of, and I fully understood General Solderelli's *cri-de-coeur* to us.

Up until now we had been the sole British representatives for four days. The day after this we went in the MAAS to meet General Arnold and his second-in-command, Colonel Greer. We met them just outside Turkish territorial waters, a few miles to the west of Kushadasi; this was to obviate any chance of a major diplomatic incident by them using Turkish waters.

General Arnold was thrilled with the way the operation had gone, and I was greatly relieved that he accepted my position as a *fait accompli* without so much as a bat of an eyelid, although I knew he was fighting for my cause with Colonel Simonds in Cairo.

He insisted that I remain in Samos until they were fully established, after which he planned to apply for me to move my fleet of caiques to Samos and to continue my MI9 work from there. At the same time I was to use my ships for ferrying supplies from Turkey to Samos, as there was an abundance held by the Royal Engineers units operating, in mufti, under his command.

From now on the build up of arrivals from Egypt and Cyprus began. General Anderson, known as 'Squeaker' Anderson, who was going to command Force 100 for the invasion of Rhodes arrived, and expressed himself extremely satisfied with the way events had shaped, and said he would consolidate the position with a limited number of troops before taking further action.

The following day my friend Captain David Sutherland, Black Watch, arrived in a Fairmile, which was a large and somewhat slower, but nevertheless very useful type of MTB with a party of Special Boat Service Commandos on board. He was second in command to George Jellicoe's Special Boat Service and had just left Jellicoe in Leros.

The next day was spent liaising with the Italian Command and the two British Generals, and that afternoon we arranged for General Arnold to return to Turkey in the MAAS; a journey not quite as smooth as we expected.

During this time I was constantly expecting to hear the vital news that the Allies had successfully occupied Rhodes, which would have completed the hat-trick and changed the whole course of the war. This I believed, was Churchill's great over-riding strategic conception, but it was not until many years later that I read the following excerpt in his book *Closing the Ring, Volume 5, The Second World War* – written on September 13th, the very day we were with General Solderelli:–

'Prime Minister to General Wilson, Middle East:

The capture of Rhodes by you at this time with Italian aid would be a fine contribution to the general war. Let me know what your plans are for this. Can you improvise the necessary garrison out of the forces in the Middle East? What is your total ration strength? This is the time to think of Clive and Peterborough, and of Rookes's men taking Gibraltar . . . Lest it should be thought that I pressed this mood unduly I cite the final summary of the combined Chiefs of Staff of our decisions recorded in Washington.

Eastern Mediterranean.

The combined Chiefs of Staff have taken note of the action which the Commander-in-Chief Middle East is taking in respect of Rhodes and other islands in the Dodecanese. They approve this action, and are considering what further can be done.'

(Some years later I met a friend Colonel Sandy Scratchley, who had been my opposite number whilst working on my Denousa plan in Cairo; he told me that Churchill had been quite exasperated by the fact that Wilson had some one million men in his Middle East command, and yet seemed reluctant to produce a few thousand for the all important invasion of Rhodes. Hence Churchill's biting, caustic remark 'Please let me know your ration strength.')

Now back to Samos, on the 18th September – nine days since we set sail from Turkey with Milton. It was a heavenly day; the Grecian islands were at their best (and their best is something quite out of this world) and it was a glorious day for us –everything had gone perfectly. A million to one gamble had come off in total fulfilment, and I was getting ready to return to Smyrna with Milton on the *Evangelistria,* to rejoin my lovely Ninette. I had been unable to notify or warn her of my sudden departure into the blue, from her point of view, on the 9th September.

After breakfast the inevitable dispatch rider came screeching up to our HQ asking us to go urgently to see General Solderelli. Throughout all these meetings David Pawson had handled the situations with great skill and firmness. The new crisis was the Black Shirt Regiments, who were fighting the *Andartes* on the island of Ikaria (an island some thirty miles west of Vathy), as they had revolted and threatened to seize the islands from Solderelli's regular forces and go over to the Germans. Solderelli asked us, in fact almost begged us, to go as quickly as possible to speak to the Black Shirt Regimental Commanders and persuade them of the folly of their plans, and to fall in with the orders of Field Marshal Badoglio which were being executed by their Divisional Commander, General Solderelli.

After leaving Solderelli I explained to David that I must return to Smyrna to continue my operations from there, as all hell would be let loose from Simonds and Middle East HQ. David replied that on this very tricky operation I would be badly needed until it was completed. Colonel Greer, whom General Arnold had left behind, and who was now the acting commander of us all, said, 'I personally will clear you with General Arnold in Ankara as being essential to this particular mission, and I therefore authorise you to accompany David Pawson, Admiral Levides and the Italian Second-in-Command, General Pejrolo to proceed forthwith in the MAAS to the capital of Ikaria.'

We left in the MAAS at about midday, and roared along the north Samosan coast, due west, until we reached the small harbour at the capital of Ikaria, Agios Kerikos. Accompanied by General Pejrolo, we ordered the Black Shirt Regimental Commanders to report to us immediately, and after a discussion lasting about two hours we achieved our objective of bringing them back on the combined Allied front.

Our business completed, we re-embarked and set off for Samos via the small island of Fourni, where we had some business to do with the Mayor about food supplies etc.

14

Change of Fortune

We pulled in to a most attractive horse-shoe shaped bay in the late afternoon, where there were about fifteen small Greek children in their birthday suits, diving off the rocks into the crystal clear blue Aegean water. We settled down to have an evening meal before returning to Samos, and after dinner David, who was extremely tired, went below deck to the cabin to have a short sleep. Alex was up in the forward part of the ship, also resting, and I was sitting on the starboard torpedo tube enjoying the most beautiful restful scene; but not for long.

Suddenly the MAAS Captain Beghli and most of his crew rushed up on deck, firing their Tommy guns wildly. My revolver was in its holster on my Sam Browne belt, and I automatically put my right hand to my left side to draw it out. Alex and General Pejrolo were both seized when one of these unpleasant gentlemen shot me just below the left hip, near my revolver. The bullet, after many months in hospital and numerous operation to try to extract it, actually passed the whole way across my body from left to right, and was eventually extracted from above my right hip.

However, for now, all four of us were prisoners on the MAAS 522. I was streaming blood and the Captain said he was going to take us straight back to the nearest German garrison, which was about fifty miles away on the island of Syros, the administrative capital of the Aegean islands. The engines were started and we headed north-west instead of the three miles north-east to our wonderful island and comrades on Samos.

After going for about twenty minutes I called the Captain

over to me and, with General Pejrolo, explained the enormity of his action. We were under safe conduct on his ship, by order from his divisional commander. To have seized and captured his own General was a certain death sentence for him and all his crew when we won the war, which we unquestionably would. The only way he could save himself from a certain ultimate death was to head for the Turkish coast and drop us ashore, before returning to his German friends in Syros.

The Captain stopped his ship about five miles north-west of Fourni where, as I have said, the treacherous attack took place, and was on the point of agreeing to dump us on the Turkish coast when his engineer appeared on deck and became party to the discussion. He, extremely unfortunately, reported that their fuel supply was very low even for the trip straight to Syros, so it was out of the question to go to Turkey and then another fifty miles to Syros. With that, our last chance evaporated.

At this stage I must endeavour to explain what I later discovered which was why the MAAS Captain Beghli so treacherously attacked us and his own General on the evening of the 18th September, when for the last nine days he has taken us, and others some two hundred miles. General Arnold and Colonel Greer were very much bigger game than us and would have earned him even more praise from the Germans, as to have seized a British Major-General and Number One in Turkey – which was strictly neutral at that moment – would have been a major coup. It would also have created a major diplomatic disaster for the Allied cause, of world-wide proportions.

Evidently what had happened, either while we were ashore at Ikaria or whilst we were having supper, was that the Captain had been listening to his radio in his cabin, or with the Black Shirt Sergeant in the afternoon. He had heard the all-important, to him, broadcast from his beloved Il Duce Mussolini, who had been rescued from his mountain prison by the fantastic rescue operation organised by Hitler's Colonel Skorzeni. 'Scarface Skorzeni' was far and away the greatest and most intrepid Commando fighter on either side throughout the entire war (as shown in *Commando Extraordinary* by Charles Foley, published by the Special Forces Library).

The message on the radio was that 'All Italian Forces were to ignore any previous commands from the traitor Marshal Badoglio', and they were forthwith under the command of Il Duce and their allies the Germans.

This was for me the first stroke of intense bad luck, as this amazing man not only put paid to us but was also instrumental in prolonging the war by many months.

During the whole of my four years at war I had been blessed by very good fortune, and, up until this Fourni disaster I had been successful and lucky.

My thread of good fortune, however, had now been irretrievably broken, and the MAAS limped along on one engine until we reached Ermoupoli, the large harbour and capital of Syros. In happier times this was a place of great beauty, but now it was completely deserted, apart from a few German guards and an extremely tough-looking German naval captain on his ship.

On the quay there were some fine houses, probably built in the 18th century by the Venetians, and as we were ordered off the boat I noticed an elderly lady looking out of an upper window of one of these houses. Within a second a huge guttural shout came from this naval captain, and he swung his Tommy gun around and sprayed not only that house but also the other surrounding buildings with thirty or forty live rounds. The elderly lady immediately ducked down behind her window sill; hit or not I do not know.

Once on shore David and Alex were taken to some kind of guard room by the Germans and I was taken to a small makeshift hospital in a house, where an Italian doctor was sent to examine me. This he did in a rather casual way, at the end of which he pronounced me not seriously wounded, only a superficial graze, and that I would be ready to leave in the morning with the others. Presumably he thought I just had a surface flesh wound, and it had not occurred to him that the bullet had actually gone three-quarters of the way through my body, where it remained.

The next day we were taken by sea-plane to Piraeus and then by German military transport to the Averoff prison in Athens. Once in the prison we were duly interviewed and searched. I was allowed to keep my fine Longines wrist watch and the gold cross and chain that Ninette had given me; they were apparently within the Geneva Convention regulations.

Over my uniform I was wearing a sheepskin jacket which I had bought in Turkey, and into which I had carefully sewn forty-eight gold sovereigns. I always travelled with this when on my MI9 work, and at first it appeared that the German officer who was searching us had not spotted the jacket's contents. Alas suddenly, just as he was finishing his search, he felt a hard object under the wool and immediately ripped the jacket off me, thereby exposing my treasure trove which might have been invaluable to me in my later months of incarceration.

We were all put into the main ward where there were iron beds and grim-looking horsehair mattresses and there we were left to await the next move. This came two days later, when we were taken off to the Athens aerodrome and told to sit on the floor of a JU52. I remember this was intensely cold, accentuated no doubt by my still untreated wound.

We were flown to Salonika and taken to the notorious Gestapo Headquarters, where the young Captain Kurt Waldheim, future head of the United Nations and now the Austrian President, is reputed to have been.

On arrival we were marched into the main reception room for our first period of interrogation, where to our amazement and absolute horror we saw Lt. Levites, who was one of David's SOE people. He had been working with him from Smyrna and had never returned from a mission. I had always suspected he was a double agent, as I had never been over-impressed with the quality of some of the people used by SOE.

From that moment onwards it was evident that the Gestapo knew exactly who we were and where we had come from, and that our previously planned story of how we had come up from Cyprus to take over the islands had been blown by Levites. I can see him there now, in that big room, with a guilty smile on his face as he looked at us. However, I could not be completely certain as to whether his presence was voluntary or whether he had been through fearful tortures in the six weeks that had elapsed since he left the Consulate.

(In this respect it is vital that all should know the suffering meted out to guerillas and Special Service people of all races when caught by the Germans. In the Appendix an excerpt

221

from *The Charioteer* describes exactly what was happening at the Gestapo HQ in Salonika and Athens while we were there.)

I did not then realise that the Germans thought we were much more important captives than in fact we were. They knew, through the Italian MAAS 522 Captain Beghli, that we were the three officers who had taken over the islands of Samos and Leros thirteen days before, beating them to it. They knew too that their supreme commander, Hitler, had personally ordered that Rhodes and the islands should not be surrendered under any circumstances, and he had counter-manded all defeatist talk by the Wehrmacht supreme command who had been in favour of withdrawal. The likely punishment for any officer not complying with the Führer's wishes could be one of immense severity, such as when they hung disloyal Generals on a butcher's hook from their lower jaw, with Himmler and possibly Hitler himself witnessing their slow death.

We were also unaware that the Germans themselves were in a state of some panic, fearing that, with the imminent attack on Rhodes, we would also have advanced up towards Salonika. They were therefore making preparations to move all prisoners of any importance to Germany as soon as possible; we evidently fell into that category.

As for the Italian prisoners – our splendid General Pejrolo had already been segregated from us, to await unspeakable horrors for his loyalty to Great Britain. The ordinary Italian soldiers were mercilessly shot in their hundreds, and rolled over into the sea from the main Salonika waterfront, while many thousands more were rounded up and shipped in overcrowded cattle trucks to work as slave labourers in Germany.

After our first hasty interrogation we were each forced, separately, into small wooden cells. These were not unlike the inside of a giant cigar box, measuring about seven feet high by seven feet long by seven feet wide, but instead of being full of cigars, the room was totally bare, with the exception of one black bucket. A very brutal and unpleasant-looking SS guard, carrying a big white stick, shoved me into this unpleasant box and then slammed and bolted the massive, double-lined door with a large steel lever.

222

With the slamming of the door came the lowest point of any period in my life.

I was well aware of Hitler's edict that guerillas, saboteurs and all those engaged in subversive warfare were to be tortured, interrogated and liquidated by the Gestapo, his SS – such as the tragic Major Tucker, Coldstream Guards, and others captured in the SBS (Special Boat Service) MTB off Rhodes. They had been taken to Germany from Salonika, where they were murdered by the SS.

Scarcely a week beforehand I had been happily married, working in a thrilling job that I understood and loved and had just instigated something that I believed then, and still do today, could have brought this terrible war to a victorious conclusion within months.

Now, incarcerated in the Gestapo cell it seemed certain that I would not see that glorious victory, and knowing I had no real courage, unlike so many others had shown in similar circumstances, I knew that my end would be that much worse.

As I looked around the cell I saw blood smears all over the walls, and somewhat naturally I assumed they must have come from the lashings received by previous unfortunate occupants. I was left alone for twenty-four dreadful hours; time enough to contemplate what was likely to happen to me when the door was next opened.

I was convinced that if, as seemed inevitable, they started to torture me, I would be unable to stand it, and began to consider various possibilities of saying goodbye to this world.

The next day the same guard reappeared, noisily opened the door and ordered me out. Apparently we were high ranking prisoners in their eyes, having provoked the wrath of their Führer by seizing those vital islands, and we were to be flown as quickly as possible to the Wehrmacht's main interrogation centre at Luckenwald, in Germany.

Once again we were rushed off to the airport, and once again made to sit on the very cold and hard corrugated zinc floor of the JU52.

By this time almost a week had passed since I had been shot at Fourni and I was running a very high temperature, 40.5 degrees C. The bullet had turned its surroundings septic and

223

the gangrene that had already set in was most noticeable by the stench.

Our first stop was Belgrade, where we all got out and went to sit in the Luftwaffe Officers' Mess whilst waiting to be transhipped in another plane to Lukenwald. I always remember how impressed I was with the *esprit de corps* of these young fighter pilots; very similar to our 601 and Battle of Britain pilots. They were very friendly and showed no animosity towards us.

During this wait our escort officer showed some concern as to my condition, and went off in search of the Luftwaffe Austrian Medical Officer. They both returned in about a quarter of an hour, and within five minutes the Austrian doctor had informed our guard (who had been expressly detailed to guard us with the closest security and deliver us direct to the interrogation centre) that he could perfectly well fly us to Lukenwald but 'He,' pointing at me, 'would be a corpse before he arrived.'

This, of course, was not what the top brass in Germany would have wanted.

The doctor said the only solution was to have me taken to the Belgrade National Hospital for an immediate operation and treatment. After a great deal of argey-bargey they very reluctantly agreed to do this, and after saying goodbye to poor David and Alex I was rushed, in a military ambulance, to the hospital.

I was carried in to a very clean, private room, and was not surprised to find an SS officer seated on a chair at the end of my bed. It was in this room that I was destined to spend the best part of the next six months, having operation after operation to try and extricate the bullet which was causing so much trouble.

The first evening I was taken on a trolley to the operating theatre, where I was told to kneel, in my birthday suit, while five doctors and surgeons probed about trying to find the bullet. This was not so much painful as immensely undignified, although never once were any of the doctors anything other then most courteous, painstaking and professional. The same went for my wonderful German nurse Johanna Mulbauer, who came from Bitterfeldt, in Eastern

Germany, and also Sister Urabyder from the Order of the Sisters of Mercy; she was Yugoslavian, and they looked after me devotedly during the whole period that I was there.

The bad and always ominous, part of this was the ever-present SS officers who were stationed in my room around the clock. Largely Austrian by birth, they were not personally unpleasant to me, but what was most disconcerting was when the inevitable interrogation officer came in. He was always armed with a large leather dispatch bag, out of which came the usual questionnaire. This always began with 'It would be interesting, Major Parish, to know . . .'

In between these Mr Fagin-like visits the surgeons were having no success in extricating the poisonous bullet, in spite of repeated operations and seemingly endless fishing about in my innards. As a result of this I very soon developed internal abcesses, and had to have six inch rubber tubes inserted into my body to drain off the pus from them. This is itself made complications and I had to be raised from the bed to lie across a network of linen trusses, thereby leaving the rubber tubes free to drain the fluid.

This routine continued much the same for many months, broken only by the constant striving of the doctors to locate the bullet which entailing a succession of major operations to remove it and to cut out the gangrenous flesh.

My trips to the operating theatre were interesting experiences; one was first given a sedative and then wheeled off to the theatre. I was then always given an apparently fairly new anaesthetic which was called 'Evipan'. This, to me, was highly attractive, as seconds after it had been injected into a vein in my arm there would be a pleasant click in my brain, followed by a very satisfactory and pleasant oblivion. I would remain in this state for several hours, only to wake up and find myself back in my room, with Johanna attending to me as usual. Each time I asked her if they had succeeded in extricating the bullet, and for the first few months the reply was always *Nein*. As this was in the days before Dr Fleming's discovery of penicillin had reached Germany, I was well aware that the internal abcesses, poisoning and constant high temperature would continue.

The days went by with fairly monotonous regularity and I thought a lot about my father and about what had happened to Ninette after my disastrous abandonment of her. Perhaps most of all I was desperate for news as to whether Rhodes, and the whole string of islands from Cyprus to Istanbul, had been secured, the start of which we had initiated on September 9th. I was confident that this should have happened within days of our capture.

At the end of November an SS guard was sitting on the end of my bed reading a German national newspaper, and I saw huge headlines about the recapture of Leros. That, to me, was the next unutterably low point of the war. I realised that Churchill's great ambition of capturing Rhodes and the other islands, thereby opening up the route through the Dardanelles and thus bringing Turkey into the war which would enable us to attack Hitler from the soft under-belly of eastern Europe, must have failed. It had failed despite the terrific resistance on Leros put up by the British forces under Brigadier Tilney, and the excellent fighting qualities of the Italian garrison who had so recently, through our mission, joined the Allied war effort.

Not long after this my first companion from the outside world arrived at the hospital, in the form of a badly wounded corporal. He was one of the fifteen hundred British soldiers captured after the fall of Leros, but had somehow got out of the mainstream of ordinary prisoners of war who were all shipped straight to Germany. He had received a shrapnel splinter in his right eye and had been taken, after the battle, to the Italian underground hospital.

The Italian surgeon had cut out his eye without anaesthetic, as apparently they had run out of it.

After this he was brought into my room and put in a bed to the right of mine, where he stayed for about ten days before being shunted north to Germany. He was a cheery and very likeable Cockney who, understandably enough, had little idea of what the Leros campaign was all about.

My only other companions were the ever-present SS guards in their black uniforms. They wore slightly baggy black breeches and black jack-boots, and their coats had silver skull and crossbones neatly displayed thereon.

They told me about their campaigns right up to the Baltic ports in Estonia and Lithuania, and showed me the most dreadful photographs of what they found in the Russian

OGPU prisons after they had pushed the Russians out.

One such photograph was of, presumably, an Estonian, who was standing up in a wooden cradle. He was in the most appalling condition, with a great slit across his stomach and most of his bowels hanging out. This poor wretched man was obviously still alive, and was awaiting further treatment from Stalin's OGPU. This was just one of the many quite terrible photographs they showed me of the Russian-perpetrated atrocities.

Stalin and his Soviet Bolsheviks had already exterminated fifteen million Russian Kulak farmers in 1928-1930, followed by a further seven million Ukranian farmers in 1930-1933 and twelve million political prisoners from 1919-1949, making a total of thirty-four million – without counting any war casualties. No doubt the man in the wooden cradle was just one such example.

Whilst I was in hospital my SS guards never once showed me any physical violence or outward animosity. In fact the majority, who like me were in their mid-twenties, were friendly, and longing to talk about and discuss the war. The one exception was a huge north-German from Hamburg. He told me with great bitterness and anger how his wife and family had just been burnt alive when my countrymen bombed their city, using fire bombs which had set alight not only a large number of houses but also the streets. These, surfaced in tar, became raging infernos and I could see him boiling with rage, barely able to control himself from taking it out on me with his huge arms and fists. He would probably have been quite justified in doing so as the fire bombing of Hamburg killed more than 50,000 men, women and children.

My medical treatment went on as usual, with the wounds being dressed and the rubber tubes being removed and replaced every evening. This was quite a painful experience, sometimes excruciatingly so. Suddenly one day my water-works packed up and I was unable to pass water, which was not only painful but exceedingly frightening. I have no idea why it happened, but Johanna immediately sent for my doctor who attended me every morning and evening. He gave me an injection of something which felt like a red hot stream of liquid coming into me, and within seconds I was back to normal, physically and mentally.

Many high-ranking doctors and specialists from Germany used to visit the hospital, and on one occasion just before Christmas Professor Doktor Hammil arrived to see me. He had worked under the brilliant Professor Sauerbruck, who operated on, and saved the life of, King George V, when he was desperately ill at Bognor. (The King referred to it as 'Bloody Bognor', although it was subsequently called 'Bognor Regis'.)

Professor Hammil was one of Hitler's personal doctors and was a most charming person. He spent quite a lot of time with me each day after he had examined me and we would chat about the war and many other things. He was aware that the Allies were gaining the initiative even though the Second Front had not yet opened, and he expected the pressure to continue in our favour although he remained confident that the Germans would ultimately win the war. This was because of the enormous importance which he and Hitler attached to the then entirely new invention of the V1 and V2 rockets, which they expected to devastate London and industrial Britain. As this was all completely new to me it was naturally somewhat depressing.

Professor Hammil did me the good service of damping down the visits of the interrogation officers, saying that I was too ill to withstand the strain. This was probably true, as I was continually running a high temperature and fever.

Beyond all this the only noticeable activity in the hospital was the constant arrival of Tito's wounded guerillas and, likewise wounded Germans. I do not think Tito's men ever got much further than the nearest firing squad, as every day the papers were filled with headlines such as *Terroristiki Tito*, together with all the dreadful things he was doing and they were about to do with him.

Christmas approached and the hospital was gaily adorned with all the usual decorations and festive fare. My food was really very good, probably better than I had been accustomed to whilst in the 15th Scottish Hospital in Cairo; every day during my stay in Belgrade hospital I was given a bottle of lager beer with my lunch and red wine with my dinner. Johanna told me this was because it was meant to be most beneficial for clearing the blood.

January passed, the bullet still lodged somewhere close to my pelvis at the base of my spine; yet another attempt to remove it had failed, and it was not until the middle of February that I was taken up once again to the operating theatre, on the usual trolley and with the all usual procedure, although this time the operation was to be carried out by Professor Doktor Hammil.

This time when I came to, Johanna was standing over me, holding in her hand the nasty-looking stub-nosed bullet that had been causing so much trouble for the last five months.

From then on I very slowly began to recover and to regain a little of my strength. In due course the rubber tubes were removed and I then had to spend the next couple of months lying on my stomach, not able, or allowed, to turn over until the several large wounds from the operations and the gangrene had healed somewhat.

By now my teeth had become terribly decayed due to all the poison in my body, and it was therefore arranged for me to be taken to Belgrade to visit the dentist. This was to be my only trip outside the hospital; I went there scarcely able to walk and feeling incredibly shaky, and returned utterly exhausted. Thereafter I was allowed to sit up on my bed a little bit every day, until I had gathered enough strength to be able to walk down the passage, propped up by Johanna, to be bathed in the proper bathroom. After five months of bed baths this was quite a step forward.

By early March I was a little more mobile, and I was informed that I would soon be leaving Belgrade and sent up, as a stretcher case, by rail to Germany.

Just as I feared, it was to be to the notorious interrogation centre at Lukenwald.

15

North to Germany

After saying goodbye to all my doctors and Johanna (to whom, somewhat emotionally, I gave Ninette's gold cross and chain) and Urabyder I was taken by ambulance to the main Belgrade station and put on the train. There were several whole compartments with stretchers laid one after another, through the whole length of each compartment. I was allocated one of these and then off we steamed for the next three days and nights until we reached Vienna. There were a number of medical orderlies on board the train and I had my own guard watching over me.

As we made our way through the open rolling Bosnian countryside I thought continually about making a break for it at one of the many night stops, when the guard – and everyone else – was less alert. However, while this may perhaps have been feasible, I realised that suddenly finding myself on the plains, in mid-winter and being scarcely able to walk would not produce a good chance of survival, even if I were undetected. I therefore reluctantly watched the Yugoslavian countryside slipping away as we wended our way north to Austria.

On arrival in Vienna I was marched slowly off through the main entrance, to where all the incoming passengers were accustomed to arriving by car or taxi. I was surprised to see the whole of the front entrance deserted, except for one old T model Ford taxi which was standing outside.

My guard and I were taken off in a military vehicle to a large Nissen hut type military camp for interrogation. I was dumped in one of these huts and given a bed amongst half-a-dozen others. One of these, I gathered from his companions, was an American Warrant Officer who had obviously gone over to the Germans and was a stool pigeon. He was a very unattractive and rather coarse fellow, who told me all about Lukenwald and what to expect.

The sanitary conditions in the ablution block were quite disgusting; every lavatory was full to over-flowing and there were always a number of Italians, and others, roaming around and queueing up.

This was another very low point for me; having heard the American's account of what to expect and again knowing that I would be quite unable to stand the full treatment of torture, I was on the verge of cutting my wrists in the revolting lavatory. However, that takes a good bit of courage, and being torn between the devil and the deep blue sea I decided to wait a little longer and see how events unfolded.

Nothing happened for the first two or three weeks, apart from near-starvation. We were fed on bowls of rudeboka soup, which was made by boiling a few turnips in a huge cauldron. This would be acompanied by a piece of black bread, and, as far as I remember, nothing much else. My weight went down to about six stone, well under half of what I normally weighed.

We were allowed to wander round the camp confines, within which there were a number of prisoners of several nationalities, such as General Michaelovitches who had fought the Germans in their original onslaught against Belgrade, and also some senior Russians.

These Yugoslavs and Russians, and most of those who survived until the end of the war, were the subject of Count Nicolai Tolstoy's and Nicholas Bethell's books. These very fine human beings were bayoneted, some by British soldiers, into the railway trucks, to be either taken back to certain death from the Red Tsar, Stalin, or to be burnt alive in their railway trucks on the orders of Marshal Tito, as many were. Fifty years later, I remain convinced that Count Tolstoy's views are correct in that these events rank as among the most disgraceful in British history and spawned the current horrors in Yugoslavia.

Article from the *Sunday Express* 30th July 1978:

Shame

At last the veils are lifted from the shabby story of how, in the latter days of the war, unwilling Soviet refugees were repatriated to almost certain death in Stalin's labour camps.

Listen to the words of an official document bearing the signature of career diplomat Sir John Galsworthy.

'It was, I thought, agreed that when a Soviet deserter came into the hands of the civil police the latter should more or less assume, or pretend, that the man in question was willing to return voluntarily to his camp and hand him over to the local military authority accordingly.

'Any misunderstanding about the man's real wishes was, I thought, to be attributed to "language difficulties." If the deserter makes it abundantly clear that he is not willing to return, the civil police are to release him more or less into the arms of a military escort who will then bundle him away to the nearest Soviet camp.

'Once back in a Soviet camp the unfortunate individual will have no access to any civil authorities (unless, of course, he escapes again), and will not, therefore, be in a position to protest against this rather rough justice.'

That document, with its weasel words, was initialled in agreement by Sir Patrick Dean.

Both he and Sir John have since enjoyed distinguished careers. Maybe they have enjoyed them. Maybe they have never woken up in the night with the cries of tortured souls ringing in their ears.

But there are surely men who have done a 24-hour shift shovelling up the slime from the Amoco Cadiz who have cleaner hands.

I made friends with some of them, including a Major Miskovitch, who had been Captain of the Yugoslavian Royal Guard. He had been captured early on, when the Germans had attacked Yugoslavia, and had been treated, along with many of his fellow officers, as a prisoner of war. Somehow he

232

managed to get out alive. (After the war he came to stay with us when we lived in Oxfordshire and he was billeted in the displaced persons camp near Bicester. He said that I had been a great source of strength to him and his comrades by assuring them that there was no question of a German victory, and that the Allies would be victorious within a year. Thankfully, as events turned out, I was not too far wrong.)

As the days passed I was continually amazed that I had not been marched into the interrogation room; I could not understand why. It later transpired that Brigadier Kenyon, who was captured after the fall of Leros, had reported to the Swiss Red Cross the inhumane conditions at Lukenwald interrogation centre, and their total disregard of the Geneva Convention applicable to prisoners of war. Because of this the whole centre was closed down shortly after my arrival. Luckily for me my case, which was already six months old, had evidently gone somewhat cold, and the interest shown in me appeared to have evaporated.

Some time later I was told that I was to be on the move again, and with a single corporal guard I was taken to the nearest station where we were put on a train. The train was full of ordinary civilians, and we sat in a compartment with six or more largely (and large) German hausfraus, who kept on looking rather curiously at me, in my French soldier's blue trousers.

We went right up to Berlin, and through the entire city. This, in March 1944, was an unbelievable sight of desolation. It was almost four years since my brother Charles had led the first Pathfinder Wellington bomber over Berlin on the very first raid, and it seemed that eighty per cent of the whole area had been devastated. My fellow female passengers kept looking out of the window at the devastation, and then giving me the benefit of their looks as a reaction to what I had apparently done.

After passing through the city we changed trains and went on for a longish time to my hitherto unknown next destination. This, as I was soon to find out, was to be a pukka prison of war camp in an old Czechoslovakian castle at Marischtrubau, but at the time I had no idea whether it was going to be a concentration camp or what horrors were in store for me.

My guard escorted me from the train and we motored a few miles, in military transport, to the main gates of this large and most formidable-looking encampment which was surrounded by a fifteen-foot barbed wire fence. After talking to the sentry the gates were thrown open and I was handed over to, and signed for, by the duty officer in charge; the corporal, I presume, then returned to Lukenwald.

I was taken into the main building which consisted of a number of rooms all occupied by about twenty other prisoners of war, and then into the orderly room. Here, I gave my name, rank and regiment before being photographed and having my finger-prints taken.

These formalities over, I was told to go and find accommodation in any of the rooms. I therefore went to the first door I could see, and entered – rather shyly, as I had been out of circulation for six months, virtually in solitary confinement.

I found about fifteen or twenty officers of different ranks lounging about. Suddenly I saw the familiar face of Tony McCraith, the younger brother of my very close friend Patrick, who had been with me in the Sherwood Rangers from 1938 until I left them after the fall of Crete.

Tony looked rather embarrassed at my arrival, and after a few minutes their conversation continued as before, completely ignoring me. David Stirling was sitting at the far end of the room with his friend Pringle and a tall officer who I got to know very well, David Crane from Nottingham. Tony appeared to be not the only person who was embarrassed by my appearance; in fact they all seemed to be, as if I had surprised them in the middle of some black magic séance.

At this point someone with a remarkably deep voice, and a typical Oxford accent, started talking. I looked round but was unable to trace the voice because there was a very tall Indian Officer standing in the way, near where the voice appeared to be coming from; I thought I knew that such a voice could not possibly come from an Indian. I therefore gave up until Tony had pulled himself together, whereupon I explained to him that I was supposed to be finding myself a bed, but if that was not convenient perhaps he could find me somewhere else? That rather broke the ice and he took me off to another room where there was a spare bunk.

What had apparently happened was that I had appeared in the room whilst they were all in the midst of listening to their secret radio. Immense effort had been made to build one, and they had thought that I was a stool pigeon, being used by the Germans to catch them red-handed. David Crane was one of the top people on the illicit radio, and somehow managed to communicate with Whitehall.

It took quite a little time for Tony to recover from the shock of suddenly seeing me, and to re-establish confidence with his colleagues. The last time he had seen me was at the Galatas prison of war camp in Crete, two-and-a-half years previously.

From then on I quickly settled into the routine which was basically, I suppose, doing nothing.

I shared a room with the deep voiced officer who was, after all, the Indian. He was Major Para Kumaramangalam, (known as 'K') who, after receiving a DSO at Buckingham Palace was flown back to India after the war by Field Marshal Auchinlech, the new C-in-C Indian. When he was staying with my father after the war I told him that he would one day become General Kumaramangalam, Chief of all the Indian Armed Forces, which indeed he did. His son was eventually to marry my eldest daughter.

Also sharing my room was Major Roger Hallam, a regular officer from the Royal West Kents whose grandfather wrote *Hallam's History of England*. Another inmate was John Tennant; he was older than the rest of us and had served at the Battle of Jutland as a midshipman. Early on in the war he gallantly joined the Army and was in an Ack-Ack regiment at the fall of Tobruk, where they were all captured and shipped to an Italian prison of war camp in Italy. He very nearly escaped to the Allied lines after the Italian Armistice but, unfortunately, was recaptured within sight of freedom and sent to Marischtrubau by the Germans. John was a great conversationalist; his father had been War Minister in the First World War and his Aunt, Margot Oxford, was the wife of the Prime Minister, Lord Asquith.

Then there was Michael Cubitt, captured at Leros, with whom I had many long walks in the camp, discussing future business after the war and the possibility of escaping over the wire.

In the room opposite me was the very likeable and highly

235

intelligent Jewish Officer, Captain Ben Aaron, whom I got to know very well. I think he was in the Pioneer Corps and, luckily for him, his officer's uniform – although not a guarantee – did save him from joining many others of his race in Auschwitz. He was a very deep thinker and entirely single-minded in his determination to play a major part in the liberation of Palestine and the formation of the new State of Israel. After the war he took this determination to such an extent that he was arrested by the British authorities in Palestine. It was only after his appeal from his prison to David Stirling and me, that our joint approach to the powers-that-be obtained his release. He later became Minister of Labour in the new state of Israel.

Amongst others were Roger Berry, from the South African Gunners; and Major Herbert Taylor, always known as Trotty, from the Royal Tank Corps, with whom he had won an MC in the desert. Trotty was a remarkable military historian and gave marvellous hour-long lectures on, for instance, Alexander the Great, or the American Civil War – without a note – bringing Ulysses C. Grant and Stonewall Jackson back to life in front of two or three hundred officers. We would discuss at length our interests in the mining world and he was to remain one of my closest friends.

' There was also Geoffrey Goschen; he was a regular of the Royal Horse Artillery of which his father, General Goschen was the Commander in Chief. He was a splendid person and a wonderful companion in the camp, although he had been captured in the desert after the battle of Bir Hakin, losing all his gun crews and this had a profound effect on him, from which he probably never fully recovered. He was an exact contemporary of Kumaramangalam's, both having been at Eton and Woolwich. We too, became very close friends.

Another life-long friendship formed in this most unfriendly of places was with a delightful young 2nd Lieutenant from the Indian Army, Saheb-zadeh Yaqub Khan, younger brother of the Maharaja of Rampur. I was always certain that he, like K, would go a very long way. After the war he was appointed ADC to Field Marshal Lord Wavell, and later to the new Viceroy of India, Lord Mountbatten, who organised the partition of India and Pakistan. Whilst his brother remained in India Yaqub took the difficult decision of opting for the

Moslem State of Pakistan. There he progressed rapidly in the Army until as a young Colonel he was selected to go to England to do the Imperial Defence College course. This was the élite of officers drawn from the Commonwealth, and having completed this with a distinction he returned to Pakistan and commanded a Brigade.

Shortly after this he was selected for the great Saint Cyr defence college course in Paris, organised by the French Army. (I think he was the only officer to have been chosen for both these courses.) After this he returned to Pakistan where, as a Major General, he was involved in the Seven Day War – against one of his closest friends, General Kumaramangalam, who was commanding the Indian Army. It was probably these two officers' behind-the-scenes communications which brought peace to the sub-Continent of India, out of what could have been a long-lasting and horrific blood-bath.

Now a Lt. General, he was given command of East Pakistan (now Bangaladesh) with a view to holding it against any forthcoming attack from India. All along he knew, and tried to persuade President Ayub Khan that it was untenable. He held the position, under mounting pressure from Mrs Gandhi, for six months, whereupon he informed the President that unless his Government were prepared to come to a settlement with India short of war he would have to resign his command.

This he bravely did, telling me shortly afterwards that it was a most terrible period in his life. When demoted to civilian status he returned to Karachi, where he was treated by all and sundry as a pariah. However soon after this India attacked East Pakistan and, as he correctly forecast, military resistance collapsed within a week and the President resigned. This brought Zulkifar Bhutto into power as Prime Minister and he immediately reinstated General Yaqub Khan, appointing him Ambassador to Paris, and then to Moscow.

After Moscow came Washington where, incidentally he hit the headlines during a notorious hijack when he volunteered to go, unarmed, to the hijackers and parley with them. This he did, persuading them to hand over their hostages and surrender. By now General Zia (who was also in the camp with me, as a 2nd Lt.) was in power, and he appointed him Foreign Minister which brought him the immensely complicated responsibility of the Soviet invasion of Afghanistan and the resulting three million refugees. In this capacity he served his country brilliantly, and after President Zia's death Benazir Bhutto asked him to remain as her Foreign Secretary, which he still is today. Also in the camp was Gordon Barker, who some years later, I was to find as my neighbour in Shropshire after he had taken Holy Orders. When he first saw me in Shropshire he was rather amazed to find I had survived, and greeted me with, 'But you are not supposed to be alive!'

Returning to the camp, life became, for me, very pleasant. I no longer had the sword of Damocles hanging over me in the form of SS guards and the constant threat of further interrogation together with everything that could stem from that; this had been my main fear ever since being captured. My remaining worry, however, was would I be court-martialled on my return to England, for having disobeyed orders and sailed to Samos?

There was a great spirit of comradeship and I made a great many life-long friends. Having no possessions – apart from the monthly Red Cross parcel, for which I will always be grateful – one really got to know people for what they were. Three years later I wrote the following description, 'Life in the camp, whilst I was there, was much like what I imagine over-fed ladies and businessmen seem to enjoy at these modern health-cure farms, perhaps slightly less boring and with a far better *esprit de corps* . . . being without anything in the world save for a monthly Red Cross parcel enabled one to really judge people on their own merit.'

We paraded around, all looking scruffy and untidy except for my new-found friend Major Willie Forbes, a regular Scots Guards officer. He was always immaculately turned out and as such was known by all and sundry as 'The last of the Britons'. I wore. every day, my thick wool French soldier's trousers, which I must have somehow picked up, or had donated, either in Belgrade hospital or in Lukenwald. They became known by K and Geoffrey Goschen as my lucky trousers. This they proved to be, as they eventually took me home, via Gothenburg and Liverpool.

On the daily roll call parades, when the German Hauptmann walked down the lines to count us, I was always very amused to think of what happened at a nearby camp when Tony McCraith had been there. He was standing near

Douglas Bader, who had two artificial legs. When the very serious humourless captain reached Bader in the line Bader suddenly flung his arms around the German's neck, cast his two legs away and hung there in front of four or five hundred officers on parade. There was nothing the German could do, other than march on down the line in this absurd position, carrying Bader with him, to the cheers of the 500!

The countryside surrounding Marischtrubau was beautiful, with rolling hills stretching into the distance. Behind the camp there were always very hard-working Czechoslovakian peasants tilling the hillside, whilst at the front, on the flat ground, there was a large sports field. Here we could enjoy watching twenty-four Hitler Jugend girls, in very brief and tight blue shorts, playing basketball. This was the nearest we got to the female sex during imprisonment, and many of my fellow officers had already been there for nearly four years, since Dunkirk.

One day I was suddenly called to the Camp Commandant's orderly room and told to report back at 10 am the following day. Apparently I had been selected, together with some thirty others, to be sent for examination by the Swiss Red Cross Medical Team for possible repatriation to Britain. This was most interesting news, and the following day we duly reported to the orderly room again. We were taken by bus to the hospital in the nearest town, where we found a team of Red Cross doctors awaiting us who put us through a rigorous examination, including X-rays.

Amongst our party was a Captain Radcliffe, a commando officer who had been fairly badly wounded in the head but was otherwise immensely strong physically. He had got himself on to the repatriation group by continually complaining of fearful headaches, and saying that the bullet which had hit him was still in his head. Ratty, as he was known, was subjected to head X-rays, and had contrived to put a pellet made of compressed silver paper and the same size as a bullet, between the back of his head and the X-ray table upon which he was lying.

All went well for Ratty; a beautiful clear photograph showed the bullet lodged in his brain and after we were all being evaluated as to the extent of our war wounds and disabilities the head Swiss surgeon came into the room and asked if

Captain Radcliffe would mind having a further head X-ray. Apparently the surgeon thought, from the picture in his hand, that it was quite inconceivable for Ratty to be physically or mentally normal. Poor Ratty went scarlet and was escorted back to the X-ray table where he had to quickly fumble around in his pocket for the bullet. Just as he was managing to get it in the right position it fell off the table, landing on the floor at the feet of the surgeon. Without further ado poor Ratty was shamefacedly marched out in front of us and into the waiting bus, to spend the rest of the war as a prisoner in Germany.

The rest of us returned to the camp; those of us (myself included) who had passed the rigorous repatriation criteria were told so, but at the same time were warned that the actual chances of being repatriated were very remote. This was because the whole operation had to be done on an international scale, with a similar number of repatriates being returned to Germany from England. We therefore returned to our rooms and thought not much more about it.

16

Oflag 7B Brunswick

Some three weeks later we suddenly had orders to pack up, as the whole camp was to move to central Germany, to what became known as Oflag Seven B Brunswick. At the time we had no idea as to why we were moved but it later transpired that our newly formed camp immediately adjoined Hitler's giant underground factory for making the engines for the new V1 and V2 rockets. The idea being that when the massive thousand bomber raids took place, which was an almost daily occurrence, we would be plastered with all their near misses. This happened on several occasions, killing a number of prisoners (including Lt Colonel Kilkelly, 8th Hussars) and guards.

The actual move was quite an experience with the entire camp being marched down to the railway station and ordered in to the cattle trucks – sixty officers per truck. Before entering the cattle trucks everyone, with the exception of the twenty-eight repatriation candidates, had their braces removed and handcuffs applied to their wrists. Once loaded, the train pulled out en route for Dresden, where our bombers had just done their worst, killing some two hundred thousand civilians and desecrating one of the most beautiful cities in Germany. Consequently there were many repairs needed on the railway track, causing a few days' delay. This made conditions for the cattle trucks inmates highly unattractive, to put it mildly. Understandably perhaps, the German guards (having just seen what our bombers had done) were in a particularly aggressive mood, frequently lashing out with their sticks and ready to shoot at the slightest provocation. Eventually we moved on, arriving at Brunswick Oflag Seven B sometime

241

around the beginning of June.

Oflag Seven B consisted of a number of fine, clean and large buildings, separated into blocks rather like chess men on a large chess board. I think the camp had been a Luftwaffe camp, rather like the big Air Force establishments you see near the A1 in Lincolnshire and Huntingdonshire. We soon settled in, and from memory the senior British officers were Colonel Waddilove and Captain Micklethwaite RN – the latter had been a prisoner of war since his destroyer was sunk when leading the abortive Tobruk raid in 1942. Each block had its own personalities: David Stirling and his friend Pringle, who was from Jamaica, were forever beavering away with elaborate 007-type plans for escaping. One was for a mass break-out over the fifteen-foot perimeter wire by about 150 officers during the night. The assumption was that in the general confusion a certain percentage would be able to get clear of the area, thus infiltrating the countryside and getting through France to the neutrality of Spain, or heading south to swim across the Rhine and thus into Switzerland.

This was exactly what Stanislaus Mardinkski did in 1944, when escaping from his Polish *Arbeit* party. He had been captured at the age of eighteen after his Cavalry regiment was destroyed when charging the German Panzer division in the first attack against Poland in 1939. Stanley was a man of immense spirit and charm, who eventually, through the good offices of the British Ambassador in Berne, turned up in England, where he joined one of the many Polish units. After the war he was disbanded but was not, like so many others, dumped in a Polish displaced persons' camp; he somehow contrived to get into civilian life and first came into my life in Shropshire, in 1957. Two years later I managed to get him a British passport and British nationality and he remained working with us until he died in 1985, a great character known throughout Shropshire and beyond.

Fortunately none of David's exciting schemes came to fruition; I say fortunately because a young and supposedly South African captain, Jerry van Zuko, made friends with many of us. He infiltrated himself into the holy of holies, where Pringle and others would be beavering away on ever-more exciting get-away schemes. I say 'fortunately' because

242

Jerry, who had considerable charm, was nothing other than an extremely clever Gestapo agent, of Belgian nationality who had spent a short time in Southern Africa, probably the Congo, before the war, and he passed back every single escape scheme to his headquarters. Shortly after the end of the war David and some of the others gave evidence against him, and he was either shot or hanged.

The Brunswick camp was much bigger than the one at Marischtrubau, with a far larger area in which to walk and exercise. It soon became rather similar to a university, with many people studying to become chartered accountants, lawyers, surveyors etc. – often with success. There was also a major theatrical group; they called themselves amateurs but were actually very professional and there was often a good play or musical available in the evenings. The theatrical side was organised by Peter Wills and several others who became actors after the war.

These soirées were not without the occasional drop of alcoholic refreshment, thanks to a young Captain called Ian Howie who had learned a little about distilling alcohol. Before long he had set up a business brewing up the raisins which arrived in our monthly Red Cross parcels. Next, with some judicious bribing of the German guards, and using the coffee and cigarettes which also came in the parcels, he was able to get enough near whisky-making ingredients to produce an occasional ration for anyone who was prepared to swap their ration for his product.

After the war Ian used his experience to start the lucrative Merrydown Cider Company.

Another sideline was a considerable amount of gambling, which was organised by Paul Coutts-Trotter, Philip Kindersley, Brocky Mytton and others. By the time I left the camp this was rapidly getting out of hand, and many young officers were getting fearfully into debt by signing IOUs up to ten, twenty and thirty thousand pounds – to be satisfied, presumably, by their parents after the war.

Politics began to creep into the camp, albeit in a small way. A number of officers were openly expressing their hopes of a socialist Britain after the war and their hero was Beveridge, later Lord Beveridge. At the time he was working on the future Welfare Society with, amongst others, Harold Wilson, in the bomb-proof cellars under Admiralty Arch. This small group was aptly named by K as the 'Beveridge Boys', and they were the precipitators of Churchill's landslide defeat in the September 1945 election.

Yet another side of our so-called University POW life were the lectures, given in the great hall to three or four hundred officers. This is where Trotty Taylor came into his element; going from Belisarius to Genghis Khan to Stonewall Jackson. One day Captain Micklethwaite, the SBO, asked me to give a major lecture on the Middle East, Greece and the chances of bringing Turkey into the war. I worked extremely hard for two or three weeks preparing this lecture, pointing out that President Inonu and Turkey were most unlikely to join our war until we had captured Rhodes and the other islands leading to Smyrna and Istanbul; unfortunately history proved me correct on this forecast.

On the overall war front the Allies had successfully begun their Second Front, despite huge losses, and throughout the months of June and July had made steady advances towards Germany, averaging, I think, some ten to twenty miles per day. Partly as a joke, and partly to raise morale, I drew up a large map – starting at Caen and going right up to Berlin, with the weekly advances showing quite clearly – also, assuming the same rate of advance, the estimated weekly progress right to Berlin, where I showed the Allies arriving through the Brandenburg gate in 1945. I kept this graph going for several weeks on the passage wall outside our room, so that everybody could see it. Eventually, just after an air raid, a furious camp commandant ordered it to be taken down immediately for insulting Hitler and the German Reich, and he wanted to know who the perpetrators of this crime were. However, in the post-raid chaos the matter was not pursued, luckily for me.

The main daytime excitement was seeing the huge fleets of Flying Fortresses on their way to bomb various strategic targets in Germany, and as they flew they looked exactly like two or three hundred Canada geese. These massive air armadas brought terrific cheers from us as they passed overhead, but it was not long before we were laughing on the other side of our faces.

Towards the end of June the first influx of prisoners began

to arrive from Arnhem, and the so-called 'A Bridge Too Far' disaster. Amongst them were a few of my friends, namely Gavin Astor and Arthur Cranley, later the Earl of Onslow, who had for a short period after I was captured, commanded my regiment. Also John Harvey, whose father was our Ambassador in Paris after the war.

Amongst the new arrivals was a young and very brash American who had been with the US Airborne Forces. He reckoned he knew all about – and probably did – the new, immensely accurate bombing technology of the Flying Fortresses. One day he gave a lecture in the open recreation area on how the new bombing technique could pin-point a target with such accuracy that they could hit a dollar bill from 25,000 feet. He told us all to watch, when the next raid flew over, to see this accuracy in action on the big German underground factory just south of our perimeter wire. This we duly did, and watched string after string of silver bombs falling nearly horizontally towards their target. However, almost before we realised it, a whole string of bombs landed the whole way along the southern perimeter of the camp and its buildings, killing a number of Allies, including Colonel Kilkelly, and Germans and wounding many more.

The American Lieutenant had been in the centre of the crowd watching the magnificent spectacle of precision bombing, giving a running commentary of the bombs as they were released from the planes, and pointing out how they would fall exactly on target. Although he was one of the fortunate ones who escaped unhurt he then totally collapsed and had a psychological breakdown, remaining in the camp hospital, a nervous wreck, until long after I was repatriated.

As a result of this bombing living conditions in the camp deteriorated immediately, as a number of buildings were unserviceable. The water supply had been destroyed and there was a lot of doubling-up and over-crowding; all most unattractive after our previous relatively peaceful regime.

Furthermore, it was alleged that around June 1944 the Canadians had shot some SS soldiers whom they had taken prisoner. This, coupled with a rumour that some British paratroopers from the 6th Airborne Division had shot their German prisoners whilst they were asleep, infuriated the Führer. He decreed very harsh treatment for escaping

245

prisoners of war, and for discipline within the existing camps to be made much more rigorous.

It was about this time that Foley, the splendid mining engineer officer, effected an escape through a tunnel with some companions. They were all captured and shot by the SS.

Likewise the great mass escape from Stalag Luft 111, where upwards of one hundred Air Force officers were all rounded up and shot. Hitler's orders were further motivated by a large amount of guerilla activity behind the lines on the Russian-Eastern front.

Soon after this, possibly as a result of Jerry Van Zuko's activities, David Stirling and one or two other marked men were taken off to the fortress prison of Colditz, and I was not to see David again until after the war. A few days after their departure I was sitting with Geoffrey, K and Philip Morris-Keating, when the German orderly officer came in and asked me to report to the camp Commandant's office, about a quarter of a mile away. Immediately I suspected trouble of the Salonika/Belgrade type, thinking – correctly – that my past was again catching up with me. It was therefore with some trepidation that I was ushered in to the office.

The Commandant wasted no time in getting straight to the point: in view of my record I was to be sent to Colditz on the following Friday.

I replied, to his astonishment, that whilst at Marischtrubau I had been passed by the International Red Cross Board of Swiss doctors for repatriation to England, on account of the severity of my war wounds. Thanks to my friend David Crane, who was in touch with Whitehall, I was actually in possession of the vital knowledge that my name was amongst the twenty-eight officers due to be repatriated within a few days.

This first major repatriation of the war had taken a very great deal of organization between the two warring sides, and unless both sides adhered strictly to their part of the bargain – as to names and number already agreed and signed for by the International Red Cross – the whole operation would collapse.

With this the Commandant's jaw dropped, realising that he was at the wrong end of a major bungle. He told me to return to my quarters while he reconsidered the matter.

Some weeks later I was informed by the same Commandant of the not unwelcome news that the repatriation party was to be ready to leave Oflag Seven B on September 9th 1944 – almost exactly one year after I had been captured.

The Almighty had done me a great service because, had I been shipped to Colditz, there was a chance that I would have shared the same fate as my friend Commander Mike Cumberledge. In 1943 Mike had been dropped by submarine with a load of explosives – with which he was to try to blow up the Corinth Canal. This would have worsened the strain on German shipping resources, making them increase every journey by the two hundred miles around Cape Matapa and Cape Malea. Tragically, he and the others involved were caught in the act and very badly treated, eventually ending up in Colditz and then Flossenburg concentration camp.

Two days before the Germans surrendered they were all shot.

I knew that the Germans linked me with their huge losses of manpower, material, ships and planes in their re-capture of Cos, Leros and Samos, and therefore they would possibly have meted the same treatment out to me.

In spite of all this I had very mixed feelings during my last days in Brunswick. I had made a number of what were to be enduring friendships and it was very sad and touching for me to see how wonderfully kind and generous K and all my room mates were to me that final evening, before we left in the dark. I knew only too well what their feelings must have been like, particularly as some of them had been in prison camp for two, three, and sometimes four years. They gave a party for me and I promised to visit all their families, which, I am glad to say, I did.

At about 6 pm we, with our meagre possessions (me in my blue trousers) climbed into an ordinary thirty-seater bus – and very nearly did not get out alive. We hung around the main gate with the engine going, all the windows and doors shut, and an appalling smell of carbon monoxide coming from the exhaust. When it became intolerable there was a minor riot to somehow open a window, which – gasping for fresh air – we finally managed to do. We then proceeded without further incident to Brunswick railway station.

Amongst our party was someone I had made great friends with, Major Richard Knight, 4th Hussars, who was a regular Cavalry Officer and quite a bit older than me. He and his wife were later to play a major part in a 'Help the Tibetans' campaign. This included adopting several Tibetan children, following the deposing of the Dalai Lama.

Once at the station we got into a comfortable civilian train with passenger coaches, much the same as every train in England in the thirties. To us, however, it was the Ritz on wheels, and away we steamed, heading due north.

This Ritz on wheels took us through Hannover, Schleswig-Holstein and Denmark, ending up in Göteborg, where we were welcomed by the Swedes amidst a rather cold atmosphere – many of the Swedes were rather pro-German at that time I think. We spent two days there being entertained, before embarking on the Red Cross ship which was to take us right round to Liverpool, fully lit up and covered with enormous International Red Cross markings and flags.

When we sailed we were told that the ship had had to change its original sailing plans. This was because the Germans had ordered it to go right up the Norwegian coast as far as Christiansund, some 700 miles due north, where they were going to have a final inspection of everything and everybody before finally releasing the ship to sail to Britain.

I was shattered by this news as, having got so near – and yet so far – from freedom, I now fully expected to be hauled off the boat at the last outpost of Christiansund.

We spent some twelve hours there, while the Germans came aboard and made their inspections.

I was relieved when finally, with three blasts of the ship's siren we headed west for home.

Home meant the wonderful prospect of being reunited with my father, with Ninette, and with my sister Elizabeth. My brother Godfrey was in the Far East and I had not seen them for five years – I had not had a single letter from anybody since being captured, and no-one had heard anything from me, as I always had the stigma of being *Persona non grata* with the Germans.

We had a very enjoyable voyage which was a million light years away from barely one week ago, but in no way did I ever forget all my friends left behind in the camp.

They were already beginning to be subjected to far more unpleasant conditions than I had experienced, and it was not long before the monthly supply of Red Cross parcels was terminated and the screw gradually tightened. John Tennant, for example, who had entered the war weighing eleven stone, was now reduced to six.

The constant threats issued by Sir Robert (later Lord) Vansittart who was the head of the British Foreign Office, against the Germans, and indirectly against the German POWs, was creating a major backlash against all my recent friends and, in fact all prisoners of war held by the Germans. I made it one of my top priorities that the moment I was in a position to do so, I would seek a meeting with Vansittart. We had a long discussion and he soon got my message, which was basically to pipe down before he so infuriated the Germans that all our POWs would be in great danger. Despite his vitriolic hatred and outspoken opinion of the Germans he was a reasonable man, and I did not hear any more of his sabre-rattling speeches at that critial period of the war.

17

Home At Last

On September 20th 1944 we arrived in a grey, overcast Liverpool dock, and I clearly remember thinking of Byron's poem about the Aegean:

> 'The Isles Of Greece! The Isles of Greece!
> Where burning Sappho loved and sung,
> Where grew the arts of war and peace,
> Where Delos rose, and Phoebus sprung!
> Eternal summer gilds them yet,
> But all, except their sun, is set.'

I suddenly realised that I was not only in love with my Greek wife Ninette, but also with Greece, where I had spent nearly three years.

After disembarking we went through the usual military procedure of names, regiments etc. and were then allocated a certain amount of money and ration cards, identity papers and a modest amount of clothing. We were then brought down to earth with a bump, and politely reminded that although our future was undecided we were still officers on active service, but in the meantime we were each allocated three weeks leave.

At last we were finally able to contact our next of kin and I immediately rang my father at Bateman's, his home in Sussex where he had been living for the last five years, but to which I had never been. After various complications I eventually got through to my father who, it transpired was fishing on the Spey. He said, 'Come up here right away' – which I did, travelling by train through the beautiful Highlands in a railway carriage empty save for one other occupant.

He happened to be the naval hero of the time, Admiral of the Fleet Sir Philip Vian DSO, who was also going for a short fishing holiday in Scotland. We sat opposite each other talking pleasantries – me having little knowledge of his exploits and he little realising that one week before his companion had been in the heart of Germany. On arrival at Grantown-on-Spey we both went our separate ways, with me feeling most unlike the Spey salmon – very much a fish out of water both mentally and physically – and in entirely different surroundings.

Nevertheless I had a very happy and relaxed ten days, hearing all the family news and writing to Ninette. Godfrey, in the Fleet Air Arm, was currently fighting the Japanese in the Far East, having sailed with the Malta convoys and the Arctic convoys to Murmansk. Elizabeth had left school and was now working as a VAD in London.

I contacted all the families of my fellow prisoners so recently left behind in Germany, and told them I would do my best to visit them all when I was discharged from hospital.

I was, of course, intensely interested in hearing how my father had managed to keep alive what I had always considered to be my group of companies, which we had bought from the Rothschilds in 1938 – conceived by me but executed with the great help of my father.

Since before the war, and throughout it (with the exception of my years in prison) I had continually written to Clement telling him under no circumstances was he to let the companies be killed off or snatched away before I returned to take over and endeavour to make them my life's work. I wanted to build them up into their former glory, or, rather, to make them worth, for the shareholders, an investment that would stand four-square against any similar investment.

This was quite an ambitious undertaking because, as a result of the war, and the depression before the war, their assets and valuation had fallen dangerously towards zero.

I shall always be grateful to my father and to Major W.M. Henderson-Scott who managed to keep the companies afloat for almost five weary war years, waiting for me to return to take over the helm as my first great ambition in life.

251

After my three weeks leave were up I had orders to report to the big military hospital just outside London. We were all to spend two or three weeks being rigorously examined and treated before it was decided what, if any, military duties we were going to be allocated.

After I had broken my skull on the island of Milos in 1941 my right eye was more or less permanently paralysed, and my right ear totally deaf; apparently the nerve had been killed as a result of the fall. To discover if this was indeed the case the doctors in the hospital made me lie down on the theatre table with my head resting on my left ear. They told me that they would be pouring cold water into my right ear and that I would probably feel faint, or might even faint, in which case I was to tell them immediately. I had no idea what they were up to, but presumed that if I felt faint I would be giving them the answer as to whether I was deaf or not.

After two or three minutes of this water trick, and still feeling perfectly all right, I shamefacedly said that I was not feeling in the least bit faint. To my surprise the doctors replied that that was exactly what they wanted to know, and they therefore regretted that the blow to my head had killed the nerve commanding my hearing – making me totally deaf in that ear.

As for my right eye, arm and wrist, all of which I had only partial use of, they would remain in the same condition also *ad infinitum*.

My internal wounds were far from happy, as they had not healed up completely and the doctors were worried that the internal abcesses would start up again. In this they were completely right, as the following year I had to be rushed to St George's Hospital for a further, and thankfully final, operation by the great surgeon Ivor Black.

At the end of my period in hospital I was unofficially told by the medical board that I was to be invalided out of the army as 100 per cent disabled. With this knowledge I sat down and wrote a report to Brigadier Crocket, the overall head of MI9 in London and for whom I had been indirectly working for the last three years.

Despite my 100 per cent disability I desperately wanted to return to my old command position in the Middle East, even as a liaison officer or consultant. This was for several reasons, the most important being to reward – and also to identify – all my Greek friends and agents who had served Britain so loyally, and who were largely known only to me. I also wanted to rejoin Ninette, whom I had not seen since September 8th 1943.

This request was sent to my successor, Commander Taffy Rodd, who continually refused any offers of assistance, which was a pity as for many years afterwards I was to get many letters and requests from splendidly loyal Greeks and Cretans asking for some help, or acknowledgement, of their services in the war.

Whilst in hospital I had spotted and made friends with a tall and very badly wounded Greek officer named Stathis Kalamidas. I immediately took to him, and realised that he was an unusually fine person of great depth of character. He had been shockingly wounded both in his legs and his head – in his forehead there was an indentation where you could see his pulse beating.

Being far from his home country, and knowing no-one in England, I invited him to come back home with me to Batemans.

Here he met my sister Elizabeth, home on leave from her VAD work, and they promptly fell in love.

As I had been abroad for seven out of the last ten years I did not know my sister as well as brothers and sisters usually do, but she was now extremely attractive, intelligent and capable and had been brought up virtually single-handedly by our father, whom she adored, since the tragic loss of our mother when she was only six.

Soon after I arrived home a long-awaited letter from Ninette appeared for me, postmarked Cairo. Evidently she had gone to stay with her sister Madame Brunner, at the Swiss Embassy. My heart leapt as I went off to the quiet of my room to read my precious letter. Ninette began by saying that after I had so sadly disappeared more than a year ago, during which time she had had no news of me, dead or alive, she had suffered great depression. She went on to say that in my absence, she, a young girl in Cairo with life then seeming so short, had met somebody else and wanted to marry him.

I remembered my doubts before the wedding, but they

were only fleeting and did not alter the fact that I was very much in love with her; more so than I had ever been with anyone ever before. However, the very nature of my work, and the state of the war on our doorstep had played a major part in distracting me from my young bride.

This was the greatest emotional blow that I had experienced since the death of my mother; comparable, I suppose, to my first night in the Gestapo cell in Salonika, but that, I suppose, was the extreme emotion of fear. Two of these awful experiences were directly created by none other than Colonel Skorzeny when he liberated Mussolini in 1943. Unknown to him he had deprived me of my lovely wife and at the same time given her to a Greek, who had, to call a spade a spade, stolen my wife.

I am not given by nature to hate or seek revenge, and even if our roles had been reversed, with me being left alone and falling deeply in love with someone else, I do not think I would have ditched her because I am just not made that way. The marriage vows were, for me, for life.

This bitter blow was so paralysing that I could not tell my father straight away. He had been longing to welcome Ninette into the family and it was about three days before I was able to break this appallingly dreadful news to him.

In the meantime Elizabeth and Kalamidas were blissfully happy together, and it was during one week-end, when they had gone to stay with one of Elizabeth's friends, that I broke the news.

My father was no longer the gay, wonderfully happy father I had known before the war – he had felt the loss of my brother Charles most terribly, and this was yet another blow.

Elizabeth and Kalamidas returned to Batemans very much in love and secretly engaged, and Kalamidas, unaware of my disaster, asked my father for Elizabeth's hand in marriage. He hoped to take her off to Greece, where he was about to embark on the Greek diplomatic ladder. Poor Kalamidas was met with icy coldness as Father, thinking of me, felt that one Greek in the family was one too many, and he flatly refused to allow an engagement.

I made every effort to get out to Cairo somehow and win Ninette back. As late as January 1945, long after I had agreed to grant her a divorce, she was writing that she was in a very mixed-up state of mind, on the verge of a nervous break-down. However, with my rival ever-present, the chance of reconciliation slipped away.

Here I was, stuck in England, half in and half out of the army, half married and half not married.

I was based at Batemans, where my father and my stepmother Eva, whom he had married in 1936, were kindness itself. There was, however, an atmosphere of sadness in the lovely old house, which I partly attributed to its previous owner, who was, of course Kipling. He also had suffered immense personal sorrow when his nineteen-year old son was reported killed within a few weeks of going to the Western Front with his regiment, the Irish Guards. This happened at the very same time as Kipling himself was touring the battlefields, giving morale-boosting speeches at the request of the Prime Minister.

Hence by December, seeing little hope of a reunion with Ninette, I agreed to her request for a divorce. However, she did not seem to understand that having been married under both Greek and British laws, it was not just a case of 'off with the old and on with the new' – the English divorce laws were highly complex.

I had no knowledge of how divorces were effected, only that I wanted ours to be with as little unpleasantness and waste of time to Ninette as possible.

At this stage I was still unaware of the identity of the lucky man who was going to supersede me; he had been lying very low throughout. Ninette said that she had heard it was customary in these matters for the husband to go off to Brighton and spend the night with a female who specialised in such fictitious operations, so that I could then be cited as the guilty party, with no moral or other troubles for me.

This, I felt, was really going too far, and suggested that the only way to do it correctly was for her lover to stand up and be counted.

I was extremely fond of Ninette's mother, and apparently she was of me. Years later I was told how angry she was when Ninette told her the news. She said in horror: 'What! Swapping sterling for drachmae!' This, coming from an eminent banker's daughter, said it all.

From then on the horrible business unfolded and, thanks to

my old friend Mr G.F. Higginson of Bird and Bird, the divorce was set in motion. Mr Angelos Vlachos was cited, and two years later the divorce document was signed, but the heartache was still present.

In this respect I was very fortunate that I had work to occupy me with the nucleus of my pre-war business, namely the Exploration Company, the El Oro Mining and Exploration Company and their small satellite companies. They were scarcely ticking over, but the all-important point was that they were alive, and thus presented me with a great challenge to build them up into something that not only I could be proud of, but also for the two thousand shareholders to do better than in any comparable investment.

This partly took my mind off sadder matters, and I soon became engrossed in my businesses and their affairs.

18

My POW's Relatives

Socially, I soon began to circulate in my pre-war crowd. I went down to stay with Colonel and Lady Violet Astor at Hever Castle in Kent, and told them all about Gavin. I greatly admired Colonel Astor, who had a magnificent First World War record, and was very tall and distinguished looking. He had been badly wounded, but stood as erect as when he had been in the Coldstream Guards thirty years before. Colonel Astor was chairman of *The Times*, and one day he asked me to one of their luncheon parties in Printing House Square, which was a great occasion for me, as they were very exclusive, attended by most interesting people. He was very modest and kind and was married to the equally charming and lovely Lady Violet. Her daughter Lady Margaret Myddleton was there; of her and her husband I saw more when I moved to Leicestershire to hunt with the Quorn and Belvoir.

There was a houseful of very distinguished and interesting guests which included Sir Harold and Lady Zia Wernher and their most amusing second daughter. Also there were Lord Herbert, later the Earl of Pembroke, and Princess Marina, Duchess of Kent. She was a most lovely person, very beautiful and very kind, and being a Greek Princess seemed fascinated by the fact that I knew her native country so well.

I saw quite a lot of this charming Princess in the weeks ahead, and often went dancing with some of these friends in the evenings.

Frequently I visited John Tennant's mother at week-ends; she lived in Kent near the great house called Maytham that Lutyens built for her husband. May Tennant had done a great deal for the factory workers in England and was made a

257

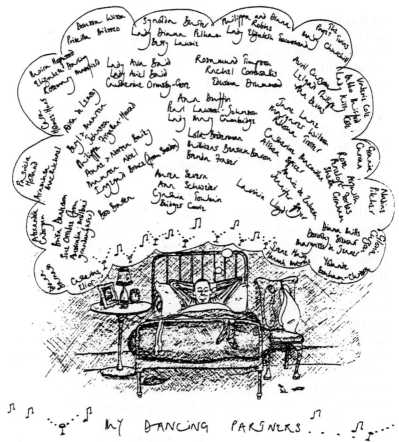

MY DANCING PARTNERS...

Companion of Honour for this work, which included initiating the Safety in Factories Act, and other social measures.

I also went to stay with General and Mrs Goschen, Geoffrey's parents, at Marconi Downs farm, near Lechlade. There we all entered into the spirit of things by helping with the farm work, and felling trees etc. From there I went to visit Eleanor Morris-Keating, Philip's wife, at her house Estcourt, in Gloucestershire. She spent most of her time working in St James's Palace on POW parcels and other things for prisoners. I also went to see Trot Taylor's wife, Marianne, and told her all about her Herbert and his impressive military lectures.

Next came a very special person, Lady Ava Baird, who had been a close friend of my brother Charles and was now more or less engaged to Ronnie Chance, of the Sixtieth. While we were in Oflag Seven B Ronnie had asked me to make certain that she would wait patiently for him to marry her as soon as he was liberated. They have now been happily married for forty-five years and live in Wiltshire.

My next visit was to Nottinghamshire, to see Sir Douglas and Lady McCraith, who were Tony's parents.

Their elder son, Patrick, had joined the regiment with me in 1937. He remained with the regiment from Palestine through to Alamein; the whole campaign along the Western Desert, through intensely fierce fighting with all my old comrades such as Stanley Christopherson, Stephen Mitchell, Myles Hildyard, Michael Laycock, Lawrence Biddle, John Walters, Roger Sutton-Nelthorpe and others. They went right through to the D-Day landing in France, and were eventually the first regiment to cross the German border. Patrick was there until the end, and later became honorary Colonel of the Sherwood Rangers. He succeeded Lord Barnby, who was with the regiment at Gallipoli in 1916, the year of my birth, and attended all the regimental dinners at Claridges – immaculately turned out and 100 per cent fit – until he was ninety-seven.

The next person I went to stay with was Sydney Morse's wife, Dorothy, at their home near Ipswich. From there I contacted Micky Revere's and Tony Holden's families. These were all Sherwood Rangers from A and B Batteries in Crete, and had sadly been swept into the bag by the oncoming German tide after the fall of Crete. They had already been locked away in Germany for nearly four years, and I had last seen them on that long, hot and thirsty march from Sphakia to Galatas prison camp.

I told them how, on the long evacuation from our gun sites above Hania through to the embarkation point at Sphakia and then back to Galatas, I had carried one of my most treasured possessions – my Jaegar camel-hair sleeping bag. On very cold nights this was worth a million to me – and also to Myles, who somehow managed to squash himself into it as well. Before escaping from Galatas I gave it to Sydney, and it must have been invaluable to him during the next four years of bitterly cold imprisonment in Germany.

Before the war Sydney had been managing director of a

259

large private brewing company in Suffolk. He was also to become a director of the prestigious Norwich Union Insurance Company. Sydney's wife, Dorothy, was the daughter of the chairman and controller of the Royal Mint, and she also did wonderful work for the SRY Association.

Amongst many other parents I saw were those of Michael Cubitt. His mother was very beautiful and his father worked in the city, running an investment trust.

Equally enjoyable was visiting David Stirling's mother, who lived in a very fine old-fashioned flat in Down Street. Her husband, Colonel Stirling of Keir, had died several years previously.

After the war, when David had returned, I went there on several occasions. There always seemed to be a conspiratorial atmosphere involving some new adventure that David and his close friends were planning. His mother seemed to be very much *au fait* with what was going on, and appeared to me as a kind of *eminence grise*.

Contacting K's parents (who were in India) was more difficult, but by the end of November news of my return to the land of the living has reached my brother Godfrey – whom I had last heard of when he was doing the Malta convoy.

Godfrey had now done nearly five years continuous service since he wrote this very prophetic letter to our father:

'18.VI.40 . . . I feel rather relieved that the French have packed up – we know where we are now, and having got rid of that procrastinating old fool Chamberlain we can now get to work. It will be six months before anything appreciable comes out of the USA and a year before we can turn the policy of defence and blockade into attack. It is no good underestimating AH – he does not give a damn how many people starve next winter as long as his armies are fed. He has ample stores to do that.

We are indeed fortunate to be alive in such interesting times; they only occur every century or so and it is the greatest luck to be here now. What an honour it is to be the sole champions of such a cause. Love to all, Godfrey.'

I now had a letter from him in the Far East, where he was fighting the Japanese – still with the Fleet Air Arm aircraft carriers. In it he congratulated me about Ninette and explained a little of his life; I quote it here, as he had achieved a really quite remarkable record.

'Ceylon, 5.4.45. I consider that business, like flying, is a precision job; an inaccurate pilot prangs sooner or later. I always do my cockpit check before taking off. Only one other member of my course of eighty starters is still on full flying duties. Sixty odd are dead. I intend to survive the peace as well – the same method will serve.'

In my reply to him I gave him my sad news about Ninette, and mentioned that if he ever went near Madras he should endeavour to call on K's father, Dr Surabaya. I asked him to tell the doctor that his son was doing noble work, in a big prison of war camp in Germany keeping the flag flying and lifting the morale of the camp.

Several weeks later Godfrey wrote the following:

'21.4.45. I went up to Calcutta in my own plane the other day. Leaving here in the dark I was there at 12.30; in time for lunch. On the way back I stopped for gas at Madras, and stayed the night. I did not have the name of your friend with me, but remembered he lived at White something or other, so spent forty-five minutes going right through the telephone directory. In the end I found a name that rang a bell, so phoned him. It was him, and he had a major pongo son so I called on him. Very charming highly cultured lawyer, played cricket in England. Left Congress in 1942. Has considerable political influence. Smallish house furnished in Indian fashion. He wore a sarong etc. Interesting library of topical books, generally a clued up bloke – bang on type as we say. I wish I had known more of his son. He does not know where in Germany the camp is, or what else goes on.'

261

Thanks to Godfrey I had been able to get through to the Indian continent.

Godfrey survived his sixth and final year in the war against the Japs, and was very impressed with the American Navy and Fleet Air Arm, but perhaps not quite so impressed with his own.

After the Hiroshima and Nagasaki bombs and the capitulation of Japan, the run-down of the Navy was beginning, and the fine fighter planes on Godfrey's aircraft carrier were being shoved overboard and sunk. Godfrey immediately stuck his toes in and got permission from his Admiral to fly his plane the whole way back to his original Fleet Air Arm base at Yeovil, in Somerset. This was a distance of some seven thousand miles, the sort of thing that Amy Johnson had been hitting world headlines for a few years previously. His Corsair is now in the Fleet Air Arm museum at Yeovil.

Godfrey duly arrived back early in 1946. Before leaving France on his refuelling stop he took on a full load of the very best Armagnac, Cognac, Burgundy and Claret. Knowing the Customs officers' routine at Yeovil he timed his arrival for 6.30 pm, and carefully circled the airport until he saw the Customs officer leave for home. He was thus able to land, load his priceless cargo into his ancient Bentley in the dark, and be well on his way to Batemans before the Customs man returned.

19

Roosevelt, Marshall and Eisenhower

By early 1945 I had finished contacting the remaining families and I then received my official 'Order of the Boot'.

My role had now come to an end.

I much regretted Wilson's failure to capture Rhodes and to bring Turkey into the war on our side, which would have enabled the war already to have been victoriously ended, with a massive Allied attack sweeping up through Romania and along the Danube right through to Berlin. This would have obviated the Second Front and storming the Atlantic Wall, which probably cost a million or more lives on both sides. The massive loss of life and material during the invasion of Europe on D-Day need never have taken place, likewise the immense destruction of civilian and war property and material throughout France, Holland and Belgium.

Russia would have been restricted to her original boundaries, whereas now the brutal communist monster was slowly pushing through the lands of our heroic Allies the Poles, Czechs, the Baltic states and many others – all the countries to the east of the Iron Curtain would have been free Sovereign states. Instead of this, a hundred million or more of them were imprisoned, including the remaining Jews trapped in Stalin's new empire. There they remained for the next half century, sealed within by that grim satanic barrier, the Iron Curtain, stretching for a thousand miles. Britain and her Empire would still have been the most powerful on earth.

Lastly, and by no means least for the Jews, had Churchill's plans for the Dardanelles of 1916 been superimposed on September 9th 1943 (under vastly more favourable conditions, with a friendly Turkey as opposed to a Turkey at war with us) – which he intended doing – the Holocaust would have been largely avoided, because Germany would have capitulated to the Allies long before the Red Army ever crossed the Polish border.

All this was a direct result of, firstly, the failure to capture Rhodes on September 9th. Secondly it was as a result of President Roosevelt and Generals Marshall and Eisenhower's refusal to help, even though Churchill had provided Eisenhower with ninety per cent of his entire Middle East forces for the incredibly stupid manoeuvre of fighting the whole length of Italy, with no obvious reward other than to reach the Alps – and come to a full stop.

On this front alone the Americans and the British, under Eisenhower, employed, and had at their disposal, more aircraft – fighters and bombers – than Hitler had for deployment on all his fronts put together.

It was at that moment, in early September 1943, that the first and unrepeatable heaven-sent opportunity to capture Rhodes, whilst the iron was still hot – and all foreseen and forewarned by Churchill – had been monumentally bungled.

Having already occupied three of the islands, the fall of Rhodes into Allied hands would have presented Churchill with a unique gift of the whole coast cleared from Rhodes to Istanbul – all in the space of three days.

So that there should be no feelings that I have 'over-egged the pudding', I quote from Churchill's *Closing the Ring, Vol. V – Island Prizes Lost* –

'When the tremendous events of the Italian surrender occurred my mind turned to the Aegean islands, so long the object of strategic desire. On September 9th I had cabled from Washington to General Wilson, Commander-in-Chief of the Middle East, "This is the time to play high. Improvise and dare".'

These last words were most appropriate to our adventure, particularly as it was on September 9th that we were sailing to capture the islands.

Churchill continued . . .

'The essential steps were completed in the formal Armistice terms, but there were other fruits to be gathered in this dread harvest: the Italian fleet must be transferred to Allied ports; there were many Italian divisions in south-eastern Europe whose equipment would be valuable to the Allies in the continued struggle against Nazi Germany, and there were still more important bases in the eastern Mediterranean. It was essential that these islands should not fall into hostile hands. I was acutely aware of this danger.'

Fifty years later, armed with all the records and speeches of Churchill, Stalin and others, I find it essential to give the full history and effect on us all in Britain and the world, and I therefore continue with the story, particularly as the two major histories of the Second World War, by John Keegan and Martin Gilbert scarcely give twenty pages (out of 1,000) to the Rhodes, Leros, Samos story, whereas Churchill himself wrote over 100 pages and says it created for him 'The sharpest pangs I suffered in the war.' The probable reason is that the exact true story had never been told before.

20

Cairo, Dardanelles and Rhodes

The Middle East Command based in Cairo under General Wilson was a mammoth military HQ with every type of different department, whose individual commanders were often devoting time to increasing their own personnel, with an eye to the ensuing elevation in rank. These numerous swelling octopuses had been named by the fighting soldiers on the Western Desert 'The gabardine swine', named after their smart gabardine drill uniforms.

I would be very surprised if, in his command – even after Churchill had assisted Eisenhower in Italy, there was much short of half a million men, which Churchill was rightly suspicious of ('Please let me know your ration strength').

On the overall war front it must be remembered that for the first two-and-a-half years of the war Britain and her Empire had stood up alone to Hitler's superb and ruthless military machine, the like of which, in its brilliant efficiency and fighting qualities, had never been surpassed in all history.

During these early years Churchill had had to fight both on the war front and on the home front, as there were many rocky periods after various disasters when he could have been thrown out.

After the fall of Tobruk, for instance, a motion was put forward in Parliament by a conservative MP to sack Churchill and appoint the Duke of Gloucester as Commander-in-Chief.

Moreover, the failure – through no fault of his own – of his Dardanelles campaign in 1917 had cast him into the political wilderness for the next two decades, and made him in many quarters a hated man. He had had to resign from the Cabinet and take up a fighting soldier's position on the Western Front, and was damned by all and sundry for his adventures into Turkey and beyond.

Despite history subsequently showing that he was right all along, and therefore missing the rewards and justification of his correctness by a matter of days, he was branded with a stigma that prevented him proclaiming – other than in a muted and diplomatic way – his desire and preference for a Turkish and Balkan front. From William Manchester's book *The Caged Lion* I quote the following:

'When the Central Powers, led by Germany and Austria-Hungary, plunged all Europe into the Great War of 1914-1918, Churchill had anticipated it. Since 1911 he had been First Lord of the Admiralty. The fleet was ready. But on the Western Front the great armies were locked in a bloody, hopeless stalemate. It would be years before either side could hope for victory in the west. Churchill saw a way to break the deadlock. He proposed that the Allied navies open a new front in the eastern Mediterranean, exploiting the weakness of the Central Powers unstable ally, Turkey. If the Dardanelles strait were forced by battleships, Constantinople would fall within hours. The French and British could then join hands with their Russian ally and sweep up the Danube into Hungary, Austria, Bavaria and Wurttemberg, ripping open the Second Reich's undefended southern flank.

Today military historians agree that the Dardanelles strategy could have ended the war in 1916 with a German defeat. But a timid British admiral, who had been sweeping all before him, turned tail at the first sign of resistance – even as the Turks, believing themselves beaten, abandoned their forts on the strait and began the evacuation of their capital. Then equally incompetent British generals botched the landings on the Gallipoli Peninsula, which flanked the Dardanelles. The British demanded a scapegoat, and Churchill, as the stratagem's most flamboyant advocate, was dismissed from the

267

Admiralty. He joined the army, crossed to Flanders, and, as a lieutenant colonel, commanded a battalion in the trenches.'

Consequently any mention of the Dardanelles, Turkey or the Balkans created terror in the minds of both the US and the British Chiefs of Staff. That is why he had to play this card with extreme diplomacy, and had his hands tied behind his back, so to speak, when pressing the eastern advance.

From *The Aegean Mission*, Jeffrey Holland writes:

'From his own statements, it would appear that Winston Churchill really hoped to open a Balkans front in preference to an Allied assault in north western Europe. His intention went well beyond "cover and deception". However, in either event, the assignment of a single infantry brigade into the Dodecanese, without first ensuring the capture of Rhodes, was intolerable and insupportable – a vain gesture, soon dispelled by superior force of arms.'

Returning to Rhodes on September 9th, the courageous George Jellicoe landed by parachute accompanied by an Italian-speaking officer, Major Count Drobski (Dolby).

Their first attempt on the previous night had failed because of poor visibility, and so they had had to return to Cyprus and try again the following night. They landed successfully; however Major Drobski (Dolby) broke his leg on impact and they then heard the sound of gunfire nearby and were uncertain as to whether it was friend or foe. George Jellicoe, who had instructions not to let General Wilson's letter to Admiral Camponi fall into enemy hands under any circumstances, decided that there was no alternative but to eat the letter there and then, which he did – making him feel somewhat the worse for it.

Shortly afterwards a party of Italian soldiers came upon them, and – exactly similar as had happened to us – proved friendly, offering to take George and his injured companion to the Commander-in-Chief, Admiral Camponi.

During their discussions Camponi asked what assistance the Allies could give in holding Rhodes, but apparently he was not offered anything substantial immediately, which in my opinion was a grave mistake. Here they were, safely in Rhodes, ready for striking NOW. Had Camponi been given the same treatment that General Solderelli had been given by David Pawson, Alex Levides and myself, I am convinced the situation would have been very different.

To be fair to Admiral Camponi it is essential to understand his position. He had served his country and Government honourably and well – having risen to C-in-C of the Italian Navy – and was at that moment commanding Italy's most important strategic island base, Rhodes. He had just received an order from Marshal Badoglio which must have been one of the most equivocal messages that he, accustomed as he was to the thousand and one pitfalls of Italian orders, had ever seen. In a nutshell, after nearly four years of war, fighting alongside his German allies, he was suddenly told to fight not with, but against, the Germans. It was exactly as if, for example, General Wilson had been ordered to stop fighting Field Marshal Erwin Rommel and to fight the Americans instead, taking his orders from Rommel.

Camponi had Hitler's own terrific and extremely tough General Klemann commanding the 5,500 beleaguered Germans, recently sent by Hitler as a fire brigade force when he suspected treachery from the Italian King, with orders to hold Rhodes at all costs. By late evening on September 9th, having managed to procrastinate in giving a 'yes' or 'no' answer to Klemann, he was suddenly confronted by Major Lord Jellicoe and Major Count Drobski (Dolby) with messages from General Wilson asking him to resist the Germans. With Klemann breathing down his neck he naturally asked Jellicoe what assistance he could give, and – of utmost importance – how soon. Jellicoe's answer left him more depressed than ever when he was told no help could come for a week. This despite the fact that Churchill had given Wilson thirty-seven days clear warning to be ready for this exact emergency.

Camponi knew that with Klemann at his back a few hours was too long, and a week was eternity – so he wrote to Wilson begging for the least he was entitled to expect, namely immediate support. Wilson, like Jellicoe, offered him nothing in under a week.

From then on his tragedy unfolded to its bitter end in front of a firing squad in Parma.

In Rhodes there were nearly forty thousand Italian troops who could – and would – fight, and in some important areas already were fighting the Germans, with no assistance from us at all.

Klemann had no hope whatsoever, as events proved, of getting immediate sea or airborne assistance from the German command in Athens (or anywhere else) due to the chaotic conditions ruling as a result of the Italian Armistice forty-eight hours before. The whole of Italy, from Sardinia to Florence, to Naples and on throughout Yugoslavia, from Zagreb to Albania, and from Yanina in Greece to Corfu and Cephalonia to the Peloponnese and throughout the whole of the Aegean was in a state of total convulsion.

The Germans were desperately short of almost every form of shipping, which in any case would have been subject to destruction by our Navy and Air Force – favoured, as shown in the maps, for the first time in that theatre of war. They had to contend with the entire British Mediterranean Fleet based just 300 miles away in Alexandria and consisting of at least ten cruisers, twenty destroyers and numerous submarines and MTBs.

They were also down to 500 planes on the Italian front, against some 4,500 Allied and American planes.

Having been offered no help earlier than a week away, Admiral Camponi said that he would see what could be arranged. In the meantime, he put a MAAS, together with his Chief-of-Staff, at Jellicoe's disposal to take him off the island with the injured Count Drobski.

(I am reminded of a conversation I once had with Colonel Jack Churchill, who had commanded the forces in Yugoslavia and was stationed way up the eastern coast of the Adriatic, and off the coast of Yugoslavia. He had with him such interesting people as Evelyn Waugh, Randolph Churchill, David Karmel QC, Admiral Cowan and others. At that stage in the war he was given a free hand to recruit any nationality, including expatriate Germans, and his experience was that the German soldier, in a corner, was unbeatable. Apparently, if you sent three Germans to hold a hill they would remain there indefinitely, holding the hill. If you sent three British soldiers to undertake the same task they would by the third day send a message back 'When is the ENSA coming?') (Entertainment National Service Association.)

In the meantime General Klemann, in his perilous position, did not send any messages out as to when the ENSA was coming, but he stayed put.

Jellicoe, the Italian Chief-of-Staff Colonel Fanetza and Drobski now left Rhodes – the only place that mattered – and never returned.

Firstly they went north-west to Symi, dropping off Drobski for medical treatment; they then raced one hundred miles due east back along the Turkish coast to Castelorizo. Here Jellicoe collected a detachment of SBS Commandos before doubling all the way back to take over Cos, Leros and Samos.

This was a complete wild-goose chase as we had already taken these islands – and had we not done so, beating the Germans to it, the Germans would have been there to greet Jellicoe when he arrived on the 14th. After our capture of Leros at 4 am on September 12th General Klemann had contacted Admiral Maschera and asked him to surrender Leros; Maschera refused, having already given the island to us. It was also a tragic waste of vital days and hours – during which time, so to speak, 'Rhodes was burning'. Wilson and GHQ Cairo knew from our signals on the 12th as his letter to Churchill on the 14th shows that Samos and Leros were in our hands and in any case it was suicidal for Wilson to order troops to the north without securing Rhodes first.

In terms of strategic gain this goose chase was to prove as useless as the Charge of the Light Brigade, from which the appalling disaster unfolded, with no assistance whatsoever being given to the Italians on Rhodes. Rhodes had been abandoned by Wilson and from then on it was lost to Churchill.

The following is quoted from the Italian Ministry of Defence, Rome 1975:

'Between 9 and 11 September, on Rhodes, 8 officers and 135 sub-officers and soldiers fell in combat; a further 300 had been injured. The losses suffered by the German forces are unknown.

271

Perhaps a timely intervention on the part of the Allies could have prevented the surrender, and would have ensured that the generous sacrifice of so many young lives were not in vain. Among the courageous men of that time mention should be made of Captains Eza Geloni (infantry) and Luigi Viviani (artillery), slaughtered by the Germans at the end of the resistance effort.'

Jumbo Wilson, meanwhile, sitting tight on his enormous white elephant (within easy bombing range of Rhodes) of staff and troops had just received Churchill's cable.

On 14th September Wilson replied to Churchill in an unbelievably futile letter, saying that the situation in Rhodes had deteriorated too rapidly for them to take any action (it had only deteriorated because he had done nothing during four vital days) and that only an assault landing was therefore practical. However, the 8th Indian Division which had been trained for this operation had now diverted to the central Mediterranean, and its ships and craft had been dispersed by the Admiralty. He went on to say that they had occupied Castelorizo island, and had missions in Cos, Leros and Samos (presumably referring to us – misleading as it implied that he had initiated the action). A flight of Spitfires was to be established in Cos that day, and an infantry garrison that night, by parachute. An infantry detachment was also proceeding to Leros. He therefore proposed to carry out piratical war on enemy communications in the Aegean, and to occupy Greek islands with Hellenic forces as opportunity offered. Since the New Zealand Division was also to proceed to the central Mediterranean the 10th Indian Division, partially equipped, was the only formation immediately available.

As all Middle East resources had been put at the disposal of General Eisenhower they had no means of mounting an assault landing on Rhodes. Wilson ended this letter with the most incredible and stupid sentence possible in the light of the utmost urgency of the situation – 'But I hope to reduce the island by the methods adopted by the Turks in 1522, though in less time.' He was referring to the seige which began on July 28th 1522 under Suleimen the Magnificent, against the

Knights of St John under Villiers de L'Isle Adam who, despite appalling hardship and famine, held out until December 21st.

General Wilson had, perhaps, not made it clear to Churchill that Leros and most of the Aegean islands were already safely in our hands. Because they were in our hands – fully equipped and armed with 20,000 Italians ready to fight any aggression from the Germans – it was quite unnecessary, therefore, to dissipate forces on looking northwards to Leros, Samos and Cos etc. Furthermore he painted an unfair and defeatist picture about the Italians on Rhodes, and did not mention that he had done nothing, in response to Churchill's letter, to prepare for this eventuality. Wilson had had more than enough time to fully equip the 10th Indian Division from his vast canal-based armament store which, with the 5,000 troops he was about to send to Cos and Leros would have given him 20,000 in all, or three times Klemann's force – without counting the 40,000 Italians. All Wilson had to do was to get Rhodes, which, with the forces at his disposal, was entirely possible and relatively easy.

Here was a situation screaming for immediate action, with the Italians valiantly resisting the Germans (who were almost out of fuel and ammunition) on their own.

They held out for five vital days, with no help from Wilson or Jellicoe; 143 men were killed and 300 wounded. One main airport, Maritza, was already largely in their hands. Here the Italians destroyed on the ground some Cant Z1007 bombers, thirty MC202 and CR42 fighters and fighter bombers. They were to die at their gun positions when Klemann's Stormtroopers charged with fixed bayonets (From the OKW War Diary).

The Germans were outnumbered by six to one (5,500 Germans to 40,000 Italians), and yet Wilson planned to send Spitfires to Cos with a paratroop landing to Cos that night, and an infantry detachment to Leros to occupy Greek islands with Hellenic forces as opportunity offered. Nothing for vital Rhodes, in spite of it having been Churchill's number one target for four years.

Furthermore, the Navy based on Alexandria had proved, in the evacuation of Crete in 1941, that in three nights it could take off over 10,000 British troops on a very much longer journey – and under massive air attack. With virtual command of the air and a much smaller distance they, together with the Air Force, would have had no problems in landing the necessary troops and paratroops. At that moment they could have landed them anywhere on Rhodes, which is a large island, (thirty miles long by fifteen miles wide) unopposed – in fact welcomed – by their 40,000 new-found Italian allies; exactly as we had found on the same day on Samos and Leros.

The arrival of paratroops and ships on the night of the 9th, well publicised by radio and leaflets to the 40,000 Italian troops on the island would have electrified the whole situation and they would then have fought heroically against their erstwhile Teutonic allies, whom they loathed. Given any lead from Wilson they would have put up a resistance comparable with the magnificent fight, two months later, when the Germans mounted a massive air and seaborne attack to recapture Leros.

In war one can never expect one's objective to be handed over on a plate completely without a fight, but here was almost just such a situation. Was advantage taken of it? Did they do what Churchill begged them to do? Improvise and dare?

No, not a single British soldier was landed on Rhodes during those few vital days. No immediate assistance to the Italian garrison was given and worse still the entire plan as outlined in Wilson's letter to Churchill was utterly useless. Whilst he was writing this letter we were actually there, in Samos and Leros. Wilson wasted vital time planning to merely take over what we had already taken, without even attempting to capture the all-important island of Rhodes (apart from asking the young George Jellicoe – he was only twenty-four at the time – to carry a letter to Admiral Camponi from himself) – without which all the troops he was planning to send by sea or air would ultimately be cut off and either killed or taken prisoner – which indeed they all were within two months.

There was absolutely nothing to stop this being a resounding success, with Turkey anxiously watching on their grandstand five miles distant. Success here, on top of the great success achieved by Montgomery in clearing the entire Italian and German armies out of the whole of North Africa, was also having a profound effect on Turkish thinking.

Major-General David Lloyd Owen, LRDG, writing after the war said:

> 'I believe we made our first of many blunders in so impotently failing to assume control of Rhodes. The failure to get airfields on the island should have been the signal that those Aegean operations were doomed to disaster unless Turkey could be persuaded at once to come on the side of the Allies.'

Meanwhile, during this complete bungle, both Hitler and General Klemann were expecting the worst. In spite of the Italians putting up an unhelped and unguided resistance for the next five days, Hitler, to his great relief and utter amazement, saw his command of the eastern Mediterranean – and therefore the whole of south-east Europe – and the neutrality of Turkey maintained, as no landing was made on Rhodes.

We now pay a visit to the Führer's HQ a few days later, and I quote again from Churchill's *Closing the Ring*:

> 'We now know how deeply the Germans were alarmed at the deadly threat which they expected us to develop on their south-eastern flank. At a conference at the Führer's HQ on September 24th both the Army and the Navy representative strongly urged the evacuation of Crete and other islands in the Aegean while there was still time. They pointed out that these advanced bases had been seized for offensive operations in the eastern Mediterranean, but that now the situation was entirely changed. They stressed the need to avoid the loss of troops and material which would be of decisive importance, for the defence of the continent. Hitler over-ruled them. He insisted that he could not order an evacuation, particularly of Crete and the Dodecanese because of the political repercussions which would follow. He said, "The attitude of our allies in the south-east, and Turkey's attitude, is determined solely by their confidence in our

strength. Abandonment of these islands would create a most unfavourable impression." In this decision to fight for the Aegean islands he was justified by events. He gained large profits in a subsidiary theatre at small cost to the main strategic position. In the Balkans he was wrong. In the Aegean he was right.'

From the above it is clear that practically never in the history of warfare have the odds been so heavily stacked against the defenders, and in our favour, as they were in Rhodes on that fateful day. General Klemann had of necessity the bulk of his troops – which were very mobile – in two or three strategic localities, including the one vital airport, Maritza, which the Italians had already partly captured. Throughout the whole fifty-mile coastline of Rhodes we could have made many individual sea-borne landings by night, without serious resistance, as the Italians were friendly and willing collaborators.

We had the might of the British Navy, with some ten cruisers, twenty destroyers and six submarines, and also the whole of the special boat service with their fast Fairmiles and MTBs immediately available. There was also a paratroop regiment which had been wasted by being dropped on Cos four days later, instead of onto Rhodes airport which was already in the hands of our new allies the Italians. (In addition there was also the whole brigade which had been sent to Leros – numbering some 3,000, plus the 2nd Royal West Kents and the fearless Greek Sacred Heart Regiment who had been sent to garrison Samos; in all over 5,000 troops immediately available.) As well as all these there was my MI9 caique fleet which, given the thirty-five days adequate warning – and the specific mention of caiques – given to Wilson by Churchill, could have been greatly increased. They could then have been operated from adjacent Turkish inlets, all of which I had photographed. Over the last year we had enticed over £100,000 worth of large caiques from the enemy-occupied Aegean to Khiosti, from where we sent them down to Cyprus.

These were all squandered in these islands because in the early stages, after our taking over Samos, Cos and Leros, the

Italian High Command had virtually burnt their boats. They knew that if the Germans attacked them and triumphed they would all be shot immediately. Furthermore the Germans did not have the facilities for capturing any of those islands at that time, nor, indeed, would have for the next two months. They then actually accomplished it, at huge cost, but only after having previously first secured their base in Rhodes. The whole pivot was, and remained, Rhodes, and it was essential to capture it now, or in the next few days. This, as the German Wehrmacht HQ in Berlin knew perfectly well, was a virtual certainty, despite Hitler's countermanding order to the beleaguered General Klemann. He was cut off, isolated, heavily outnumbered and had no hope of immediate assistance.

The next few hours and days would have been the first, and the ideal, moment when everything was in our favour to change the whole course of the war and as Churchill knew, history.

21

Roosevelt and Smuts

Given victory now, on September 13th 1943, with open country ahead right up to Odessa and the borders of Romania and the Black Sea, Churchill would have come out of his self-imposed subserviency to his new-found American allies. He would have switched the axis of the attack from the northern boundaries of Turkey in Europe and the Macedonian plain. From here he would have had, as he knew only too well, the supreme advantage of having Hitler and his German forces fighting and spread out over a gigantic front of 3,000 miles, stretching from the north of Finland right down towards Istanbul.

On this southern front Hitler would have been at his most disadvantaged position in the whole war, due to the immense distance from Berlin – 1,500 miles, largely along unmade roads and with pitifully inadequate railway communications with which to have to meet a new and fresh army of forty-five rugged Turkish divisions and possibly another forty-five Allied divisions, released from the planned Second Front in Normandy. They would all be easily supplied by sea to within a few miles of their front, with further disaster looming for Hitler in the loss of his only natural oil supplies from the Ploesti oil fields which were situated only 200 miles from the Allied front.

Likewise, roughly half of his grain supplies would immediately be in jeopardy with the loss of the continent's greatest corn-growing area stretching from the Ukraine west into Romania and on into Hungary. This would create the certainty of a famine stalking right across his continental European fortress, thereby making the old adage of 'An army marching on its stomach' a realizable nightmare for those in control at the Wehrmacht HQ.

Even after this first chance had slipped away Churchill was still desperate to capture the island, although it was the first chance that could have changed the history of the war.

There was now a second chance, as Churchill had asked Wilson to effect 'Accolade', the code name for the invasion of Rhodes, which had been planned and rehearsed for the last year. To do this it was necessary to have only a tiny fraction of the forces which Churchill had given to Eisenhower for his Italian campaign returned to him for a quick and successful capture of Rhodes.

Tragically, despite Churchill's enormously magnanimous offer to put the whole execution of the war on the back burner and to fly out with his Chief-of-Staff to meet Roosevelt and, or, his Chief-of-Staff General Marshall, in Algiers, where he would explain the vital reasons for capturing these islands, all his appeals were turned down flat.

On October 8th 1943 Churchill wrote the following to Roosevelt:

> 'I earnestly pray that my views may receive some consideration from you at this critical juncture, remembering how fruitful our concerted action has been in the past and how important it is for the future... I am sure that the omission to take Rhodes at this stage, and the ignoring of the whole position in the Eastern Mediterranean would constitute a cardinal error in strategy ... We must find some means of resolving these difficulties and making sure what is the right thing to do. I am willing to proceed to Eisenhower's HQ with the British Chiefs-of-Staff immediately, if you will send General Marshall, or your personal representative to meet me there, and we can then submit the results of a searching discussion to you and your Chiefs-of-Staff. We can be there Sunday afternoon (October 10th).'

The following day Roosevelt sent a totally unsatisfactory and unhelpful reply, ending with a virtual refusal to meet

Churchill – so much that Churchill noted in his book that: 'Mr Roosevelt's reply quenched my last hopes.'

In his letter Roosevelt also showed that neither he nor his Chief-of-Staff or advisers cared – or had the slightest idea – of the military situation in the eastern Aegean.

> 'We have almost all the facts now at our disposal on which to judge the commitments probably involved in the Rhodes operation. As I see it, it is not merely the capture of Rhodes, but it must mean of necessity, and it must be apparent to the Germans that we intend to go further. Otherwise Rhodes will be under the guns of both Cos and Crete.'

At the time this letter was written, we still had contol of the islands to the north, including Samos and Leros. There was nothing south of Rhodes except for Cyrenaica and Egypt, both of which were firmly in British hands. There was nothing east of Rhodes except for Castelorizo and Cyprus, both of which were British bases. As for 'Otherwise Rhodes will be under the guns of Cos and Crete' – not even a ten-year-old schoolboy could have made such a fantastically stupid remark. The nearest point on Crete, on its extreme eastern tip, was 130 miles. No gun in the world, either then or since, has ever covered even half that distance. Likewise Cos was fifty-five miles north of Rhodes, and therefore also totally out of range. Furthermore on October 9th we still had British troops fighting on Cos.

As a legacy of their own War of Independence the Americans had no love for the British Empire, but with their active participation in the war it would become a question of 'He who pays the piper calls the tune.'

Roosevelt, Eisenhower and Marshall had little or no strategic knowledge of global war compared with the two greatest soldiers/statesmen of this time, namely Churchill and Field Marshal Smuts, both of whom, with gross impertinence they ignored and over-rode.

Smuts's brilliant campaign for his own country, South Africa, had, in 1901, kept the whole British Empire and five hundred thousand troops under Lord Kitchener at bay for four-and-a-half years, with his eighty thousand Boer farmers.

Likewise, when he gave total allegiance to Britain in her greatest struggle of the first Great War 1914-1918, his military and stateman-like ability made a profound impression on Churchill and the British War Cabinet.

He proved to be the only one who foresaw the disastrous effect of not matching the Russian war effort from the east, up through the Balkans and Turkey and obviating Overlord and the Second Front, thus ending the war on a par with Russia, possibly a year earlier. All this he almost unbelievably and prophetically forecast in a letter to Churchill, dated August 31st 1943:

'General Smuts to Prime Minister.

For your private ear I should like to voice my personal misgivings about the progress of the war. If you don't agree with me please forget my grouse. But if in any way you share my feelings you will take your own initiative in the matter. While our Middle East campaign was conducted with conspicuous vigour from El Alamein to the end in Tunisia, I sense a slackening and tardiness in operations since then. It took us several months between Tunisia and the Sicilian landing, and there is now another strange pause after Sicily at a stage in our affairs when the urgency is very great. To compare the Anglo-American effort with all our vast resources, with that of Russia during the same period is to raise uncomfortable questions, which must occur to many others. Our comparative performance on land is insignificant, and its speed very unsatisfactory. There is much and constant boasting of our production effort, especially of the colossal American production. And after almost two years of war the American fighting forces must be enormous. But still, the Russians account for the vast bulk of the German army on land. Shipping and other troubles account for this difference in part, but that is not the whole story.

I have the uncomfortable feeling that the scale and speed of our land operations leaves much to be desired. Our Navy is acting up to its usual high standard, and our Air Force is magnificent. But almost all the honours on land go to the Russians, and deservedly so considering the scale and speed of their fighting and the magnificence of their strategy on a vast front.

Surely our performance can be bettered and the comparison with Russia must be rendered less unflattering to us. To the ordinary man it must appear that it is Russia who is winning the war. If this impression continues, what will be our post-war world position compared with that of Russia? A tremendous shift in our world status may follow, and will leave Russia the diplomatic master of the world. This is both unnecessary and undesirable, and would have especially bad reactions for the British Commonwealth. Unless we emerge from the war on terms of equality our position will be both uncomfortable and dangerous . . . I do not yet know what was being planned at Quebec and assume the best programmes have been worked out and approved. But what about the rate of their execution? There is grave danger in delay, in tardiness of performance on our part.'

This was followed up by another letter three days later:

'General Smuts to Prime Minister, September 3rd 1943.
After sending my previous message criticising our war progress I must frankly express my disappointment with this Quebec plan as being an inadequate programme for the fifth year of the war, and especially after the enormous change that has taken place in our war fortunes recently. This plan has only added to my misgivings and fears for the future. It does no justice to the real strength of our position, and may gravely affect public morale as well as future relations with Russia. We are capable of a much greater effort, and should face the position with greater boldness.
In effect, the plan merely proposes to continue

and increase the present bombing and anti-U-boat campaigns, to take Sardinia and Corsica and the south of Italy and bomb northwards from there. We are then to fight our way northwards through Italy, over difficult mountainous terrain, in a campaign which may take much time before we reach northern Italy and the main German defence position. Next spring we shall cross the channel in force if the air and military situation in France is favourable, and we may invade France from the south if only as a diversion. We leave the Balkans to the guerillas with air encouragement from us . . . If by the end of 1944 we have done no better than merely nibble at the enemy's main positions we may experience a dangerous revulsion of opinion, and rightly so. It would compare most unfavourably with the grand effort and achievement of Russia, who may conclude that her suspicions of us are justified.

In the absence of inner staff information it is difficult for me to suggest alternative plans, but I feel convinced that we can and should do much more and better than the Quebec plan, which would unduly drag out and prolong the war, with all its attendant risks and possibilities I have indicated in my former message. The bombing policy, the anti-U-boat campaign, and the large scale attack across the channel I approve . . . We should immediately take southern Italy and move on to the Adriatic, and from a suitable point there launch a real attack on the Balkans and set its resurgent forces going.

This will bring Turkey into the picture and carry our fleet into the Black Sea, where we shall join hands with Russia, supply her and enable her to attack Hitler's fortress itself from the east and south-east. With the vast change in the war situation on the Russian front I do not think this too ambitious a programme to work to . . .'

Churchill's opinion of Smuts can be no better summarised

than in his letter to Eisenhower of September 19th 1943:

> 'Field Marshal Smuts will be in Cairo Monday
> September 27th, staying with Casey, and will be in
> your theatre about four days later, on his way here.
> He possesses my entire confidence, and, everything
> can be discussed with him with the utmost freedom.
> He will stay some months in London, taking up his
> full duties as a member of the British War Cabinet.
> He will carry great weight here with public opinion.
> I shall be grateful if he is treated with the utmost
> consideration. He is a magnificent man and one of
> my most cherished friends.'

Roosevelt's reply of October 9th was written at the exact
moment when the USA succeeded, through President
Roosevelt and Generals Marshall and Eisenhower, in not only
destroying the British Empire and the greatness of Britain, but
also condemning the world to a totally unnecessary extra year-
and-a-half of horrific war. It handed over to communist
Russia, the most brutal and bestial power the world has ever
seen, all of Europe to the east of the Iron Curtain. It is
accepted that since 1930 they have been responsible for the
murder and liquidation of nearly fifty million of their people.
The others were condemned to half-a-century of slavery and a
virtual non-existence (with the exception of members of the
Polit Bureau or an active Commisar).

We can now see what was happening in the wolf's lair, Hitler's
headquarters in Prussia, for the two weeks preceding
Badoglio's capitulation. Hitler, with his sixth sense, suspected
the Italian King's and Badoglio's coming treachery, despite
promises from them that they would fight on until the end of
the war. Field Marshal Kesselring and General Richthofen
were also advising Hitler that the Italians would fight on with
them.

When the bomb burst on September 8th 1943, and the BBC
had just announced Italy's unconditional surrender, the
whole of the German position in Italy and the Balkans was one
of the utmost gravity. If it had not been for the quite amazing
recuperative powers shown by Hitler, Jodl and Rommel, the

whole of the Italian peninsula, and the German troops within it, might have been lost – particularly as the Americans, after being badly mauled, had just managed to hold on to their bridgehead at Salerno, largely as a result of the enormous support they received from the Royal Navy who were shelling the beach heads, and the enormous weight of bombs dropped by the Air Forces.

Hitler's staff rejoiced at the thrashing meted out to the Americans. Jodl set their value far below that of Montgomery's seasoned troops.

> 'Although the British and Americans had been committed in equal numbers, over nine-tenths of the prisoners who surrendered were Americans. American paratroops were usable, but the rest surrender the moment their position is hopeless, and never attack so long as a single gun is left firing from the German lines.'

Hitler wrote off the threat of an enemy invasion elsewhere for many months to come (and in that he was proved absolutely correct).

> 'No more invasions for them! They are much too cowardly for that. They only managed the one at Salerno because the Italians gave their blessing.'

The bungled Allied planning comforted him greatly over the next weeks –

> 'Why did they not immediately invade the Balkans, where the natives were waiting for the Allies with open arms? . . . Why had they not ventured a bold invasion north of Rome when Badoglio defected? . . . Why had they not at once occupied the islands of Rhodes, Cephalonia and Corfu?'

From this it is absolutely clear that Hitler and the High Command were convinced that had the Allies immediately captured these islands (as Hitler himself would have done had the boot been on the other foot), they could have immediately invaded the Balkans through Yugoslavia, where Colonel Jack Churchill was operating with Tito's large force of guerillas. They numbered many thousands, and were capable of destroying all the German lines of supply, namely rail, road, and telephonic communications.

To the east the capture of Rhodes would have enabled Churchill to achieve his objective of getting Turkey into the war and opening up the sea route to Russia in the Crimea, thus saving 10,000 miles on the vastly more hazardous Murmansk route.

As Hitler saw it, if we had acted instantly, we would have had, in a very short space of time, a second and third front operating against him in south-east Europe, with very little that he, with his fully extended lines of communication, could have done; any question of an Atlantic Wall attack i.e. 'Overlord', would be quite unnecessary.

The threat of landing in the west would, and did, keep some thirty to forty of Hitler's divisions permanently deployed on guard to protect the Atlantic Wall. On the eastern front, which was far and away his largest battlefield, stretching for some 1,500 miles from north to south, he had already lost the battle of Stalingrad, which was the turning point of the war. In Germany itself the destruction from the Allied air forces was almost beyond belief, as I saw on my way through Berlin in early 1944.

It was about now that the seeds of treason were being planted throughout the top officer corps and German High Command at the Ober Kommand Wehrmacht, with Colonel Count Schenk von Stauffenberg acting as liaison officer to the conspirators who, it later transpired, numbered about 6,000 top-ranking officers and officials.

Their objective was to depose Hitler, seize power and immediately surrender to the Western Allies. Almost all of this they could have effectively and efficiently done on July 20th 1944, when the Count placed a bomb underneath the map table within a few yards of Hitler in his conference hut. The bomb successfully exploded, killing and injuring some of Hitler's top officers and blowing up part of the building, but, by a million to one chance, Hitler was only slightly hurt.

The Count, who had another bomb in his briefcase but did not use it, having seen the building blown up sky-high, immediately telephoned his headquarters at the OKW giving the watchword 'Valkyrie' (meaning 'into action') to the leaders of the conspiracy. He explained that he had just seen the building, in which Hitler was, destroyed by his bomb, and that they should put their long planned operations into immediate effect. This they did, with the code word being transmitted to all the conspirators. For the next two days the OKW virtually ceased to exist as an operational HQ. It was exactly as if the War Office in London, or the Pentagon in Washington, were totally paralysed in an instant.

It was then that Colonel Skorzeny (who was present at the OKW HQ, which was about a hundred miles from Hitler's Wolf's Lair Supreme Operations HQ) took over command of the whole of the OKW on his own initiative directly it became evident that Hitler had survived the bomb.

With Himmler Hitler rooted out all the conspirators (even those remotely on the fringe such as Rommel and Kluge) by extreme Gestapo interrogation and torture methods.

As an example, when discussing General Fellgiebel, whom he believed had betrayed his secrets to the enemy, he screamed 'Fellgiebel must confess if he has to be skinned alive!'

The previous pages show what a monumental and seemingly insuperable task Hitler had in front of him on September 8th 1943.

Had the two new fronts been opened up, as I have outlined, there was nothing Hitler could have done to stop Churchill's thirty-year-old – but still correct – vision of defeating Germany from the weak underbelly of Europe: the Balkan front, which would have advanced from Colonel Jack Churchill's area in Yugoslavia, via Belgrade and the Danube. It was scarcely 300 miles to capture Vienna, Berchtesgaden (Hitler's eyrie) and Nuremberg, in the heart of Germany, and was 1,000 miles west of the nearest Russian-German front.

The third front would advance with Turkey's forty-five fresh divisions, and another forty-five Allied divisions up through Macedonia to Thrace, and through Bulgaria to capture Romania and the Ploesti oil-fields – upon whose supplies Hitler's whole war effort was then largely dependent, since the Allied bombing had greatly reduced the output from the huge synthetic oil from coal plants within Germany. The application of a tourniquet on the oil and wheat would in itself have largely paralysed Germany, now that the Russian oil fields were lost.

This was the situation that Churchill saw in September 1943 when he was frantically moving every administrative lever he could lay his hands on to capture Rhodes and the Dodecanese islands.

Now, thanks to the total lack of co-operation from the Americans, the failure of Wilson to move like a tiger (or a Patton, a Rommel or a John Hackett), and deviating away from Churchill's wishes to capture Rhodes, the key to the Aegean and the Eastern Mediterranean was lost.

I quote Churchill, from *Closing the Ring,* chapter XII:

'The surrender of Italy gave us the chance of gaining important prizes in the Aegean at very small cost and effort. The Italian garrison obeyed the orders of the King and Marshal Badoglio, and would come over to our side if we could reach them before they were overawed and disarmed by the Germans in the islands. These were much inferior in numbers, but it is probable that for some time past they had been suspicious of their allies' fidelity and had their plans laid. Rhodes, Leros and Cos were island fortresses which had long been for us strategic objectives of a high order in the secondary sphere. Rhodes was the key to the group, because it had good airfields from which our own air forces could operate in defence of any other islands we might occupy and complete our naval control of these waters. Moreover, the British air forces in Egypt and Cyrenaica could defend Egypt just as well, or even better, if some of them moved forward to Rhodes. It seemed to me a rebuff to fortune not to pick up these treasures. The command of the Aegean by air and by sea was within our reach. The effect of this might be decisive upon Turkey, at that time deeply moved by the Italian collapse. If we could use the Aegean and the Dardanelles the naval shortcut to Russia was established. There would be no more need for the perilous and costly Arctic convoys, or the long and wearisome supply line through the Persian Gulf . . . I felt from the beginning we must be ready to take advantage of any Italian landslide or German round-up.

. . . Once Rhodes was denied to us our gains throughout the Aegean became precarious. Only a powerful use of air forces could give us what we needed. It would have taken very little of their time had there been accord. General Eisenhower and his staff seemeed unaware of what lay at our fingertips, althought we had voluntarily placed all our considerable resources entirely in their hands.'

This terrible failure could have been avoided by using our own forces, (which, as I have shown, were ample in the circumstances) unaided by the Americans.

However, this in no way exonerates Roosevelt, Marshall or Eisenhower for their deliberate refusal to help Churchill in his vital task both then and later – even after Churchill had given them ninety per cent of his available forces for their Italian campaign. In this respect I can not do better than quote from the diaries of Field Marshal the Viscount Alanbrooke, KG, OM, as quoted in Arthur Bryant's book *Triumph in the West 1943-1946:*

'November 1st 1943: When I look at the Mediterranean I realise only too well how far I have failed. If only I had sufficient force of character to swing those American Chiefs-of-Staff and make them see daylight, how different the war might be. We should have had the whole Balkans ablaze by now, and the war might have finished in 1943. I blame myself, yet doubt whether it was humanely possible to alter the American point of view more than I succeeded in doing. And what I did I would never have achieved had it not been for Dill's help, his close association with Marshall, his deep knowledge and the implicit confidence I had in him.

I was suffering from a heavy cold and had not fully recovered from the strain of the Quebec

Conference. Reading between the lines, I think I cannot have been far off a nervous breakdown. Nevertheless, there is a great deal in what I wrote. Just when there were fruits to be gained, the Americans selected that moment to damp down our efforts; troops, landing-craft and transport were removed and re-allocated. At very little cost Crete and Rhodes could have been rendered possible operations without affecting Italy, whereas as matters stood these were only possible at the expense of Italian operations and were consequently ruled out. Success in Crete and Rhodes might have had the happiest repercussions in Turkey and the Balkans without ever committing a single man in the Balkans!'

And then – on November 18th in Malta, we see from Alanbrooke just how deep the wound created by America's stupendous folly had gone:

'Had a talk with Alex (Field Marshal Lord Alexander) in the garden, which was good value. We then had our conference with the PM in bed: Chiefs-Of-Staff, John Cunningham and Tedder. The PM gave a long tirade on evils of Americans and our losses in the Aegean and the Dalmation coast. He was not at all at his best, and I feel nervous as to the line he may adopt at this Conference. He is inclined to say to the Americans: "All right, if you won't play with us in the Mediterranean, we won't play with you in the English Channel".'

By going north into the Aegean and leaving Rhodes unconquered in their rear (despite every possible plea from Churchill), Wilson effectively prepared a noose (which was obvious from day one) for the necks of the 5,000 British troops that Wilson was to send up to these islands, instead of landing them on Rhodes that night. Likewise the same noose became, during the next two months, the hangman of half of the entire British Mediterranean fleet based on Alexandria.

They were transporting and supplying these troops and

sustained devastating losses – to such an extent that Captain (later Rear-Admiral) Percy Todd, in command of the flotilla sent up to supply, and subsequently to evacuate, the troops from Leros, castigated Churchill for this operation, which was not in accordance with his orders.

He also said quite plainly that this was the only occasion in the war when the British Navy was on the point of mutiny.

Up to and during the subsequent German assault on Leros in November the Italians lost some 50,000 men. Some of the officers were shot by the Germans, including the heroic Admirals Maschera and Camponi shot by firing squad in Parma on 24th May 1944. The gold medal for military valour was awarded in memory of Admiral Maschera (the trial of the Admirals is in full in Gianni Rocco's most moving book) and the men were sent to work in slave camps in Germany.

Thirty-two vessels were sunk, crippled or captured – double the number that Admiral of the Fleet Lord Jellicoe had lost in the world's biggest naval battle, the Battle of Jutland, in 1916. Virtually the whole expeditionary force was lost, captured or killed, together with much of the Air Force, as a result of not capturing Rhodes. Britain lost some three or four thousand who were killed, wounded or taken prisoner, plus the total loss of all the huge quantities of supplies and war material on Leros, Samos and Cos; also a retribution bombing on Gregory Marc's house and the beautiful capital of Samos.

A.J.P. Taylor, referring to Churchill, says:

> 'He stirred up General Sir Henry Maitland Wilson, the Commander in the Middle East, to seize the Italian islands in the Aegean. Wilson obeyed. The Americans refused to authorize reinforcements. The British forces were overwhelmed by the Germans. Most of them were taken prisoner. This was not only an unnecessary misfortune. It shattered another of Churchill's dreams: that of bringing Turkey into the war.'

22

Batemans: Church Bells and Tin Mines

Now that I was living at Batemans with my father and step-mother Eva, I slowly readjusted to civilian life after my retirement from the army. I had been given a 100 per cent disability pension which was a great help, and with it I was given a small, green, rehabilitated ex-Army Austin. This was a great blessing, as after five years of war cars were worth their weight in gold.

Gradually I got over the misery of my broken marriage and began very quickly to pick up the reins of my companies. Throughout the war they had been based, with their staff, at Major Henderson-Scott's house in the middle of the New Forest. Fortunately they had all survived four years of the blitz without any casualties, and they had now returned to London. Picking up the reins was not difficult, but making progress for the companies was a different matter. This was due to the state of the economy and the mining industry throughout Africa and Malaysia, over and above which every possible bureaucratic government restriction was in force. Thus it became a period of marking time, and holding our heads above water until long after hostilities had ceased with V.E. Day.

In 1920 my mother had bought for £400 a freehold house for her children – 21 Halsey Street, which had been let. By mid-1945 it became vacant and I was able to move in, which could not have been more convenient. I soon established a bachelor household, and was able to have many of my pre-war friends and POWs who had been with me in Germany to stay. These included Lt. Yacoub Khan and Major Para Kumaramangalam; whilst Para was staying with me he had a command from His Majesty King George VI to report to Buckingham Palace, where he received the Distinguished Service Order. Life after V.E. Day soon became an exciting social whirl, with many old friends returning from the various fronts. There were cocktail parties, and dancing the nights away at the 400, the famous nightclub in Leicester Square – always with a bevy of young and very attractive girls. A number of them used to come down to stay at Batemans with my family.

Batemans was a delightful house in a wonderful setting, with an enchanting garden which included a rectangular trout pond. This was enclosed by a brigade of my father's favourite pollarded poplars, standing like so many guardsmen to attention on all sides. Further down through the water garden, and over the small stream, brought one to Kipling's miniature Aswan dam and hydro-electric plant. They had been installed by Kipling's great friend Sir William Willcocks, KCMG (1882-1932), who had built the Aswan dam. Kipling's plant had been commissioned in 1906; one of the very first in the United Kingdom, and it provided Batemans with electric light and power from then until the early 1960s, when the mains arrived to light up Kipling's many masterpieces.

To the east of the house, about two hundred yards away, were the old and completely overgrown remains of a quarry. This formed a horse-shoe indentation into the hill, where, amidst beautiful carpets of primroses and other wildflowers my father kept his immaculately painted white beehives, forming a crescent at the back of this delightful secluded spot. Every visitor to Batemans had to undergo the ritual of a visit to my father's beloved bees, accompanied by him. He was President of the Sussex Bee-keepers' Association, and guests would later enjoy hot scones with honey from the combs for tea. This, eaten during the austerities of war-time rationing, was a treat still vividly remembered half-a-century later.

My father had found his Porkellis tin mine not only romantic but very profitable – until the great slump of the thirties. Like all other Cornish tin mines Porkellis had been going, on and off, since the Phoenicians, but was brought to the edge of disaster and closure when the price of tin collapsed, like all other commodities, to below £200 per ton. Father rallied the leaders of the Cornish tin industry together with the MP for the Porkellis district, Commander Agnew, and was appointed head of the Cornish Tin Producers Association. In 1937 Clement, who knew the Prime Minister Neville Chamberlain, visited him in this capacity. He explained that the industry was on its death bed after centuries of massive and profitable production, and that unless immediate steps were taken there would be no tin mines operating in Cornwall.

This was the time when the first rumbles of Hitler's Nazi Germany were being clearly heard throughout Westminster, and Clement explained to Neville Chamberlain the strategic importance of having our own indigenous supply of this vital metal in the event of war, with U-boats disrupting our normal supply from the massive low-cost open-cast and dredge-operated tin mines of Malaysia.

With due respect to the Prime Minister the penny dropped instantly, and he made arrangements for the Minister of Defence, Sir Thomas Inskip, to see Clement and to review the whole situation. The plan that father submitted to the Minister was simple in the extreme, namely that the Government should guarantee a fixed price of £200 per ton to the Cornish tin producers while the market price remained below £200. As and when the price exceeded £200 per ton the Government would be able to pocket the difference. Thus, at very little immediate expense, and with the likelihood of a substantial future profit, the Cornish tin industry would continue in production.

Sir Thomas, after discussion with his civil service and ministry advisers, came back with the sad news that he had been advised that there was an abundance of tin in Malaya, and in any case it was not a metal of any strategic importance. He therefore regretted that the Government would not accept his proposals. I have heard it suggested that the appointment of Sir Thomas as Minister was similar to Nero making his horse a Senator.

Father replied that in that case there was no alternative but to close down the industry, withdraw the pumps from the mines and let them flood. He made it quite clear to the Minister that this irrevocable step would mean that if he (or his successor) came to him in a few years time in the event of war and the loss of ships carrying tin to the Liverpool smelter, it would be no good asking him to re-open and start the Cornish tin mines again. Regardless of how much assistance was offered, this could not be achieved in less than two or three years.

Subsequently, in the third year of the war when one freighter carrying 20,000 tons of tin from Malaya had been sunk by a U-boat on its voyage to Liverpool, my father received an urgent call from the Ministries of Supply and Defence offering him (for the Cornish tin industry) millions of pounds in immediate aid to rehabilitate the mines, as Britain was virtually out of tin.

It was at this time that church bells were removed from their belfries throughout the Kingdom and melted down for their tin content: each bell contains some eighty per cent. The crash programme of financial assistance was accepted in the interest of the war effort, but my father again warned that no tin would be forthcoming for at least two or three years. Nor did it until a year after the war had ended, when the peal of bells my father gave in memory of Charles were hung in the ancient Burwash Church of St James's, from where they have summoned the faithful to worship ever since.

Some years later there was a Service of Dedication for the hanging of these bells, taken by the vicar, Sir Henry Denny. While matters were proceeding with all due solemnity there occurred a sudden crisis of no mean proportions. My father had invited many of his friends and neighbours, including the Astronomer Royal from Herstmonceaux Castle. He had brought with him his American opposite number from California, who had only arrived that morning after an uncomfortable and delayed flight from America via Gander in Newfoundland.

This gentleman was sitting in the pew immediately in front of me, when there suddenly burst forth upon us a loud outbreak of snoring, and the august person of the American astronomer from Pasadena Palo Alto slumped gently sideways, coming to rest in Godfrey's lap. I am ashamed to say that both Godfrey and I collapsed in ill-smothered giggles as Godfrey turned round to me and asked for help in carrying the by now prostrate figure down the length of the pew at shoulder level, without disturbing those sitting in it. This we somehow managed to do, and despite our by now uncontrollable laughter we carried him the whole way down the aisle, plonked him in our father's two-door Morris 8, and took him straight back to one of the spare bedrooms at Batemans, leaving him, still unconscious, in the capable hands of Mrs Webb.

Godfrey and I then returned to the church for the remainder of the hour-long service, after which we all went back for a buffet supper. Half-way through this the astronomer, who had no doubt been dreaming about his beloved solar system, surfaced once again, and we were all delighted to see him enjoying a rather good meal and some excellent wine.

23

The Exploration Company Ltd. and The El Oro Mining and Exploration Company Ltd.

During the week I worked from the very fine mahogany-panelled Victorian suite of offices on the second floor of Finsbury House. Just behind this was the prestigious River Plate House, which my great-uncle, Frank Woodbine Parish, had built. From there he administered many of the South American railways, such as the Buenos Aires Great Southern, of which he was a director and Chairman for many years. He also looked after many industrial and land companies, such as the Argentine Southern Land Company, which had in excess of a million acres of some of the finest cattle and sheep pastures in South America.

The Exploration Company, after various reconstructions, began many diverse activities and the history portrayed in my speech of May 23rd 1988 (see Appendix) was – and still is – consistent and relentless for the next forty-five years. The objective was never to aim for a massive billion pound organization. It was simply to keep the issued capital of the companies as small as, or smaller than, they were when the Rothschilds and Barings had floated them a century before. But – and this has always been the target – I proposed to make the worth of the individual shareholders' shares increase year by year, without asking them or anybody else to put up more of their hard-earned capital. It was to be done by self-generated growth. The following article in the Bulletin in the Appendix portrays the end result.

Weekends would often be spent staying with various friends, and I sometimes used to go to Mrs de Courcy and her son Kenneth at Iccomb Manor, near Stow-on-the-Wold, where one always met many interesting people. My old friend of Smyrna and Cairo days, Colonel Billy Maclean DSO was often staying there.

Kenneth was a somewhat controversial character, with many friends and many enemies, and when they were enemies they were often vitriolic. He and his mother kept a London establishment at 11 Eaton Place where, during the week, there were constant lunch and dinner parties. I often attended these and alway greatly enjoyed them, along with other frequent visitors such as Colonel David Stirling and Princess Marie Louise (a granddaughter of Queen Victoria). One evening party was especially memorable to me – there were about eighteen people to dinner, which began at a quarter-to-eight and went on late into the night. Among the guests were the Duke and Duchess of Windsor, whom I sat next to; it was the day after she had been robbed of her jewels. Lieutenant Jack Kennedy, in naval uniform, and his sister Kathleen, the widowed Marchioness of Hartington were also present.

One evening Robin Maugham (son of the Lord Chancellor) took me to a party given by Sir Harold Nicolson and a number of politicians and hopefuls who were standing as candidates for the General Election which Churchill's Government had called for September 9th 1945. Although not unduly interested, I went to speak in the days ahead for some of the candidates, including Lord Astor who was standing for a south London constituency. I would certainly not have won him any votes, possibly the opposite.

Several days before the election Robin Maugham very kindly rang me up in Halsey Street and said that Mary Churchill had invited him to join her and her family after dinner at 10 Downing Street to stay late into the night hearing the final election results as they came through, and that he had asked her if he could bring me too. I was surprised but rather thrilled at the prospect of being with the Great Man in his seat of power, amidst his closest Cabinet and other colleagues. I also looked forward to meeting this youngest daughter of the Churchills who was, at the time, generally considered by the press and much of the country, to be a wonderful person, in addition to being extremely good-looking.

We duly reported to number 10 around 10 pm and stayed until the early hours of the morning. For an account of what happened I cannot do better than quote Robin's article in the Appendix which appeared in the *Daily Telegraph* 'Churchill's Hour of Defeat, 26.1.65.'

Throughout the evening Mary was every bit as delightful as I had anticipated and Winston, the focus of attention in his boiler suit, was much as I had envisaged him both in character and personality. Brendan Bracken and Duncan Sandys were there throughout and Anthony Eden came in at intervals; Robin, who evidently knew Churchill well, had long conversations with him.

So ended a memorable evening and night, when we were present at a most tragic occasion.

The victor of nearly six years of war was rejected by the electorate of his own country. Yet had it not been for his courage, tenacity and strategic leadership, Britain would doubtless have been divided up with the rest of the British Empire between Hitler and Stalin, with most of the male population being sent to work in Germany and Russia. In those totalitarian societies the words 'Morrison' and 'trade unions' would have counted for nothing. Winston had told us during the course of the evening that of all his colleagues in the Government Herbert Morrison was by far and away the most dangerous. (One afternoon Winston's secretary had come in to tell him that Herbert Morrison had been taken ill and would not be attending Cabinet meetings. Winston replied, 'Nothing trivial I hope?')

As the night wore on some of the Ministers left, and Winston, standing with his back to the Reuter's machine, beckoned Robin and me to come closer to him, which we did. I was standing looking straight at him, about four feet away, when he said, 'It is up to you young men to carry on because I have led the horse of Britain to victory and now they (meaning the socialists) are going to drive it over the cliff into the quarry and destroy it.' I then made my only remark that evening to the great man, 'Well Sir, you won the race for us', which momentarily seemed to light him up, but he went on to say, 'I shall now have to lay down all my responsibilities, and what I shall miss most of all are the despatch boxes and cables being brought in at the start of every day.' He then quietly moved off, no doubt to bed.

In this sombre setting Robin and I stayed a while with Mary, who was greatly moved, before taking our leave and returning to our respective homes.

The next day I went to the office as usual, where there was beginning to be a number of new propositions for us to look at. I remember lunching with Herbert Latilla and my father in the River Room at the Savoy, where I recounted the historic evening, and added that a few people had suggested that I should go into politics. Herbert was adamantly against it, saying that I should stick to building up my business. Perhaps it was this advice that confirmed my inner conviction that I was better suited to business than politics, and I therefore kept the engines at full speed ahead in my business world.

At this time Britain was suffering from an acute fuel and coal crisis; all households were rationed to a few shovelfuls of coal daily, with little hope of getting the British coal mines back to pre-war production rates for several years. The Government had appointed a Minister for Fuel and Power to handle this grave crisis. While I was a prisoner of war in Czechoslovakia I had noticed that every room was given a small amount of lignite, or brown coal as it was known, to burn in the fires. The BTU of poor quality lignite is only one third of that of the best British coal; nevertheless it did give a reasonable amount of heat – along with a lot of black smoke and a nasty odour. It was also very high in ash content, and about twenty-five per cent of its original weight would be left in the grate by the morning, but in those grim days of every form of rationing beggars could not be choosers.

One day Mr H.J. Wilson called on us at the Exploration offices with a proposition to mine the lignite deposits of Bovey Tracey in Devon. With my Czechoslovakian knowledge I naturally showed some interest, particularly after he had shown me his full report with plans of all the bore holes drilled in the Great War, indicating many millions of tons of relatively easily worked brown coal by open-cast methods.

I put this to Major Henderson-Scott, who was a mining engineer and had won the gold medal at the Royal School of Mines. He and W.W. Varvill (until recently Manager of the Kanongo gold mines on the Gold Coast) both considered that from the mining point of view it would be a satisfactory

300

proposition to undertake, particularly as the by-products from the Bovey lignite were very valuable – one being Montan wax, much needed by the chemical industry, and one of the main attractions.

We decided to go ahead and put the proposition into one of our dormant companies in the office, a company called Bellfield Works. I brought in a partner in the form of Commander Rex Janson RNVR, Chairman of Jantar Tin Company. Rex was a great help in the early days as he was a friend of Hugh Gaitskell, who was, I think, deputy to Mr Shinwell, Minister of Fuel and Power, and Rex brought Hugh Gaitskell to lunch with me at Eaton Square.

Bellfield Works got off to a flying start, once Shinwell had arranged for us to have priority for our open-cast machinery and other equipment. Within a year we were mining and shipping to coal merchants – and to my long-suffering friends throughout the southern half of England at the rate of several thousand tons a week, loaded into railway trucks at the Bovey Tracey siding.

I remember we had a press conference at 35 Eaton Square, and most of the national papers were represented. It became quite a feature in the financial world and the shares of the parent company, El Oro, more than doubled.

As the Government and we ourselves were most anxious to increase production rapidly, we asked Sir Godfrey Mitchell, Chairman and founder of George Wimpy (probably the leading open-cast coal operator in the Kingdom) if he would put up additional money – I think £60,000, and bring his know-how and equipment down to Bovey Tracey. All of which he did. Shortly after his arrival the coal situation began to improve, and due to the low quality of our product and its obnoxious smell it began slowly to lose the goodwill of our customers. The solvent extraction plant erected by our Russian chemical engineer Dr Ivanovsky ran into a succession of teething troubles, and he was unable to produce a Montan wax product of 100 per cent purity, which was what the manufacturers were demanding. It soon became evident that more sizeable finance would be needed, and due to our still very limited resources I did not think we should, or could, match the large finance which Wimpy and the Jansons were prepared to put up. This they did, and we withdrew, remaining a minority shareholder.

The operation continued for several years, with Sir Godfrey Mitchell at the helm. However, as the real British coal became increasingly available it unfortunately became evident that our market would gradually fade away after we had failed, by a small majority, to get the power contract for the supply of lignite to the huge Newton Abbot coal-fired power station. This would have given us a captive market, on our doorstep, of at least five thousand tons a week. In the end it was a question of putting up the shutters and writing off our substantial investment, after much sweat and tears.

Since my first meeting with Mary Churchill I had seen an increasing amount of her, and this coincided with the arrival in England of my old wartime colleague Captain Emmanuele Vernicos. He was full of ideas about getting the contract from the Admiralty to salvage some of the merchant ships sunk in Tobruk harbour. It was known (from the ship's mainfest) that at least one of these had seven thousand cases of whisky on board, which had been destined for the Naafi canteens on the Western Desert.

Captain Vernicos was the eldest son of Nicholas Vernicos, who had the largest tug-boat and salvage vessel business in Piraeus. His plans for Tobruk were eminently sound, and he was one of the few people with the necessary technical knowledge and ability to complete the salvage successfully.

Amongst his many achievements Vernicos was also a remarkably talented painter. While he was continuing our work in Athens he was betrayed by the Lili Marlene of Greece, Ntiritaoya, to the Italian police. He was imprisoned, tortured and sentenced to death with Frank Macaskie, and although his death sentence was commuted he was not released until well into 1943. During his period of captivity in the Calithea prison in Athens he had painted a remarkably good portrait of Winston Churchill, and he asked me if I could arrange for him to present it to the great man. I asked Mary if she could arrange it, to which she readily agreed. However, on the appointed day Churchill was suddenly called away on one of his vitally important meetings, and asked if the Captain would mind if he were to present it to Mary, as his proxy. The Captain was thrilled, and we therefore visited Mary together and made the presentation.

After the Captain had been liberated from prison he went to Cairo to see Colonel Simonds and his other senior officers in MI9, and whilst he was there he called on my great friend and fellow-officer, Colonel Patrick McCraith. At our regimental dinner at Claridges in 1988 Patrick related to me, over several glasses of port, their meetings in Cairo and subsequently at his home in Nottinghamshire. The next morning I rang Patrick and asked him if he would write it all down, which he did, and I reproduce it here.

'*Captain Emmanuele Vernicos,*

It was either you and/or Myles who introduced me to Vernicos. I thought that he was a splendid fellow and I took to him immediately.

Sometime afterwards I met him on my way to lunch at Shepheards Hotel and asked him to join me.

This must have been in the latter part of 1943 and just before we returned to the United Kingdom to prepare for D-Day.

We had a pre-lunch drink on the terrace of Shepheards. The sight of me sitting with a Greek naval officer with gold teeth attracted the attention of my friends and acquaintances as they entered the hotel for lunch. But my embarrassment was as nothing when, without warning, Vernicos put his head in his hands moaning very loudly. When the moaning had ceased I asked him what on earth was the matter. He told me it was of no moment and I gave him another drink.

After he had ceased his loud moaning for the second time he told me that on a recent spying trip into Europe the Italians had become extremely suspicious of him and, as a consequence, had tortured him. They beat him with rubber truncheons in his kidneys and applied a wooden vice around his head. They tightened the vice slowly until he passed out, when they released the tension and allowed him to recover. After recovery the vice was again slowly re-tightened. This treatment lasted on and off for a fortnight. Whether he then escaped or was released I cannot remember.

As a result he could eat very little and suffered fearful head pains.

I telephoned the hospital and made an immediate appointment for him to be examined by a doctor there who I

303

knew to be a specialist in head wounds. I hailed a taxi and he went off at once.

He returned after I had had my lunch and told me that the doctor could find nothing physically wrong with his head and had come to the conclusion that the Italians had carried out their torture in a very professional and experienced manner.

Vernicos later invited me to lunch at a Greek restaurant. This was a greater embarrassment than the terrace at Shepheards. The restaurant appeared to be in the Cairo Red Light District, the table was outside on the pavement, his other guests were Greek men and women of fearsome appearance, the lunch consisted of many courses and lasted all afternoon and allied soldiers (including Sherwood Rangers) passed by continuously. I ate food which I had never seen before and which, fortunately, I have never seen since.

Pip and I married in February 1946 and after our honeymoon in Ireland we lived in a small cottage called 'Cotswold' in Normanton on the Wolds, Nottinghamshire. Our visitors' book discloses that:

On the night of the 1st/2nd October of that year you came to stay.

On the night of the 12th/13th October Emmanuel Vernicos came to stay, apparently on his way to the United States. He gave his address as yours, at 35 Eaton Square.

He brought with him a vast quantity of mussels which he insisted on deep frying. The mussels were delicious but he used up Pip's entire stock of cooking fat carefully built up from the then meagre monthly ration.

He himself ate nothing. He told me that his kidneys had been permanently damaged. He was unable to sleep due to severe headaches.

I asked him what had happened to the Italians. He said nothing had happened to them. When I asked him why he told me that he despised them so much that he couldn't be bothered to give evidence of their cruelty. They thus got off scot free.

About a month later Vernicos died in (if I remember rightly) New York, no doubt as a result of this torture.'

Vernicos was very excited about his plans for raising the ships in Tobruk harbour and I had done a detailed calculation of the salvage value of the cargo which would not have been destroyed by the sea water in the main ship. This contained the 7,000 cases of Scotch whisky, at that time virtually unobtainable anywhere in the world. I thought that this sort of exploration was exactly what our company, the Exploration Company, had been formed for in 1886, and I agreed that we would help in the financing of the operation. We formed a limited company, the Vernicos Exploration Company, of which he was to be Managing Director, and he immediately began to search the world for a suitable salvage ship capable of raising the ships from the bottom of Tobruk harbour.

Unfortunately his family salvage vessels, including the *Irene Vernicos* had been destroyed in Souda Bay in 1941 by the Germans' relentless bombing in their fearsome Stukas. I can still see them now, coming in at about 1,000 feet, then, with their terrifying screech, suddenly nose-diving to within a few hundred feet, at which point they jettisoned their bombs. These would invariably be on target, or otherwise very near misses, which brought up huge plumes of water as the bombs exploded.

Vernicos eventually located the ideal vessel for his purpose in New York Harbour, called the SS *Brandt*. Thereafter a lot of time and energy was spent on administrative details and arranging the necessary 80,000 dollars to purchase the ship. He went to his family's old and much respected shipping brokers and agents in the City of London, P. Wigan Richardson, who greatly assisted in all the details necessary for bringing this large ship from New York to Tobruk harbour. On the finance side we went to see my old friend Commander Adrian Seligman.

Although Adrian was not in the family firm of Seligman Brothers, he was well known to me as before the war he had sailed around the world before the mast, on the equivalent of a windjammer. With the advent of war he had commanded an MTB in 1939 off the east coast of Britain, and operated in the North Sea against German reconnaissance aircraft. He first became famous when Lord Haw-Haw announced over the radio from Berlin that they 'Would get the Jew Seligman' – which they actually failed to do throughout the war. Adrian went on to do notable work in the Aegean whilst commanding a section of the Levant Schooner Squadron, similar to George Jellicoe's Special Boat Services. I used to see him quite frequently during this period.

Seligman Brothers arranged a draft for the purchase and victualling of the SS *Brandt,* and all was set up for the Captain to sail from Greece, where he was making final preparations as to crew etc. to New York.

He sailed on a liner that called at Marseilles before crossing the Atlantic, and a few days later I received the ghastly news from his family that he had suddenly died on board the liner.

This was to me a very deep personal loss as, over the six years that I had known him, we had become very close friends and were on the same wavelength throughout.

Emmanuele Vernicos died as possibly one of the least rewarded Allied officers operating in the Middle East with the British.

After the collapse of Greece he followed the White Ensign in his ultra-modern salvage vessel, the *Agia Irene,* to Souda Bay, where he remained with the Navy from January until the beginning of the great German onslaught, on May 20th 1941. Weeks before the main assault intense bombing of the battleships in Souda Bay had commenced, and by the time of the paratroop landing many ships, including the cruisers *York* and *Ajax* had been badly crippled and were in danger of sinking.

Vernicos anchored alongside the *York,* endeavouring to save her from total loss. Throughout the Battle of Crete, from my position on St John's hill overlooking the great Souda harbour, I saw wave after wave of Stukas bombing these helpless ships, with the Commander's salvage ship tied up alongside the *York.* Huge plumes of water spurted up after each salvo, until his ship too was likewise crippled.

In the evacuation of the island by the British he remained behind to look after his young Newfoundland wife and family. Having settled them in he went into the hills, from where he sent out messages to any British who had not been evacuated or captured to contact him. His message reached us, as already recorded in Myles's diary.

Despite abandoning his wife and family and everything he had in the world for the British war effort, he never received any recognition, posthumous or otherwise. Meanwhile many of his countrymen – politicians, diplomats, service people – had been enjoying the fleshpots of Cairo, stealing other men's wives, and intriguing in cliques for, or against, their King. This is described in full by Churchill in *The Greek Torment.*

I now found myself with a perfectly good salvage ship lying in New York harbour, with no human dynamo to man and run this large operation, which was now a total void. As in military matters, withdrawal is very much more difficult than advancing, and a number of months were wasted in the very complicated closing down of the Vernicos Exploration Company. I remember the auditors, Deloitte, Plender Griffiths, were somewhat suspicious on hearing that the Greek Managing Director had died in what they thought to be suspicious circumstances on the liner, and they insisted on seeing the death certificate before they would complete the balance sheet.

24

Spartamint and Grey Steel

Spartamint certainly was the finest horse that Marcus had ever bred, but after six years of carefree careering around on Marcus's huge and lush pastures, he did not take kindly to being broken in.

In due course, however, Willie Pickard completed the job, and I returned to try him out with the local pack. It turned out to be an experience that I never wanted to repeat. He was enormously strong, as keen as mustard, and virtually uncontrollable.

After one or two more flirtations with death on the hunting field I reluctantly decided that he was too much for me in my state of health, which, at that time, was none too good. At Marcus's suggestion that he would make a champion steeplechaser I sent him to Charlie Bell, at Epsom.

After a few months with Charlie he began his steeplechase career by winning at Fontwell Park and coming in second at Leicester. Then, having thrown his jockey at Newton Abbot, he led the field by a considerable margin before deciding to try to jump the canal. He landed right in the canal, causing something of a palaver in getting him out again – we had to use a crane.

I was never completely devoted to horse-racing though, and when Jimmy Seely made me an offer for Spartamint, I reluctantly accepted. I then proceeded north again to buy, from Marcus, a first class (but slightly less energetic) hunter on which I could really enjoy hunting. This I did for several seasons with the Quorn and Belvoir.

My new horse, whom I had named Grey Steel after Kemal Ataturk, was, although I say it myself, the envy of many. He was the most perfect jumper and had a wonderfully placid temperament. A child of six could have handled him, although he stood almost seventeen hands high. It was only when, some years later, we moved reluctantly down to suburbia that I had to say goodbye to him. He was bought by Mrs Bishop of Shipton Hall in Shropshire. She told me how impressed she had been when he was loaded into his horse box, which had a canvas hood flapping around. Most horses would have been terrified, but Grey Steel quickly, without any fuss, put his head right down under the canvas and stepped into the box. This decided her and she immediately made her purchase. He later won, amongst other events, the jumping competition at the Royal Cambridge Show. Harry Llewellyn, who had been with me in Palestine in the first year of the war, wanted to ride him in the Helsinki Olympic Games, but unfortunately he had gone lame by that time and was never able to show the Finns how a real horse jumps. He ended his days happily with Mrs Bishop at her lovely manor house where we visited him – I for one with a lump in my throat.

On my return to London from my first visit to Ness Hall after the war I was not feeling very well, and developed my first bout of most unpleasant asthma on the train. This and bronchitis were beginning to place something of a damper on my evenings.

Nevertheless I saw a considerable amount of Mary Churchill, who had recently accompanied her father to the Potsdam Conference in Berlin; she told me how very charming, and how beautifully turned out in very well-cut suits Stalin was.

I have never forgotten this, as at that time he must have had the blood of ten million or more of his fellow countrymen and neighbours on his hands.

Also at that time Stalin was planning his secret war to capture and enslave us and the whole of Europe. This would have given him – with the hammer and sickle – the vast heartland of the world, stretching from Vladivostock to Calais, and with a population of 500 million people – all of whom would be nothing more than slaves under the Red Tsar. Yet only a few months before Churchill had intended to capture

309

Berlin and drive as far east as possible, thereby squaring up with the Russians.

Again he was defeated by Roosevelt, Marshall and Eisenhower, as is evident from the diaries of Field Marshal Viscount Alanbrooke KG OM, quoted in Arthur Bryant's *Triumph in the West*:

'March 29th. A very long COS meeting with a series of annoying telegrams. The worst of all was one from Eisenhower direct to Stalin trying to co-ordinate his offensive with the Russians. To start with, he has no business to address Stalin direct, his communications should be through the Combined Chiefs-of-Staff; secondly, he produced a telegram which was unintelligible; and finally, what was implied in it appeared to be entirely adrift and a change from all that had been previously agreed on ... At 5.15 pm we were sent for by the PM to discuss Ike's telegram to Stalin, and our proposed action ...

... March 30th Good Friday. Had a long COS meeting in order to finish off all the work for the weekend. Matters, however, looked rather ominous owing to Eisenhower's wire to Stalin ...

... For the British, Eisenhower's telegram was one more disappointment and source of disillusion. Having gone to war in defence of Poland and the liberties of Europe at a time when Russia was in league with the aggressor, and America concerned only with her own neutrality, they were now, with six years of struggle crowned by victory, forced to witness at the dictate of one of their principal allies the needless subjection of the whole of Eastern Europe to the totalitarian tyranny of the other.

On March 28th four days after Montgomery had crossed the Rhine and while strong German forces still barred the Russians' road to Berlin and Vienna, the Western Allies were confronted only by spasmodic resistance from a disintegrating, defeated army whose mobility had been broken by their overwhelming air power, and whose morale by the Battle of Rhineland and Westphalia in which it had lost, since the beginning of the month, 300,000 prisoners. On that day Montgomery's bridgehead was thirty-five miles wide and twenty-five miles deep, with twenty divisions and 1,500 tanks already across the river, while the Americans had taken Frankfurt and Mannheim, and Hodge's and Patton's armour was sweeping northwards to encircle the Ruhr and join Simpson's Ninth Army in the rear for the long-awaited drive across the Hanover plains to the Elbe and Berlin – the goal of every Allied soldier since the start of the Western counter-attack at Alamein two-and-a-half years before.'

'My intention,' Montgomery had cabled the CIGS on March 27th 1945, 'is to drive hard for the line of the Elbe . . . I have ordered Ninth and Second Armies to move armoured and mobile forces at once and to get through to the Elbe with utmost speed and drive. The situation looks good and events should begin to move rapidly in a few days . . . My tactical HQ moves will be Wesel-Munster-Herford-Hanover – thence via the autobahn to Berlin, I hope.' Yet on that very day, without reference to the Combined Chiefs-of-Staff or a word to the Commander-in-Chief of the British forces which still constituted nearly a third of his army, Eisenhower dispatched a telegram to Stalin informing him that he proposed, after encircling the Ruhr, to concentrate in central Germany for an advance, on an Erfurt/Leipzig axis, towards the upper Elbe, there to await the arrival of the Russians. His object, he explained, was to cut Germany in half, separate its northern defenders from its southern, and thereafter to concentrate his main force against the supposed 'National Redoubt' in the Austrian Alps, in which, it was rumoured, Hitler and the Nazi fanatics intended to hold out until new secret weapons or a split in the Grand Alliance came to their aid.

This unexpected message, of which copies were sent to London and Washington, received a cordial welcome from the Lord of the Kremlin, who had been perturbed by his Allies' sudden triumph and feared that the collapse of the Germans in the west would enable the British and Americans to reach Berlin while his own forces were still held up on the

Oder.

Churchill saw this clearly – 'There is very little doubt in my mind,' he wrote to Roosevelt on April 5th, 'that the Soviet leaders . . . are surprised and disconcerted at the rapid advance of the Allied armies in the west and the almost total defeat of the enemy on our front, especially as they say they are themselves in no position to deliver a decisive attack before the middle of May.' (*Churchill VI.*)

He at once cabled back his approval of the Supreme Commander's intention to ignore Berlin, which, he declared, had 'lost its former strategic importance' and towards which, he assured him, the Soviet High Command now planned to allocate only secondary forces, and then not till the middle of May. At the time of Eisenhower's intervention in the international scene the relations between Moscow and London had been strained almost to breaking point by the Kremlin's bad faith over the Polish elections and by the arrogance with which it was imposing its rule on the nations of Eastern Europe, while even Washington's faith in Russian liberalism had been shaken by the treachery with which the Polish patriot leaders had just been tricked and kidnapped and the accusations of bad faith which Stalin was levelling against his erstwhile companions of Yalta over the German peace overtures in Italy.

Of all this, however, the Supreme Commander was unaware. To him, as he put it in his memoirs, 'In his generous instincts, in his love of laughter, in his devotion to comrades and in his healthy, direct outlook on the affairs of a workaday life, the Russian seemed to bear a marked similarity to . . . the average American', and he apparently assumed that the rulers of Russia were equally guileless. But the British war leaders – the Chiefs-of-Staff for military reasons and the Prime Minister for political ones – viewed his abandonment of the direct drive on Berlin as yet another sacrifice on the altar of American military prestige of sound strategy and of Britain's war aims. These included the early liberation of Holland, the occupation of the North German naval ports, and the freeing of Denmark.

For Brooke and his colleagues did not believe the Germans could maintain any serious resistance in the Austrian Alps, and saw in Eisenhower's plan to exchange a concentrated

British-American thrust across the Hanover plains to Berlin for an all-American advance in central and southern Germany the same danger of logistical dispersal which had dissipated the Allies' resources after their breakthrough in August, and thrown away the opportunities presented by Montgomery's earlier victory. Apart from this they regarded Eisenhower's direct approach to Stalin as a usurpation of their authority. The Prime Minister, who attached much less importance to the strategic defects of the Supreme Commander's plan than his military advisers, was much more concerned at Eisenhower's readiness to minimize the importance of the German capital and to leave its capture to the Russians, who would then, as the captors of both Berlin and Vienna, appear as the real victors in the war and the sole 'liberators' of central Europe.

'I deem it', he wrote to Eisenhower on April 2nd 1945, 'highly important that we should shake hands with the Russians as far east as possible.'

And later:

'The Japanese war and its incompatibility with the country's desire for a speedy return to peace-time conditions were not Brooke's only worry. Victory over Germany had put an end to the fighting in Europe but not to Britain's responsibilities there. Having been allowed to march into the heart of the Continent as a result of America's and Britain's scrupulous adherence to their agreements, the Russians were now making it plain that they not only intended to stay there permanently but, in defiance of those agreements, to deny their Allies any say in the future of the vast areas and national populations – Polish, Balt, Czech, Slav, Croat, Hungarian, Bulgarian, Romanian, Austrian and German – which they had over-run. Everywhere, under cover of the Red Army, Communist satellite governments were being set up and a ruthless proscription instituted by the massacre and deportation of all elements capable of giving leadership to the helpless peoples now being incorporated into the Empire of the hammer and sickle. Meanwhile the Communist Yugoslav leader Marshal Tito marched his partisans into Italy and tried to take possession of the provinces of Venezia Giulia and Istria and the ports of Trieste and Pola. Only the Prime Minister's firmness and Alexander's swift action prevented Britain and

America from being presented with a *fait accompli* there.'

Yet, although they might protest at their ally's aggression, the British and American leaders were at a hopeless disadvantage. Unlike Stalin and the Communist puppets whom the Red Army had sat in the saddle, they could only do what was likely to be endorsed by the electors on whom their power depended, and to whom, for the past few years, they had presented the Russian Communist leaders as champions of democracy. They were prisoners of their own propaganda; and to resist the breaches of faith of the Kremlin Imperialists by force was out of the question. Those who constituted their own fighting forces were themselves electors, whose one desire now that they had beaten the Nazis was to get home and leave the peoples of Europe to settle their own destinies. Churchill, with his historic sense of Christendom's unity and his far-ranging and prophetic imagination, saw the peril of the European situation:

'I moved', he wrote, 'amid cheering crowds or sat at a table adorned with congratulations and blessings from every part of the Grand Alliance, with an aching heart and a mind oppressed with forebodings.'

His former Labour and Liberal colleagues, aligned against him now in electoral battle and, still more, his American allies, failed to share his vision or, if they did so, felt it to be of small importance compared with the immediate practical problem of meeting the electors' demands for peace and disengagement.

The new American President Truman, a modest man devoted to his former chief's memory, held himself bound to carry out Roosevelt's policy of trusting the Soviet leaders. He was surrounded by advisers, both civil and military, who looked with the utmost suspicion on Churchill's wish to halt the Russians until they had honoured their agreements, and while the democracies still possessed the forces in Europe with which to do so.

'If the situation is handled firmly before our strength is dispersed, Europe may be saved another bloodbath.' (Prime Minister to President, 12th May 1945 – *Churchill VI, p.484*)

Despite the change in the Soviet attitude since the demarcation lines for the Occupying Armies had been agreed in 1944, Washington now insisted on withdrawing its troops from the Elbe to the west of Leipzig and Erfurt, thus handing over to the Russians a further large slice of Christendom at the very moment when they were extinguishing the last remnants of Polish independence 300 miles to the east. To the Prime Minister this retreat, which was carried out at the beginning of July, established Soviet tyranny permanently in the centre of Europe, bringing down, as he put it, 'an iron curtain between us and everything to the eastward.' But the only American reaction, expressed by the dead President's confidential adviser, Harry Hopkins, was that it was of vital importance that the United States should not be manoeuvred into a position where she would be aligned with Great Britain 'as a bloc against Russia to implement England's European policy'.

It was these three, Roosevelt, Marshall and Eisenhower, who had swept aside Churchill's *cri-de-coeur* about capturing Rhodes, thereby, on that occasion, prolonging the war by almost two years and enabling Russia and Stalin to occupy the whole of Eastern Europe as far as Berlin. Now, two years later, they did the whole thing again, by tying Churchill's hands and allowing the Russians to reach Berlin, thereby sealing the fate of the world by consigning it to fifty years of cold war and untold hardship, murder and cruelty throughout the bulk of Europe.

25

The Consequences

The penalty that Roosevelt, Eisenhower and Marshall brought to Britain and Churchill was the unnecessary loss of the flower of their manhood and the ultimate total destruction of the British Empire and Pax Britannica, which for two hundred years had provided the world with the happiest and most peaceful period in its history. Look at those once proud and happy lands today: the Middle East in turmoil – Palestine and the Lebanon in continual internecine war of the most vicious kind; most of Africa in poverty and often localised war. The sub-continent of India (and the once peaceful and happy island of Ceylon) is now split by racial and religious hatred and poverty, hidden under a paper covering of political dogma aimed at decrying the mote in other nations' eyes in order to hide the much larger mote in their own.

Looking back on the last half century we can clearly see the appalling cost to America of their refusal to help Churchill. Since 1943 the American debt has risen from $142.6 billion to $3319.2 billion; most of which was spent on defence in an endeavour to keep level with the most ruthless and evil power on earth, the communist state of Soviet Russia. The monster they helped to create and whose 250 million near-starving people they are now having to help feed.

The communist plague was to infiltrate the world, starting in Greece where, as early as 1945, the germ had created a civil war. This caused the death, often under excruciating torture, of over one million Greeks – enormously exceeding any casualties they had suffered in the war, and the kidnapping and deportation to behind the Iron Curtain of thousands of Greek children, torn from their families, many never to be seen again.

The germ then spread to Vietnam and Indo-China, where the Americans, in an utterly useless war, were defeated by a country with less than four million ruthless Vietcong, led by Ho Chi Minh and commanded by the brilliant General Giap. This was was to prove the United States' greatest military disaster, and far and away its most costly was of all time, splitting the country from top to bottom. Had the Russians been halted at the end of the war and made to revert to their original frontiers – leaving Poland and all the other states living in freedom – this disaster would never have happened, since the North Vietnamese would not have been supplied by Russia (as Mao Tse Tung had been during his 'Long March' in 1935).

The disease then spread to the Caribbean, where Castro was able to turn a friendly and prosperous Cuba in to a moored communist aircraft carrier within fifty miles of America's east-coast state of Florida, from where Marxist propaganda was exported throughout Central and South America, down to the once-prosperous and peaceful Chile, where they enthroned Señor Allende.

Turning east, the process continued in the immensely rich and lovely British Malaya, where, had it not been for General Templer and the steadfast British planters and their loyal workers, the whole area would have gone the same way as the Dutch East Indies. Their home government, ravaged by war, and prevented by Mountbatten from coming to their rescue, saw all their possessions torn from them – like the Greek children who were forced to march over the Epirus into captivity.

China and Burma with its oil, wolfram, rubies and teak went the same way, followed by the Seychelles and Madagascar; not content with their achievements they then applied the same technique to the whole continent of Africa.

The French, after a fearful struggle, were ejected from Algeria; Egypt almost succumbed and her neighbour Libya became the Cuba of North Africa, sworn to eliminate and destroy all Jews and the state of Israel. From there the evil monster fixed its eyes greedily on the mineral wealth of southern and central Africa, and saw the necessity of

317

overturning the governments and peoples of the British, French and Belgian Colonies and Dominions.

In Abyssinia the Christian Emperor Haile Selassie (a direct descendant of the Queen of Sheba) was overthrown and his family, princes and statesmen were tortured, imprisoned and murdered – apart from the fortunate few who happened to be abroad, by the Marxist revolutionary Colonel Mengistu.

Sweeping through Tanganyika, Zanzibar and Kenya the tide reached the immensely rich Congo. For a while President Tshombe stood out like a rock amidst the rising water, but partly submerged by it, was aided by the misguided efforts of the United Nations under Dag Hammarskjold and his Irish henchman, Conor Cruise O'Brien. President Tshombe was shortly to pay the price of having stood up alone against the communist avalanche; he was seized and kidnapped on a Spanish airliner heading for Madrid, from where he was eventually sent to Communist Algeria. He died there some months later without any British or western government lifting a finger to save him. Their failure to act was an abrogation of the moral responsibility of the world in the first air hijack of all time – the success of which has enabled terrorists to plague the world's airlines on an ever-increasing scale.

Next in the net were Angola and Mozambique – each a country the size of Europe – thus enabling the whole weight of the spearhead to be launched against Britain's model self-governing colony of Rhodesia – happy and well-administered, as I had seen for myself, since 1935. Rhodesia proved a harder nut to crack; Ian Smith and his loyal Rhodesians were able to fight off this well-nigh insupportable attack for twelve years, in spite of Russian and Chinese arms pouring into the country and the imposition of sanctions by Mr Wilson, Alec Home and the United Nations. Eventually, however, through the Trojan horse laid on by the Americans under Dr Kissinger and the British under Lord Carrington, they were beguiled into the Lancaster House death trap.

This cleared the road to the ultimate target of South Africa – the richest area in the world for the all-important and vitally necessary strategic minerals. The popular slogan and battle-cry 'Apartheid' was adopted by the United Nations Central Committee and the naive, gullible (and so-called Liberal and democratic) Americans and British.

As their terrorist army the communists use the ANC, based on so-called front-line states now firmly in their camp. They continue to pour what they describe as 'freedom fighters' – armed with limpet mines and Kalashnikov rifles into South Africa whilst working up a crescendo of world venom against that country's government. Their sole objective is to destroy the country which is the best governed in the whole of Africa (and certainly better than any other communist state), and is more prosperous and has more industry than the rest of Africa put together.

To pick this plum after forty years planning would make the Soviet Union incontestably the master of the industrial world, because if they were to establish an ANC-controlled communist government in Pretoria they would control between eighty and ninety per cent of the most important industrial and strategic metals on earth namely platinum, paladium, irridium, manganese, chromium, vanadium – and a host of other. Within a matter of months, and without firing a shot, the Soviet Union would bring every industrial country in the world to a standstill, hence producing millions of unemployed people, starvation and poverty, unless those millions are prepared to deal on their terms.

We are now being served with a delicious menu of *perestroika* by the Kremlin in an iron fist covered by a velvet glove in the form of Mikhail Gorbachev, with the western world swooning over him as it did in 1945 and 1946, when every pub in England was drinking the health of 'good old Joe Stalin'. If America fails to reverse its policy of allying itself with Russia and the ANC in their sanctions and every other policy aimed at destroying South Africa, they will only have themselves to blame for having handed over control of the most important sea route in the world, that around the Cape, and total industrial power through the irreplaceable control of all the major strategic minerals on earth, the power of which Stalin foresaw fifty years ago. However, the internal rottenness of the USSR is likely to save the USA by collapsing first. As has just happened at Christmas 1991.

Not even harmless Afghanistan escaped. Although they devastated a country of 12 million people, fortunately – despite the deployment of 120,000 Russian troops – the

319

Russians were, in the end, soundly thrashed by the Mujahidin guerillas.

The aforesaid are the fruits from the seeds of gratitude to Britain and Churchill from Roosevelt and the Generals. Gratitude for what, one may well ask? – From being narrowly saved by Britain from being defeated and finding themselves in much the same position as occupied France and Poland.

As I have shown, the battle for Crete delayed Hitler's massive Barbarossa offensive against Russia by possibly six vital weeks. Even then, as is seen from Stalin's *cri-de-coeur* letter of September 4th 1941 to Churchill '. . . He stared defeat in the face . . .' – had the offensive been six weeks earlier it would have given Stalin and Russia the *coup de grace*. Without the Cretan delay Hitler's forces would have far over-run Moscow, which would have encouraged the Japanese part of the Axis to attack Russia in the Far East, the Vladivostock area, which would unquestionably have given total victory to the Axis Powers dominated by Germany and Hitler.

They would then have controlled everything from Christiansund to Vladivostock in the north, and from Cape Town to Sydney in the south. One thousand million people, organised by the two most efficient and hard-working industrial nations on earth, ready to harness the immense reserves of raw materials to the gigantic workforce.

A then isolated USA would have been left with two alternatives – to capitulate or co-operate.

It was for saving them from this that Britain and Churchill deserved gratitude and co-operation. Neither of these did they get, even though they had sacrificed everything, and had fought alone against the Nazi monster for almost two-and-a-half years while America enjoyed full peace and prosperity – selling arms and equipment to us – and would have continued to do so had the Japanese not bombed them into the war.

I was born in the same year as the Russian revolution, when Russia was bankrupt and, in world terms, an insignificant power. Since then I have seen the whole relentless progress of the communist monolith, whose only road-blocks appear to have been their own self destruction.

26

Mary Churchill

The latter part of 1945 saw my health steadily deteriorating. However, Mary Churchill, whom I had now known for about eight months, was kind enough to come out with me on several occasions and to stay at Batemans. One evening she asked me to collect her from her father's house in Hyde Park Gate. When I arrived I was shown into the drawing room and the butler told me, 'Miss Mary is changing and will be down shortly.' I thus waited for a few minutes, admiring the imposing room and the pictures on the wall, when in walked her father, looking rather rotund and cherubic whilst smoking a cigar and dressed in his usual boiler suit. We were left alone for a quarter of an hour, during which we talked about world affairs and I explained my views that Britains's future lay in her great dominions and colonies, with particular reference to Southern Africa.

I knew that a number of Officers, contemporaries of mine under Freddie de Guingand, in his closing months as Chief-of-Staff to Field Marshal Montgomery, had been given an exercise. They had to select the most promising country – anywhere in the world – for a young man to go to live and make a career. After six months they reported to de Guingand that they had, after the most careful planning, chosen Southern Rhodesia. The General and many others responded to this by deciding to up sticks and go too, doing sterling work there for the rest of their lives.

I have always wondered – probably entirely incorrectly – whether Churchill had asked to be left alone with me to weigh me up, and to see if I was any improvement on Vic Oliver. I had a nasty feeling the answer was probably 'No'. I was still legally married to Ninette and although by now I was extremely close to Mary I was in no position to make any suggestions in that direction without being grossly unfair.

Shortly after this my health went up the spout, and I had to be rushed to St George's Hospital at Hyde Park Corner to have a major emergency operation.

After the interminable operations performed by the German surgeons in Belgrade to remove the Italian bullet so long lodged in the centre of my body, and the draining of the ever-growing internal abscesses thereby created, I had appeared superficially to be cured. At that time Dr Fleming's miraculous penicillin had not reached the Germans so the poison was still present, lying dormant until now, eighteen months later. It now resumed its onslaught with a vengeance and the internal abscesses all recurred, accompanied by a very high fever.

Fortunately I was lucky enough to have the great surgeon Ivor Black to operate on me this time, accompanied by Doctor Fleming's wonderful penicillin. After massive injections for several weeks, plus all the old draining-tube paraphernalia, I began slowly to recover. After a month or two the worse was over, not for a day or two but, thanks to the Almighty, right up until now, nearly fifty years later.

It was about now that Mary went on a visit to Paris and met my cousin Christopher Soames. (His mother was Hope Woodbine Parish, later Mrs Soames and later Lady Dynevor.) Christopher was about four years younger than me and I had had to look after him when he was a new boy at Eton. He subsequently asked me in Cairo if I could give him a job in my operations, about which I was not too enthusiastic. At a later date he joined Colonel Simonds in MI9, where he remained until almost the end of the war, before becoming Assistant Military Attaché in Paris. It was in the City of Light that the great romance began and they were married at St Margaret's Westminster in 1947. (I attended the wedding with my fiancée, to whom I had recently become engaged and who was to prove the great and lasting love of my life; we have been married now for forty-five wonderfully happy years.)

1946 saw me well recovered and fully established at Friars Wells, Wartnaby and also back at 35 Eaton Square again (having foolishly sold Halsey Street). I was very active on the business front with many irons in the fire and several gold-mining ventures on the Gold Coast, namely Kiankor Gold Mine, Central Wassau Gold Mines, and Ashanti Obuasi. These projects took up a great deal of time, entailing several long and arduous flights to the Gold Coast which in those days took three days, plus a great deal of badly-needed capital and mental anxiety. Unfortunately they all failed, and in my office Central Wassau soon became known as 'Central Washout'. Some of the other ventures, fortunately, did bring a certain amount of grist to the mill, but it was none the less a difficult period.

In Leicestershire I entertained most weekends and had very happy parties with many friends staying. One of them was Amaury de Riencourt, who was shortly to set off for Tibet. There he wrote his first of many books, *The Roof of the World,* which was a best seller both in Britain and America and has recently been re-published.

Towards the end of June I was invited up for a weekend to stay with Sir Douglas and Lady McCraith at Plumtree in Nottinghamshire; a most delightful house, where Patrick and Tony had spent most of their lives until the war. Phyllis McCraith was still running the Nottinghamshire Sherwood Rangers Yeomanry Welfare Association. This entailed a huge amount of work, as five years of war had caused many broken marriages and kindred emotional problems for families. A large part of this landed on Phyllis's plate, not for a few months but for the next thirty years, and if anyone deserved a medal she did.

One afternoon at Plumtree Lady Trent motored over to tea with the McCraiths. Afterwards on the lawn, bathed in warm evening sunshine, she said how much she had enjoyed having my brother Charles to stay with them before the war in Scotland at Glenborrodale, and asked if I would be free to come up and stay in August. I already knew quite a lot about Glenborrodale from Charles and his excellent colour cine films of the house parties they used to have there, so I gladly accepted. As I was already going to stay with my Colonel, Lord Yarborough, at his shooting lodge at Kingussie I said I would be delighted to come on from there, and would arrive on August 25th.

Although I did not know it at the time, a seed had thus been planted which was shortly to become a tree of the greatest happiness.

June and July were very busy months in the office, with a number of new ventures and also our weekly newsletter called *Trends,* which was edited by Trotty Taylor and later by Ian Howie, both of whom had been in Oflag 7B with me. *Trends* soon generated quite a large following, and in due course I sold it to Bill and David Stirling.

Soon it was time to head north, where I had a very happy week with the Yarboroughs.

I remember one of the many attractions of the property was going to the top of the hills with Diana after the ptarmigan, which, even at that time of year, were completely white. They were very sporting, dodging about behind boulders. The tops were very rocky, with sparse-growing heather. To reach them took several hours of hard climbing which Di thought nothing of, but which I found rather tough going after my fairly sedentary life in London. However it was all great fun, and we had lovely parties in the evening.

I left Kingussie after breakfast, and motored for many hours through beautiful highland scenery in my friendly ex-Army baby Austin, still painted khaki green. Unfortunately I had not realised that there was a ferry at Ardgour and had therefore driven the extra hundred miles around Loch Linnhe, becoming increasingly anxious throughout as I was well aware that my hosts were expecting me in good time for dinner. Running true to form perhaps, I arrived an hour and a half late.

Glenborrodale Castle was a most impressive sight, with a wonderfully romantic atmosphere enhanced by its divine setting.

My host, Jack Trent, came out to meet me in his dinner jacket and was wonderfully cheery and welcoming to someone who had had bad manners enough to arrive late.

The assembled company having finished dinner whilst I was still hurtling round Loch Linnhe, Jack took me into the dining room and sat with me while I ate an excellent meal; something I am ashamed to say I have never done with any of my late-arriving guests!

Glenborrodale had been built by C.D. Rudd, who had bought the whole of the Ardnamurchan peninsula in 1906 after having founded the great De Beers Diamond Corporation with Cecil John Rhodes. Together they had formed and floated the Consolidated Gold Fields of South Africa in 1887. Not content with these great achievements, Rudd, with one native, had gone up alone to negotiate the land south of the Zambesi known as Matabele Land, which was ruled over by King Lobengula. He negotiated alone for nearly two months, surrounded by 10,000 of Lobengula's fully armed Impis, who were an off-shoot of the Zulu tribe in South Africa. He successfully concluded a treaty with Lobengula in the name of the great white Queen Victoria, for the territory which was shortly to become the British self-governing colony of Rhodesia, named after his partner and co-director Rhodes.

On his way back with the signed treaty documents, during the thousand-mile walk to Kimberley and Cape Town he and his servant got lost in the bush. After three days without food or water he was literally dying of thirst. Before collapsing he cut a small vein in his body and wrote, in his own blood, a note telling whoever found him that the treaty documents were hidden under a large boulder near his body. Fortunately some natives came across him unconscious but still alive, and looked after him, hence the document was saved and the country of Rhodesia came into being.

Rudd eventually returned to Glenborrodale and lived there until his death in 1916, known and liked by all the locals who had initially mistrusted him, as they mistrusted anyone from England. He was a terrific walker and none of the stalkers or ghillies could keep up with him for a whole day on the hill. Kenny Cameron, who had the Achetiny Beat, told me once when we were out stalking that even though he used to win the running at Kilchoan Sports he could not keep up with Mr Rudd, who, he said, went at a wolf's trot all day. Indeed, when Mr Rudd and his son Bevil used to go over the hills from Shielbridge to Glenborrodale, a distance of eight miles, he always beat his son – who went on to win a gold medal running in the Antwerp Olympic Games in 1928.

When Rudd had bought the peninsula he ordered two magnificent mansions to be built on the two finest sites; one was Glenborrodale and the other was Shielbridge House, which overlooked the Shiel salmon river. Shortly after Shielbridge had been completed Mr Rudd was travelling by coach and horses to Fort William, en route for London. Suddenly his factor rushed up behind him with the awful news that the house had burnt down. The arsonists were the salmon poachers, who feared they would be deprived of their livelihood.

Quite unperturbed by the news, Rudd asked his coachman to stop outside the Salen Post Office. In he went, drafted a one-word telegram to his architect saying 'rebuild', and continued his journey. The house, meanwhile, was rebuilt.

After my dinner Jack gave me some delicious port and took me into the drawing room. This was a most lovely room, with entrancing views across Loch Sunart and the small islands of Risga and Carna to the Morvern Peninsula – where I had spent many happy holidays as a boy. Looking westwards one could see Tobermory and the island of Mull.

Yet it was not these wonderful views that riveted my attention, but a tall slim girl of outstanding beauty and freshness. She was wearing a lovely long red close-fitting evening dress, and Jack introduced her to me as his youngest daughter Elizabeth, known always as Billa.

In the course of life things sometimes happen in a blinding flash; years of normal routine and nondescript occurrences can pass by, but once in a lifetime one is targeted by a bullet which scores a direct hit. This evening I was on the receiving end of that one in a million bullet.

This ravishing creature reminded me of my boyhood heroine, Alison, from John Buchan's book *Castle Gay*. I knew there was no turning back, and as far as I was concerned, here, on this beautiful evening fading into the long Scottish twilight, rose – God willing – the ardent hope of an everlasting supreme happiness stretching far into the distance beyond the Morvern hills.

The rest of this momentous evening was spent meeting my fellow guests. Amongst them was Captain Wilfrid Bruce, one of my host's brothers-in-law. His brother-in-law was Captain Robert Falcon Scott, and he had commanded one of Scott's ships, the *Terra Nova,* on the South Pole Expedition. Wilf was a very engaging, tough old man, and a very keen fisherman. He usually returned from the hill lochs with a good catch of brown trout, invariably accompanied by a ghillie and a highland pony to carry his large frame for the two hour journey up to the lochs.

(One week later a minor crisis arose when Wilf's pony bolted whilst he was fishing, and seemingly disappeared off the face of the earth. It happily managed to fall to me, on my way south in my green Army Austin, to overtake this very same pony careering down the road beyond Strontian, presumably heading for an assignation of love. Apart from the undoubted pleasure the pony's recovery would give Captain Bruce and my host, it also gave me a wonderful opportunity of sending a telegram to my newly-found dream girl, with all the obvious excuses it would afford for future correspondence.)

Staying at Glenborrodale was like a pre-war house party at its very best. There was plenty to do and plenty to see, and I was in my element there, having spent many similar holidays in Scotland with my family before the war. Every morning before breakfast we would go swimming from the castle jetty, in freezing cold water. We visited many of Jack's extensive highland farms, which I particularly enjoyed as this necessitated long motor drives invariably sitting next to the beautiful Billa.

27

Marriage

Back in the office I had to devote my days to the small but emerging group of companies. When some of my seemingly promising operations failed to come up trumps, in spite of a great deal of hard work and worry, they went down on my mental balance sheet as goodwill gained from experience. One used to be told, 'There is a fool born every minute,' but on the other hand omelettes cannot be made without breaking eggs, and my general investment policy for the companies, operating largely on individual initiative and inspiration, was beginning to bear fruit.

Also bearing fruit was a series of letters to Billa, who proved an excellent correspondent. I finally invited her to the theatre, followed by a romantic evening's dancing at the 400.

It was little more than a month since I had first been enchanted with Billa in the drawing room at Glenborrodale and, as the Duke of Wellington once said, 'It was a damn close-run thing' – as my adorable girl was leaving for Lausanne in the morning, to polish up her French and to have singing lessons for her beautiful voice. As personal contact was no longer possible a prolific correspondence ensued – culminating in my driving out to Switzerland in January, taking Billa's sister Mary with me by way of a smoke-screen to allay any parental flak.

Our journey out was quite something in mid-January, and we drove the 1,500 miles – much of it through deep snow – in my newly acquired pre-war Jaguar, which I had bought from my cousin Patrick Parish. We somehow managed to get there in one piece, staying a night en route at the Beau Rivage Hotel at Ouchy where Billa joined us for the drive to Grindelwald.

There we were joined by a large party of cousins and friends.

The next few days were spent hopelessly and deliriously in love, and we were completely oblivious to the outside world, even to poor Mary, who had been a wonderful travelling companion to me during our drive out.

As far as I was concerned this was IT; we were fantastically happy. We were also virtually impregnable from the long-range missile which was soon to arrive from Billa's dear mother in response to my formal letter asking her parents for their youngest daughter's hand in marriage. To darling Billa's eternal credit she had great courage and, although wounded by this correspondence, had no intention then or later of hoisting the white flag. We were greatly helped by the encouragement of the Trent second eleven in the form of Billa's elder sisters, Mary and Ann.

Our happiness to me was so great and all-enveloping that for the first time in three years the anguish caused by Ninette's letter of September 1944 was superseded by this new-found heaven. This wonderful happiness has continued unbroken ever since.

Billa was to be the great and lasting love of my life.

In Grindelwald we spent enchanted days and evenings, when we went out to various restaurants to dine and dance.

The time to strike camp and reluctantly head for home came all too quickly, and off we set in the Jaguar again. I remember one particularly terrifying episode when we were at the top of one of the lesser mountain roads, which had a one-in-three incline covered in snow, and underlaid with sheet ice. The good Jaguar would not respond to the brakes, even when in first gear; nor indeed, was it possible to steer with any accuracy. I was soon in a cold sweat of fear which I tried to hide from my companions, visualizing all sorts of appalling horrors that I would have to report to their parents. I therefore asked the two girls to kindly get out and walk down, whilst I, fairly terrified, took the car down what amounted to something much steeper and icier than the Cresta Run. As on practically every other occasion the Lord Almighty was on my side, and somehow the car and I slithered down in one piece. They later told me that I had given the impression of being supremely confident and it had never occurred to them that they might be in any danger – I apparently resembled a pilot at the controls of a Dakota!

We then spent the last night at the lovely Beau Rivage Hotel, in rooms overlooking the small quay where the exquisitely beautiful Empress of Austria was murdered by a lunatic. It was a very happy last evening but in the morning we had to say our sad goodbye. I shall always remember the poignant farewell; having to leave Billa to return to Lausanne whilst I returned to face alone the inevitable barrage of attack from Lenton House, Nottinghamshire to prevent Billa entering into a rash and hastily considered marriage. En route to London via Paris I fell prey to thoughts of being horse-whipped across Eaton Square by Lord Trent, whom I had so admired.

Once safely back home I had to wake myself up and gather up the reins of my business, greatly helped as usual by my father and Major Henderson-Scott.

One weekend at Friars Wells I had an American friend, Bobby Roberts and, I think, David Stirling to stay, and I asked Billa's parents to come over for dinner.

This was a great success, and I remember during dinner Bobby asked Jack Trent what he did, to which Jack replied, quite correctly, 'I am in the drug business.' Bobby was unaware that he was talking to the Chairman and Managing Director of Boots Pure Drug Company and, as it happened, the Regional Controller of Industry in the Midlands and the Chancellor of Nottingham University. Although in those days drugs had not acquired the notorious associations that they have today, I was not altogether surprised to see Bobby raise his eyebrows in obvious surprise – but he was too much of a gentleman to press the matter any further!

The dinner party ended on a very amicable note and I was invited to lunch at Lenton House about a fortnight later – where, I imagined, the whip would be pickled ready for my arrival.

Only Billa's parents and myself were present at this lunch; I was evidently going to be put through the hoop. Lunch was charming and delicious; all smiles and the height of kindness and friendship. Then came the ominous invitation to come into Jack's study. This instantly reminded me of an incident twenty-two years earlier when W.J. Oakley, the Headmaster of Ludgrove, asked me to come into his study. He said that although it would hurt him more than me, he was going to have to cane me for some misdemeanour that I had most definitely committed. He was a very likeable person who, I am certain, meant what he said. That, however, was no consolation for me in my present position.

Jack was kind and charming as usual, and began by saying that Billa was still very young and would also be very hard-up, which would make for hardship in an early marriage and he obviously wondered what I would be able to offer in maintenance. I replied that that depended on what, if any, success I had in building up my small group of companies.

I felt very much like a beggar on horse-back at this stage in the proceedings as, although they were quoted, Jack's solicitors Allen & Overy, had never even heard of my companies.

I also told Jack that I had expectations from my grandmother, Mrs Bonham-Christie. She lived on Brownsea Island, and was the original naturalist (or 'Green'): her love of animals, birds and trees far exceeded her love for her fellow human beings. Her father, C.J. Sofer Whitburn's trusts were destined to come to Godfrey, Elizabeth and myself via our grandmother. (As it happened none of them did, but luckily neither Jack nor I were to know this.)

Happily, by the end of our meeting Jack agreed that our marriage would be allowed to take place later in the year. I immediately sent a progress report to my unofficial fiancée, who, stuck out in Switzerland, was very anxious for news.

This all having been settled, I returned to London and waited for my golden girl to return. This she did fairly shortly, having cut short her stay in Lausanne, to the detriment of her French. The next few weeks were interrupted on two occasions by my having to fly out to the Gold Coast to visit our hoped-for mines, and also to Rhodesia and Elizabethville, in the Belgian Congo. The latter was particularly unfortunate as I got stuck there, as there were no planes coming back for over a week. I used this wasted week in buying some rather lovely embroidered silks, crêpe-de-chine and other dress materials, all of which were at a huge premium in clothes-rationed England. This store fortunately made up the bulk of Billa's trousseau, so I was forgiven for these tiresome faraway flights at a very crucial time.

On my return I found that Billa and her mother had arranged a visit to her grandmother, Florence, Lady Trent at her beautiful home Villa Millbrook, in Jersey. She loved giving large house parties, and if people were not staying in the house they would often come for lunch, tea or dinner. By the end of the day she was inclined to sit in her large armchair, a perfect example of a *grande dame* holding court.

Luckily she seemed to take favourably to me, and one evening she asked Alfred, her butler, to go to the silver cupboard and get out a pair of silver peacocks. She then presented them to me in front of the assembled company.

A visit to Villa Millbrook during the rationing in England in early 1947 was an experience never to be forgotten. Every afternoon one of us would go through the ritual of accompanying the Dowager in her green Rolls Royce for a drive around the island – driven (at never more than 16 mph) by her green-liveried chauffeur called Boris. Boris was a White Russian. He was always immaculately turned out and looked the dead spit image of a Cossack Guards Officer, which he probably had been.

Now only a month remained before our wedding, and of course there were many things to do. My father was, as he always had been, a pillar of affection and kindness, and it was he who arranged, through his old friend Canon Hannay (the author George E. Birmingham) to marry us in his church, Holy Trinity, Prince Consort Road. In 1947 it was virtually impossible to get married in a church if one had been through the divorce courts, regardless of whether or not one was the guilty party. We therefore had a brief ceremony in Caxton Hall, followed by a service of blessing in the beautiful church which, with our friends and loved-ones present, gave our marriage an aura of happiness in which each and every one of us could feel and enjoy.

We then led the thousand guests to Claridges Hotel, where my new parents-in-law had laid on a superlative reception, during which – rationing or no rationing – nearly a thousand bottles of champagne disappeared.

When the reception had nearly drawn to a close I brought Billa, looking quite wonderful and now in her going-away outfit, down the main staircase to a large limousine waiting to take us away for the start of our honeymoon. Actually this was really to throw the hounds off the scent, as we were merely driven to Hampton Court, on this beautifully hot June evening, where we walked through the gardens, got lost in the maze, and returned to Claridges for a quiet dinner in our suite.

The following morning we were up early in readiness to catch our long flight to Athens. This was the first stage of fulfilling the promises I had made to Billa to take her on a sailing honeymoon in the Aegean, guarded by my wartime Greek pirates. We were met at the airport by many of my friends and taken to the Grande Bretagne Hotel, there began our glorious honeymoon. (It was from this same 'GB' that General Student and other members of the German High Command had launched their massive airborne attacks on Crete, and later Cos, Samos and Leros – providing me with interesting memories.)

Ten happy days were spent in and around Athens and seeing many of my old friends, including my erstwhile comrade David Pawson and his wife Pam. We visited many beautiful sights and swam in the clear and unpolluted waters of the Aegean.

Most importantly we saw my wonderful friend and colleague Alex (now Admiral) Levides, whom I had not seen since September 1948, when he bravely joined me on the epic capture of Samos and Leros – an exploit for which he in particular apparently suffered most grievously at the hands of the Germans. They often treated Greek officers and men as second rate people. In the early days of his incarceration I think he was forced to remain standing day and night, followed by having to stand, sleep or sit in several inches of water. As a result of these and many other exceptionally unpleasant barbarities, a huge toll was taken on his health in later life. It was a great pleasure to meet the Admiral's wife, and their daughter Yolanda. We also met his cousin Colonel Levides, who was Controller of the King's Household – and, as a dyed-in-the-wool Royalist, at the opposite end of the political spectrum from the Admiral, who was a dedicated Venizelist.

As our first ten days drew to a close it was necessary to

purchase a few items for the sake of a minimum amount of comfort on Captain Miltiades Houmas's small and rugged boat, my old friend the *Evangelistria*. She had somehow survived being the first and last operational caique in the war, and her Captain was now an OBE and DSO. (See Appendix.)

Milton arrived, as usual, exactly on time.

With him came a hand-picked crew of two, and ample provisions for a fortnight's nostalgic cruising – we were going to retrace part of my wartime journeys to some of the lovely islands which had befriended me.

We set off from Turcolimano, the small harbour containing the Royal Hellenic Yacht Club, and headed east past Cape Sounion with its temple. The first evening brought us to Agios Georgios, a small barren island some thirty miles beyond Sounion where there was a large sunken warship half protruding out of the water, and here we anchored for the night. It must have been something of a shock for my poor bride, so recently tucked up in the highest quality linen sheets, to find herself sleeping next to the engine in an all-male boat with no washing facilities other than the ocean.

Each morning we would breakfast on deck and then swim in the clear, clean water. In the afternoons we would wander through the olive groves which ran right down to the blue Aegean; a truly Arcadian honeymoon whose memory we still treasure. We visited several islands, including Syphnos, where Emmanuele Vernicos's grandfather came from and about which he had told Myles and me so much during our escape from Crete. It lived up to his best descriptions as the most beautiful island, abounding in fruit and honey. We were met at the port and escorted by mule up the hill to the Vernicos's house, where we spent a comfortable night looked after by an elderly Greek housekeeper, dressed, as all Greek widows are, always in black.

Unfortunately the weather turned against us and our old friend the *melteme* came to meet us, blowing hard, and soon became a *fortuna* which accompanied us back to Piraeus. Luckily Billa was far too frightened to think about feeling seasick. (I, who used to suffer from acute air and sea-sickness, had been cured from this most unpleasant affliction since my very first day on our escape from Menes in Crete, in August

1941; this immensely traumatic experience somehow cauterized the feeling and I have been completely impervious to it ever since.)

Shortly after our return to Athens Billa was struck down by a severe attack of sand-fly fever, and we both suffered from 'gippy tummy'. Consequently, our last week was spent with a doctor in attendance and dear Pamela Pawson translating our symptoms and his instructions; nevertheless it was an epic honeymoon which we will remember all our days.

On the return flight, in my anxiety over Billa, I somehow managed to lose my beloved camera which had been with me throughout the war, and in 1947 the loss of the Mark III Zeiss Ikon camera was quite a loss.

We landed at Rome to refuel, where we were met by my old friend Edward Oliver, who was working at the British Embassy in Rome.

After this we flew on towards England, but as she was blotted out by fog we had to land in Aix-en-Provence. We spent the night in a charming old-fashioned hotel, with large brass beds, feather mattresses and pink cabbage roses climbing up the wallpaper. Billa was by then almost recovered, in spite of having lost two stone in ten days, and thoroughly enjoyed the Aix interlude.

The next day we reached England safely, and for me it was straight back to the grindstone. I had to keep my companies and their many activities on the rails and hold off the many sharks and predators who, even in those early days, were always eyeing lustfully any small group of potentially valuable companies with full Stock Exchange quotations.

The next rather thrilling move was to help my young bride establish a family home at Friars Wells.

Here we had a flourishing farm with a herd of Lincoln Red cattle, several of my Colonel Donny Player's Percheron horses, a Ridgeback lion dog that he had brought back from Rhodesia, and his faithful labrador. I remember the former disappearing in one bound out of the dining room window, with our fortnight's meat ration clamped between his jaws. We also had five or six hunters, which I bought from Marcus Kendal in Yorkshire, and a wonderful harness room. This was exactly as Donny had left it at Christmas 1939, when we had all sailed together with our Colonel Lord Yarborough and the

Sherwood Rangers, from Brocklesbury Park in Lincolnshire to join the Royal Scots Greys in Haifa.

His saddlery consisted of about a dozen very best pre-war Whippy saddles, bridles, attractively coloured and initialled horse rugs – in fact everything necessary to make up the full complement of items needed in a hunting establishment. Most of them I still have today, and in spite of them being at least seventy-five years old they are still as fine as anything available today.

One day we had a disaster, when my fine Lincoln Red cattle broke into the garden. Seven of the prize beasts were found several hours later dying a very unpleasant death, after enjoying eating the yew hedge.

Billa and I had a very happy two years at Friars Wells; our first child, Suzanne, was born there, assisted into the world by our regimental doctor, Geoffrey Brooks, GM. We were surrounded by many old friends and having Billa's parents nearby at Hambleton Hall near Oakham, where they had moved to, made it all the more agreeable. Life was very pleasant and happy, with two days hunting a week, hunt balls and numerous lunch and dinner parties. My stud groom, Baggaley, also looked after Billa's sister and brother-in-law's hunters, taking them in at livery, and it was fun all going off to the meets together.

In the district there were some of the giant figures of industry of the day, such as Harold Bowden of Raleigh Cycles, the Hope-Morleys of Morley's 'spinning wheel' knitting mills chaired by Lord Hollenden, Sir Eric Gore-Browne, the eminent banker and the Birkins, with their famous Nottingham lace. We saw most of these Napoleons in their own industry. Another couple we saw a lot of was George and Marjorie Earl; he ran Earls Cement, now called Blue Circle. They lived at Bagrave Hall, recently the home of Asil Nadir, who has made the headlines with his Polly Peck company.

Marjorie and George lived for hunting, and, if I remember rightly they were both joint Field Masters of the Quorn. On one of my first days out with the Quorn or Belvoir Marjorie introduced me to the Master, Toby Daresbury. He, like James Hanbury, looked exactly like a fox, and one felt they operated on the same wavelength. After a brief conversation with the Master I moved on, closely followed by Marjorie who, when we were alone, took me aside. In the nicest possible way she informed me that one never, simply never, came out with a leather case of sandwiches strapped to one's saddle. If you really had to eat you could have one small sandwich in your pocket, nothing more. I had to take the hint and so my very expensive Swaine and Adeney case was relegated to the attic, where it has remained ever since.

The unwritten rules were strictly adhered to. I remember one afternoon when the whole field of some two hundred came to a check while the Master, Lord Belper, was casting hounds just beyond a strong post and rail fence. Suddenly a young David Burghersh and Rupert Watson charged forward and cleared the fence, landing just short of hounds. Belper halted the entire field some hundred yards behind and shouted abuse at them, ordering them not only to jump back over the fence but to leave the field. For a few moments they showed signs of mutiny, but their resistance was short-lived and they were obliged to retreat in front of the whole field. I have never witnessed a more devastating public rebuke, and hope never to be on the receiving end of anything like it.

Much as we revelled in this life, however, it could not be indefinitely sustained. My ever-growing business commitments and the obvious necessity of earning enough for the support of a growing family convinced us that we must move nearer to London.

My cousin Tom Cottrell-Dormer was shortly moving from Newbottle Manor near Banbury, to his main property Rousham, near Steeple Aston, and he kindly offered to lease Newbottle to me.

Off we went – packing up the Jersey cows, the horses (including my beloved Grey Steel and Billa's adored Gascony, whom she had had since she was eight) and all our belongings – descending on Newbottle and Horace Hopcroft in the spring of 1949.

We were sad to be leaving Friars Wells and Melton, where we had been very happy, but after Suzanne was born Billa was no longer able to come to London with me. I was working very hard and it meant an enforced separation for four days a week. She was by now an expert on the *Nursery World*, and an absolutely outstanding mother, believing in the methods used since time immemorial of feeding her baby and looking after her herself.

Newbottle was a quite outstanding Elizabethan manor house, abutting on its own church and beautifully situated on the edge of a plateau, with meadows gradually falling away towards Kings Sutton. There was a very fine garden – with a quite remarkable asparagus bed, planted at the time of Waterloo and producing prolifically ever since. About 600 acres of let farmland surrounded us, over which we had the shooting, and I threw that in with my yeoman farmer neighbour Phil Bull. Phil was a great character and known to everyone in the district. He took us to a most enjoyable dinner at Blenheim Palace, given by the Duke for the coursers of the county. My cousin, Lena Shennan, won the Waterloo Cup.

Billa was soon busy running the estate, and she used to take the garden produce to the Women's Institute in Banbury market. In 1950 our little family was enlarged by the arrival of our son Robin, who was christened in Newbottle church.

Whilst Billa was keeping the home fires burning I commuted daily to London; from Bicester to Paddington and thence to the city. However, after two years I began to find the journey – three hours a day – too much, and reluctantly decided to move closer to London.

We therefore descended on suburbia, in the form of Rose Cottage, Mogador, near Lower Kingswood in Surrey. Rose Cottage had been built by Sir Thomas Sopwith's mother at the time of the Great War, and was an attractive seven-bedroomed house with four acres of garden. Here we spent the next six years, during which time our second daughter Caroline was born. I commuted every day to the city, holding together and building up the group of companies, which was proving a far from easy task. I was discovering that being in the Army was an infinitely easier life than fighting one's way upwards in the City of London.

Michael Woodbine Parish and Billa on the occasion of
their wedding, seen here leaving the Holy Trinity Church,
Prince Consort Road, London on 26 June 1947.

Lieut. Commander Godfrey Woodbine Parish DSc marriage to Roly Ruck Keene, Admiral Ruck Keene's daughter in 1946 after six years of war with the Fleet Air Arm. This included the Malta convoys and swimming for two hours after the aircraft carrier HMS *Eagle* was sunk. Then the Murmansk convoys and finally in the Far East against the Japanese.

Spartamint with my Jaguar in the background having just been to Switzerland and back – almost all the way in snow. January 1947.

Billa with Suzanne and Rev. Buswell at Florence Lady Trents St Matthews Lalique Glass Church in Jersey after the christening in 1948.

Michael Woodbine Parish with Billa and Air Vice Marshal and Mrs Somerled Macdonald, sister and brother-in-law, 1960.

Michael Woodbine Parish with Elefteris Rosmaris in Crete, 1960. He rendered enormous help on the author's escape from Crete as described in Myles's Diary.

Left to right: Lambris, the author, Suzanne, Lambris's daughter Lakkos, together in Crete, 1966

George and grandson Constantinos Zegos at the wedding of Emma Parish to Charles Houston in July, 1987.

Michaelis and Elefteris Rosmaris, 1988.

Costa Rosmaris at the 50th Anniversary of the Battle of
Crete in May 1991. He is Elefteris's and Michaelis's
eldest brother.

Zur Vergeltung der bes-
tialischen Ermordung
eines Fallschirmjägerzuges
u. eines Pionierhalbzuges
durch bewaffnete Männer
u. Frauen aus dem Hinter-
halte, wurde Kandanos
zerstört.

ΩΣ ΑΝΤΙΠΟΙΝΟΝ ΤΩΝ
ΑΠΩ ΟΠΛΙΣΜΕΝΩΝ
ΠΟΛΙΤΩΝ ΑΝΔΡΩΝ
ΚΑΙ ΓΥΝΑΙΚΩΝ ΕΚΤΩΝ
ΟΠΙΣΘΕΝ ΔΟΛΟΦΟΝ-
ΗΘΕΝΤΩΝ ΓΕΡΜΑΝΩΝ
ΣΤΡΑΤΙΟΤΩΝ ΚΑΤΕΣΤ-
ΡΑΦΗ
Η ΚΑΝΔΑΝΟΣ

Kandamos, Crete, 50 years ago the author's party had passed the village of Aghia Irin after Omatos, while going over the top of the mountain. They looked down on their left where the German parachutists under Max Snelling were wiped out. The beasts, for vengeance, burned the whole village and killed the men. This notice is written in Greek and German. The comments Commander Vernicos wrote on the back of the photo are shown on the facing page.

Kandanos (Crete)

I do not know if you remember the place. Just after we passed the village of Aghia Irini, after Omalos, and while going on the top of the mountains, we looked down on our left the ruins, where the Germans parachutists under Skimelling were wiped out, and the beasts for vengeance, burned the whole village and killed the men. It is written in German and Greek.

E. Neily

The New Zealand guard of honour at Galatas on the 50th
Anniversary of the Battle of Crete, 26 May 1991.

Mr and Mrs Albert Stokes of the Sherwood Rangers
Yeomanry (ex Y Battery in 1941). Trooper Stokes was
captured by the Germans and spent four years working
in the Polish coal mines.

The memorial case of the *Evangelistria* and Capt.
Miltiades Houmas in the National Maritime Museum,
Piraeus, Greece, 1990.

The Greek Distinguished Service Medal awarded to
Michael Woodbine Parish.

The *Evangelistria* made in bronze by the Hellenic
Maritime Museum, the first was presented to Major
Michael Woodbine Parish.

Charles and Emma Houston depart from their wedding reception on a hump.

Florence Houston, the author's granddaughter aged 2 years.

Glenborrodale Castle where Billa and Michael Woodbine Parish met on 27 August 1946.

Back row, left to right: Lord Trent, George the piper, Dr Beckett Overy. Middle, sitting: Fraser, Head Stalker. Front row, left to right: Colin Pitman, Ian Campbell, Bruce Campbell, Ashley Player.

Billa and Michael Woodbine Parish at Glenborrodale Castle in 1990. The author proposed to Billa shortly after their first meeting here.

28

The Dead Hand of Socialism

The companies had survived the post-war period and, although still small in relative terms, now had assets approaching £2,000,000 in contrast to their nadir in the early years of the war of some £200,000.

Although it was probably a mistake in terms of my working access to the city, we had for some time now been looking out for a home in real countryside, such as that of my youth at Little Danby in Yorkshire. We visited several properties within about a hundred miles of London but one day we saw in *Country Life* an attractive looking house for sale in Shropshire. Neither of us had ever been to Shropshire, and had barely heard of it save from Housman's poems; nevertheless we decided to visit it.

One glimpse of the house, in its magnificent setting with wonderful views over the lake to the Long Mynd, was enough. After brief negotiations the conveyancing was completed and we moved in.

The next thirty-three years, despite the worries and anxieties of maintaining and improving a large estate and turning it into a profitable operation, were ideally happy for a young wife and growing family – our youngest daughter Emma had now arrived. It was something of a nightmare for me, torn between Shropshire and a growing business in London.

Business was a continuous struggle, not helped by being confronted for many years by confiscatory taxation – which has continued to the present day: in other words, fifty years hard slog to get the companies heading for the top of their league instead of languishing on the verge of bankruptcy, which was the position when I took over. Over this half-century I was forever being invited out to lunch by numerous take-over specialists, all of whom fortunately went away empty handed.

On the world economic and political front things were not so bright. Britain and her Empire were entering what was to prove a period of long decline, which has continued over some fifty years to the present day. The fiasco and disaster of Suez in 1956 was recognizably just another downward step in this process. Suez did more, thanks to Dulles and Eisenhower in America, to undermine Britain's standing throughout the world than any other single event. To such as myself, who had seen Britain and the greatness that had been in pre-war days, this was like a dagger in the back.

I was shocked and horrified to see two hundred years of wealth and Empire being obviously destroyed in front of me. Post-war Britain and the early fifties were, for anyone able to glimpse down the road to the future, an horrific experience. I had seen Churchill swept away, and rememberd his words on the fateful day of his defeat – how he had led the horse of Britain to victory, only to see it being driven off the cliff, and how it was up to young men like us to re-light the torch of Britain's greatness. The speed of our decline was visible on every front.

Even so, we were still one of the two great powers of the world, and gradually the seeds were being sown in my mind for the formation of a new political party that would endeavour to halt the dissolution of everything I believed in. Harold Macmillan was now in power, after Eden's collapse, and I wanted to try and reverse what was rapidly becoming a Cresta Run decline into insignificance, with Macmillan in the driving seat of the toboggan.

Thus in 1958, I formed the British Party, later to be called the New Party. Despite its very limited financial backing it achieved supporters from all over the United Kingdom, as well as from abroad. However, it was a forlorn hope, and quite unable to compete against the wealth and established party headquarters of the big parties in every town in the kingdom. My supporters and I were left, therefore, to watch the accelerating decline of our once-great country, as I described in *20 Years On*.

Keeping pace with Britain's decline were two erstwhile enemies, Germany and Japan, who were already drawing level or ahead of us, and at least half-a-dozen other countries were running their affairs as well as, or better than us.

In 1964 the dead hand of socialism appeared, with Harold Wilson becoming Prime Minister – beginning his term with a trumpet call of the great things he was going to do in the first hundred days with his erstwhile friend George Brown. These hundred days proved nothing more than an hundred days of hot air. He then commenced a profligate spending policy of the great wealth that remained in the national coffers, having been created by British industry, the merchant princes and the City of London.

Within a few years he had reduced our country to the verge of bankruptcy and had to introduce a major devaluation of the pound. We were confronted by confiscatory taxation and exchange controls which were vigorously applied. Wilson then proceeded to lay the foundations for the continuing and speedy dismemberment of the British Empire. Whether or not that was a good thing only time and history will tell. He opened the floodgates to immigration from many parts of the world, thus sowing the seeds for changing the whole ethnic basis of the British people, with law and order steadily deteriorating seemingly in inverse proportions to their arrivals.

Next came a strike-torn Britain, near bleeding to death under the dominant greed of the trade union movement. Wilson's solution to strikes was to settle them amicably – i.e. after the inevitable capitulation, which in turn would increase inflation and the cost of living. This usually took place over tea and buns at No. 10, and was hailed as a brilliant victory.

By the late 1970s and early 1980s Britain was very low. Interest rates had reached South American proportions – twenty-two per cent and more – War Loan was down to seventeen-and-a-half from one hundred and eight after the war, and the value of shares quoted on the South African market exceeded the total value of shares quoted on the London market.

Our once-great country would have hit the rock of bankruptcy in the latter years of Wilson's and Callaghan's governments, which had already had to beg the IMF for help,

341

had it not been for the Almighty's gift of self-sufficiency in oil – realised by the discovery in 1960 of some £10,000 million worth of oil reserves in the North Sea; just enough to keep the wolf from the door.

With the election of Mrs Thatcher, to use an American expression, 'The buck had to stop', and it did.

Robbo Robinson, Arthur Scargill and many others, including dedicated communists, fought her in a fearfully expensive rearguard action costing Britain, through the coal strike and British Leyland, billions of precious pounds. This did no good to the workers, the country or anyone else, whilst at the same time the instigators were busy lauding the conditions and envying the lot of the peoples in the eastern bloc.

This battle slowly won through, and with victory a new spirit emerged. This was embodied in the message of Thatcherism, which was simplicity itself: give everyone an equal and fair chance.

In 1982 the Falklands affair blew up, costing both countries much loss of life and bloodshed and at least £10 billion of wasted money and assets. The battle was won on the ground and on the sea, greatly helped by arms from the USA. In spite of all this the fruits of victory never materialized and nothing was resolved or achieved (apart from enabling Mrs Thatcher to be re-elected); leaving the situation the same as when my great-grandfather left it in 1830.

The message of Thatcherism has continued; but it takes a superhuman effort to regain the position lost through forty-five years of inflation and squandermania. Politicians and the Foreign Office have poured billions of pounds down the bottomless sink of Nigeria and countless other ill-governed African and Asian ex-colonies. Our big banks have irrevocably lost billions of pounds of their money – indirectly Britain's money – in the course of their supremely foolish lending to Africa, Russia and its communist satellites, and many South American countries – all for no possible gain, and now some £2,000 million to Robert Maxwell.

Worse still, over the last forty-five years politicians and the Foreign Office have continually backed the Russians and communist states, most of which have now disintegrated. The £400 million or more a year that it costs to keep these smooth gentlemen in office has not only been wasted but has actually done great harm in helping to keep these regimes in power.

The depths of communist depravity were revealed in the murder of Father Jerzy Popietuszko thus igniting the hearts of the very nation for whom we originally went to war.

The fruits of Foreign Office policy are best illustrated in the front page cover of *Private Eye* dated January 5th 1990. It says a lot to have made Ceaucescu a Knight of the British Empire and to have entertained him at Buckingham Palace, when everyone with the slightest knowledge of world affairs knew what horrors this man was inflicting on his once-rich and happy country. Not a finger was lifted to help during these years of suffering, although with its demise the Archbishop of Canterbury and others were swift to jump on the bandwagon and denounce its excesses. I had seen it for myself in 1937, and what applied to Romania applied to almost all the others.

The triumph of freedom was a miracle from God and of the people alone.

It is small wonder that so many people admire Nicholas Tolstoy's crusade to have the instigators of the worse crime in Britain's history exposed – for having sent 70,000 Cossacks and Yugoslavs either to their deaths or to years of indescribable misery and lingering extinction in the Gulag Archipelago; graphically described by a prisoner of the regime, Alexander Solzhenitsyn.

To my certain knowledge the Foreign Office backed the Russian Government in keeping this appalling crime at Katyn hidden for twenty-five years, and it took twenty-five years before Lord Barnby and others were allowed to erect the Katyn Memorial in London at Gunnersbury, about which Bernard Levin wrote in *The Times* on 23 April 1990 Britain's complicity in a chronicle of shame.

Parliament is now in favour of a War Crimes Tribunal of octogenarian Nazis living in Britain. I would suggest that it is equally right and proper to hold the equivalent for those responsible for the murder of 70,000 Yugoslavs and Cossacks in 1945. A similar tribunal exposing the Soviet perpetrators of Katyn and countless other hideous war crimes, many of whose results are comparable to the Holocaust would also be justified.

29

Full Circle

Our first visit to Greece after our honeymoon came thirteen years later. We returned, somewhat naturally, to the White Mountains of Crete and the Menes Peninsula, where my Grecian life had really begun. Our initial search was to find those two gallant brothers, Michaelis and Elefteris Rosmaris. Their elder brother, the equally stalwart Costa, had not been in the Cretan campaign as he was with the Greek army in Albania, fighting the Italians. (The Greeks decisively defeated the Italians, capturing 250,000 of them with the loss of 2,500 Greeks. Had Hitler not sent the German army to save Mussolini's forces they would have been swept out of Albania.)

We reached the lovely little village of Rodopou, nestling in the foothills of the White Mountains, and were told that all three brothers still lived there, exactly as before. Elefteris was staying with his father-in-law, Kynatis, who was the local priest – and also a war hero. When we found Elefteris he was thrilled, and overwhelmed to see us, and gave us a true Cretan welcome. We also tracked down Michaelis and Costa, who were away tending their flocks on the mountain plain of Omalos for the summer grazing.

Having remade contact with our Cretan friends we returned to Heraklion and spent the night in a nice old-fashioned hotel, opposite the Cathedral, whose bells rang almost continuously from 6 am for the whole of Sunday. So, with the peal of bells in our ears and plans laid for future visits with more Cretan friendships and adventures we sailed back to Athens.

Next we went to perhaps my favourite island; Kimolos. I

have always considered the north coast of Kimolos to be one of the most beautiful places in the world, comparable perhaps with the views from Glenborrodale Castle over Loch Sunart. From here we visited, among other places, the island of Milos – the scene of my accident in 1941. On our return we had to wait for six hours in a queue as the boat was late due to a terrific storm. When it eventually arrived, at midnight, we had to first scramble into the tossing tender, to be rowed out to the island steamer. In the pitch dark with jostling crowds all trying to catch the boat Billa fell and badly twisted her ankle. She has reminded me ever since that instead of giving her sympathy all I said was, 'How can you do this to me?' However, in her usual sweet and magnanimous way she forgave me, despite being in excruciating pain, and we got safely back to Piraeus, blown along by the *megala fortuna*.

Since then we have had many lovely Grecian holidays, one of which was taking the children on my old war-time boat the *Sentosa*. Sailing out of Glyfada, we headed first for Paros, after which we passed Spetsapoula, Niarchos's island, where we saw long lines of rope tied at intervals with cloth, such as is used in shoots to make the pheasants get up. On the aeroplane coming out I had noticed a huge load of pheasants in crates, obviously bound for Niarchos's coming pheasant shoot. From there we went to Spetses, with glorious bathing and boating in the numerous small bays; a paradise for children and parents. Next came Hydra and Nauplion, from where we visited Epidaurus and on to the father of all medicine, Hippocrates's hospital, and thence away from the lovely Byronic islands.

We arrived back in Phaleron Bay just as the young Princess Anne-Marie was arriving on the Danish Royal Yacht for her forthcoming marriage to the young King Constantine of the Hellenes. She was escorted by squadrons of Greek and Danish naval units and fighter aircraft; a most impressive occasion for our young family to be inadvertently involved in.

On a subsequent visit to Crete we re-enacted the exact evacuation route from the 'Y' gun battery position on St John's Hill right down to Sphakia, through such well-remembered places as Souda, Stilos, Vrisses, Alikambos, Kares, Amoudani and Imbros. We followed the same mountain road, which had been somewhat improved. We saw the house where Myles had caught and cooked his chicken, before taking a small fishing boat for a few miles westwards along the coast to the delightful little fishing village of Loutro. There we were proudly shown a Roman coin by an elderly lady who had just found it in her garden.

From there we went to Maleme and Hill 107, where Freyberg had lost the momentous battle for Crete, and then on to the Rosmaris's at Rodopou, where we were given a massive Cretan feast at Elefteris's house. After lunch Costa and Michaelis showed us their houses and then we retraced the epic twenty-four hour non-stop journey mentioned in Myles's diary. Going up through villages such as Vrisses, Alikianos, Skines, Meskla, Lakkos – some of which still showed the marks of when they were burnt by the Germans after the villagers had been taken out and shot – we eventually reached the plain of Omalos, still looking just like the roof of the world with the romantic Gorge of Samaria leading down from it to the south coast port of Agia Roumeli, on the Libyan Sea.

In later years some of our finest holidays were with Marcus and Lola Mander on their Camper Nicholson yacht, the *Mariola,* on which we had many delightful cruises through the Aegean Mediterranean, Ionian and Adriatic seas.

Our daughter, Caroline, was the first to take to the matrimonial road – to a most charming Greek, George Zegos. They have four very entertaining children: Constantinos, Elizabeth (Bettles), Dimitra and Rose (pure dynamite). Next was Suzanne, who, at the tender age of twenty and endowed with great beauty and intelligence was tragically paralysed in a road accident. So cruel a blow at such a young age had given her much to endure, but in 1983 she married the charming Junior Kumaramangalam, son of my old friend K, and they have two children, Kim and Zoe.

The departure of Suzanne left Robin, an apparently confirmed bachelor and inveterate world traveller, and Emma. She also had travelled the world, but returned from celestial space with a bump in 1987, when she married the charming – and English – Charles Houston. Their wedding was on a beautiful summer's day in our 11th century church of St Michael and All Angels which had been transformed into a bower of sweet-smelling flowers. This immensely happy occasion was rounded off by their leaving the reception on Miriam, a fine camel. While they were proceeding down the drive a fisherman, fishing quietly by the lake, happened to glance up – getting more than he bargained for. 'Now I've seen it all,' he declared. In 1989 their little girl Florence was born, known always to me as Flossie Florenze, and in 1991 Michael.

With Caroline now settled in Greece our annual holidays have naturally pivoted on her family, at their home on the island of Salamis.

In 1988, whilst visiting our old friends Andrea Alevra and his daughter Eleni, Eleni mentioned that the Vlachos's lived nearby and gave us their telephone number. I had not seen Mrs Vlachos (Ninette) since September 9th 1943, and Billa said she would be intrigued to meet her after all these years, so Caroline kindly rang her and I then spoke to her.

We arranged for them to dine with us. I was in a considerable state of trepidation, not knowing if I would even recognise my ex-wife after so abruptly and sadly abandoning her. All went well and we spent a delightful evening with them and their daughter Eleni.

To me it was an occasion of great significance – let any married person imagine how they would feel if, in an instant, after four months of marriage, that happiness and the marriage itself was abruptly terminated and you were not to see each other again for nearly half a century.

When seeing Ninette and her Ambassador husband, Vlachos, the intervening half century did not prevent remembering the appalling sadness I suffered when, after repatriation from Germany, having heard nothing for a year, Ninette wrote that she wished to marry Angelos Vlachos, whom on the very day I was captured was himself being liberated from Greece by Captain Costa in my MI9 caique. This tragedy made me at the time, fifty years ago, think that Menelaus was right when he waged his Trojan War to regain his Helen stolen by Paris in the very area where my Helen was stolen 2,000 years later.

During a recent visit to Greece we returned to the island of Samos, arriving on the night boat just as the sun was rising over the Turkish mainland. We checked into the Hotel Samos in Vathy (now renamed Samos) and after a delicious breakfast we quickly located the British Vice Consulate and the Vice Consul Mrs Garoufali-Marc OBE. The Marc family have been the Consuls in Samos for 170 unbroken years; the longest of any British Consulate in the world.

Mrs Garoufali-Marc kindly arranged for us to see Captain Milton's widow, Eleni Houmas. In Eleni we found the most lovely, serene and peaceful person you could ever wish to meet, surounded by memorabilia of her gallant husband. Her charming house, in which both Milton's parents and grandparents had lived, is in the small town of Chora; the main street of which has been re-named Miltiades Houmas Street.

We spent about half-an-hour with Mrs Houmas and then asked her to join us for lunch in Tigani at a restaurant adjoining the quay where her husband had brought in the *Evangelistria* to liberate his island after four years of harsh enemy occupation – I would suggest that a memorial be erected on the wall of this Tigani Quay to record the arrival of the *Evangelistria* to liberate Samos the first area in Greece to be liberated. Sadly, but understandably, she declined, as she was still in mourning for her husband. However, before we left she telephoned three of her four sons (the eldest being in Zaire) and arranged for us to meet them in Athens.

After lunch the Garoufali-Marcs motored us up over the mountain road to Vathy, exactly as Alex Levides, David Pawson and I had motored in the Italian military vehicle to General Solderelli's large HQ – on the site of which is now the Xenia Hotel. Mr Garoufali-Marc, senior lawyer in the island, told us that the Italian HQ, along with much of the rest of Vathy, had been destroyed by forty German bombers in a reprisal for having joined the Allies two months after we had taken over Samos. After they had devastated this beautiful island by air the German ground troops then pursued the townsfolk up the mountainside, indiscriminately machine-gunning them as they fled.

After this we drove to the German Consul's house which we had requisitioned on the day of our arrival, and which was our HQ for nine days. The whole scenario came vividly to my mind, as if it had all happened yesterday instead of forty-seven years before.

The following day we made the seventy-mile sea voyage to

Chios; the same journey but in reverse as I had done on the *Evangelistria* with Milton. Just as before we stopped at Karlovasi, the western port of the island, before turning due north to Chios. On arrival we were in sight of Chiosti, from where we had started, and Egrilar in Turkey.

After two pleasant days we returned to Athens, where we were taken to the Hellenic Maritime Museum at Passalimani, near Piraeus, by Christos and Yanni Houmas. Here we saw the beautiful model of the *Evangelistria* and an oil painting of Captain Miltiades Houmas OBE, DSO, CC. I was given copies of the official *Naval War 1941-44* and of *Agenda 1943.* The latter was Milton's log book, in which he wrote every day on the *Evangelistria,* including his full account of the vital day, Thursday 9th September 1943.

In the ensuing days Christos and John's brother Nico drove the 300 kilometres from his hotel at Pylos in the Peloponnesos to see us, and we also met Christos's wife Sophia and their three children – Milton's grandchildren, who have since become friends of my grandchildren.

Our most recent visit was on account of the fiftieth anniversary of the Battle of Crete, for which the Greek, British, New Zealand and Australian governments were organizing a two-week memorial. Myles wrote to me about it and suggested we should go together. I was delighted, and told him that Billa and I would go via Salamis, where we would collect George and Constantinos, and bring them along too.

We all stayed at the Dôma Hotel in Hania, one of the most delightful old-fashioned hotels in Greece.

On the first day George kindly motored me out west to Maleme and Hill 107 and surveyed the area where Colonel Andrews VC commanded the New Zealand Battalion which was responsible for holding Maleme aerodrome. Not only had the Colonel held out, but he had defeated an immensely fierce attack during the first twenty-four hours by the brilliantly efficient German paratroop division. By the morning of the second day the Battle of Crete had been virtually won, with General Student on the verge of withdrawing and accepting personal disgrace from Hitler. Had General Freyberg answered Colonel Andrew's urgent and repeated calls for reinforcements, of which there were ample supplies, the Battle of Crete would have given Churchill his first great and resounding victory.

Next we went up, via Kolimbari, through the mountains Myles and I had known so well, to the village of Kandanos. In 1941 the Germans had rounded up all the men, women and children who had not escaped and shot them, before destroying the entire village as a reprisal for the resistance put up against them. We lunched at a nice taverna opposite the memorial to those killed by the Germans. The previous day there had been a large ceremony and the memorial was now covered in freshly-laid wreaths.

The following day we headed along the south coast of Souda Bay as far as Kalives, where Myles had been stationed with 'A' Battery in the fort at the entrance to the bay. We lunched at Vrisses, under the same trees overlooking the river where, fifty years earlier, I had joined General Weston as his liaison officer. Another day took us to a reunion at Kolimabari Monastery and then on to Kastelli. Here the Greek Gendarmerie had put up an amazingly heroic fight against the paratroops and were completely victorious, but subsequently paid with their lives for their bravery. That day we lunched at the charming little harbour of Kastelli and the couple nearby asked if my companion was my daughter.

Another day George took us over the mountains to Sphakia, where, although the sea front had been greatly developed for tourism, the background remains much the same as the day Myles captured his chicken.

One evening we went to a reception given by the Greek Government; Myles had arrived by boat from Kalamata, where he had seen Patrick Leigh Fermor, George Jellicoe and Xan Fielding and they had invited all of us. During this reception I suddenly saw someone wearing a Sherwood Rangers blazer coming towards me and he introduced himself as Trooper Albert Stokes, of 'Y' Battery SRY. I was amazed, because I also had been in 'Y' Battery. Albert, like me, had failed to be evacuated and had spent the rest of the war in the Polish coal mines, working as a prisoner. He and his wife both looked very fit and well, and I greatly admired his *esprit de corps*.

We went also to a reception at Kolimbari, where we called at the Hotel Rosmaris. There we saw the stalwart Costa, and went with him to the memorial ceremony at Galatas, scene of some of the fiercest fighting. Lastly we went to Lakkos where Myles and I had spent many a night, before going on to Omalos and then the Menes Peninsula where we visited Elefteris and Michalis.

On our previous visit to Greece George had told us that Greece had been turned down as the site for the 1996 Olympic Games, in favour of Atlanta, Georgia.

The Olympic Games are of course Greek, having started at Olympia some 2,000 years ago and then begin again in Greece in 1896. Sadly, the games have now become a multi-billion dollar business, with money being the main objective. In my view Greece should bring an action against the Committee of the Games for using their name, and insist on having a ten per cent royalty paid to Olympia every time their name is used – including on television programmes, or on goods sold. They should succeed in exactly the same way as the French champagne growers succeeded in banning the use of the name 'champagne' on wine grown anywhere except in the Champagne area. If people want to call the Games the 'Atlanta Games', or the 'Birmingham Games' then let them do so, but they have no right to call them the Olympic Games.

The world should remember that the only other country in early 1941 apart from Britain who stood up to Adolf Hitler was little Greece, with a (then) population of scarcely eight million – long before America came in, forced off the fence by Pearl Harbour. In their heroic struggle Greece lost about 500,000 men, a far larger proportion of its population than the losses sustained by America.

Before ending the long saga it is appropriate to write about the Gulf War.

The Gulf crisis is another example of how western governments and the United Nations did nothing – when Saddam Hussein attacked Iran in 1980. This fearful war cost a million young Iranians their lives, many of whom – including, in 1988, his own Kurdish women and children from Halabja – were massacred by poison gas and other banned chemical warfare horrors. The Iranians sent many of their poison gas victims to London and other European hospitals for

351

treatment and verification.

The West watched all this, but instead of helping they merely continued to arm their then-friend Hussein to the tune of eighty billion dollars – some of which is still owing.

For ten years the main concern was to defeat Iran and her fundamentalist revolution which threatened Saudi Arabia, the Arab Emirates and Israel (and whose surrogates took over 100 US Embassy officials hostage).

The Gulf War was initiated by President Bush, goaded on by much of the press and by Mrs Thatcher, exactly as she did over the Falklands. The war was precipitated by Iraq's invasion of Kuwait on August 2nd 1990; not that it was ever anything other than a regional threat to small third-world states, as Auberon Waugh showed in his article in the *Spectator* of January 19th 1991.

There was little reason for Britain, self-sufficient in oil, to waste her resources of men and materials in helping to pick America's hot chestnuts (Israel, oil and self-interest).

President Bush, under threat of public opinion not to repeat America's Vietnam casualties, ensured that 99.9 per cent of deaths were Iraqi. To this end, preliminary to the land offensives were six weeks of the most concentrated bombing of military and civilian targets the world has ever seen, probably approaching one hundred thousand tons of bombs or more than ten times the amount that created total collapse and a bomb-happy rabble of us in Belgrade, Athens and Crete.

This decision was taken by President Bush and resulted in the cold-blooded premeditated murder (similar to the sinking of *The Belgrano*) of Iraq, ninety per cent of whose population were as innocent as any of their neighbouring Muslim states. (It would be interesting to know what, if any, cash inducements were offered by the USA to the leaders of Egypt, Syria, Turkey and others for their co-operation.)

As many people of similar age to me know from experience, 100,000 tons of bombs is an almost unbelievable weight of bombs for the USA and her mercenary Allies, with a combined population of some 350 million to drop on a small country of 16 million. This, combined with the timely collapse of Iraq's long-term ally, Russia, made certain that the outcome was never in doubt. To talk of a brilliant victory comparable to Hannibal's over the Romans is nonsense.

Despite the brilliant performance of the Desert Rats and the British forces who sailed for the Gulf Campaign 40,000 strong, and returned 39,982, half the casualties were killed by their own side. It was, however, America's war and to put it into perspective Britain provided scarcely ten per cent of the men and materials somewhat likening our position to that of the Kingdom of Sardinia who was allied with Britain and France against Russia in the Crimean War.

The USA (under the guise of the UN) created a second holocaust in Iraq, devastating the country and Kuwait as well while planting the seed of hatred in the hearts of the Muslim world.

'Operation Desert Storm' may possibly have gained the Americans some temporary material advantage, but at a cost of unparalleled human and ecological suffering, with about two million human beings killed, wounded or displaced and now to add to these horrific figures we have the following announcement in the press on 23rd October 1991 'Child mortality surges in Iraq. Infant and child mortality in Iraq has increased 380 per cent due to the Gulf war and 900,000 children under five are starving, says an international study team. They found almost a completre breakdown of services and widespread epidemics', and an almost similar situation amongst the Kurds all of which is the sole responsibility of the USA and their lacky the United Nations for withholding medical supplies, food and machinery to a beaten and devastated country who waged two wars, one against Iran and one against Kuwait in both cases probably given a nudge by USA. The warning of 'Iraq disaster' appeared in *The Independent* article 22nd March 1991 as 'UN report on Iraq forsees disaster'. To all who have children or grandchildren look at them and imagine the size of the crime in starving possibly to death 900,000 children nearly a year after the war ended. A war which in its new role of 'rent-a-thug' cost the USA financially nothing, in fact with the contributions from Japan, Germany and others of some $75 billion, it may easily have made a monetary profit. (A war which Sun Tzu would have handled with negligible loss and much gain.)

Furthermore America, having eliminated her recent ally

353

Iraq, may lave laid herself and much of the Middle East open ultimately to a far more sinister force – the Ayatollah's Iranian fundamentalist revolution. He destroyed the Shah from a villa in Paris. On this occasion America's ally and friend the Shah was abandoned by the USA.

This is what the war began about ten years ago, when I pinpointed the significance of Khorramshahr and the threat to Israel.

Iran today, without having fired a shot, is the real winner of the Gulf War – an immensely rich country with probably more oil than Saudi Arabia, Iraq and Kuwait put together, and no external debt.

With a population of over fifty million compared with Saudi Arabia's eight million, Iran will be the main power in the Gulf – well pleased with the USA (with whom they still have no diplomatic relations), and whom they describe as the Great Satan, for having totally destroyed their enemy Iraq. In this respect the most important event at the Madrid conference has been President Rafsanjani's officially stated intention to send troops into Israeli-occupied areas to fight on behalf of the Palestinians. In view of Iran's close links with Afghanistan, Pakistan and China, numbering in all a block of 1,500 billion people over an unbroken link eastward of Teheran of some 6,000 miles it is a threat which in years to come when possibly linked to the moslem states of the late Soviet Union, Algeria and Libya, may give cause for the USA to regret their action in the Gulf war which has, I repeat, created hate in the hearts of 1·2 billion Muslims and was won by vastly superior technology.

The Gulf war was won with the United Nations being nothing more than institutionalized humbug.

With the demise of Russia the USA is the strongest country militarily and industrially in the world, and her fortunate citizens have never had to experience bombing of their homeland or being starved and frozen to death on snow-covered mountains. Until this state of affairs was achieved the Americans chose to ignore a number of brutal aggressions, since there was no oil or other monetary gain at stake. In fact as I have said before they watched with equanimity Hitler conquering all Europe with his blitzkrieg on Warsaw, Amsterdam, Brussels, Paris, Belgrade, Athens, Hania,

Heraklion and the Jewish holocaust, with the certainty that Britain would also be engulfed had Hitler not attacked Russia instead. Even so this did not happen till a year after Dunkirk, and in that year Jewish extermination and concentration camps were increasing all over Hitler's Europe, and had he decided to attack Britain after Dunkirk, he would have had some 200 divisions against Britain's possible ill-equipped 40 and would have almost certainly succeeded. Thus America, who continued to earn money and did not enter the war for a further eighteen months would have left the majority of the Jewish race to the mercy of Adolf Hitler.

Apart from those I have already covered there was China's attack on Tibet, Turkey's attack on Grecian Cyprus, Syria's attack on the Lebanon and Israel's attack on Palestine. Returning to China and Russia's combined attack, through surrogates, on Africa, it is little surprise that the Princess Royal, on 29th April 1990, appealed for help for the 27 million Africans faced with death by starvation. The starvation was created by the handing over of almost all the African states except, as yet, South Africa, to communist dictatorships.

If South Africa, the powerhouse of Africa, succumbs to Mr and Mrs Mandela it will be a case of poor Africa – and poor Britain if ever Mr Kinnock comes to power. In the fourteen months since Mandela has been realeased from prison his determination to continue sanctions, thus depriving his followers of work, there have been thousands of deaths and woundings amongst his people and the Zulus, enormously exceeding anything under the National Government's rule over nearly half-a-century.

The 'victory' of the Gulf war was the most recent of America's many follies, the most abysmal of which was depriving Britain of her great empire when she had saved America from defeat by Germany and Japan, only to be rewarded by the Americans siding with Stalin against them in 1945.

Regrettably, the USA – who may have gained the whole world, but at the loss of her soul – still remains light years away from ever being able to produce the combination of Churchill, the British Empire and Pax Britannica, all of which she helped to destroy.

☆   ☆   ☆

General Sir John Hackett's review of *Aegean Adventures:*

Disastrous decisions and equally disastrous indecision in September 1943, when Italian capitulation opened a clear route into Southern Europe through the Balkans, prolonged for another year and a half, with catastrophic destruction and loss of life, a war which Churchill was confident could be won in that year by Christmas. Rhodes was the key, dominating the Eastern Mediterranean and, with the Dodecanese and the recapture of Crete, it was ours for the asking. Deep-seated American suspicion of British imperial aims resulted in determined obstruction by Roosevelt, Marshall and Eisenhower to Churchill's plans to invade through the Balkans and thus to bring Turkey in to the war and put Germany out. The marked US subservience to Stalin which now showed itself was to enslave half of Europe for another half century. A heaven sent opportunity was thrown away in what Churchill recognized as his darkest wartime days.

Those of us with ringside seats could only look on the disastrous outcome with dismay.

This account of a young gentleman's pre-war social sporting and business life finds him in the yeomanry when war breaks out and then engaged in the high adventure of special operations in the Middle East, with wounds and captivity to follow. Its importance lies in well documented exploration in depth of the policy which, in spite of Churchill, handed Poland (for which we went to war) over to communist tyranny and took care to ensure that Stalin's troops got to Berlin, Vienna and Prague before the Western allies, and could seize the Baltic republics and dominate Yugoslavia unhindered. The worldwide eclipse of the once-great British Empire was the inevitable result of its prostration in crippling and unnecessarily prolonged warfare and of world dominance by the two victorious superpowers, the USA and (thanks to the USA) the USSR. History will almost certainly show the obstruction in the mid-20th century, of Churchill's vision, largely by Roosevelt, Eisenhower and Marshall, as that century's greatest disaster. Much of this book may be of interest to few readers. The presentation of its major theme deserves the widest public attention.

J.A.H.

APPENDICES

BANKERS MAGAZINE, 1911

THE LATE MR WHITBURN

By the death, which occurred at the beginning of November, of Mr C.J. Sofer Whitburn, in his seventy-fifth year, Lombard Street has lost one of its oldest landmarks.

To those of our readers who may not be habitures of the money market, it may be stated that the late Mr Whitburn was the senior partner in the banking and discount firm of Messrs Reeves Whitburn & Co., in Clements Lane. Mr Whitburn, however, was not merely senior partner, but was also the founder of the firm, the beginnings of which date back far beyond the years covering such famous events as the City of Glasgow Bank failure and even the Overend Gurney crisis.

Mr Whitburn was born in the year 1836, and received his education at a private school in Dunkirk. He was only just over thirteen years of age, when, owing to the sudden death of his father he was under the necessity of commencing his business career, and, in the year 1850, he started, as a mere lad, in the firm of Sanderson & Co., bill brokers, that firm, together with the famous firm of Overend and Gurney, being almost the only discount houses of importance in the City.

From the very beginning of his career at the bottom rung of the ladder, young Whitburn showed that devotion to all the details of business which, it may truly be said, characterised his career up to the date of his death. At the time when he still occupied a position as a junior in the service of Sanderson's, that firm failed, and Mr Whitburn, although possessed of an exceedingly small amount of capital, started, in 1859, when he was only twenty-three years of age, business on his own account, in connection with Mr Reeves, who had also previously been employed in the firm of Sandersons.

In spite of arduous work by both partners, the business grew slowly, in spite of energy and ambition, the transactions of the firm were, from the outset, characterised by extreme caution. Those were times, however, when caution and prudence were undoubtedly required, for within the first twenty years of the firm's existence, there occurred two of the greatest crises which have visited the City, namely, the Overend Gurney crash and the City of Glasgow Bank failure. Not only did the firm of Reeves Whitburn pass unscathed through these trying years, but it was always a proud boast of Mr Whitburn that, throughout, there was never a question even of seeking financial assistance. None the less, the strain on the nerves of the partners was severe, and shortly after the City of Glasgow Bank failure in 1878, Mr Reeves elected to retire from business. From that time for fourteen years, Mr Whitburn carried on the business himself; but in February, 1892, his only son, Mr Charles Whitburn, who survives him, joined him as active partner.

There are probably few vocations where high moral character, shrewd insight, and keen attention to the demands of business, are more truly appraised at their full value than in the banking and discount profession, and it was unquestionably the possession of these attributes in quite an exceptional degree which was responsible for the success achieved by Mr Whitburn. He commenced life as a comparatively poor man; he ended it as a very rich one; but, like our merchant princes in commerce, he achieved something more than wealth, for it is men of his calibre who have contributed to the greatness of our reputation in the world of commerce and finance. The envious onlooker will frequently describe such individuals as mere wealth-spinners; those who come more closely into touch with them know that over and beyond the natural desire for wealth is passion for the work which brings not only personal gain, but, in the aggregate, commercial and financial prestige to the country.

At the time of commencing business in 1859, Mr Whitburn, as was the fashion in those days, did not seek the sanctity of a private room, but sat in the outer office with his clerks, separated from them only by a curtained partition. The business grew, the staff increased, private rooms became necessary to see the clients who called; but Mr Whitburn, to the day of his death, occupied his old position in the outer office, feeling, as he often said, 'more at the centre of things and in touch with the stir of the details of business' than if he were in some private sanctum. His holidays were nil, his absences from business through illness were rare, for he was one to whom hard work and steady application to business appeared to bring sound health. A day off, he used frequently to maintain, had a far from beneficial effect, and to him his daily avocation, with all the complex details pertaining to a discount business, was an endless delight. There was probably no man in the City of London so familiar with the standing credit of all firms and institutions in the City as the late Mr Whitburn. His memory was marvellous, and to say that he was a walking encyclopaedia on all matters pertaining to credit simply expresses the truth. His fund of humour was considerable, but it was a humour extracted from his surroundings, and to talk over financial matters with him, as the writer of this sketch was frequently privileged to do, was to get into touch with a man who found at once his employment and recreation in his daily duties, and who had the power of communicating his enthusiasm to those about him.

It cannot, perhaps, be said that his energies outside his business were directed over a wide area, but nonetheless his interests were not entirely confined to the precincts of Lombard Street. Second only to his devotion to the atmosphere of City life was his keen appreciation of the beauties of nature, and for many years he spent much of his spare time during the favourable months of the year at his pretty summer residence in Addington Park, Kent. An intense lover of home, his circle of friends, outside business acquaintances was not a large one, for in private life he valued the friendship of few rather than the acquaintance of many. Among the interesting characteristics of his private life was his love of dumb animals which amounted to a passion, and he was never happier than when, freed from the cares of business, he was able to seek outdoor relaxation with his dumb friends.

His duties in the City were continued up to the last days of his life, his death occurring after a brief illness, so that, as most of the tributes which have been paid to him by the daily press truly said, he literally 'died in harness'.

From the premier financial house in the City, where he was most highly esteemed, down to the smallest firm with which he had transactions, Mr Whitburn was appreciated, not only for his devotion to business, but for his sterling personal qualities.

The photograph which we give to our readers of Mr Whitburn is of a more unconventional type than usually appears in the pages of the Bankers' Magazine, the reason being that the only picture taken for the last twenty years is an enlargement of a small snapshot taken a few months before his death. Although not clothed, however, in City garb, we believe that not a few of our readers will be glad to have this reminder of a face and figure which have long been familiar to so many within the precincts of Lombard Street.

OFFICIAL HISTORY OF THE MILITARY NAVY
THE ITALIAN NAVY IN THE SECOND WORLD WAR

Volume XVI
EVENTS IN THE Aegean AFTER
THE ARMISTICE

(RHODES, LEROS AND SMALLER ISLANDS)

COMPILER: DIVISION ADMIRAL (a) ALDO LEVI
REVISER: SQUADRON ADMIRAL (a) GUISEPPE FIORAVANZO

2nd Edition

ROME 1972

We shall take 18 September as the date of a painful event which, although it does not concern Leros directly, appears to relate to the damaging consequences of a general nature which this had on the relationships between our Commands and the Allied Commands, reports which, in the executive field, had been initiated on a fairly satisfactory basis of trust and comradeship. This event was the rebellion of Mas 522.

The Mas 522, commanded by S.T. C.R.E.M.c Carlo Beghi, attended the armistice on Samos, as arranged by Gen Solderelli, commanding the 'Cuneo' (Wedge) Division. It turns out that S.T. Beghi enjoyed the confidence of the General, so much so that on the occasion of a pre-announced replacement of the 522 with another Mas, the General asked the Mas fleet Command not to implement the replacement, and to leave the 522 on Samos with Beghi, who was quite a capable officer, professionally speaking.

On 12 September the 522 had transported to Leros T.C. Gaudioso, Deputy Chief-of-Staff of the 'Cuneo' Division, with the first two British officers Pawson and Parish to make contact with our Command. Beghi stayed on Leros for two days, reported to his immediate superiors, and did not give rise to the slightest suspicion as to his feelings at that time. In reporting to the officers on Samos, he had an opportunity to perform another mission of trust during the evening of the 17th, transporting from Samos, to the limit of the Turkish territorial waters, General Arnold, British military attaché in Turkey. It was Arnold who raised some suspicion about him, and did not trust him, but the Samos Commander did not give any heed to the warnings.

On the 18th it was considered necessary to send a mission to Nicaria, where one or two difficulties had arisen for the Greek guerillas as well as in their relations with the Black Shirts, whose behaviour and attitude were by no means reassuring. It was also necessary, however, to coordinate the defensive action of both parties, and to this end Gen Solderelli, by agreement with the British mission, decided to send to this post General Pejrolo, Second Commander of the 'Cuneo' (Wedge) Division, together with Col Pawson of the British mission. Most of them requested authorisation for this from Gen Arnold, Commander of the British forces on Samos, but they did not await his reply, which was received in fact after their departure, and was affirmative. In the telegram reply Gen Arnold suggested that one or two 'Commandos' also be taken along. The General and the Colonel were also joined by the British Major Parish and Captain Levidis from the Greek Navy.

The Mas 522 departed from Vathy (Samos) on the 18th. It first called at a place called Armenistes (northern coast of Nicaria), then reached Kerikos, the capital of the island. The Allied officers, having disembarked, spoke to the civil authorities and those representing the guerilla bands. General Pejrolo spoke to the officers of the Black Shirts to explain to them the situation, and to remind them of their duty to and cooperation with the Allies. The Commander of the Mas, so it seems, had no contacts with the Black Shirts, except for a short discussion with a Sergeant Major. They left at around 16.30. The Greek officer left his pistol in the office of the Postmaster, where the discussions had taken place. The Mas 522 headed for Fourni, and this took some time because S.T. Beghi had difficulty in identifying the landing place. They reached Fourni at 18.15. The Italian officer who commanded the small garrison (one platoon) went aboard. They departed at 18.30 telling the officer who had offered food that they did not need it because they would be having lunch at Vathy (Samos) in one hour. The Cape Phanari lookout (northern point of Nicaria) caught sight of the Mas towards 19.00 hours, sailing in a regular northerly direction (course), but a few minutes afterwards, in the half light of twilight, it saw the Mas approach the west, i.e. on the opposite course to that taken at Vathy. There was a strong wind and the sea was rough. The failure of the Mas to arrive on Samos was initially due to damage or causes of a nautical nature. Every means was tried to establish radio and telephone contact, but to no avail. Once the alarm was also sounded on Leros, since the sea conditions did not allow another Mas to be sent, the Camogli was sent to patrol the waters of Nicaria and two seaplanes were also sent as soon as possible. The reconnaissances continued throughout the 19th. Finally, on the morning of the 21st, it was ascertained from a fisherman who had escaped from Sira, and who had reached Mykonos, that the 522 had reached Sira. The assumption was made (but not supported by firm evidence) that the criminal action had been agreed by radio and telephone by the German Command on Sira. Some sort of agreement with the Black Shirts on Nicaria is also possible.

It seems from the testimonies given that S.T. Beghi, after arriving on Sira, took control of the situation, saying that he had the agreement of his crew, and that his plan was to take the first favourable opportunity to get through to the Germans with his Mas, and in doing so to capture some high-ranking officer. It seems that Beghi was referring to Gen Solderelli. The action was taken suddenly at dusk. Having switched off the engines on the pretext of a breakdown, the crew, armed to the teeth, surrounded the four officers, fired some shots into the air to intimidate them, and took them prisoner. Major Parish made to pull out his pistol, but someone prevented him and delivered him blows on the side and on the arm, which were apparently not serious. There were no shortage of attempts at a reaction, and to persuade the men to return to their duties, on the part of the officers, particularly General Pejrolo, but this was to no avail. The four officers were put under close guard by an armed sentry in a small room in the bow of the ship, and the Mas made for Sira, which it reached during the night. Sira had already been taken by the Germans, and the arrival of the Mas, with its booty, was the cause of great satisfaction. The prisoners were sent by air to Greece, and from there to a German prison camp. The Mas remained in the service of the Germans. S.T. Beghi was given promotion and German honours, which were the prelude to other honours which he was eventually given for services rendered in the Black Guards of the Republic of Salo.

The details of the episode involving the defection of the Mas 522 have been gleaned from the report of Gen Pejrolo and from the depositions made in the trial which was brought in due course against Beghi for 'collaboration with the enemy.'

EXTRACT FROM 'the BULLETIN' – APRIL 1991

An Example of the Long Term Virtues of Equity Investment
Two of the neglected charming by-ways of City investment are

The Exploration Company with shares priced at 190p and El Oro Mining & Exploration with shares priced at 420p. El Oro holds 45% of Exploration and it in turn holds 49 · 9% of El Oro. Do not waste time looking for the share price in the FT. Mr Michael Woodbine Parish who chairs both companies is far too careful with shareholders' money to waste it on paying for a price quote in their pages. It is fair to say that he is one of the 'old school' as he has now been in charge of the two businesses since 1951 and connected with them before that. When he took charge in 1951 the shares had been at 2d – two old style pennies and the total assets were under a quarter million. Now they are nearer £60 million.

To mark this remarkable record of service Mr Woodbine Parish is due to produce a book which he has been working on for the past two years. This will cover a half century of his own experience and a century of City affairs. As we have explained before in this Bulletin in spite of their names the two companies are no longer mining shares but investment trusts. The results have just been published and Exploration has pre-tax profits of £3 · 18 million and El Oro has profits of £2 · 5 million. In both cases the dividend has been raised, in the case of The Exploration Company to 12p on shares now priced at 190p and in the case of El Oro to 24p on shares priced at 420p, a very reasonable return for an investment trust. The list of shares held does include some mining investments but is mainly blue chips. But the history is even more fascinating for it was The Exploration Company which, as a mining finance organisation, sponsored the construction of the Central Line on London's Underground with Sir Ernest Cassels and his friends finding £2 · 17 million for this purpose 'despite public apathy'. This is of course today a line so busy that it is considered to be dangerously overcrowded with trains carrying 2,000 passengers at a rate of 30 an hour during peak period. It also helped to finance the Paris Metro.

In making a comparison of past progress Exploration Company's price of 190p would come to nearer twice that when allowance is made for bonus and rights issue and dividends paid. So, after allowing for decimalisation, one could say that the return over 40 years has been around 400 fold. Certainly an investment of £1,000 in 1950 would now be worth nearer £200,000, whereas had the £1,000 gone into War

Loan it would be worth about £380.

The original company started in 1866 and was known as the Rothschild Exploration Company and specialised in mines. In 1899 it helped to start the El Oro mine in Mexico with Col Baring as chairman and John Hayes Hammond, Rhodes's famous mining engineer, as consultant. This became one of the world's great gold and silver mines but as the mine was worked out its assets declined and by 1940 were down to £37,131. They are now about £20 million. When Mr Woodbine Parish became sole managing director in 1951 net assets of The Exploration Company had also fallen to £107,000. On the last balance sheet available they were £32 million. It is a remarkable example of the value of long term investment in equities.

CHAIRMAN'S STATEMENT
The Group profit, before tax, including £919,933 (*£995,914 for 1989*) share of profits applicable to Related Companies was £3,182,301 for 1990 against £3,062,501 for 1989. Group assets, taking investments at market value, were £26,581,117 (equal to 220·54p per stock unit) against £32,328,183 (268·22p per stock unit) for 1989. After taking into account the full effects of the cross-holdings, as detailed in the circular of 1st December, 1965, the asset value, on a going concern basis, was approximately 262p per stock unit against 325p per stock unit for 1989.

The year under review has been one of considerable difficulty not only in the United Kingdom but in the world at large, with probably more bankruptcies of all sizes than in any other period in the last decade. It is therefore somewhat pleasing to produce results showing the highest profit in your company's history and an increased dividend. Although the asset value was down at the year end it is probably, at the time of writing, higher today.

Regarding the future, only a fool, which I am generally considered, would make a categorical forecast in present world conditions. I can, however, say that your company is in an exceptionally strong position, and I look forward to being able to weather whatever economic blizzards are in store for us better than most and as good as some. If history is any guide to the future, a study of my 53 years' service to your

365

company mainly shown in the progress table on page 4 may be helpful.

In that respect, when the Exploration Company was having a rights issue in 1957 to shareholders at par 1/- (5p) the Investors Chronicle did a major article on July 26th 1957 on The Exploration Company and the El Oro Mining & Exploration Company, headed 'Wanted: £100,000'. This reminded me of notices put up in glass frames outside police stations. The article included the following excerpt: 'Mr Michael Woodbine Parish says in a statement to shareholders "That the board (of each company) will definitely make a distribution to shareholders in the next one to two year period." It would be interesting to hear how he proposes to do this.'

This approach reminded me of my war-time experience of being guarded by the Gestapo for some 6 months. During interrogations the same procedure always began with: 'It would be interesting, Major Parish, to hear . . .'

The answer to the question in the *Investors Chronicle* lies in the table on page 4 in the Report and Accounts showing that in 1958 a dividend of 5% was paid. Dividends have continued every year for 33 years, with the 1991 dividend being 320%.

The advice at the end of the article was as follows: 'The record, no less than the below-par quotation of the existing Exploration and El Oro shares, suggest that shareholders in these two companies would do best to ignore the offers now being made.'

A number of stockholders, myself included, did not take their advice, taking up their rights at 1/- or 5p per stock unit. These stock units now stand at 225p and, allowing for the 1 for 2 bonus in 1961 the price comes to 337p. In the intervening years substantial dividends have been paid and this year, on the original cost of 5p stockholders will receive 12p. Stockholders who did not take the *Investors Chronicle* advice and invested £1,000 in the rights issue would this year receive a net dividend of £3,600 and own shares worth £67,500. Those who did take the *Investors Chronicle* advice might feel a little nostalgic, and if human, a tinge of envy.

To revert to Gestapo phraseology, 'It would be interesting to hear' how many of the recommendations of the *Investors*

Chronicle, over a like period, show an appreciation of over 60 times, or 6,000%.

As a further matter of interest The Exploration Company, since 1958, will have paid out by the end of 1991 £13,081,000 in tax and dividends, and on 31st December 1990 its net assets amounted to £26,581,117 against the £107,261 it had in 1950, almost self-generated. The profit before tax was £3,182,301 against £2,991 in 1950. At no time have any of your Directors been granted free options to buy your company's shares, a practice which is widespread today and which I am on principle against. If Directors believe in their company they can perfectly well buy shares like any other shareholders without having the company's issued capital watered down, and thus lowering the value of many companies in which your company is interested. The progress of the El Oro Company was largely similar to The Exploration Company and in my speech of 20th May, 1982 I said, 'If I had to hazard a guess, I would say that my wife and myself have waived for your company and associated companies, either in dividends or directors' fees, getting on for £100,000 and the market value has risen from 2p to the equivalent of approximately 60p.'

As usual I have to thank my co-directors and our minute staff of one: Mrs Smith, our secretaries BDO Binder Hamlyn, represented by Mr Watkins and Mr Allan Evans. I would once again like to congratulate my former co-director Anthony Tennant, and Alice Taylor on the outstanding results they have achieved for their Guinness Shareholders.

In due course I hope my book, which will contain something about the 100 year history of your company and much else, will be available, and if you require a book please indicate the number on the enclosed proxy card.

P.S. A shareholder has sent me the enclosed extract about your company from 'the Bulletin' – April 1991 which I enclose.

Michael Woodbine Parish
1st May, 1991

CHAIRMAN'S STATEMENT, Exploration Company plc, 22nd April 1992, by Michael Woodbine Parish.
The Group profit, before tax, including £908,116 *(£919,933*

for 1990) share of profits applicable to Related Undertakings was £2,518,820 for 1991 against £3,182,301 for 1990. Group assets, taking investments at market value, were £29,877,400 (equal to 247·88p per stock unit) against £26,581,117 (220·53p per stock unit) for 1990. After taking into account the full effects of the cross-holdings, as detailed in the circular of 1st December, 1965, the asset value, on a going concern basis, was approximately 282p per stock unit against 262p per stock unit for 1990.

The above in the worst recessionary year since 1930, speaks for itself. It is now 55 years since I joined your company and with the exception of the war years I have piloted it ever since, with the results shown in the column on page 4. All stockholders who were with me in 1950, have seen the value of their holding increase approximately 211 times and have received 1,648% in dividends. My book, which a large number of you have ordered, will hopefully be published by February 1993, and will cover the whole period.

I will think aloud about what has happened to us all and Britain and your company since 1937, when our country was leading the world; with Adolf Hitler came war and the sacrifice of many of our finest for Britain. They were immortalised in Noel Coward's evocative poem *'Lie in the Dark and Listen'*. The last lines of which were, *'There is one debt you'll forever owe. Lie in the Dark and Listen'*. He meant us all.

Churchill having saved the world from Hitler's Germany would have finished the war in 1943/4 by a replay of his correct Gallipoli strategy of 1916 had it not been for the constant obstruction of the USA. At that moment on the 9th September 1943 Britain, the Empire, and Churchill were lost. America set out to back Stalin and the USSR against Churchill, which resulted in a half century of untold suffering, which continues today.

Britain's decline accelerated with Churchill's defeat on the 25th July 1945 by the Socialists. I was present at 10 Downing Street on that fateful night when he said to Robin Maugham and myself, 'Hardly had I put down the reins of office, when the horse was taken from me, only to be ridden into the quarry'. From then onwards, I believe, thanks to Macmillan, Wilson, Callaghan, Healey and others, our great country has declined from first to last amongst Industrial Nations, and was only saved from bankruptcy in the 1960s through the gift of the Almighty of $20 billion a year from North Sea oil. Which brings me to this general election whose result I correctly forecast, as I was convinced, after forty years of experience the average Briton could no more trust Mr Kinnock or John Smith to take and invest his money in their crack-pot ideas anymore than their predecessors from Wilson onwards had achieved with such devastating results for their country.

This in no way endorses Mr Major or Mr Lamont whose politics have created great suffering for 86,000 householders having their homes repossessed and their marriages in jeopardy, 50,000 firms bankrupted last year and an increasing number this year, and over 2½ million unemployed for no apparent gain, no wonder inflation came down. We were only saved, not by Mr Major or Mr Lamont, but by the average Briton not being prepared to be fleeced yet again by Socialist squandermania. The purchasing power of the pound in 1937 was 64·5p and 1990 was 2·2p.

Now turning to your company, we have been able to steer safely through dangerous waters for over half a century, and I have every confidence of being able to continue so to do. Any of you who have not ordered my book can do so on the enclosed prepaid proxy form.

As usual I have to thank my co-directors, the company secretaries and Mrs Smith.

Michael Woodbine Parish
27th April, 1992

Letter from a shareholder:

Sir,

I write to thank you most sincerely for your historical, factual and interesting report. Aged 86 I have lived through the period and can confirm every word.

What a pity it is that men of your calibre cannot control our future.

Unfortunately my holding in your Companies is small but I thank you for the generous way you have looked after my investments.

Yours sincerely
Henry A. Howard
11th May 1992

CITATION
Captain Miltiades Andreou Houmas, DSO OBE

Captain Houmas is undoubtedly the outstanding figure among Special Service caique skippers in the Eastern Mediterranean. From January, 1943 to September, 1944 he has made no less than 40 journeys to enemy occupied territory. During this period, Captain Houmas was selected to operate on all missions requiring more than normal courage and ability and in 90% of these missions he was successful. In no case can failure be attributed to him. His seamanship is magnificent and his courage of the highest quality. He is always the first to volunteer for any expedition of an unusually hazardous nature, and because of his skill as a sailor, his iron nerve and the great resource and common sense he shows in emergencies, he has always been selected for such expeditions.

In May, 1943, he was selected to go to Cephalonia, on the western coast of Greece, to pick up Stoker Capes, the sole survivor of HM submarine *Perseus*. It would be unnecessary to enlarge upon the hazards of such a long trip through enemy waters under constant patrol from ships and aircraft. Upon arrival in Cephalonia, Captain Houmas was submitted to most detailed interrogation by the Italian Harbour Police. With extraordinary ingenuity he managed to lull their suspicions of the obvious irregularities of his arrival there and the lack of necessary permits in his possession. Having landed someone, whose duty it was to contact Stoker Capes, Captain Houmas was ordered by the Italians to another port. Upon arrival there, his caique was again boarded by Italian police. Once more by adroit replies and judicious bribery he contrived to maintain comparative freedom of movement for himself and his caique. Later he deemed it necessary to

370

contact Stoker Capes in person. This entailed a long journey over land, which he completed successfully. Finally, in pursuance of a plan he had evolved himself to suit the exigencies of the particular situation, he returned in his caique to his original port of landing, where Stoker Capes was embarked and, although the caique was by then under special observation, Captain Houmas set sail for Turkey, where he arrived 12 days after he had set out, having completed a journey of 1,000 miles.

On 10 days after his return from Cephelonia, he was sent to search for escapers on Samos. On arrival in the island waters, he left his caique and started to row ashore alone in a dinghy. He was surprised by an enemy patrol boat which he proceeded to engage single-handed with his Tommy-gun. Although his frail craft provided no cover or protection he closed with the patrol boat and succeeded in killing four of the Italians on board and escaping himself in the subsequent confusion. His caique had sailed, as the crew were alarmed by the sound of shooting, so Captain Houmas, after 15 days in hiding on Samos, during which he searched unsuccessfully for evaders, stole a rowing boat and rowed back to Turkey, where he arrived still carrying his Tommy-gun.

It is difficult to find adequate words of praise for Captain Houmas's superb behaviour during the Aegean operations in the autumn of 1943. During this campaign he made a total of 25 trips to the islands and rescued no less than 48 Imperial personnel as well as bringing out 100 Italian military personnel and many Greek refugees. On one occasion the engine of his caique broke down but, nothing daunted, he proceeded to pick up some British escapers and then completed the return trip from Kos to Turkey by rowing the whole distance, a feat difficult to surpass for determination and courage, not only on account of the mileage involved but because of the danger of enemy interception. In reviewing the part played by Captain Houmas in the Aegean operations, it is essential to bear in mind that the Germans were concentrating every effort to prevent British escapes, that the waters between Turkey and the islands were, therefore, keenly patrolled from land, sea and air were also heavily mined. Yet Captain Houmas continued to sail these waters to bring British personnel to safety.

In 1944 too he has continued to serve with all the skill, courage and resource he can command. He has made many trips to Greece and the islands to rescue Imperial personnel. In July 1944, he piloted a High Speed Rescue Launch, which went to Mykonos to collect 2 British airmen and brought them safely to Turkey.

Extract from Daily Telegraph 26.1.65.

CHURCHILL'S HOUR OF DEFEAT

ROBIN MAUGHAM recalls the evening of July 25, 1945, which brought to an end Winston Churchill's first Premiership. This account is based on notes made shortly afterwards.

After dinner on the evening of July 25, 1945, I had been invited round to the annexe of No. 10 Downing Street. The following day we would know the results of the first General Election to take place since the war had begun.

Though his son Randolph was frankly pessimistic, Churchill was still optimistic about the result of the election. So much so that Mary Churchill asked me to come in for a drink after dinner the following evening, and to take her out to the Orchid Room later to celebrate.

By noon on the following day it was clear that the Labour Party had won and that Churchill had been heavily defeated. I rang Mary to ask if she still wanted me to come round. Yes, Mary said, she did. So I put on a dinner-jacket and came round after dinner, bringing a friend, Michael Parish, with me.

A few people were sadly gathered in the living-room of the annexe when we arrived – Diana and Duncan Sandys, Mary Churchill, Brendan Bracken and Jack Churchill, Winston's brother. But the defeated Prime Minister was not present.

Suddenly the door opened and Winston Churchill appeared. Silence fell over the room as he walked in. He was dressed in his open-necked boiler suit and embroidered slippers.

He looked stricken. No one said a word. We were all like a lot of actors who had dried up on their cues. He turned towards me. I was the newcomer. So I walked across to him.

372

'Good-evening, sir,' I said, 'I'm so very sorry about what has happened.'

For some reason this trite remark pleased him. For an instant the sorrow left his face.

'Oh!' he said, smiling at me. 'So you are sorry! And your father? And how is he? Is he sorry?'

Before the war, when my father had been in the Cabinet as Lord Chancellor, he and Churchill had had a violent row at the time of the Munich Pact.

'Yes, sir,' I said, 'he is sorry too.'

'The only thing that matters is England,' Churchill muttered.

He then sat down, beckoning me to a chair beside him. At that moment Anthony Eden came in, looking very fit and bronzed. He stayed only a few minutes.

'I expect I shall see you one of these days,' Churchill said as Eden was leaving, accentuating each word ponderously.

'I don't think it's as bad as all that,' Eden replied.

'The Labour Party have inherited a tough proposition,' Churchill said, after Eden had gone. 'We cannot stop these strikes. They will be better at it than we were . . . But hardly had I put down the reins of office, when the horse was taken from me . . . Only to be ridden into a quarry,' he added.

I had the impression that Churchill was anxious to be fair to the victors, but he could not resist the suspicion that his defeat was the result of a secret Socialist conspiracy against him. And he gave instances of some of the more malignant behaviour of various members of the Labour Party.

The future was grim, he said. England had been through two great wars and had incurred large debts. America could be counted out on the grounds of Lease-Lend. But India and the Middle East countries were important and would have to be paid.

'We must be fair to the Labour party,' he said, turning to Brendan Bracken. 'They have inherited terrible difficulties. We must lay off them for a few months and give them a fair chance. But if they start to tamper with the Constitution then we must go out into the streets and protest.

'That wretched man Morrison is the most dangerous man of them all, mark my words. He delighted and revelled in the power of 18B. He was determined to oust me. An election was bound to come after this tedious war, and the Labour party were determined to get rid of me.'

'The Tories would have been nothing without you,' Braken replied. 'If you hadn't been their leader they wouldn't have polled more than 15 votes.'

Suddenly Churchill swung round towards me as if I had just spoken.

'So this little *contretemps* has surprised you?' he asked.

'Yes, sir,' I replied.

'Did you speak in the election?'

'Yes,' I said. 'On two occasions, and both were for Harold Nicolson.'

'He is out, too,' said Churchill, 'and I am sorry for it.'

He was still turned towards me, so I felt that I must at least say something. He seemed to expect it.

'Thousands of men who've been through this war will always look to you for leadership,' I said. 'I believe, sir, that you've been overthrown by an ill-educated mass of discontented people who will presently try to overthrow the Labour party in its turn.'

'I have only a few years to live,' Churchill replied. 'I am finished. It is up to people like you to carry on. I will never return to power. I have left my name to history, and I have no regrets.'

'Will you lead the Opposition?'

'I am not quite certain that the Tories want me,' Churchill answered. 'But I can tell you this. The leaders of the Labour party will try to go slowly. But they will find the tail of their party will lash them into precipitous acts. The people in front will be shoved on by the men behind.

'There will be more difficulties when the Japanese war ends, which will be soon. *We* have made arrangements on that score. But the Socialists will claim the credit for it. However, the main difficulties are internal. England has been bled white by the strain of these two great wars.'

As he spoke, I felt that it seemed as if sometimes he would forget for a moment that he was no longer Prime Minister. But then like a nerve starting up in a tooth, back would come the memory of his defeat, and almost in the middle of a sentence he would refer once again to his own position.

'Throughout the last six years I have grown accustomed to

374

rise early and start work at eight and go on working until four in the morning. Indeed I suppose I shall find it strange to have no labour on my hands. It seems incredible that tomorrow I have nothing to do.'

Then, as if trying to convince himself, he added: ' But it will seem odd on the morrow when all the great affairs of State are no longer brought to me. Now it is up to you young ones. I have a short time to live. But I feel that history will give me a fair reading.'

At that stage Diana and Duncan Sandys said goodnight and left. Presently, Jack Churchill got up to go.

Winston went on talking. But the flashes of his usual good humour died quickly. And he now shook his head wearily.

'For five long years the reins of office have been in my hands,' he said.

He fell silent again, and Michael Parish spoke for the first time.

'Well, at least, sir, you won us the race,' Michael said.

This cheered him up, and for a moment he was back on his old form.

'I won the race,' he said. 'But now you've warned me off the turf!'

Once more he fell silent. He was obviously exhausted. And Mary decided it was time for her father to go to bed. But he would not listen to her. He still lingered. There were now only four of us left in the room – Mary, Brendan Bracken, Michael Parish and I. Churchill looked desperately old and sad.

'I cannot go back to Potsdam,' he said. 'But unless Attlee and Bevin go back immediately, the conference will crash itself into nothing before reaching maturity and decision.

'Attlee came and asked Eden to help him out. But Eden was rather severe, perhaps too severe, and said, "Let me have it in writing and I will put it through the usual channels." '

Churchill looked vaguely around the room.

'I expect my leisure will worry me at first,' he said. 'But at least I shall be able to devote proper time to my painting.'

Suddenly he turned to Mary.

'Bring me my sketch of the Black Prince's house,' he said.

Mary fetched his picture of Marrakesh and stood it on the floor, leaning against the sideboard. Brendan Bracken stood up to look at it.

'You're standing too close,' said Churchill.

So Bracken moved back.

'And now you're standing in my light,' said Churchill. Patiently Bracken moved aside once more.

For a while we stood in silence looking at the gaily-coloured painting. Churchill was motionless. He was far away in his own imaginings.

When, presently, he began to speak it was clear that his thoughts now flickered to and fro between the portrait and the memory of his defeat.

'Another few days and I shall be proud of it,' he said, staring at the picture. 'And I shall be able to spend quite a time painting during these last few years which are left to me . . . Yes, it needs a little mauving in . . . But the term of my mandate has been withdrawn by the people . . .

'Yes. It does need touching up a bit . . . And certainly leisure will be pleasing. And I am grateful for having been given the chance to rest during the few years left to me . . . But it will be strange on the morrow when the great affairs of State are no longer brought to me.'

Then with an effort he raised his head from the picture and moved slowly towards the door. Each step that he took seemed heavy with pain. At the door he paused.

'But I have no regrets,' he said.

For an instant he hesitated. His eyes were bleary with tears. Slowly his gaze wandered round the four of us. But he was heedless of our presence. His mind was far away, ranging perhaps over lobbies and battlefields, assemblies and oceans, palaces and the broken slums of London.

'I have no regrets,' he repeated.

'I leave my name to history.'

And he walked out of the room.

TO THE POPULATION AND THE MILITARY FORCES ON CRETE

It has been brought to the notice of the German Supreme Command that German soldiers who fell into the hands of the enemy on the island of Crete have been illtreated and even mutilated in a most infamous and unhuman manner.

As a punishment and reprisal therefore it is announced that:

1) Whosoever commits such crimes against international laws on German prisoners of war will be punished in the manner of his own cruel action, no matter be he or she a man or a woman.

2) Localities near which such crimes have been perpetrated will be burned down. The population will be held responsible.

3) Beyond those measures further and sharper reprisals will be held in store.

The German Supreme Command

SOLDIERS, SAILORS and AIRMEN of the ROYAL BRITISH ARMY

There are many of you still hiding in the mountains valleys and villages.

It is useless to resist.

All efforts to flee are in vain.

The coming winter will force you to leave the mountains.

YOU are to present yourselves AT ONCE to the GERMAN SOLDIERS. ONLY those who present themselves AT ONCE will be sure of an HONOURABLE and SOLDIERLIKE captivity of war.

On the contrary, who is met in Civilian Dress will be

treated as a spy.

Signed THE COMMANDER OF KRETA.

COPY of a leaflet dropped by the Germans after the surrender of Crete

ORDER
Of the German Military Commander of CRETE

Because the town of Anoyia has been the center of British Intelligence in Crete, and because the Anoyians committed the murder of the Military Commander of Geni-Gave, and his guards. Because the Anoyians took part in the sabotage of Damastas, because the Anoyians give shelter and protection to the different resistance groups, and because Anoyia was used as a stop-over during the abduction of General Von Kreipe, we order the total destruction of this town and the execution of every male Anoyian within the village and within one kilometre radius.

Hania 13.8.44
The German Military Commander
of Crete

X MILLER

KINGDOM OF GREECE

On the 3rd May 1946, awarded to the village of Anoyia
WAR CROSS FIRST CLASS
For the destruction suffered during the German occupation 1941-44, and the admirable conduct, endurance and unparalleled heroism until self sacrifice.

THE MINISTER

K. MANETAS

COMMENDATION FOR AWARD
OF MILITARY CROSS

77954 Leiutenant (Loc.U/Capt) Michael Woodbine Parish of Nottinghamshire Yeomanry (Sherwood Rangers)

Captain Parish was captured during the operations in Crete and was taken to the POW camp at Galatas.

On 17th June, together with another officer, he escaped from the camp and took to the hills. The intention of these two officers was to make for the Eastern end of the island and there endeavour to find a boat in which to escape to British Territory. However, before they had gone very far, they were shown a note from Lt-Cmdr Vernicos, asking that any escaped British or Imperial officers who had escaped should get into contact with him and he had good hopes of arranging their passage to Egypt. Accordingly, the two officers met Lt-Cmdr Vernicos who arranged for their accommodation and hiding in the Cretan hill villages. On discovering that there were still a large number of Imperial Service personnel at large in Crete, it was decided to organise a headquarters for all such personnel, from which the passages to British territory could be co-ordinated and which, under the direction of Lt-Cmdr Vernicos, could arrange the shelter and hiding of the Imperial troops. After several fruitless attempts to arrange for a mission to reach Egypt to arrange the evacuation of the Imperial Service personnel, a way was discovered through a clandestine organisation that was transporting Cretan soldiers from the Greek Mainland to Menes, the northern-most point of Cape Spartha.

After a very arduous wait of ten days, during which severe hardships were undergone, finally a 20ft sailing boat arrived. This set out to take the whole party to the Peloponnesos, but on the way they encountered bad weather and were forced to make Cythera Island, and on the next day, Elaphonis. By various ways and after a number of difficulties the party managed to sail in a small boat by way of the Aegean islands to the Turkish mainland.

At one of these islands Captain Parish met with an accident in which he broke his arm and fractured his skull.

In spite of his injuries, Captain Parish volunteered to return to Greece in order to help, in cooperation with others, in evacuating numbers of other Imperial Service personnel known still to be at large in Greece, and he is now behind the enemy lines doing courageous work.

J. Shearer
Brigadier, DMI

FROM THE CHARIOTEER

HOURS OF LIFE by Ange Vláchos *(translated by Peter Bien)*

> *Endure my heart. You have*
> *already endured worse than this.*

Odyssey XX, 18

CHAPTER ONE

In a hidden corner of the body—there in the centre of his breast—a spark of life remained, just exactly to keep the heart beating softly. A shudder passed through him, as though from the final discharge of the horrible pain which would be expelled now, little by little, at his every breath: a memory, only, of those terrible hours of his past. And yet, an indelible stamp would remain forever on his face.

He had not talked. When you saw the preparations around you—the thick whips, the meat-hook hanging from a ring on the ceiling, or those planks which looked like operating tables, with the curved iron at one end for gripping your neck and immobilising your head—the fright was enough to break you even before they started.

But Dimitri had no time to see these things, because one of the two half-naked giants had rushed directly at him, trying to rip off his shirt to bare his back. After he had been pushed from the interrogator's office into the large basement room with the high ceiling, Dimitri had whirled abruptly to prevent the door from closing. But it banged loudly shut and he found himself alone in front of the two monsters. As soon as the first colossus fell upon him to strip him, that was when it

380

happened: a sudden impetus propelled Dimitri's whole body atop the huge half-naked torturer. With one punch, he drew blood from the giant's face; perhaps he also broke one of his teeth, for although Dimitri was slight of build, he had worked up momentum and his clenched fist had found the other man unprepared. The torturer's astonishment was so great that for an instant he gaped at Dimitri stupidly, as though trying to discover the meaning, if any, of what had happened. But the second torturer seized the cowhide. Bellowing loudly, Dimitri fell to his knees, his back deeply striped. He tried to defend himself with his hands, clasping his open palms together over his face. But he was forced to release them quickly under the burning blows of the two giants, who were flogging him maniacally. His excruciating screams were loud and prolonged; his voice began to lose all human characteristics. Sagging to his knees, sitting half-upright, trying to roll himself into a ball, he collapsed at last to the ground in his efforts to escape the blows. But this was worse, because now the tip of the cowhide was what found him, and the pain was more biting than ever. The longer the flogging continued, the heavier each blow became, and he felt each time as though inside him an explosion had been set off which took away his breath and sent sparks flying before his eyes. Finally he fainted; but he had endured to the end. He had not talked.

For this brief account of my brother's life and death I have relied heavily upon the memorial book written by my father a few months after Charles's death in action. The book was meant to serve as a tribute to a brave and loving man and also as a link with Charles for all those who knew and loved him.

CHARLES WOODBINE PARISH D.F.C. RAF
12 APRIL 1915
22 APRIL 1943

(PATHFINDER FORCE)

Charles was my parents' first child born a few months before my father went off to France to serve in the First World War. In 1916 I was born and Godfrey three years after me. We lived first in London and then in Paris where our sister Elizabeth completed the family in 1923. Then followed almost eight very happy years in the North Riding of Yorkshire where we had thirty or more acres to run wild in when we were at home from school in the holidays. We rode and swam, played tennis and cricket, kept bees on the moors – an idyllic existence, until suddenly and bravely in 1931, our mother died. Our bereavement meant the family moving to Knightsbridge where, overlooking Hyde Park we all lived in the school holidays. It was during this time that the quiet humour and absolute unselfishness of Charles's personality began to manifest itself. However, complementing his gentleness was his vigorous enthusiasm for many practical activities. After Eton he went off to Munich to learn German, and following that travelled to India.

One summer holiday in Scotland Charles and I both swam across the Sound of Mull. We completed the crossing in an hour – a feat said not to have been achieved since 1745. It was this kind of endeavour as well as the pursuits of stalking, shooting and sailing which was to prove invaluable to both of us during the Second World War.

When in 1936 my father remarried, and we acquired a delightful stepmother, the family moved to 35 Eaton Square. By then Charles had been working in the City for two years, but his heart and mind were much more deeply involved in the flying he did at weekends as an RAF volunteer. The outbreak of war in September 1939 found Charles with me, touring Rhodesia and South Africa, where I was already achieving some success in the world of 'big business.' We arrived back in England in October. I joined the Yeomanry and was soon posted to the Middle East while Charles spent ten months in training before his first operational flight with the RAF. In the spring of 1940 Rudyard Kipling's beautiful old house in Sussex – Bateman's – became our family home, and Charles spent all his leaves there in that lovely and historic part of England.

The first of Charles's fifty-four bombing missions – a rarely equalled record at a time when we suffered the loss of many bombers – was the first raid on Berlin in August, 1940. He flew low enough to recognise buildings he had visited during his student days. A month later Charles returned unexpectedly to Bateman's. He seemed well but tired. When pressed by my father for the reason for his unscheduled leave he reported that he had been forced to bale out of his aircraft over the North Sea and that he was the sole survivor of two Wellington bomber crews which had crashed in the Channel during atrocious weather conditions. His aircraft had been struck by lightning; one engine failed and the other caught fire. Charles swam seven miles in darkness in his Mae West flying jacket, trying to reach the English coast, and using the North Star as a guide.

After about an hour he could see the beams of coastal searchlights and he swam towards them. Suffering from severe cramp and sickness he almost gave up twice, but when at last dawn came, finding that he was less than a mile from the shore he made a last effort to rally his strength. At last he gained the beach, but was too weak to drag himself out of the sea. He lay exhausted at the tide's edge until some soldiers in a nearby pillbox heard his shouts for help and came and hauled him from the water.

Within a week he was back flying a new Wellington over Germany with a new crew. None of his previous crew had survived. On 21st September under half-inch banner headlines the *Daily Mail* ran the whole story; but Charles himself treated the episode with characteristic modesty.

In 1940 in an effort to obliterate this vital armament-producing area, our bombers made sustained attacks on the industrial centres of the Ruhr. Charles was in the thick of it all. This first series of thirty raids resulted in hospitalisation due to a frost-bitten foot, but after a brief period of recuperation he resumed flying – this time in a Stirling which he proudly announced was the biggest bomber in the world. Miraculously his hazardous career was to continue for another two-and-a-half years.

Then on 22nd April 1943 the BBC news informed us that the RAF had attacked the Baltic port of Stettin: thirty-one of our bombers were missing. Charles had told us that flying casualties were always quickly notified and this proved all too true because at three o'clock that afternoon the grim telegram arrived from his air-station reporting him as missing. Two days later a confirmatory letter which emphasised the outstanding qualities of Charles and his crew arrived, and encouraged a faint hope that he may have baled out over the sea, as he had in 1940.

We held on to that slender optimistic thread until early in June when a twenty-one year-old Canadian engineer Sgt Smith, who had accompanied Charles on nineteen 'sorties' went to see my father at Bateman's. He said that he was the sole survivor of the eight crew members. The Stirling had caught fire after having been attacked at about 2 am by a night-fighter ME110. Charles, unwounded and perfectly calm, said, 'Sorry boys – we'll have to jump . . .' Smith, however, was the only one who was able to escape. His parachute had not even had time to open, when in less than sixty seconds, with its guns still blazing at the enemy fighter, the aircraft had crashed and exploded. Smith landed in a field and wandered about miserably for two days without food or drink. He was eventually found by a group of those brave resistance fighters who, at the risk of their own lives, helped and harboured our airmen who landed in enemy-occupied territories. Thus he escaped to England. Using Smith's information, his resistance helpers found and identified the Stirling, M for Mother, which had crashed near a farm house without damaging it. The smouldering wreck contained seven bodies. Together with his crew Charles had perished at his post doing his duty to the end.

When he died he had just turned twenty-eight years old – in the vigour of his young manhood. A brave, honourable and loving brother – we mourn him still.

Excerpt from the Daily Mail 21.9.40

PILOT JUMPS, SWIMS 7 MILES
Charles W. Parish aged 25
Guided by Star When Lightning Wrecked Bomber
by Noel Monks, Daily Mail Air Correspondent

Here is one of the most amazing RAF stories of the war. It was told to me yesterday by a young pilot officer, sole survivor of the crew of a heavy bomber that crashed into the Channel when returning from a raid in Germany last week.

The machine was struck by lightning, one engine caught fire and the other failed.

The pilot officer saved himself by swimming seven miles in darkness, in his 'Mae West' flying jacket, to the English coast. This is the story in his own words:

'We were flying at 6,000ft when we ran into a storm – thunder and lightning. We went up to 9,000ft and turned on the de-icers.

'Suddenly there was a terrible clap of thunder right over us, and for a few seconds we were completely out of control.

The aircraft was badly iced up and we began losing height at the rate of 2,000ft a minute, though the ship's nose was up.

'Because of the thickness of the ice on the windscreen we were flying blind, and just as we turned course to head for home, the port engine packed up. We tried the de-icers, but without effect.

'The rear gunner then reported the the engine was on fire, but this didn't worry us much, and we went on until we saw searchlights, which meant the coast of England.

'At this moment the other engine conked out. We were flying then at 7,000ft. The captain decided we'd get over the coast and then jump.

'Soon he asked the rear gunner if he thought we were over land and both the rear gunner and the navigator agreed we were, though we were still flying blind.

'The captain then ordered the crew to abandon the aircraft.

WATER-PLANED
'The captain and I went on. We were now down to about 4,000ft. The ice had gone and I saw searchlights about five to ten miles away on the starboard beam. The compass was quite hopeless and no earthly use. I thought we were flying south along the coast.

'The captain ordered me to jump. We wished each other "Good luck" and just before I jumped I yelled to him, "Turn right."

'The parachute opened all right and going down I could see

The Daily Mail, SEPTEMBER 21, 1940.

PILOT JUMPS. SWIMS 7 MILES

Guided by Star When Lightning Wrecked Bomber

By NOEL MONKS, Daily Mail Air Correspondent

HERE is one of the most amazing R.A.F. stories of the war. It was told to me yesterday by a young pilot officer, sole survivor of the crew of a heavy bomber that crashed into the Channel when returning from a raid in Germany last week.

The machine was struck by lightning, one engine caught fire and the other failed.

The pilot officer saved himself by swimming seven miles in darkness, in his "Mae West" flying jacket, to the English coast. This is his story in his own words:

"We were flying at 6,000ft. when we ran into a storm—thunder and lightning. We went up to 9,000ft. and turned on the de-icers.

"Suddenly there was a terrific clap of thunder, right over us, and for a few seconds we were completely out of control.

The aircraft was badly iced up, and we began losing height at the rate of 2,000 feet a minute, though the ship's nose was up.

"Because of the thickness of the ice on the windscreen we were flying blind, and just as we turned course to head for home, the port engine packed up. We tried the de-icers, but without effect.

"The rear gunner then reported that the engine was on fire, but this didn't worry us much, and we went on until we saw searchlights, which meant the coast of England.

" The captain and I went on. We were ~~possibly~~ ~~~~ ~~~~ ~~feet.~~ The ice had gone and I saw searchlights about five to ten miles away on the starboard beam. The compass was quite hopeless and no earthly use. I thought we were flying south along the coast.

" At this moment the other engine conked out. We were flying then at 7,000 feet. The captain decided we'd get over the coast and then jump.

" Soon, he asked the rear gunner if he thought we were over land and both the rear gunner and the navigator agreed we were, though we were still flying blind.

" The captain then ordered the crew to abandon the aircraft.

WATER-PLANED

" The Captain ordered me to jump. We wished each other ' Good luck ' and just before I jumped I yelled to him, " Turn right.'

" The parachute opened all right and going down I could see the searchlights about seven miles away.

" Then I realised I was over the sea and that the sergeants had probably jumped to their doom.

" When I landed in the sea I must have gone down a pretty good depth, and I came up with a terrific rush. In fact, I practically ' took off,' as my parachute dragged me along at a terrific speed.

" I lay flat on my tummy and ' planed ' across the rough water. I thought I was being blown back across the Channel, so I jettisoned the 'cnute and my flying boots and began to swim.

" The searchlights had gone out, so I tried to guide myself by the north star. I kept it on my right, and swam towards the coast. My ' Mae West ' was very useful.

ABOUT ' ALL-IN '

" After about an hour the searchlights came on again, and I swam towards them. I swam for a long time. Twice I almost gave up. But something kept me going.

" The searchlights didn't seem to get any 'nearer.' I had very bad cramp, and was ill a few times.

" When dawn came at last, I saw I was about three-quarters of a mile from the shore. I took off my trousers and made a last effort, as I was about all-in. I reached the shore opposite a pillbox.

" I was too weak to pull myself out of the water, and was rolling about half in and half out of the sea.

" I shouted several times, and at last some soldiers rushed out of the pillbox and picked me up.

" The soldiers were very good to me. I am sorry to say my five colleagues were lost."

The story of Charles Woodbine Parish's miraculous survival

387

F/L Parish List of Operations

OPS HOURS TO DATE 244 10

DATE.	No.	PLACE		DATE	No.	PLACE
25.8.40	1.	Berlin		26.9.42	30	Garden.
30.8.40	2.	Berlin		28.9.42	31.	Lingen. Day. ✓
5.9.40	3.	Black Forest		2.10.42	32	Kacfeld
8.9.40	4.	Boulogne		5.10.42	33	Aachen
16.9.40	5	Flushing		11.10.42	34	Middlefart
21.9.40	6 ✗	Dunkirk		13.10.42	35.	Kiel
23.9.40	7	Berlin		20.11.42	36.	Turin
25.9.40	8	Calais		28.11.42	37	Turin
23.9.40	9	Hanau		4.11.42	38	Baltic S.
1.10.40	10	Essen		8.12.42	39	Baltic S.
7.10.40	11.	Boulogne		14.12.42	40	Lorient
9.10.40	12	Graven Broch		23.1.43	41	Lorient
				26.1.43	42	Lorient
				4.2.42	43	Turin. PF

Charles Woodbine Parish's list of 54 bombing operations in his own handwriting. He was on the first raid over Berlin in the War and his historic attack on Dunkirk 21.4.40 is clearly marked with an X.

388

Date	No.	Target
15·10·40	14	KIEL
20·10·40	15	COLOGNE
29·10·40	16	BERLIN
1·11·40	17	BERLIN
8·11·40	18	COLOGNE
13·11·40	19	HAMM
17·11·40	20	DUSSELDORF
25·11·40	21	KIEL
23·11·40	22	BOULOGNE
8·12·40	23	BORDEAUX
15·12·40	24	MANNHEIM
20·12·40	25	DINGHY·SWEEP
23·12·40	26	MANNHEIM
29·12·40	27	LORIENT
3·1·41	28	BREMEN
15·1·42	29	ESSEN

Date	No.	Target
	45	BERLIN
13·7·43	46	LORIENT
14·2·43	46	COLOGNE
9·3·43	47	NUANBERG
9·3·43	48	MUNICH
11·3·43	49	STUTTGART
29·3·43	50	BERLIN
10·4·43	51	FRANKFURT
14·4·43	52	STUTTGART
16·4·43	53	MANNHEIM
20·4·43	54	STETTIN — MISSING

the searchlights about seven miles away.

'Then I realised I was over the sea, and that the sergeants had probably jumped to their doom.

'When I landed in the sea I must have gone down a pretty good depth, and I came up with a terrific rush. In fact, I practically "took off" as my parachute dragged me along at a terrific speed.

'I lay flat on my tummy and planed across the rough water. I thought I was being blown back across the Channel, so I jettisoned the 'chute and my flying boots and began to swim.

'The searchlights had gone out so I tried to guide myself by the North Star. I kept it on my right, and swam towards the coast. My Mae West was very useful.

ABOUT 'ALL-IN'

'After about an hour the searchlights came on again, and I swam towards them. I swam for a long time. Twice I almost gave up. But something kept me going.

'The searchlights didn't seem to get any nearer. I had very bad cramp and was ill a few times.

'When dawn came at last, I saw I was about three-quarters of a mile from the shore. I took off my trousers and made a last effort, as I was about all-in. I reached the shore opposite a pillbox.

'I shouted several times, and at last some soldiers rushed out of the pillbox and picked me up.

'The soldiers were very good to me. I am sorry to say my five colleagues were lost.'

LIE IN THE DARK AND LISTEN
by Noel Coward

Lie in the dark and listen.
It's clear tonight so they're flying high,
Hundreds of them, thousands perhaps,
Riding the icy, moonlit sky,
Men, machinery, bombs and maps,
Altimeters and guns and charts,
Coffee, sandwiches, fleece-lined boots,
Bones and muscles and minds and hearts.

English saplings, with English roots
Deep in the earth they've left below.
Lie in the dark and let them go;
Lie in the dark and listen.

Lie in the dark and listen.
They're going over in waves and waves
High above villages, hills and streams,
Country churches and little graves
And little citizen's worried dreams;
Very soon they'll have reached the sea
And far below them will lie the bays
And cliffs and sands where they used to be
Taken for summer holidays.
Lie in the dark and let them go;
Theirs is a world we'll never know.
Lie in the dark and listen.

Lie in the dark and listen.
City magnates and steel contractors,
Factory workers and politicians,
Soft hysterical little actors,
Ballet dancers, reserved musicians,
Safe in your warm civilian beds,
Count your profits and count your sheep
Life is passing above your heads,
Just turn over and try to sleep.
Lie in the dark and let them go,
There's one debt you'll forever owe.
Lie in the dark and listen.

INDEX